# PAN AM AT WAR

## HOW THE AIRLINE SECRETLY HELPED AMERICA FIGHT WORLD WAR II

### MARK COTTA VAZ AND JOHN H. HILL

Skyhorse Publishing

Copyright © 2019, 2025 by Mark Cotta Vaz and John H. Hill

All rights reserved. No part of this book may be reproduced in any manner without the express written consent of the publisher, except in the case of brief excerpts in critical reviews or articles. All inquiries should be addressed to Skyhorse Publishing, 307 West 36th Street, 11th Floor, New York, NY 10018.

Skyhorse Publishing books may be purchased in bulk at special discounts for sales promotion, corporate gifts, fund-raising, or educational purposes. Special editions can also be created to specifications. For details, contact the Special Sales Department, Skyhorse Publishing, 307 West 36th Street, 11th Floor, New York, NY 10018 or info@skyhorsepublishing.com.

Skyhorse® and Skyhorse Publishing® are registered trademarks of Skyhorse Publishing, Inc.®, a Delaware corporation.

Visit our website at www.skyhorsepublishing.com.

10 9 8 7 6 5 4 3 2 1

Library of Congress Cataloging-in-Publication Data is available on file.

Cover design by Rain Saukas
Cover photo credit SFO Museum and National Archives

Paperback ISBN: 978-1-5107-8370-6
Hardcover ISBN: 978-1-5107-2950-6
Ebook ISBN: 978-1-5107-2951-3

Printed in United States of America

*"Pan Am is an instrument of U.S. policy and a weapon of global war."*

—"Pan Am at War,"
Time magazine, May 18, 1942

To Bettylu Vaz,
my mother, for her inspiration and support
—MCV


To Renee, our son, James,
and the memory of my mother, Marianne
—JHH


*and*
To the trailblazing men and women
who pioneered global air transport

# CONTENTS

★

## PART I: AIR POWER

**CHAPTER 1:** Visions of the Future — 1
**CHAPTER 2:** Born to the Air — 15
**CHAPTER 3:** Champions of Air Power — 28
**CHAPTER 4:** Prophet of a New Era — 35
**CHAPTER 5:** The Aviator and the Airline — 48
**CHAPTER 6:** An Accumulation — 59
**CHAPTER 7:** The Miracle Year — 72
**MAP I:** Latin America — 91
**CHAPTER 8:** Life in the Air — 92

## PART II: WAR CLOUDS

**CHAPTER 9:** Across the Pacific — 109
**CHAPTER 10:** Island Stepping Stones — 121
**CHAPTER 11:** Clipper Glory — 133
**MAP II:** Pacific & Alaska — 146
**CHAPTER 12:** War in China — 147
**MAP III:** Asia — 161
**CHAPTER 13:** The Colonizers — 162
**CHAPTER 14:** The World of Tomorrow — 175
**MAP IV:** Atlantic — 188

## PART III: WARTIME MISSIONS

**CHAPTER 15:** The Secret Plan — 191
**CHAPTER 16:** Air Carrier of the Arsenal of Democracy — 206
**CHAPTER 17:** The Pan-Africa Corps — 216
**MAP V:** Africa & The Middle East — 227
**CHAPTER 18:** Far Horizons — 228
**CHAPTER 19:** Case 7: Condition A — 241
**CHAPTER 20:** Clippers at War — 250
**CHAPTER 21:** Hell Riders of the Himalayas — 266
**CHAPTER 22:** Militarization — 279
**CHAPTER 23:** "The Fastest With the Mostest" — 291
**CHAPTER 24:** Into the Congo — 301
**CHAPTER 25:** No Distant Lands — 313
**NOTES** — 319
**BIBLIOGRAPHY** — 361
**ACKNOWLEDGMENTS** — 369
**INDEX** — 371
**AUTHORS** — 395

# PART I

# AIR POWER

# CHAPTER 1
# VISIONS OF THE FUTURE

*"In a sense, the formation of Pan American Airways turned out to be the first countermeasure the United States ever took against Nazi Germany."*
—Henry "Hap" Arnold, commanding general,
U. S. Army Air Forces in World War II[1]

The Nazi blitzkrieg thundered over London, their bombs lighting up the blacked-out city as searchlights swept the sky and anti-aircraft batteries returned fire from Hyde Park. It was an hour before midnight and two Yanks were viewing the spectacle from their hotel rooftop. Juan Terry Trippe, president of Pan American Airways, would remember this day, June 17, 1941—now he was certain the United States would be drawn into the war in Europe. Major General Henry "Hap" Arnold, chief of the Army Air Force, saw grim confirmation of the prophecies of air power crusaders. Suddenly, a man stepped out of the shadows, tapped Trippe on the shoulder, and said, "The Prime Minister asks that you join him for dinner."[2]

Earlier that evening, Trippe appeared before the Royal Aeronautical Society to deliver the Twenty-Ninth Wilbur Wright Memorial Lecture. His topic, "Ocean Air Transport," detailed Pan Am's advances since pioneering commercial airways across the Pacific and Atlantic. Flying oceans was a "developing art," and with war curtailing Atlantic steamship service Pan Am provided a vital link between neutral America and besieged Britain. Trippe himself had made his crossing from New York on one of his airline's iconic Flying Clippers.

The muffled explosions of aerial bombing were audible throughout Trippe's lecture. Afterwards, Trippe was invited into the Air Ministry where Royal Air Force officials kept him talking before a gigantic world map. The topic was North Africa, where the tanks of General Erwin Rommel had cut off British supply lines and threatened Egypt and the Suez Canal. With the world map at hand, Trippe explained how a South Atlantic airway through Africa could supply the desert troops.

Trippe's ensuing meeting with Prime Minister Winston Churchill begs the question: were Trippe and Arnold on a secret mission, using the prestigious lecture as cover? Since the summer of 1940, Trippe and President Franklin Roosevelt had discussed securing the South Atlantic skies between Brazil and Africa since the Nazi conquest of France gave Hitler a foothold in French colonial Africa, making South America vulnerable. An operation across Africa had also been discussed in months of secret correspondence between Churchill and Roosevelt. The day of Trippe's lecture, Roosevelt reported to Churchill: "Army is studying possible ferry from Natal [Brazil] with idea that African landing places might be three in number—Bathurst, Freetown, and Liberia."[3] General Arnold even proposed using a commercial airline to do it.

Whether by accident or design, Trippe found himself at 10 Downing Street for a private midnight supper with Churchill. Scotch and sodas fueled two hours of poring over maps and talking strategy before Churchill gave his blessing—Pan Am would organize a ferrying and military supply operation across Africa. Churchill would cable Roosevelt and Trippe should expect to hear from the president when he landed in New York.

When a Clipper returned Trippe to New York a waiting Marine Corps officer escorted him to another plane that whisked him to Washington. Although Churchill and Roosevelt regularly corresponded by letter and telegram, the apparently serendipitous nature of the midnight brainstorming between the airline executive and prime minister is revealed in Roosevelt's first question to Trippe when he was ushered into the Oval Office: "What did you tell the Prime Minister?"[4]

Four months later, *Life* magazine took readers into Trippe's office on the 58th floor of New York's Chrysler Building. Writer Noel Busch described the squeak of a giant world globe as Trippe turned it, measuring with parcel string a new airway from Brazil's eastern hump to the African ports of Monrovia, Bathurst, Freetown, and Leopoldville. "By the time President Roosevelt was ready to talk plans for running a Pan American service across the South Atlantic to the Sudan, Trippe had already issued instructions for installing it," Busch revealed. "Trippe's latest display of his ability to transfer an extra hemispheric enterprise from blueprints to blue water on short notice was characteristic." The article's headline added: "Young Chief Helps Run A Branch Of U.S. Defense."[5]

*Time* magazine observed the airline's 1941 annual report "read like a military communiqué," and Pan Am was "an instrument of U.S. policy and a weapon of global war."[6] Trippe wrote in the report, "That Pan American today is able to serve the United Nations throughout the world, is due in large measure to the fourteen years of pioneering and scientific progress which have gone into the development of its facilities and the training of its personnel."[7] To the public those fourteen years, encompassing the existence of what was considered the world's greatest airline, were not about wartime exigencies but the miracle of commercial aviation.

Once upon a time, an airplane passing overhead made people stop and stare; even fall to their knees in wonder. Powered flight unshackled terrestrial bonds, obliterated ancient barriers of time and space. An airplane spanned distances in hours and minutes that took weeks or days by land and water. More than any other airline, Pan Am made that miracle a reality.

The "System," as Pan Am called itself, fulfilled the promise of air travel with style, serving up winged adventure with cocktails and gourmet meals. Within twelve years of its birth, Pan Am encircled the Caribbean and South America, conquered the oceans, boasted 65,000 miles of air routes serving fifty-five countries, and made its four-engine Clipper seaplanes a fixture of the skies. Pan Am was America's first and only international airline and sole possessor of the technology, infrastructure, and procedures to safely and systematically fly the oceans. By 1939, when Pan Am inaugurated commercial transatlantic flights, a print advertisement proclaimed: "It is a small world . . . by Pan American." The ad observed that the world had essentially shrunk, thanks to speedy flying Clippers binding together formerly distant lands. "Think what this change signifies . . . ," the ad rhetorically asked. "It means a new American leadership in this changing world! Those Flying Clippers are America's Merchant Marine of the Air. They are recapturing, on international trade routes, a prestige that has been lost to this country since the days of sail." The ad practically proclaimed that Pan Am was spearheading America's global interests.

Pan Am's status as "instrument of the nation" was hinted at in news describing how the airline out-maneuvered a competitor or negotiated its latest exclusive air agreement with a foreign power.[8] What was not generally reported was that Pan Am's stunning rise was promoted and facilitated by power brokers from Washington to Wall Street. By World War II, Pan Am was key to the strategic maneuvering of America and its allies.

Trippe and Arnold represented the dual forces shaping aviation since the first rickety winged gliders took flight—Trippe saw commercial potential, Arnold a weapon of war. Aviation's ability to overcome natural barriers convinced Arnold that foreign military air powers would one day fly across the two oceans that still seemed insurmountable bulwarks guarding the nation's coastlines, with those imagined enemy aircraft commanding the air space as it penetrated the vulnerable interior. Even the international expansion of commercial aviation, when operating under the flag of a hostile nation, posed a threat—and such an enterprise was operating in the hemisphere. And so, with his strategic military intuition, early flying experience, and a still uncommon grasp of the practical applications of the airplane—both among the general public and military planners—Hap Arnold formed Pan American Airways in the interests of national security.

In the summer of 1909, Hap Arnold was a twenty-three-year-old second lieutenant, two years out of West Point and heading home after a tour of duty in the Philippines. During a stopover in Paris, he saw his first airplane dramatically suspended on display over a street near the Place de L'Opéra—the monoplane of Louis Blériot, the first powered aircraft to fly the English Channel, a feat accomplished a few weeks previous. The "queer contraption," Arnold recalled, was "the forerunner of a human instrument that, for good or evil, in war and peace, was to change the face of the earth."

"I'll confess I hadn't any blinding vision of the future of Air Power at this moment, but one thought I did have was probably as good as anybody else's who looked at Blériot's plane that summer. I thought: 'If one man could do it once, what if a lot of men did it together at the same time? What happens then to England's Splendid Isolation?'"[9]

Arnold returned to New York in time to witness an exhibition of powered flight at the Hudson-Fulton Celebration marking the 300th anniversary of Henry Hudson's discovery of the river that bore his name, and the recent centennial of Robert Fulton's navigation of it by steamship in 1807. Among those marveling at the seminal aviation event was ten-year-old Juan Trippe. The boy and the soldier didn't know each other then, but the exhibition inspired their respective visions of aviation and sparked the passion that created Pan Am.

The Celebration Commission had fifty-one committees, including one to showcase "aerial locomotion." The Celebration report observed, "there was something peculiarly striking, even dramatic, in the thought that in a commemoration which recalled the days when the Hudson River was navigated only by canoes, and which celebrated the advent of Hudson's sailing vessel and Fulton's steamboat, the climax of three centuries of progress should be marked by the navigation of the river—or a part of it—by airships."[10]

The aviation star was Wilbur Wright. There had been lighter-than-air flights in hot air balloons that floated on air as a sailing ship floated on water. But flight in heavier-than-air flying machines, such as winged airplanes and gliders, depended on airflow over its surfaces for aerodynamic lift and upward thrust. In 1903, a motorized airplane designed and built by brothers Wilbur and Orville Wright lifted above the sand dunes of Kitty Hawk, North Carolina. It was the first recorded flight in a mechanically powered, heavier-than-air machine successfully flown and controlled by an onboard pilot. Six years later, the Celebration was showcasing Wright as a master of aerial locomotion. The Celebration's takeoff and landing field was Governor's Island, a military base across from Battery Park between Staten Island and Brooklyn to which Hap Arnold reported. Arnold later called Governor's Island New York's first "airport."[11]

Wilbur Wright made his first flying attempt the morning of September 29. His Model A Flyer was rolled from its shed and placed on a monorail facing due west to New York Harbor. A red canoe was strapped to the bottom as a lifeboat in case the aircraft crashed into the water. Wright lifted almost one hundred feet into the air, covered two miles, and spent seven minutes and ten seconds aloft as steam whistles of ships and nearby factories echoed cheering spectators ringing the shoreline and crowds on ship decks in the harbor. Wright made four successful flights that day, his last a spectacular trip up the Hudson and back covering almost twenty miles and lasting thirty-three minutes and thirty-three seconds in the air.

But his second flight was the most celebrated. At 10:18 a.m., Wright ventured over open water, aiming for Bedloe Island and the Statue of Liberty. He flew over the *Lusitania*, which was bound for England, as passengers on deck cheered and waved handkerchiefs.[12] As Wright made it to the Statue of Liberty, Juan Trippe and his father watched from Battery Park.

Charles White Trippe suspected his boy would be thrilled. Aviation fascinated Juan, and he had made a wooden model airplane with a three-foot wingspan that he propelled with elastic bands during outings in Central Park. (Orville also traced the Wright's aviation interest to a childhood toy, a rubber band driven helicopter from their father.)[13] It was said that Juan saw The Future as he watched Wright circle the Statue of Liberty.

The Celebration record alluded to aviation's military possibilities. Indeed, aviation's military and commercial potential were already entwined. The U.S. Army began studying the "flying machine" in August of 1907. On

February 10, 1908, the Wrights signed a contract with the War Department to develop a military plane. The first known fatality in American aviation occurred during its development when Army Lieutenant Thomas L. Selfridge died in a crash with Orville, who was severely injured. Despite that setback, on August 2, 1909, just before the Hudson-Fulton Celebration, the Wright warplane was accepted.[14]

The Wrights trained the first two military pilots for the War Department—one was Hap Arnold, who had received a War Department letter asking if he was willing. Arnold's commanding officer thought the idea suicide, which emboldened the young officer. On April 21, 1911, Arnold and second lieutenant Thomas Milling, 15th Cavalry, left New York by train for the Wright factory in Dayton, Ohio.[15]

The Wrights shared knowledge and hospitality, inviting their two students to join them for Sunday dinners. "They never took themselves half so seriously as we took them," Arnold recalled. "Still, to Milling and me, sitting at their Sunday dinner table and listening to their quiet stories[,] what they had done was a miracle. . . . Without any formal scientific training whatever, two 'ordinary' young Americans from an ordinary town in the state of Ohio had not only grasped and advanced the whole known science of aerodynamics—they had become its admitted masters, even more appreciated in Europe than at home. . . . More than anyone I have ever known or read about, the Wright brothers gave me the sense that nothing is impossible."[16]

Milling and Arnold emerged as the first qualified pilots in the U.S. Army. In the summer of 1911, Arnold flew five miles to deliver a satchel of letters in Long Island, making him one of the first U.S. airmail pilots. All the while, Arnold gained experience of aviation's peril and potential.[17] "All those early aviators knew more than they could tell anybody," Arnold later mused. "But what was it they knew, or knew they didn't know? Things happened, that was all. The air was a tricky place. The best laws, discovered and formulated by the best aeronautical brains, could still be upset, it seemed, in a second."[18]

By the summer of 1914, the Hudson-Fulton Celebration's dream of a glorious future ended with World War I. After the Armistice, America's military establishment ignored aviation's advancement in favor of warships and the security of two great oceans, while commercial aviation favored war surplus aircraft. In Europe, aviation was vital to recovery. Governments invested in national airlines, while defeated Germany saw commercial and military advantages in an air industry.

American air power advocates, led by Brigadier General Billy Mitchell, leader of American Air Forces in World War I, saw synergy in commercial and military aviation. "Air power is a composite of airplanes, air crews, maintenance crews, air bases, air supply, and sufficient replacements in both planes and crews to maintain a constant fighting strength," Hap Arnold explained. "In addition to that, we must have the backing of a large aircraft industry in the United States to provide all kinds of equipment, and a large training establishment that can furnish the personnel when called upon."

In 1923, the State Department directed the War Department to make a survey flight through Central America to consider landing fields and potential airmail service to the strategic Panama Canal Zone.[19] The resulting "Central American Flight" led by Major Raycroft Walsh on February 4, 1924, affirmed U.S. airmail service was viable.[20] The Post Office Department sent a representative to make a firsthand determination, but as Assistant Secretary of State Francis White recalled, "The man sent was extraordinarily lacking in vision; he went to the Canal Zone and to Port [Limón] in Costa Rica and then abandoned his trip saying he could see no future in the matter whatsoever."[21]

Meanwhile, a German airline was profitably operating in Colombia—too near the Canal for Arnold's comfort. He resolved to block foreign airlines by forming "Pan American Airways," a commercial airline whose name spoke to his stratagem of hemispheric security. By then, the boy who marveled at Wright's Hudson-Fulton flight had grown up into a leader of the air industry taking root in New York City.

★

Juan Trippe was raised in New York City but born in Seabright, New Jersey, on June 27, 1899. The son of Charles Trippe and Lucy Adeline Terry, he was named for his mother's stepfather, Juan Pedro Terry, the Cuban-born son of a wealthy Irish-Venezuelan.

Juan's life had just begun but two months later came within a hairsbreadth of ending. It was late August at Charles and Lucy's summer residence in Seabright, and a happy gathering of Lucy and her sisters included a horse-driven surrey ride. Juanita and Louise Terry and three-year-old brother Charles were in the front seats, with Juan, his nurse Louise Farr, and mother in the rear. Louise was holding the reins as they traversed the notorious North Borough railroad crossing, a gateless bend that concealed approaching trains—including the West End Express that was upon them, reportedly without a warning whistle, before Louise could lash on the two-horse team. The collision cut the surrey in half, instantly killing the horses and those in the front, hurtling the sheared rear section into a ditch.

"Three Killed by a Train: Son and Sisters-in-Law of Charles W. Trippe Dead at Seabright: No Warning At The Crossroads," read *The New York Times* front-page headline. Infant Juan, his mother, and nurse were injured but survived. The *Times* described the crossing as "one of the most dangerous in this vicinity" and the scene of several accidents in recent years. Lucy, found unconscious, was initially spared knowledge of her son and sisters' deaths for fear the shock would kill her. "There was much excitement in the village to-night," the newspaper reported, "and much indignation was expressed by the citizens over the failure of the railroad to place gates or a guard at this dangerous crossing . . . the matter will be thoroughly investigated."

The psychological impact on an infant, with or without conscious memory, of such a violent accident and heartbreaking loss cannot be determined. And while little spoken of in the years ahead, the incident was certainly made known to Juan.

Not long after the horrific tragedy, Lucy inherited over $190,000 of the Terry fortune. Charles, a Columbia engineering school graduate who had worked for railroads and the New York Health Department, became a Wall Street investment banker, forming Trippe & Company and buying a seat on the New York Stock Exchange. Notwithstanding a brief stint in the world of finance after college, Juan Trippe would make a firm decision not to follow his father into a comfortable Wall Street career. By then he had already accepted personal risk as an active pilot and would seek his destiny and fortune in the skies, pinning his future to the still embryonic notion that aviation could be shaped into a world-changing enterprise.

Pan Am historian Robert Daley, who spent considerable time with Trippe in his later years, might have hit upon a deeper truth in his offhand observation, "Trippe seems to have been an extremely fatalistic young man, as far as his safety was concerned."[22]

As a young man, Juan was a daydreamer with a sharp and inquiring mind. He also had a sense of patriotism and duty—a great, great uncle, John Trippe, had been a decorated naval officer who fought pirates in the Mediterranean and was the namesake of four naval ships.

By the time Juan enrolled at Yale in 1917, he was a husky six-footer and played right tackle on the freshman football team. He was renowned as a ferocious hitter with an Iron Man reputation for never being taken out of a game. Football embodied an American ethos of competition, a crucible where one's mettle was tested and success awaited the winner—and Juan Trippe liked to win. It was said, "[Trippe's] idea of the offense was—kill the other guy."[23]

The First Yale Unit, a flying club, nourished Juan's passion for aviation. Nicknamed "The Millionaires' Unit" because of their privileged backgrounds, they preferred being called "The Unit." "It was, in fact, a group of young men unified by an idea, fused together by an eager purpose, and steadfastly adhering to a conception of service," a Unit history noted.[24] By March of 1917, Yale provided immediate leaves of absence for students entering the military—the Unit was at the forefront of volunteers. "The fact that [First Unit volunteers] goes today to New London to be sworn into the Naval Reserve and is anticipating orders to enter into intensive training soon, brings the seriousness of the situation home to the members of the University," noted a *Yale News* editorial.[25]

On April 6, 1917, the U. S. declared war on Germany. A few hours after a satisfying 14-0 football victory over archrival Harvard, half the team resigned to join their classmates enlisting for the war.[26] Trippe applied with the Navy and was one of the elite nine of fifty candidates selected for night bomber pilot training. Juan, commissioned as an ensign in the U.S. Naval Air Reserve, was awaiting orders to ship overseas when the Armistice arrived on November 11, 1918.

Trippe returned to Yale in December of 1918. Although he entered Yale with the Class of 1920, the eleven-month absence for military service delayed his graduation until 1921. During his return to the university, he helped revive the Yale Flying Club (formerly the Yale Aeronautical Association), where he served as treasurer and organized the first intercollegiate air meet, his teammates including future partners John Hambleton—a Harvard man!—and schoolmate Cornelius Vanderbilt "Sonny" Whitney.[27] "Somewhere in the overlapping of the War and his college career, Mr. Trippe's slow-moving eye turned skyward, and never again were his thoughts wholly earthbound," *Fortune* magazine observed.[28]

Trippe bought a war surplus seaplane for $200 from a Philadelphia naval yard and commuted by air from East Hampton, where his family had a summer home, to New Haven, the home of Yale. He took off and landed from both spots at wooden ramps he built himself. The advantage of air travel was obvious—within minutes Juan reached areas that took a half-day or more by train or automobile. He developed practical experience over water, including flying high enough so in an emergency one could glide to a safe water landing.[29] Trippe wanted to make air travel a business when America had no international air service, few domestic routes and airfields, and practically no infrastructure, much less pilots, engineers, mechanics, radiomen, capital investment, manufacturers, and government support.

When Juan was twenty-one, his father died from typhoid. An economic downturn forced his father's firm into a reorganization that considerably reduced Juan's inheritance, but there was still enough to launch his first air company. Several items Charles Trippe bequeathed became fixtures in his son's future airline offices, notably a sturdy roll-top desk and a 19th-century Malby's "colossus globe," thirty-six inches in diameter, that put the world at Juan's fingertips as he plotted global air routes. But the world came later.

Juan formed Long Island Airways (LIA) in 1923, raising eyebrows among his social set that assumed he would become a banker, like his father. Juan envisioned LIA as a chance to develop a business model for the aviation industry. "It was on Long Island Airways that he developed his style," Pan Am's corporate history notes. "[Trippe] figured out the nature of an airline—what sort of thing it really would have to be, what conditions it would need in order to live and grow."[30]

Trippe was president, chief pilot, and sometime mechanic. The airline, a seasonal operation, had two full-time pilots, two reserve pilots, and seven naval surplus single engine Aeromarine pontoon bi-planes. The two-seater seaplane allowed for a pilot and passenger, but Juan ingeniously made an extra seat by making adjustments, including moving the gas tank from inside the fuselage to outside—now he could fly wealthy couples to the Hamptons, up the Hudson, even Albany and Lake Placid. An employee manning a motor launch at the foot of Wall Street on the East River went back and forth to a barge anchored near the Statue of Liberty, where LIA seaplanes stopped for passengers to board or disembark.[31] LIA's base and maintenance yard was an inactive naval air station at Rockaway Beach, a lonely hundred acres of salt marshes, lagoons, and islands with a view to a skyline dominated by the Woolworth Building. Trippe leased it "by benevolent permission of the Navy" for $100, and his agreement to keep four hangars freshly painted.[32]

When Trippe shut down for the winter of 1923–24, he began exploring the New York Public Library for what little there was on air transport. He set up appointments with transportation companies—ships, railroads, buses—that might provide a business model. Trippe burst into executives' offices with enthusiasm, asking smart questions and disarming the older men he met with a photograph of his fleet at Rockaway. One was Thomas D. Mitten, who upgraded Philadelphia's transport system from streetcars to buses and felt air travel was the future. Trippe contributed cost-accounting analysis to an aviation report Mitten co-authored with engineer William Stout and submitted to Secretary of Commerce Herbert Hoover, the future president Trippe would come to know.[33]

In its first two years, LIA earned about $40,000. A big slice, about two hundred hours and $12,000, came from the movie business in New York. Trippe's last professional piloting job was a movie stunt, the kind of cocksure risk that would soon rattle the nerves of conservative air executives. The script for the forgotten production called for Trippe to fly down Broadway and over Battery Park to the Statue of Liberty—he flew so low a cameraman filming from a rooftop caught the tops of his wings. When Trippe returned to Rockaway, a policeman was waiting with a court summons. Trippe's lawyer got the case dismissed—there was no law against "low flying."[34]

LIA marked Trippe's first visionary foray into other countries. When Trippe learned that United Fruit, which did considerable business in Central America, needed to make a three-day journey to Honduras's capital for paperwork that finalized transactions, Juan used his Yale connections to meet with company executives and convince them he could deliver their paperwork within hours by plane. He made a similar proposal to logging interests in the Canadian wilderness. But Trippe knew long-term success depended upon a U.S. Post Office airmail contract, and it would take "a substantial company," to get it and LIA, capitalized at only $5,000, was not that company. He closed LIA for good in 1924.[35]

With a strategy to win airmail contracts, Trippe incorporated his new airline, Eastern Air Transport, in Delaware on September 12, 1925. Trippe's team included Lorillard Spencer, a wealthy World War I combat pilot, L. L. Odell, a transportation engineer, Robert Thach, a war flyer and Alabama lawyer, and Sherman Fairchild, whose interest was aerial photography. Trippe attracted other young aviation enthusiasts, many from Yale, including friends and flying partners C. V. Whitney and John Hambleton. Within two years, Trippe, Hambleton, and Whitney were hailed as "Pan American Airways' Musketeers."[36]

The connection to capital was Cornelius Vanderbilt "Sonny" Whitney, son and heir to the fabled fortunes of Gertrude Vanderbilt and Harry Payne Whitney. "C. V.," as he was also known, was tall and handsome; a sportsman often dismissed as a polo-playing playboy who had "fatal blue eyes that are continually getting him in messes," his mother lamented.[37] Whether fate or those fatal blue eyes, his Yale years were marked by scandalous events. During Sonny's sophomore year, while driving at dawn without a license, he crashed his Stutz Bearcat into a horse-drawn wagon, killing a friend on the passenger side. In his junior year, he faced a million-dollar paternity suit brought by a former Ziegfeld Follies dancer that persisted for a decade before being dismissed. Harry Whitney, upset by his son's behavior, was determined to straighten him out. After Sonny graduated Yale in 1922, his father sent him to Nevada for a stint of hard work as an ore sampler at the family's Comstock mine.[38]

But Whitney had the patriotic resolve for service. He registered at Yale in the fall of 1917, but left to enlist as an aviation cadet with the Army Signal Corps. He was commissioned a second lieutenant and became a combat and acrobatics instructor. The Armistice arrived before he saw combat.[39]

John A. Hambleton was two years older than Juan, and from a banking family with deep roots in Maryland (Hambleton & Company, Inc. was established in 1865). Hambleton's lineage included a naval hero, and he had a passion for aviation, from piloting planes to helping found Maryland's Air National Guard. Hambleton believed that military service and the war would be waiting for him. In February of 1917, after one semester at Harvard, he enlisted in the Aviation section of the Army Signal Corps and by October was sailing for Europe, where he flew under Brigadier General Billy Mitchell in France.

Trippe, Hambleton, and Whitney were of that generation shaped by the Great War and among the first air warriors, qualities that characterized the spirit of the commercial airline that military airman Hap Arnold would form. "There was a sense of both [commercial] flight and military flight, of the white knight's code of honor," reflected George Hambleton, John's son and a Pan Am executive. "It seems that is important to the mindset that formed Pan Am."[40]

C. V. Whitney once noted another attribute characteristic of those who built the world's greatest airline: "We were born to the air."[41]

## CHAPTER 2
# BORN TO THE AIR

*"For hardship, disappointment, drama, and suspense, this 1919–27 era of civil aviation equals any that followed. It was the anvil on which the lives, characters, and skills of these very young civil aviation founders were forged . . . Trippe, Whitney, Hambleton were all [very young] in 1925. . . . [Their] old letters come alive with the eagerness, impatience, changing goals, and energy of youth—and no less, its inexperience and sometimes its naiveté. But where could one have gained experience? There was none."*

—John C. Leslie, Pan Am executive[1]

Commander Billy Mitchell later recalled April 1918 as a time when "air fighting was continuous and sharp" against German forces in the Metz area of northeastern France. During this period, a second lieutenant named John Hambleton "came forcibly to my notice," Mitchell added.

Hambleton left the Toul airdrome in command of a patrol of five airplanes, and Mitchell was on the field when three returned. As they landed and taxied to their assigned positions, Mitchell noticed each plane was ripped with bullet holes. The right body strut of the patrol leader's aircraft was almost shot away, and Hambleton himself had bullet fragments lodged in his head and shoulders. He coolly reported that superior forces attacked his patrol, they had lost two of their own but shot down three enemy aircraft, and he then led the survivors home. "In spite of the intensity of the combat he had been in this young officer made one of the best reports of the patrol that I ever heard," Mitchell recalled. "From that time on he distinguished himself in every operation. He became a flight commander, a squadron commander and soon would have been a commander of a group of one hundred airplanes [if the war hadn't ended]."[2]

Hambleton was a lieutenant with the 95th Aero Squadron in the spring of 1918, and part of Mitchell's air attack at Saint-Mihiel. It was the biggest coordinated use of airplanes in a military operation—1,481 planes flying 3,300 sorties that included observation flights, strafing, and bombing runs—and cleared the way for American ground troops at the Meuse-Argonne offensive.[3] Hambleton was eventually given command of the 95th, before leaving to command the 213th Squadron.

Harold Buckley, who flew alongside Hambleton in the 95th, attested to his bravery and leadership, observing that while under his command "there were none of us brought down." His commander always went into battle with a strategy, and he explained: "According to pre-arranged tactics, if we had an opportunity, he was to attack and I was to stay above, to guard him from a surprise attack from other planes. . . . The next occasion would be my turn; he would stay above and protect me." Buckley gave an example: "[A]fter some maneuvering, John gave me the signal and dove down on five Fokkers, shot down the end man with his very first burst, swung off and rejoined me and we made a get away [sic], being ten or so miles in Germany and well satisfied."[4]

Hambleton's greatest friendship from the war was Merian C. Cooper, a fellow air warrior similarly born to the air. Cooper recalled it was Christmas Eve, 1917 when his new friend talked about aviation's future. "I realized then—1917—that I was talking with a rare visionary genius, though an eminently practical one." After the Armistice, Hambleton returned home "on fire with the idea that man would eventually span the oceans by air, and with the direct idea of playing a part in the future of the then unknown civil aviation," Cooper explained.[5]

Cooper barely survived the war. He flew the American DH-4 Liberty plane, bitterly known as the "flaming coffin." The morning of September 26, 1918, returning from a bombing mission over Dun-sur-Meuse that began the Meuse-Argonne offensive, Fokkers attacked Cooper's squadron. During the furious dogfight, Cooper's cockpit burst into flames, his rear observer, Edmund Leonard, was wounded, and their bullet-riddled aircraft went into a flaming tailspin. Cooper opened the throttle, sucking out the flames, and miraculously coasted to a rough landing—near a German infantry camp. The Fokker that downed them landed nearby and the pilot got out—handsome and clean-cut, the spitting image of a flying ace in his crisp uniform bedecked with medals—and strode over. To the surprise of Cooper and Leonard the German pilot saluted them, followed by young soldiers rushing from the nearby camp to provide aid and comfort.

Cooper and Leonard would heal in different hospitals and prison camps until the whole bloody business ended with the Armistice. They were blessed, or damn lucky—the faulty Liberty plane and its architects would be singled out for scathing rebuke in General Mitchell's postwar air power crusade. Mitchell would declare that more Americans died from flying Liberty planes than from the guns of German pilots.[6]

Hambleton was one of those whose spirit was forged, not extinguished, in combat. Reporter Gerald W. Johnson wrote in 1929: "The average man came back tougher, coarser, more cynical, all-around meaner than he was before: but in a vast number of cases he also came back stronger, wiser, far more resourceful and more enduring. John A. Hambleton came back full of energy and ideas, able and willing to take the lead in a great pioneering enterprise, the development of commercial aviation in America."[7]

Hambleton returned to his family estate in the Green Spring Valley of Baltimore with the rank of colonel and honors including the Croix de Guerre and the Distinguished Service Cross with Oak Leaf Cluster. He took up investment banking but contemplated commercial aviation. In the spring of 1922, Cooper met Hambleton at Flat Rock, North Carolina (across the state from his sweetheart Margaret "Peg" Blow's hometown of Wilmington), to discuss a domestic airline's ideal organization and a potential American-owned foreign airline.[8]

On December 3, 1924, John married Margaret, the daughter of George Blow Elliott, president of the Atlantic Coast Line Railway. The couple took a five-month honeymoon cruise to Italy, Egypt, and ports in China, Japan, and Hawaii. Hambleton faithfully recorded each day's happenings in his diary, from the wonder of the Pyramids to a stomach ailment his bride picked up in Agra that required medical attention and persisted for months.

On May 2, they returned, docking in Seattle. The Hambletons took the West Coast Limited to the East Coast and the family home affectionately known as "Hambledune." John continued the ritual of recording, in his cramped handwriting, daily events in his palm-sized diary. His 1925 diary recorded a milestone year during which he joined his aviation dreams with those of Juan Trippe and saw a reckoning in Mitchell's controversial crusades for air power and against war profiteering. On May 8, the day after returning to Hambledune, Hambleton visited his old commander. "Found Mrs. Mitchell at home, but general [was] out exercising horses," he wrote. "They are both optimistic about the outcome of the controversy."[9]

Hambleton took a train to Washington on May 29, where he met with General George Pershing, heard a lecture from Major Raycroft Walsh on the "Hawaiian Maneuvers," a test of coordinated defense of the Pearl Harbor naval base, and visited the Mitchells. Hambleton also huddled with Major Walter G. Kilner, who agreed he would "have Sen. [William C.] Bruce write Secretary of the Navy stressing my interest in commercial aviation."[10]

The year's aviation breakthrough was the Contract Air Mail Act of 1925. Known as the Kelly Act after its chief sponsor, Congressman M. Clyde Kelly, Republican from Pennsylvania, it allowed private firms to bid for domestic contracts with the government. Trippe began working with Kelly to develop international airmail legislation.[11] But for the present, the prize was Air Mail Route No. 1, the potentially lucrative New York–Boston route.

Trippe's Eastern Air Transport was the "substantial company" he knew could make a powerful bid. He persuaded Hambleton, Whitney, and Bill Vanderbilt to put $25,000 each into Eastern, and added William Rockefeller to his board. The other contender was Colonial Airlines, led by such establishment figures as Connecticut Governor John Trumbull. The two rivals merged—reportedly, the U.S. Post Office considered the twenty-six-year-old Trippe too young to be responsible for a major airmail route.

On October 5, Trippe changed his company name to Colonial Air Transport (CAT), and two days later, after merging with Trumbull's outfit, the new airline was awarded Air Mail Route No. 1. Although agreeing to operate under Trumbull's corporate structure, Trippe got both parties to accept Colonial Air Transport as the corporate name, with himself as managing director. Trippe successfully argued that with the combined board numbering more than thirty, it would be efficient to form a seven-member voting trust. Trippe's side included himself, Hambleton, and Rockefeller. Trippe had to win over one vote to hold a majority, but that would prove more difficult than he imagined.[12]

Colonial Air Transport was headquartered in Manhattan, at the southeast corner of Madison Avenue and 42nd Street. The airline had three airplanes, two full-time pilots (including Bert Acosta, a future member of Richard Byrd's aerial expeditions), and two reserve pilots. The industry was converting from war surplus to modern aircraft, and at this point, Trippe "gave the signal to his wealthy [Yale] classmates, and said that aviation could someday be a business," Pan Am's corporate history records.[13]

As with his first company, Trippe considered Colonial a lab for developing a business model for the industry. "What sort of animal would [the aviation industry] be—would it be closer to a railroad, an international shipping line, a telephone system?" Trippe mused. "We kept our books, [payrolls], time charts. All these things were gotten right out of the bus and railroad formulas. It was trying to get a business-man's approach to what someday could be done with an airplane as a coming vehicle of transportation."[14] But as Trippe pored over mail service contracts for railroads and bus companies he realized each was "a local enterprise." As he noted, "It wasn't small thinking—there had been no precedent."[15]

On October 8, Hambleton went to New York to meet Bob Thatch, who was now part of the newly merged CAT. Hambleton's diary indicates it was the first he heard of the new company, although he was becoming deeply involved. "It appears [Thatch] is one of a group behind Eastern Airway and Colonial . . . who have originated Boston[–]New York feeder line. He wants me to take hold of the southern hub."[16]

The next day, Hambleton was driven to the airplane manufacturing plant in Hasbrouck Heights, New Jersey, recently established by Anthony Fokker, the Dutch aviation pioneer in prewar Germany who produced the fighter planes that bore his name. Waiting at Fokker's factory was L.L. Odell, an original member of Eastern Air Transport. "He impressed me favorably," Hambleton noted. He also met Fokker and was impressed with his aircraft: "Their three[-]engined ship is a corker."[17] The Fokker Tri-Motor, the first introduced in America, was a welcome advance for those distrustful of single-engine aircraft.

On October 13, Hambleton met Odell and Trippe at Thach's office to discuss expansion, notably "the southern hub." "They both feel that it would be foolish to begin operations on a Washington to Miami run but feel Jacksonville is far enough north to start from," Hambleton noted. "Finally both showed considerable interest that their group would probably be interested in going 50-50 on such a line." They were thinking big. A foothold in Florida would open up Cuba, the Caribbean, Central America—an October 15, 1925, document apportioning Eastern Air Transport stock mentions a Key West–Havana route.[18]

Trippe telephoned Hambleton on October 15 to report his group would go half on a Jacksonville to Miami run, at $300,000. That day, with "new figures and proposed schedules" for the prospective air link in hand, Hambleton and an associate caught the Havana Special train to Jacksonville for a research tour of the Florida Keys. Jacksonville was home to Merian Cooper's family, and Hambleton visited Merian's brother, a future Pan Am executive. "Called on Mr. John Cooper, Jr. who was very much interested in a seaplane line from a development he is interested in to Miami," Hambleton recorded. "It might have possibilities."[19]

The next day, before dawn, Hambleton and his associate drove a narrow brick road to St. Augustine. Hambleton made a bemused diary entry on real estate developments and "people's gullibility." They passed "Picture City," a sprawling movie studio development, Palm Beach, and Hollywood. In Miami Beach, Hambleton marveled at swamps being drained, new land emerging, tall buildings rising. "Development was almost continuous," he wrote.[20] The next morning, he was up before dawn and driving in pouring rain. It was still raining when he reached Tampa and met the mayor and city officials. "They are ready to begin an airdrome & want an engineer to build it for them," Hambleton noted. "Wired Thatch to advise him."[21]

Back at Hambledune, Hambleton met with Trippe and Odell on October 27 to draw up a "tentative set up" for a Florida airway. "We agreed that a line to carry passengers was the only profitable proposition to undertake in [Florida] at the moment and that we would have to have a record of operation before attempting to actually carry passengers," Hambleton recorded. That meeting was followed by a luncheon with aircraft manufacturer Harold Pitcairn to discuss his investing in their aviation ventures, including the proposed Florida line.[22] Hambleton met with Major General Mason Patrick, chief of the Army Air Corps, about "getting [Wall] Street to work on [Colonial] Airways." Major General Patrick replied that it was against policy for officers to be involved in a commercial venture and required the approval of the Secretary of War.[23] Pitcairn dropped out, but Hambleton had better luck with Milton Elliott, son of his father-in-law, the president of the Atlantic Coast Line Railroad. The coordination of rail and air connections would be a cornerstone of Pan Am's future network.[24]

Trippe's faction wanted Colonial to upgrade its fleet to the big three-engine Fokkers. Anthony Fokker told Trippe he was unwilling to send one of his planes to Florida unless they committed to an order.[25] There were rivals for a Florida line—on November 13, Hambleton noted a meeting with "Robertson" (possibly Major William Bryan Robertson, cofounder of Robertson Aircraft Corporation), who began talking about his own prospectus for a Florida airline. "I told him I was a competitor & to watch his step as I was competing," Hambleton wrote. That day, at noon, Trippe, Thatch, and Odell met with Hambleton to discuss his idea for purchasing Fokker planes. "[I] made Odell a proposition to buy present ship @ $20,000

& agree to buy a new one for $35,000, part of purchase price to be old machines," Hambleton recorded. "Odell did not like it. Thatch is favoring a syndicate instead of a corporation."[26]

On November 23, Hambleton, Trippe, and Odell met with Fokker and one of his sales managers. "We thrashed the matter [of buying planes] back & forth & finally agreed that Fokker was to make a trip down on Dec. 5th for 10 days," Hambleton wrote. If everything broke right, an order would be placed for the delivery of two ships in ninety days. "Trippe & I talked all afternoon & I feel very much encouraged about the whole thing."[27]

The new Fokker, considered the first true transport plane built in America, came with an eye-popping price tag of $37,500, "a large sum in the days when airplanes were uninsured," historian Matthew Josephson reported.[28] To the consternation of Colonel's cautious and conservative board, Trippe had gone ahead and placed an order with Fokker. "They were a bunch of old fogies," Trippe recalled.[29] The board became further alarmed with the news Fokker would promote his trimotored plane that December with a visit that included a survey flight to Cuba, where Trippe planned to petition President Gerardo Machado for air rights to Havana. The Fokker F-7 survey would be flown by navy flier George Ponds, with passengers Trippe, Fokker, John and Margaret Hambleton, Robert Thatch, and others boarding at various stages.

A key member of Trippe's survey was aviation industry publicist Harry Bruno. It was "a giant publicity stunt," recalled Bruno. "The real function of the flight was very neatly summed up in the orders I received from Juan Trippe himself: 'Build up public acceptance for the Fokker planes.'" It was all done "in grand style," Bruno added. Earlier in the year, Trippe had met Bruno, a go-getter who contended bad publicity might be avoided, even in the aftermath of a plane crash, if "properly handled." Bruno also had a visionary suggestion for Trippe: "One way to 'sell' the safety of air travel to the American people is to reach them through the medium of the motion picture." Bruno's concept of promoting air travel through moving pictures would be realized in movie newsreels and in advertisements broadcast on the future medium of television. Of course, the thrill of aviation was already being dramatically displayed on movie screens in dramas such as magician Harry Houdini's 1919 *The Grim Game,* which filmed an unplanned accident as two stunt planes spectacularly collided in mid-air (and miraculously made rough, but safe, landings). Pan Am insider Merian Cooper, who would forge a career as a filmmaker and Hollywood producer, captured the romance and wonder of flight in *Flying Down to Rio,* a 1933 RKO feature hailed as "A Musical Extravaganza Staged in The Clouds" (which includes Cooper's unheralded but historic pairing of dancer Fred Astaire with the little-known Ginger Rogers).[30]

The survey began with a layover at Bolling Field in Washington, allowing Hambleton's influential friends and acquaintances to tour the aircraft, including Air Corps chief Major General Patrick and Major General James Fechet, assistant chief of the Air Corps. The flight's publicity campaign got its desired headlines in Jacksonville: "Ten-Passenger Liner Reaches City at 10:40: Thousands See Huge Ship Skim Over City," read the *Jacksonville Journal* headline. "The flight was a revelation of the high degree of safety and comfort to which airplane designing and manufacturing has been developed," the paper reported. The cabin was "equipped as luxuriously as the finest yacht," with carpeting, an aisle separating cushioned wicker chairs, "ash receivers" fastened to the walls for smokers, and framed photographs of Fokker's European factories. The paper was too modest to mention the onboard toilet. Pond told the paper the flight had been "handicapped" by delays due to rain, winds, and fog, but bad weather otherwise had little effect.[31]

The pilot didn't mention the delays included one engine going out, and then another, followed by an emergency landing near Key West. Minutes before impact, Margaret Hambleton was hustled into the toilet, considered the safest spot. "We came down on one of the mangrove-covered keys, blew out our tires, and damaged the fuselage and wings, but were only jarred ourselves," Trippe recalled.[32] Margaret remembered coming down in a cornfield, but agreed they were none the worse for it: "Juan Trippe began laughing and shaking his head, so we joined in, and it all seemed a glorious joke when we . . . were picked up . . . in a very ramshackled Ford car."[33] (The

Colonial board wasn't laughing when Trippe argued the multiple engines allowed them to glide to a safe landing.)[34]

A special flight for Tampa's mayor and guests resulted in glowing comments of "amazement at the comfort and seeming safety of the trip," the *Tampa Telegraph* reported on December 19, along with news that Tampa would probably be one of the terminal points.[35] "Then, to cap the climax, the transport with Fokker and Trippe on board set a new record with a nonstop flight from Miami to Havana in 125 minutes," Bruno recalled, adding that Trippe was "thinking of an airline from Key West to Havana."[36] The Hambletons disembarked in Miami, leaving Pond to fly Fokker and Trippe to Cuba. When they met the Cuban dictator, Trippe proposed a demonstration flight. Machado's positive reaction would pay off later.

The Fokker was returning over the Keys when the left engine went out, and Pond aimed for what he hoped was a mud flat on Key Largo—it was a reef and blew both tires. This time there was no laughing as Trippe, Fokker, and Pond came ashore with the tide. According to historian Robert Daley, they lit a fire on railroad tracks to stop a train and catch a ride to Miami. Trippe recalled the plane sat on the beach for weeks until new engines arrived and it was repaired and flown back. Daley adds that the Fokker was sold and eventually flown by Richard Byrd on the first flight over the North Pole.[37]

★

In 1926, Trippe met a twenty-four-year-old chief pilot for St. Louis–based Robertson Aircraft Corporation named Charles Lindbergh. Unlike most flyers, Lindbergh was interested in radio and direction-finding equipment. "I remember," Trippe recalled, "that Lindbergh introduced himself to me and we began to review the ground triangular radio equipment which had just been developed for us by Hugo Leuteritz, a young radio engineer of R.C.A., and which we were using. Lindbergh was intrigued by the fact that the U.S. Navy dirigible 'Los Angeles' had been permitted to help calibrate our Air Mail Route No. 1." Lindbergh, Trippe added, "was extremely interested in any new developments in the primitive radio and direction-finding equipment of those days."[38]

Trippe and Hambleton wanted Colonial Air Transport to be a domestic and international airline. A key ally was Hambleton's childhood friend David Bruce, who married into the family of Treasury Secretary Andrew W. Mellon. Through Bruce's intercession, Mellon facilitated introductions to everyone from Secretary of Commerce Hoover to Secretary of State Frank Kellogg and the president. "I met Coolidge quite a few times," Trippe recalled. "Mellon would take me there. We would get in that little private elevator and go over there [Coolidge's office]."[39]

Bruce arranged a meeting between Trippe and Assistant Postmaster General W. Irving Glover. It didn't hurt that Trippe arrived with the backing of Dwight Morrow, a J. P. Morgan partner and a major figure in aviation policy. Trippe enthusiastically reported to Hambleton that Glover was interested in activating the old but now dormant airmail route from Key West to Havana. "His attitude left no doubt in my mind but that he would cooperate with us to the utmost," Trippe concluded.[40] Trippe was on fire with ambition, a December 2, 1926, letter to Hambleton reporting, ". . . I personally persuaded Messrs Weicker, Rockefeller, Whitney, Fairchild, [Richard] Hoyt and others to invest. . . . Five years from now I will turn back ten dollars for every single dollar invested, or 'bust' in the attempt."[41]

Trippe continued cultivating Yale connections that would aid the future Pan Am's development. There was Assistant Secretary of State Francis White, whose responsibilities included being Chief of Latin American Affairs. First Yale Unit contacts included founder Frederick Trubee Davison, son of a partner in J. P. Morgan & Co., whose career posts included an appointment by President Hoover as the nation's first Assistant Secretary of the Navy for Air. Another Unit star was David "Crock" Ingalls, the Navy's only aerial ace who would serve as Assistant Secretary of the Navy under Coolidge and Hoover, and become a Pan Am executive. (Ingalls's WW I missions included single-handedly destroying a German airdrome when he sprayed a balloon with tracer bullets and it burst into flames, collapsed on three hangars, and triggered an explosive fire.)[42]

In 1927 Trippe, Hambleton, and Whitney pursued their vision with a new airline. The Colonial board was content with Air Mail Route No. 1, but Trippe knew one route was not enough, given contracts under the Kelly Act lasted only four years. "I kept hearing that the New Haven Railroad had run successfully for years and why not Colonial," Trippe recalled. "They said: Why rock the boat? The boat was winning the race and why take on more. It was an ultra-conservative point of view."[43]

★

By the mid-twenties, Major Hap Arnold, now an Army Air Service information officer in Washington, was reading disturbing reports from the U.S. military attaché in Colombia regarding *Sociedad Colombo-Alemana de Transportes Aéreos*, or SCADTA, a German-Austrian airline with a strategy for expanding airmail and passenger service throughout South America, Cuba, and into the United States. The airline, established in Colombia in 1919, was the first in South America and one of the world's first successful airlines. Its seaplanes navigated the Magdalena River, which flowed north from the mountainous interior near Bogotá to the seaport of Barranquilla. Passenger fares were expensive but popular—rail and steamer could take weeks, but an airplane made the 650 miles from Barranquilla to Bogotá in seven hours. SCADTA owned its own post offices, set its own mail rates, pocketed all revenue from airmail stamps, and was securing monopoly concessions with other Latin American countries.[44]

Arnold met with Postmaster General Harry New and asked whether his office was legally obligated to grant the German airline an airmail contract. New replied that a contract would have to be awarded—unless another airline, ideally a U.S. company, could perform the service. Arnold headed to his office, took out a map, and began sketching an air route for a truly "pan" American airline. With planes limited in range, he had to consider geography. The most desirable gateway into Central America was the Caribbean Sea. Arnold envisioned flying from the western end of Cuba to the Yucatan

Peninsula, down to Guatemala, British Honduras, Nicaragua, and to the Canal Zone and Panama.

Arnold drew up a prospectus with Major Carl Spaatz, Major Jack Jouett, and former naval officer John Montgomery. "It is not generally realized," Arnold noted, "that that great international air line, Pan American Airways, was not started by any rich and powerful business combine, but actually was founded by three young Army officers and one ex-Navy officer without a dime between them."[45]

They would have to play catch-up against the "mystery man" helming SCADTA. Dr. Peter Paul von Bauer was another of that special breed born to the air and a force to be reckoned with in the struggle for air supremacy of the Americas.

## CHAPTER 3
# CHAMPIONS OF AIR POWER

*"There can no longer be any doubt that complete control of the air by any nation means military control of the world."*

—GENERAL BILLY MITCHELL[1]

When the Armistice arrived, the German pilot's first thought was his standing orders to never surrender a plane—so he pulled the fuse of a charge to the fuel tank of his aircraft and blew it up. Returning from France, he saw burning and broken planes scattered throughout the Rhineland and Germany. "It seemed the end . . . a nightmare for those of us who loved flying," he wrote. "It was worse, much worse, than all the dangers of war I had been through." Most of the destruction of airplanes came after the Treaty of Versailles, often by a starving population desperate for firewood and the pittance they might get for scrap metal. The air warrior destroyed his plane out of duty; they were destroying planes out of desperation. "You couldn't blame those people," the pilot wrote. "And, anyhow, planes to them were the very symbol of war—which they hated above all."[2]

The German pilot, writing under the alias Hauptmann Hermann, recalled innocent days when his college professor, aircraft manufacturer Hugo Junkers, told him: "The airplane will become a weapon of happy humanitarianism that will carry blessings to all people and all nations." But soon after Germany's defeat, government officials asked an outraged Junkers to design passenger planes that could be converted into bombers. Germany had begun its secret rearmament, and commercial aviation was key.

"There was also the very important task of matching development in military aviation abroad and of collecting intelligence—a task that in the beginning was almost entirely handled by [the commercial aviation] industry," Hermann wrote. "Air traffic could be subsidized without running afoul of the Versailles treaty. Air traffic lines could train pilots without arousing suspicion, since they needed pilots. Through the channel of the airlines large amounts of money could go to industry without arousing suspicion. Airline companies could build transport planes (then still considered convertible into bombers), and could fly them at night—a procedure that would amount to training pilots as night bombers. In a word, airlines would be the perfect camouflaged set-up for secret air rearmament."[3]

There was national pride and commercial potential in setting up an airline in South America, where air travel could overcome primitive roads, mountainous terrain, and jungles and rivers. With the lack of a U.S. international airline, a colossal market was open to foreign interlopers such as SCADTA. But while Europe was close to the east coast of South America by sea, by air the U.S. had the hemispheric advantage. "The route to North America was one continuous fly-way, with short hops and profitable stops," Pan Am's corporate history notes. "And so, by air, you could re-draw the political and commercial geography of the world—unhook the Latin American countries from Europe and attach them to North America. In fact, airmail to Latin America might make a bigger difference sooner than domestic U.S. airmail . . . airmail to South America would change trading conditions fundamentally."[4]

But the U.S. had not legislated an international air capacity, nor negotiated reciprocal air agreements. "It was obvious from the outset," a Pan Am document observed, "that an American-flag air transport service in Latin America could not be developed in competition with the air lines subsidized by European nations, unless the Government established a national policy of encouraging such a service by long-term airmail contracts or other financial assistance."[5]

The airplane changed the rules of military strategy and national security, but most U.S. policymakers failed to see it. The architects of SCADTA saw the possibilities.

★

During the war, Julius Klein, an observer in the German Air Corps, often held court in the officer's mess, telling tales of his former life as an emerald prospector in Colombia and the wonders of the Magdalena River, describing it as the perfect airway for seaplanes. After the Armistice, some German airmen decided to create that imagined airway. Werner Kaemmerer, who came to Barranquilla to sell war surplus airplanes, began making trips to Germany to find better planes and crews for a potential airline in Colombia. He returned with two Junkers seaplanes, pilots Friedrich Fritz Hammer and Helmuth von Krohn, and aviation technician Wilhelm Schnurbusch, who had been developing torpedo planes at the German Navy's aviation development center.[6]

By 1920, airmail service began when von Krohn, piloting a Junkers F-13, made a delivery from Barranquilla to Puerto Colombia. The all-metal monoplane, with its closed cabin capable of carrying four passengers and two-person crew, was better suited to the tropics than a rot-prone wood and fabric plane. Colombia's steaming humidity still caused radiators to boil and engines to overheat, planes lost power, payloads had to be limited to attain lift. Schnurbusch experimented with big automobile radiators, extending wingspans to improve takeoffs, and adjusting pistons to provide full throttle at sea level.[7]

Dr. Peter Paul von Bauer arrived in Bogotá in time to lead the fledgling operation. "[von Bauer] saw very clearly the essentials of the geographic set-up—the long river leading straight in from the coast to near the capital city; the incredible time savings that could be offered," notes Pan Am's corporate history. "If Junkers or somebody could come up with an airplane of sufficient performance, here was an opportunity to create something quite new under the sun: an airline."[8]

Von Bauer was born in 1888, second son of a wealthy Austrian with holdings in sugar beets and a sugar refinery. He attended the University of Munich, where he began studying engineering, but switched to geography, geology, and cartography. In 1911, he booked passage on a ship to Panama, gateway to his planned explorations of North and Central America. Onboard, he met Hamilton A. Rice, a Bostonian working for a British rubber company and headed to the nexus of Colombia, Venezuela, and Brazil to search for a new river passage to the port of Manaus. Von Bauer joined Rice's expedition, a chance meeting and snap decision that turned into two years of adventure.[9] They usually traveled by canoe, venturing into jungles where they encountered tribes untouched by the outside world. At one point, von Bauer was near death from fever, but took some sage, jungle-wise advice—drank massive quantities of *aguardiente*, the local moonshine. Whether youthful vigor, the parasite-killing properties of the intoxicating spirits, or a bit of both, he survived.[10]

Von Bauer completed his doctorate and returned to his exploration of Central America—and his destiny in Bogotá, where Austrian Consul Albert Tietjen facilitated Dr. von Bauer's introductions to Kaemmerer's team. A few days later, Tietjen proposed von Bauer as the airline's European representative charged with adding amphibian planes through a swap of stock and planes with Hugo Junkers. Von Bauer personally put SCADTA on secure financial footing through a $100,000 deal with a Peruvian sugar concern that allowed him to buy a controlling interest, which he shared with his brother, Victor. Von Bauer shunned government subsidy and entered into an airmail contract with Colombia. The airline's agency at Bogotá was in the shop of a hardware dealer who happened to be the German Consul. Customers sending airmail letters put them in chamber pots marked "Barranquilla" or "Europe."[11]

In 1923, SCADTA proved its value. A joint land survey between Colombia and Venezuela to settle a boundary dispute stalled because of mountainous terrain, jungle, and Motilones Indians likely to greet intruders with poisoned darts. But within six weeks, SCADTA mapped 2,500 square miles by air. When the newly delineated border was found rich in minerals on the

Colombian side, suspicious Venezuelans called in the French to check the data—they judged it "excellent." The following year, during one of the perennial bank runs, SCADTA airlifted tons of vital currency from Medellín to Bogotá, avoiding weeks of risky land travel. The grateful government provided about $60,000 toward the purchase of a Dornier-Wal, an all-metal sesqui-plane flying boat designed by Dornier of Germany, whose planes were usually produced in Italy to circumvent the Versailles Treaty.[12]

Von Bauer captured the public's imagination, promoting pilots as national heroes and advertising the wonder and comfort of air travel. In 1925, he led two amphibian planes on a historic survey of Central America—testament to its importance was that the U.S. granted permission to pass near to the Canal Zone via a specified airway. The benefits included a lucrative airmail proposal from Guatemala's Minister of Development. The only hitch was Havana, where a plane needed a new engine and customs made it difficult to obtain (von Bauer suspected U.S. pressure). The survey proved the feasibility of air routes from Colombia to the Canal and throughout the region. *Fortune* magazine declared the survey "over the uncharted jungles of Central America" had been a "remarkable voyage."[13]

Von Bauer traveled to New York for a fund-raising and diplomatic push through the summer of 1926. He formed a charter in Delaware for an "Inter-American Airways" and took meetings with President Coolidge and Postmaster General New to discuss a U.S. airmail contract. "As a matter of fact, Postmaster General New definitely told him that he would not give him a contract; that he would only give it to an American company using American planes and pilots," recalled the State Department's Francis White.[14] But within a year, von Bauer would return to Washington with diplomatic muscle.

Meanwhile, other German airlines were emerging in Latin America. In 1924, the Kondor Syndikat was organized in Germany and began operating as a survey company in South America and the Caribbean. Its German-owned successor, Condor, was incorporated in Brazil in 1927. "This beginning of German air transport activity in Brazil is of considerable significance, for Brazil was to become the base of German airline operations throughout the continent—a logical development in view of its strategic position on any air route to Europe and its large German population," historian William Burden explains. "Deutsche Lufthansa, the German government-owned combine which took over most of the multitudinous German air transport companies in 1926, had complete financial control of Condor almost from the first." (The airline was identified as "Luft Hansa" until 1933 when it was thereafter referred to as "Lufthansa.")[15]

Von Bauer claimed his airline was practically a private company, but in a 1929 historical background report to incoming Secretary of State Henry Lewis Stimson, Francis White wrote, "It appears . . . [von Bauer] is very close to the German Luft Hansa and, although he denies it, we have been credibly informed in the past that the Luft Hansa controls his operations."[16]

Billy Mitchell was at the forefront of air power advocates warning of foreign airlines operating near the Panama Canal, as well as another world war that would be largely decided in the air. Mitchell never forgot the young flyers who went down in flames, victims of an unholy marriage of politicians and war profiteers he publicly damned as the "Air Trust." Mitchell envisioned an autonomous air force and argued America was vulnerable to air attack—the oceans would not be a defense for long. He felt military and commercial aviation were linked and an international airline was vital to the nation's strategic interests. Mitchell's supporters included Hap Arnold, Colonel Hambleton, Major Carl Spaatz, and Captain Eddie Rickenbacker, America's famed WW I flying ace.[17]

Mitchell hailed military officers who were advancing aviation, including Navy airman Lieutenant Commander Albert C. Read, who took the "Atlantic challenge" of British newspaperman Lord Alfred Northcliffe. On May 16, 1919, Read led three four-engine Navy Curtiss flying boats on the 1,300-mile stage from Newfoundland to the Azores. Two of Read's group dropped out, one rescued at sea and the other making it to land. Read's aircraft continued through a violent rainstorm, landed in the Azores, and flew the 800 miles to Lisbon, becoming the first to cross the Atlantic.[18]

By the early 1920s, the U.S. air industry was getting traction, but Mitchell's air power campaign was complicating things. "After 1921 the aviation industry itself worked actively for Federal legislation and thereby revealed at a tender age its uniqueness among private enterprises," a Federal Aviation Agency history wryly notes. "Congress' reluctance to legislate on the matter stemmed largely from the controversy over aviation's status in the Nation's defense structure."[19]

In July of 1921, Mitchell led a team of Army airmen off the Virginia coast to determine whether aerial bombing could sink a battleship. The demonstration was officially approved, but Mitchell disregarded advance words of caution from War Department "brass heads." "Get into this thing, as if we had to sink an enemy ship attacking one of our ports," Mitchell urged his team, who were armed with 2,000-pound bombs, not lighter bombs sanctioned by the Navy, and flew to higher than anticipated altitudes. To Army and Navy observers watching from the *Henderson*, the observation ship, it seemed impossible that airplanes could sink the anchored *Ostfriesland*, a 27,000-ton German ship employed for the demonstration. But one bomb wounded it in a spectacular explosion, and the airmen went for the kill.

As the great ship sank, one plane broke from the pack and made such a low arc over the *Henderson* the observers involuntarily ducked. As one witness recounted, "Billy Mitchell at the controls, leaned perilously far out of its cockpit, and waved his hand to the gasping crowd. . . . You could see his devilish grin under his goggles. Suddenly with a choppy military salute, he swerved about and tore off after his boys."[20]

## CHAPTER 4
# PROPHET OF A NEW ERA

*"Slim Lindbergh had a curious view of life and risk. And he loved flying. He loved it from the very beginning knowing, that as an aviator in the twenties, he could not expect to live very long. He once said that if he could survive ten years before he was killed, this would more than equal any ordinary lifetime."*

—Juan Trippe[1]

The U.S. Navy was interested in the potential of airships and the U.S.S. *Shenandoah* was one of its prized dirigibles. The Navy scheduled a *Shenandoah* flight on September 3, 1925, but it was stormy that day. Commander Zachary Landowne argued that it was too dangerous, but the flight continued as ordered—the airship went down in the bad weather, crashing near Sharon, Ohio. A mob swarmed over the wreckage, scavenging for souvenirs where thirteen crewmen died, including Commander Landowne. Meanwhile, Hap Arnold's friend, Navy Commander John Rodgers, along with his crew, was reported missing while on the historic first attempt to fly from San Francisco to the Territory of Hawaii—the vast Pacific between the mainland and the islands was considered impossible to cross by air. Rodgers and his crew survived but were presumed lost at sea when the *Shenandoah* crashed. Billy Mitchell, who counted Landowne and Rodgers as friends, took it badly when Secretary of the Navy Curtis Wilbur seemed to shrug off the air disasters with the statement, "The Atlantic and Pacific are still our best defense."

An angry Mitchell issued a statement on September 5 proclaiming Landowne and Rodgers "martyrs" and blasting the "criminal negligence and almost treasonable administration of the national defense by the War and Navy Departments." Mitchell acolyte Hap Arnold called it a "remarkable statement," while President Coolidge announced that Mitchell would be court-martialed.[2]

Coolidge did establish an Aircraft Board to hold aviation hearings and asked J. P. Morgan partner Dwight W. Morrow to chair it. In the opinion of Arnold and others, the board had respectable members, including Morrow and Senator Hiram Bingham, a recently elected Republican from Connecticut and an adventurer credited with discovering the ruins of Machu Picchu. But the real purpose, Arnold felt, was to overshadow an investigation by Wisconsin Congressman Florian Lampert considered too favorable to Mitchell's air power views.[3]

"Wrote Bingham a letter advocating a separate air force," Hambleton recorded in his diary, echoing a key component of Mitchell's crusade. A week later, Bingham invited Hambleton to testify before the Aircraft Board in Washington. On September 28, Hambleton noted he "occupied front row at hearing all day." Major Kilner testified first, followed by others advocating for "[General Mason] Patrick's scheme, that is a separate [air] corp within the War Dept."[4]

Mitchell's court-martial was scheduled for October 28, 1925, in Washington, and Hambleton talked with his old commander early in the month. "He is more optimistic than ever," Hambleton concluded. "Says that all the board could be expected to disclose was that something is radically wrong."[5]

Frank Reid, a Republican Representative from Illinois and Mitchell's chief counsel, presented evidence the *Shenandoah* flight was ordered as a "publicity stunt" despite dangers that included bad weather. Reid noted faulty and obsolete planes used in the Great War, the lack of postwar investment in military aviation and air readiness, and the War Department's "almost treasonable" failure to institute proper air service to defend the Hawaiian Islands until 1923. One key defense echoed Arnold's crusade against SCADTA: "That the War Department has been guilty of almost treasonable administration in not forestalling the attempt of a foreign flight administration to secure a foothold in Central America, within striking distance of the Panama Canal, and though often requested to do so by the chief of the air service, it ignored this menace."[6]

Colonel Hambleton, Captain Rickenbacker, Major Spaatz, and Major Arnold were among seventy-three defense witnesses. During the trial, General Fechet flew over the capitol on maneuvers, allowing Arnold, who was testifying, to point out the sound they heard overhead was a flyover of thirty-five planes—the Army's entire air force.[7] Raycroft Walsh, who flew the Central America survey the previous year, testified in support of a U.S. air presence in the Americas, adding "foreign interests had gained a foothold in Central America, threatening the Panama Canal."[8] Rickenbacker's testimony assailed the War Department and government for using obsolete planes in World War I, the evidence being "the graves of men whose lives were a pitiful sacrifice." He declared the military establishment "through petty selfishness and envy," were now trying to destroy a man who served his country with distinction.

"I might as well have been talking to a stone wall," Rickenbacker later lamented. "Billy Mitchell was found guilty and dismissed from the service. That was his reward for the great service he had given his country."[9]

It was clear to air power advocates that commercial aviation was the best route to achieving their strategic vision. "[H]ealthy air transport was, is and always will be of vital importance to our country," declared Rickenbacker, whose own civil aviation interests included Eastern Air Lines. "Only through the normal demands of a growing air transport industry could a healthy aircraft-manufacturing industry grow and prosper. . . . If the government would not train large numbers of men for aviation or encourage the establishment of at least potentially greater aircraft production, then it would be up to the commercial airlines to do so. By selling air travel, by increasing both mileage and service, by working constantly to perfect the reliability of commercial aviation, we could establish nuclei of production and training that could be expanded when the need arose."[10]

Despite Mitchell's court-martial, 1926 marked a breakthrough for American aviation. Many policymakers privately agreed it was in the national interest to block foreign airlines in Latin America. Even the Aircraft Board, which rejected a separate air force, influenced a reorganization of the Army Air Service through legislation establishing the Army Air Corps on July 2, 1926.[11]

The significant achievement was the Air Commerce Act of 1926, described as "the legislative corner-stone for the development of commercial aviation in America." The new law separated military and civil aviation as well as mandated that the Secretary of Commerce encourage establishment of airways and air commerce, advance technology, license pilots, certify planes and equipment, and investigate accidents. The act stipulated all foreign aircraft, even commercial ones, had to secure permission to fly through U.S. airspace, including the Canal Zone, and that U.S. civilian planes obtain reciprocal rights.[12]

As prospects brightened, talks continued at Hambledune. Fife Symington, a future Pan Am executive, recalled listening to Trippe and Hambleton discuss ideas few dared dream. "[They] enthusiastically outlined their dreams and plans for transoceanic and transpolar flight . . . the financing, required government approval, most suitable airplanes for the routes, technical support and flying expertise of crew members charged with the responsibility of safe pilotage of the planes . . . Hambleton and Trippe's particular interest was the careful planning of those subjects for the launching of an international airline."[13]

Merian Cooper, now a Hollywood filmmaker, fixed the seminal talks at Hambledune as coming in late 1926 or early 1927, soon after his return from the jungles of Siam, where he and his production partner Ernest Schoedsack had made *Chang*, an adventure film for Paramount Pictures. "During this meeting we discussed at length the feasibility of pioneering, in the near future, Latin American commercial routes," Cooper recalled. "It was then that Hambleton proposed, for the more distant future, his vision of intercontinental Polar Flights—a dream in those days more fantastic than today's prospect of passenger flights to the Moon. It was beyond the wildest expectations of every pilot, engineer, and aircraft designer of that era. . . . It was his dream, and his alone; neither Trippe nor I (nor anyone else of whom I know) dreamed of it until then."[14]

A commercial airway from America to Europe was another dream. In the tradition of cash competition to spur aviation, a $25,000 prize awaited the first to fly a heavier-than-air powered craft nonstop from New York to Paris. The offer, made in 1919 by French-born American hotelier Raymond Orteig, seemed impossible until aviation advances made the feat feasible by the mid-1920s. In 1926, French ace René Fonck made the first attempt, flying with a three-person crew in a trimotor Sikorsky outfitted with radio equipment and red leather padded seats. The plane didn't even lift off from Long Island's Roosevelt Field, crashing down an embankment at the end of the runway and killing two of Fonck's crew. By April of 1927, Commander Richard Byrd's Fokker crashed on its first test flight. Ten days later Noel David and Stanton Wooster, sponsored by the American Legion, died in a crash during their last test flight. On May 8, Frenchmen Charles Nungesser and François Coli, attempting to fly from Paris to New York, disappeared.[15] Prize money seemed inconsequential, given the chances of wings icing over, engine failure, fatigue, or anything that could send a plane into the ocean. Only those born to the air contemplated it.

⭐

In the predawn hours of May 20, 1927, Roosevelt Field was chilly, and a drizzle made the airfield muddy, but one young barnstorming airmail pilot decided to risk all. Juan Trippe, who was there, estimated 500 spectators had come to see history, or disaster, in the making. Among them were such aviation luminaries as Anthony Fokker, Bernt Balchen, René Fonck, and Ruth Nichols, as well as rivals for the Orteig Prize: Richard Byrd, Clarence Chamberlin, and Bert Acosta. On hand to record the event was a Fox Film Corporation newsreel crew equipped with a new sound-on-film process called Movietone.[16]

The pilot's plane, covered in tarpaulin and secured to the back of a motor truck, arrived with a police escort from nearby Curtiss Field. The muddy runway had deep ruts requiring boards set across so the *Spirit of St. Louis* could be safely pulled to its starting point at the field's western end. The slow march in darkness and drizzle conjured an image that would have been a premonition of doom to anyone but the flyer, Charles Lindbergh. "It's more like a funeral procession than the beginning of a flight to Paris," he thought.[17]

Trippe wondered if Lindbergh would even make it off the field. There was a gully in the middle, telephone wires at the end of the 5,000-foot runway, a muddy field, and the air was heavy. "I did not attempt to speak to him," Trippe recalled. "I felt that he had enough on his mind. . . . I knew that his small plane was terribly overloaded with its 451 gallons of gasoline and 20 gallons of engine oil. He was well down into it, seated in a kind of wicker armchair, with extra fuel tanks built into the plane in front of his face where the windshield should have been. [The setup required a built-in periscope for Lindbergh to see in front of him.]

"The plane began to roll, very slowly at first, then a little faster. . . . Finally, he was in the air," Trippe recalled. "He cleared the telephone wires, they said, by a mere 20 feet. Then he was gone and we all went back to the city. The next evening (Saturday) we were greatly relieved to learn that Lindbergh had landed safely at Le Bourget [airfield outside Paris]."[18]

Lindbergh flew past exhaustion and human endurance—he had been in the air thirty-three and one-half hours, setting a nonstop airplane flight record of 3,500 miles—when he saw the bright lights of Paris and used the illumination to steer toward Le Bourget airfield, where an estimated 150,000 were waiting. At 10:24 p.m., the crowd heard the miraculous sound of an engine roar from the sky, followed by the *Spirit of St. Louis* caught in the sweeping searchlights. As he landed, Lindbergh saw what he recalled as a "movement of humanity" across the airfield. Lindbergh was quickly spirited away and his history-making aircraft was secured in a hangar before the frenzied crowd caused damage to the pilot or his plane (a few souvenirs from the plane were grabbed, including the clipboard with Lindbergh's flight log).

Poet and publisher Harry Crosby, nephew and godson of J. P. Morgan, was there and described frenzied "pandemonium [of] wild animals let loose, and a stampede towards the plane . . . and it seems as if all the hands in the world are touching or trying to touch the new Christ and that the new Cross is the Plane and knives slash at the fuselage."[19]

During his triumphant stay in Paris, Lindbergh met Blériot and called him "my master." The first to fly the Channel passed the torch by replying, "Ah, but you are my son, you are the prophet of a new era."[20] The Future seemed to coalesce in the twenty-five-year-old pilot who overnight became the archetypal hero of the century; a man inflated to super dimensions through the new mass media that transmitted his voice via radio broadcasts and replicated his image in newspaper photos and the flickering projected light of movie newsreels. "Slim," as his friends knew him, had a humble nature to go with his tall, lean, all-American looks, but his eyes seemed fixed on Destiny. "His glance [was] keener, clearer and brighter than anyone else's, lit with a more intense fire," wrote his future wife, Anne.[21]

Lindbergh and his *Spirit* returned home on the U.S.S. *Memphis*, a battleship sent by Coolidge. The president personally awarded Lindbergh the first Distinguished Flying Cross and promoted him from lieutenant in the Air Service Reserve Corps to colonel. Lindbergh used his sudden celebrity to champion American aviation, beginning with what was said to be his first public appearance "under roof" since his return, a gathering at the Washington Auditorium sponsored by the National Press Club. Lindbergh explained that Europe looked at U.S. airmail with "reverence," having no similar service. "But, whereas we have mail lines, they have passenger lines. All Europe is covered with a network of lines carrying passengers between all the big cities. Now it is up to us to create and develop passenger lines that compare with our mail routes."[22]

On June 13, Lindbergh was honored in New York with the kind of ticker tape parade reserved for victorious armies. At the reviewing stand at City Hall Park, he addressed the crowd and radio audience: "In regard to aviation I would like to say just a few words, that is, not to expect too rapid development. We are not going to have trans-Atlantic service in a few months. . . . It is inevitable, but it will be after careful development and experimental research. We should have it probably within five or ten years."[23]

Trippe visited Lindbergh at the Commodore Hotel. A week later, Lindbergh and his lawyer came to Trippe's 57th Street apartment for a lengthier discussion. Trippe, an ex-executive of Colonial Air Transport, asked the most famous man in the world to be involved in a new airline he was planning. "Trippe was extremely persuasive," writes Pan Am historian Robert Daley, "and an agreement in principal was hammered out that night, even though his airline did not yet exist and his prospects were far from sure. It was understood that Lindbergh would fly off on his goodwill tour through all forty-eight states, as planned. Afterward, he would swing down through Central America on a second goodwill tour, this one backed by the State Department. By the time he came back, Trippe's airline should be better defined."

On July 20, Lindbergh's air tour of the continental United States began as the *Spirit of St. Louis* left Long Island's Mitchel Field. The route headed to Connecticut and Maine, crossed the continent to Washington and down to California, returning through the South to New York. Lindbergh logged 22,350 miles and two-hundred and sixty hours in the air, visited eighty-two cities, rode in 1,285 miles of parades in his honor, and made 147 speeches—tens of millions saw him, what Lindbergh biographer Scott Berg estimates as "one-quarter of the nation." Throughout, Lindbergh extolled aviation as a key industry and symbol of progress. When Lindbergh returned to Mitchel Field on October 23, the fate of Trippe's airline was decided.[24]

★

The battleground for U.S. international aviation—"FAM 4," the Foreign Air Mail route from Key West to Havana—was not virgin territory. Aeromarine Airways, an American company started in 1919, began flying first class mail from Key West to Havana under contract with the U.S. Post Office in November of 1920. However, Aeromarine's schedule was somewhat "on demand," notes Pan Am executive John Leslie, and folded in 1924.

Assistant Postmaster General W. Irving Glover, the man Postmaster General New put in charge of airmail, wanted to revive the route.[25]

Hap Arnold officially formed Pan American Airways on March 14, 1927, and set his sights on FAM 4. Arnold had been quietly developing his airline throughout the Mitchell affair, with plans to install himself as president and general manager, Carl Spaatz as operating director, Jack Jouett as personnel manager, and John Montgomery as field manager. Arnold recalled "our plans for Pan American had progressed so well that I had made up my mind to resign from the Army." But the aftermath of Mitchell's court-martial included payback for his supporters, with Hap banished to Fort Riley, Kansas. "That was the end of my plan to resign [the Army] and become president of our newly founded Pan American Airways," he wrote. "I couldn't very well quit the Service under fire."[26]

With Arnold's withdrawal, Richard D. Bevier was installed as president, John Montgomery as vice president, and George Grant Mason as secretary. Pan Am was an airline on paper only—other than a purpose and mission imparted by Arnold, the new company had no aircraft and no commercial aviation experience among its corporate officers.

The battle for FAM 4 included the new airline begun by Trippe, Hambleton, and Whitney. On June 2, 1927, Robert Thach presented papers in Delaware forming the Aviation Corp. of America (ACA). The partners each put in $25,000, but capital investment totaled $300,000 thanks to backers who followed them from Colonial, including Grover C. Loening, W. Averell Harriman, William H. Vanderbilt, Edward O. McDonnell, Sherman M. Fairchild, John Hay "Jock" Whitney (C. V.'s cousin), William A. Rockefeller, and Seymour H. Knox.[27]

A third group led by Richard Hoyt, rising star in Wall Street and aviation circles, dealt itself in, forming Southeastern Air Lines on July 1.[28] Trippe had urged Hoyt to invest in Colonial, but he backed Florida Airways, founded by Eddie Rickenbacker and Major Reed M. Chambers. Their airline was struggling, but the "Chambers-Hoyt group" hoped they could turn things around by winning FAM 4. (Back in 1925, when Trippe and Hambleton were laying groundwork in Florida, Chambers "called up & wanted to know how things were going," Hambleton noted. "Told him there wasn't much chance of us getting together now.")[29]

There was an impetus for a merger, but the Pan Am group of Montgomery, Bevier, and Mason were determined to win outright. Even without airplanes, they had leased airfields in Key West and Havana and were negotiating with Cuba for a mail delivery agreement. Montgomery and Bevier met with Trippe and Hoyt for token talk about consolidating but were confident Arnold's groundwork would win them the prize.[30]

The Aviation Corporation of America was similarly determined. On July 12, the board passed what John Leslie calls "a remarkable resolution" authorizing Managing Director Trippe "to submit bids for any contract airmail route *in his own best judgment*" [Leslie's emphasis]. Trippe was even authorized to invest in Pan American Airways if it won the Key West–Havana mail contract.[31] "The next break," Leslie added, "came when the Hoyt group gave up their aspirations and agreed with the Trippe group to mount a tripartite effort."[32] Hoyt gathered all parties for a cruise on his yacht off the coast of Florida, along with Assistant Postmaster General Glover, who supported a merger.[33]

Pan American Airways won the contract on July 16, but there was a catch—they had to make an airmail flight no later than October 19, or forfeit. Of course, they had no planes.[34] And then a shocker—Trippe and Hambleton revealed they had secretly negotiated exclusive Cuban landing rights with President Machado, nullifying Pan Am's lease on the Havana airfield. Pan Am was left "in a poor position to operate the route and seemed destined to default on their U.S. mail contract," Leslie noted. "So it was that three groups were deadlocked over the Key West–Havana situation, each lacking some essential element with which to operate[.]"[35] The wrangling continued for months, even as the deadline approached. The stakes were huge, and *Fortune* noted: "Already a sizeable percentage of the financial interest in aviation was aligned behind the venture." The Trippe-Hambleton-Whitney faction had the inside track, having raised $500,000 in operating capital.[36]

Trippe turned up the heat in negotiations with Richard Bevier and his brother, Kenneth. The brothers offered to make the Trippe and Hoyt factions minor partners, then suggested a merger, with Pan Am holding the controlling interest. Trippe turned them down. As the Beviers wilted, Trippe kept his cool, never yielding an inch, repeating talking points over and over again. "Like a good chess player he knows precisely what effect a given move will have," *Fortune* once observed. "People who cannot see ahead are always amazed by Mr. Trippe. They think that he is either shot with luck, or else exercises diabolical cunning, or else indulges in lobbying of the more obvious sort, or even in graft. He does none of these things—because he does not have to. He has a better technique."[37]

Pan Am finally agreed to merge on Trippe's terms. But there is the strong possibility, at variance with historical accounts, that Hap Arnold secretly facilitated his airline's absorption by ACA. "[Arnold] knew Trippe was young and ambitious, he knew he was smart and extremely patriotic," notes Kathleen Clair, who joined Pan Am in 1948 and was Trippe's personal secretary for more than thirty years. "Trippe did not go to Arnold and ask to merge with his Pan American Airways—Hap Arnold called him in! . . . Trippe had already been over to Cuba and got the return contract from [Machado], the dictator down there, so he was halfway home."

This scenario explains how a company without planes or aviation experience won a foreign airmail contract and why the ACA board voted to invest in them. Arnold's vision was rewarded, and waiting in the wings was the Trippe-Hambleton-Whitney coalition of veteran airmen and wealthy investors to run it.[38]

Trippe later confirmed that Arnold "approached us as a military man about this airline problem." Arnold and Secretary of War Dwight F. Davis, among others, helped secure an airfield at Key West, Trippe added. "They wanted to do it because it was in the national interest and we wanted to do it because we needed an area big enough in Key West for the airplane to land." Trippe also talked with Arnold and Spaatz about expanding from Cuba to Central America: "We discussed the problems of terrain and climate and weather with them. They certainly were bitten with the idea that a service could be made down there."[39]

The merger began on October 3. Southeastern had reincorporated as Atlantic, Gulf & Caribbean, which was absorbed by Trippe's new company—and had a subtle name change to Aviation Corporation of the Americas (ACA)—along with Pan American Airways, Inc. Trippe later referred to ACA as "just a corporate shell . . . Pan American was the company that conducted the entire business." The name of the operating company, Pan Am, was publicly used from the start and later became the official name.[40]

The final terms "must have been a melancholy one for the Bevier group," Leslie reflected.[41] Trippe became president and general manager, Hambleton vice president, Whitney chairman of the board, and the brothers were out.[42] But time was almost up and the Post Office refused to extend the deadline.[43]

But ACA had been preparing. Trippe hired André A. Priester, former flight manager of the Royal Dutch Airlines, as chief engineer. They assembled a staff, made arrangements to purchase Fokker planes, and J. E. Whitbeck was picked to manage their Key West airfield.[44] The military field included surrounding acreage to be leased for a new airport with the stipulation it be named after the seller—so Meacham Airport it was. Fred Gelhaus was hired to build the runways, and there were coral boulders to demolish, rough surface to level, gaping potholes across the runway to fill. "When the tumult [of negotiations] subsided on 13 October 1927," John Leslie writes, "only six days remained until the mandatory first mail flight on 19 October 1927—a deadline which the new company had no visible means of meeting."[45]

On October 18, pilot Edwin C. "Eddie" Musick and a Fokker land plane were ready in Miami, but Key West's airfield was still in poor shape. Priester and Whitbeck frantically worked the telephone to find an amphibian aircraft. Whitbeck got a lead—a Fairchild FC-2, dubbed *La Niña* and owned by the West Indian Aerial Express Company was being repaired in Miami. Pan Am chartered the seaplane and its pilot, Cy Caldwell for $175 (accounts go as high as $250). The flyer landed at Key West before sunset on the 18th. The next morning—deadline day—Caldwell departed, reaching Havana in just over an hour and delivering seven mail sacks with 30,000 letters.[46] If the seaplane had not been found in time, the contract would have been canceled, opening the way for other competitors to win the prize—and, perhaps, relegate Pan American Airways to a footnote in history.

The first Foreign Air Mail contract with the U.S. government was signed at the Mayflower Hotel in Washington. Howell French, an old friend of Bob Thatch who signed as a witness alongside Trippe, Thatch, and Hambleton, recalled that aircraft designer and manufacturer Igor Sikorsky's first amphibian airplane was then being tested for the overwater route from Key West to Havana. "Incidentally, that plane . . . was accepted and ordered by Pan American immediately, because it gave them the only piece of equipment that could be flown over water safely and thus opened up the extension of Pan Am's routes to Central and South America," French recalled.[47]

"When Pan American came to us, we were very small and they were very small," recalled Sikorsky, a Russian émigré. "We knew about them. They [Trippe, Hambleton, Whitney] had some reputation because they had been in Colonial. But we did not question whether or not we thought they could make a go of it—what counted for us was that they were able to pay $35,000 for an airplane."[48]

CHAPTER 5

# THE AVIATOR AND THE AIRLINE

*"Only a year after the start of actual flying, Pan Am found itself far beyond that of a mere business firm, even a firm in the glamour business of flying. It [had] become an instrument of the nation."*

—Pan American Airways, unpublished corporate history[1]

On October 28, 1927, a Fokker Tri-Motor named the *General Machado* rose from the finally completed runway at Key West, bound for Havana with Captain Huestis "Hugh" Wells at the controls and Eddie Musick navigating.[2] It was the first scheduled flight of an international air service under Juan Trippe's direction, and a proud moment given he was courting a girl whose father, Edward R. Stettinius, a J. P. Morgan partner, had doubts about him. Elizabeth "Betty" Stettinius, who had been sent to Paris to forget her suitor, wept with joy when she received Juan's cable: "FIRST FLIGHT SUCCESSFUL." The happy couple married in 1928.

By December, Pan Am and its parent company, Aviation Corporation of the Americas, moved into a suite of rooms at the Chanin Building at 122 East 42nd Street, across from Grand Central Terminal. Trippe had one office, Chief Engineer André Priester the other. Chief Communications Engineer Hugo Leuteritz's "office" was a chair pulled up to Priester's desk. Trippe's roll-top desk was against a wall with a table behind him—when he had a visitor, he turned and talked across it. Trippe never left without closing his roll-top, leaving some wondering what secrets lay within. One "old-timer" recalled, "Trippe was more like our God" and Priester was "our boss," particularly at Key West, where he was the face of the company.[3]

André Priester's early life was out of *The Arabian Nights*. He descended from a sea captain shipwrecked off the coast of Java, where André's father was provincial governor. When André was born in 1892, his birth certificate was witnessed and signed by several Rajahs. He grew up in surroundings akin to a royal court, a privileged life that ended at age sixteen when his father died. Eager to see the world, he signed on with the crew of a cargo ship.[4] Before Trippe hired him, Priester distinguished himself at Koninklijke Luchtvaart Maatschappij Voor Nederland an Kolonien, also known as KLM, or the Royal Dutch Airline. He was considered the first employee at the East 42nd Street office.[5]

Priester helped transform aviation's barnstorming culture into a business through strict rules of operation and emphasis on safety. As the airline expanded, he pragmatically favored flying boats, as the aircraft "carried its own airport," a necessity as there were no airports or emergency landing fields in the Caribbean or Brazil's coastline, but plenty of bays, rivers, lakes, and lagoons. Priester demanded that pilots reserve fuel and daylight—a flying boat landing at night in dark harbors risked crashing into driftwood or unlit fishing boats—and he would cancel an over-water flight if seas were too rough.[6]

Priester also believed radio, a technology starting to come into its own, was the answer to tracking and reporting changing weather conditions to airborne planes and airfields on the Key West to Havana route—and points beyond. He brought aboard Leuteritz to lead Pan Am's radio communications effort.[7]

Hugo Leuteritz was one of the promising young wizards in the field when he joined the Radio Corporation of America (RCA) in New York. He acquired his amateur radio operator's license at age thirteen, researched radio at the Pratt Institute in Brooklyn, and served as a Junior Radio Expert Aide in the Navy during World War I.[8] When Leuteritz arrived at RCA, radio was about transmitting dots and dashes, equipment was bulky and heavy. For eight years, he focused on long-distance communications with less bulky equipment, developments vital in adapting radio to aircraft. Finally, RCA directed the twenty-eight-year-old to investigate radio's aviation possibilities. The company was not ready to commit, Leuteritz discovered when he requested $25,000 to research a lightweight transmitter-receiver. "They said aviation was not ready for spending that kind of money," Leuteritz recalled.[9]

Fate intervened when Leuteritz got a call from Grant Mason and John Montgomery of Pan American Airways, around the time of the merger with the Trippe-Hambleton-Whitney group. They were investigating "this radio thing," Leuteritz recalled. "They had no idea what they wanted—they [only] knew they wanted radio for communications and perhaps some navigation."[10] Leuteritz, still an RCA employee, took a train to Key West to begin experimental work for the airline. RCA was interested—their research indicated Key West was a bad static area and would provide a good equipment test. The day after Leuteritz's arrival at Key West a boat followed with a 100-watt RCA transmitter.[11]

Leuteritz had done radio work for Colonial Air Transport in 1926, but when he met Trippe for the second time the conversation took an unexpected turn, and he was offered a job: "André will have nobody else but you."[12] Leuteritz replied that Pan Am had only a few planes and wondered if that would keep him busy. "We will have a fleet of airplanes, fly to Latin America, the Atlantic, the Pacific," Trippe answered.

"What you are talking about is a gamble," Leuteritz said.[13] He also thought, "[O]ne of us is nuts!"[14] Flying the oceans! Perhaps it was the audaciousness of Trippe's vision, but Leuteritz discussed the job offer with his boss at RCA, C.H. Taylor. Leuteritz decided to take the gamble and Taylor graciously allowed a one-year leave of absence. The leave became permanent—Leuteritz was the start of Pan Am's Radio Division. It was a humble beginning, Leuteritz recalled: "The only thing I had was the transmitters in Key West and they were the property of RCA!"[15]

Another indispensable figure was Colonel Charles Lindbergh. Even as the airline was settling into its East 42nd Street office, Lindbergh and his *Spirit of St. Louis* was flying the aerial survey of the Caribbean and Central America he promised Trippe.[16] The aviator was warned it was "foolhardy" to fly his famous land plane instead of an amphibian aircraft. But, Lindbergh later wrote, "My greatest safety reserve with the *Spirit of St. Louis* lay in the amount of fuel it could carry. (If fog had covered Paris, when I arrived nonstop from New York, I still had enough fuel to reach Rome.)"[17]

Lindbergh began in Mexico, where he was the official guest of Dwight Morrow, who was handling Lindbergh's finances at J. P. Morgan and had accepted Coolidge's appointment to be ambassador to Mexico. Morrow invited Lindbergh to spend Christmas with his family.[18] He would fall in love with the ambassador's shy daughter, Anne.

The morning of December 28, the family saw Lindbergh and the *Spirit of St. Louis* off on a mission that would last through February, cover more than 9,300 miles, and visit sixteen countries. The flight advanced aviation beyond the astounding achievement of a solo transatlantic flight—the possibilities for travel and commerce became clear to the public, policymakers, and investors. By January, when Lindbergh stopped in Havana, the obstacles against a U.S. international air program were largely overcome, thanks to Pan Am and the antagonist that was the reason Hap Arnold created the airline.

★

Toward the end of 1927, the State Department received a petition from Colombia, signed by most of the U.S. businessmen operating there, requesting support for SCADTA's bid to expand to the Canal Zone and Key West. In response, Coolidge appointed the cabinet-level Interdepartmental Aviation Committee to help write legislation to expand U.S. aviation into the international sphere. Its importance is clear in the government branches represented: Assistant Secretary of State Francis White, Assistant Treasury Secretary Carl Schunemann, Assistant Postmaster General Warner Irving Glover, Assistant Secretary of Navy Edward P. Warner, Assistant Secretary of Commerce William P. MacCracken, General George Simonds, and Admiral F. H. Scofield.

The first meeting was held in White's office on November 23, 1927. Secretary of State Kellogg opened by announcing Colombia's pro-SCADTA petition, a request difficult to refuse—unless an American company offered similar service. Kellogg left to let the committee get to work on the confidential recommendations they would make to their respective Cabinet officials.

"It was the unanimous conclusion of the Committee that *from both a military and economic point of view* [authors' emphasis] it was essential that air transport service between the United States and South and Central America be established without delay, that it should be exclusively owned and operated by our citizens," the minutes recorded. They suggested establishing two key routes in cooperation with foreign airlines in the region. The Key West to Havana line would serve all Central America north of the Canal Zone and south along the west coast to Santiago and across the Andes to Buenos Aires, where connections could be made with France's national airline to Montevideo and Rio de Janeiro. The second would pick up the Key West to Havana line, but fly southeast to Trinidad and Venezuela "where a connection would be made with the operations of the Colombian company." The committee recommended amending statutes for awarding foreign airmail contracts so the postmaster general could "award the contract to that company which he believed would best serve the interests of the United States."[19] That company was the new airline led by Trippe, Hambleton, and Whitney.

The next day, Hambleton was in Washington lobbying for foreign airmail service. He first saw Secretary of the Treasury Andrew Mellon, a meeting arranged by David Bruce. He met Francis White at the State Department. At the War Department, First Yale Unit veteran Frederick Trubee Davison shared Army air reports of weather conditions and geography in Latin America. During lunch with Andrew and Richard Mellon, Hambleton mentioned problems getting gasoline to Key West, which the treasury secretary promised to discuss with Gulf Oil's president—his nephew, William L. Mellon. On Bruce's advice, Hambleton asked Andrew Mellon to introduce him to the Secretary of Commerce, and Hambleton's busy day ended with Herbert Hoover, who invited him back the next afternoon.[20]

Pan Am promoted itself as the instrument of U.S. foreign air service. After all, the State Department didn't know how to do it, and the Commerce Department's purview was licensing pilots and checking planes, not negotiating with foreign governments to forge airways into uncharted airspace and establish airports and infrastructure.[21] "None of them had the practical experience with the problems of how to get rights in these foreign countries," Trippe explained. "How was the carrier to get along out in this world? There was nothing out there but jungles. And these people weren't quite clear; it had to be shown to them that the carrier had to get out there and make these arrangements."[22]

The December 16, 1927, board meeting of Atlantic, Gulf and Caribbean Airways/Pan Am featured a wide-ranging report from Juan Trippe. The Interdepartmental Aviation Committee would "assist in the development of commercial aviation in Central American and South American countries," he reported, adding that Senator George Moses and Congressman Kelly had introduced, in the Senate and House respectively, a bill to authorize the postmaster general to make ten-year airmail contracts with U.S. companies operating in foreign countries. Trippe outlined negotiations underway for airmail contracts in Cuba, Peru, and the north coast of South America. He then proposed purchasing the Sikorsky Amphibion because, in order of importance, it could survey Central and South America, be a reserve aircraft at Key West, provide experience in operating and maintaining a flying boat, and be used for a potential airmail contract between Key West and Miami.

Trippe's report included the "von Bauer situation" that dovetailed with the Aviation Committee's recommendations of sharing foreign routes with the Colombian airline: "Negotiations under way with SCADTA interests, looking to the joint operation of certain 'key' routes on the northern coast of South America and in the Canal Zone, and exclusive mutual contracts for handling through traffic in that section of the world."[23]

Even as they were quietly negotiating with SCADTA, the lobbying push made good use of the specter of "German interests" in the hemisphere. "I [knew] that von Bauer and Lufthansa and Condor were working together and the [German] government was giving them pilots and equipment and so forth," Trippe recalled. "This didn't just happen." During congressional testimony, Trippe testified that SCADTA was operating near the Canal, but had a comeback: "Why not us?"[24] Pan Am was a "100% American owned Corporation," Trippe told Francis White, and evoked the German threat when he asked White's help in getting the American Embassy in Havana to secure Cuba's domestic mail concession for his airline. White not only helped, he echoed Trippe's talking point: "We are most anxious here to have American aviation as prominent as possible in the Caribbean region. . . . The Pan American Airways is a hundred per cent American owned and managed company and for that reason we would be glad to see it, rather than Germans, have the contract in Cuba."[25]

Meanwhile, Lindbergh's survey flight was generating massive news coverage and public interest. "People's scales of distance had not yet changed," Pan Am's corporate history explains. "In the Caribbean region this was doubly dramatic because the places were so remote and exotic. . . . Every move of the super-famous man was followed by the press, and thus the flight served as a lesson in air geography. We cannot now recapture the magic of the airplane in those days—how it could jump in hours between places that were 'in reality' days or weeks apart."[26]

The press called it the "Goodwill Flight," a term Lindbergh later said "had a connotation of namby-pambiness that was distasteful to me." His survey flight was evaluating terrain and weather, planes and payloads, potential ground facilities and radio stations, all while flying over jungle as dangerous as the ocean he crossed less than a year before. "In 1928 you could fly a long time over jungle without even a native hut and clearing showing up below," Lindbergh recalled. "Flying over hundreds of miles of jungles in Central America, I was constantly aware of the great height of tree trunks under the blanket of green foliage below me. What would happen in the event of engine failure? Of course I would stall down into the thick branches. Would my plane hang up in them, or crash on through?" And if he crashed through to the jungle floor and survived, where would he go, what direction would he take, how would he survive in that virtually impenetrable green vastness?[27]

In January, when Lindbergh landed in Havana, he met Trippe and Hambleton behind closed doors. A subsequent newspaper article noted they discussed "the possibilities of an international air mail service."[28] Lindbergh arrived in time for the Sixth Annual Pan American Conference, where Trippe was technical advisor to the U.S. delegation headed by future Supreme Court Justice Charles Evans Hughes—it was a measure of Pan Am's influence that the delegation flew to Havana in the airline's *General Machado*. Mrs. Calvin Coolidge, in the presence of her husband and Cuba's president, christened a Pan Am Fokker the *General New*, in honor of the postmaster general, beginning a tradition of first ladies christening Pan Am planes.[29]

It helped the airline's cause that Eddie Musick and former Colonial Air Transport pilot Hugh Wells were delivering airmail safely and on schedule. From October 28 through December of 1927, an estimated 131 flights were completed between Meacham Airport and Havana's Camp Colombia Field. "During this time," an *Aviation* article reported, "no engine trouble of any kind was encountered and no interruption on account of weather was suffered."[30] Pan Am's passenger service began on January 16, 1928. The fare was $50 each way, with Hughie Wells and Gus Alfonso flying seven paying passengers, arriving in Havana at 9:38 a.m.[31]

The daily schedule was departure from Key West at 8:00 a.m., arrival in Havana at 9:15 a.m. The return flight at 3:45 p.m. made Key West at 5:15 p.m. The one-way fare included transportation to and from the airport and thirty pounds of luggage. The timetable brochure proclaimed, "Travel the Comfortable Way," contrasting steamer travel over "the endless rolling and pitching of a spiteful sea. . . . But now man has mastered the principles of flight and may enjoy the comfort, speed and safety of aerial transportation."[32] That was a stretch, as airplanes suffered rolling air currents. Still, it seemed miraculous that one could have breakfast in Florida, lunch in Havana, and be back home in time for dinner.

The Foreign Air Mail Act, authorizing the postmaster general to enter into foreign airmail contracts, became law on March 8, 1928. Trippe had a hand in its key features—he was again accused of writing the legislation—but he hailed it as "the Lindbergh law," feeling Lindbergh's survey flight and subsequent congressional testimony carried the day.[33] In addition to ten-year contracts, rates were steady, so the U.S. Post Office paid in full for its reserved space, whether or not it used the designated amount. The act allowed an out from competitive bidding by empowering the postmaster general to award foreign routes to low bidders "that can satisfactorily perform the service required to the best advantage of the Government."[34] It was tailor-made for Pan Am.

Lindbergh not only inspired aviation legislation at home, but his international celebrity helped aviation worldwide, including the Latin American market Pan Am hoped to conquer. "[F]lying was the glamor thing of the era," Pan Am's corporate history noted. "It was wonderful and lifted the soul. A person might be anti-U.S. politically, and might find Americans not simpatico, but he could not be against airplanes, or against pilots."

Francis White later acknowledged the symbiosis between Lindbergh and Pan Am as a catalyst for advancing American aviation, explaining the industry "languished until 1927 when private interests, the Pan American Airways, established a service between Key West and Havana, which was very successful and prompted them to explore the possibility of extending their lines still further. Lindbergh's trans-Atlantic flight greatly increased interest and developments followed very rapidly."[35]

On March 30, 1928, the postmaster general advertised bids for six Foreign Air Mail routes into the Caribbean and South America. Pan Am and its new affiliate, Pan American-Grace Airways (known as "Panagra"), won them all. The new contracts included FAM 5, Key West to Cristóbal in the Canal Zone via Cuba, Mexico, British Honduras, Nicaragua, and Costa Rica (with provisions for extensions); FAM 8, from Brownsville, Texas, to Mexico City; and FAM 10, from Paramaribo in Dutch Guiana to Santos, Brazil, via intermediate points.[36]

Early in 1928, Trippe was invited to Washington for a private meeting with Secretary of Commerce Hoover, who would soon be elected president. Hoover had sent trade representatives to explore new markets with foreign nations, and foreign airmail service fit perfectly into his efforts at increasing trade and advancing aviation. The only awkward note was Hoover's tendency to look at Trippe's feet as he talked, leaving Trippe wondering if his shoelaces were untied.

Hoover believed an airline could be an instrument of U.S. trade expansion into South America, but he wanted a "Community Company," operating like a public utility, not a government airline. Trippe had similarly concluded an airline had to operate like a government-regulated public utility, servicing unprofitable routes as well as popular ones, keeping prices down, and staying in business through all economic conditions. Pan Am's corporate history summarizes Trippe's position as "One Field," meaning an exclusive franchise. Trippe accepted government regulation but was adamant that, in such a model, competition was counter-productive.[37]

Hoover asked Trippe if it suited him to have a list of companies that could financially support his airline, even join the board. "He thought we could do much better as a regulated public utility provided the utility had all these components of strength behind it," Trippe recalled.[38]

Back in New York, some voiced the same fears heard at Colonial—they were making money, why rock the boat? Trippe felt *now* was the time to expand, with everyone in the thrall of aviation's potential. The costs of foreign expansion were staggering, but Hoover had already begun telling business firms to get behind the young airline.[39] "[Hoover] knew international business, had been in it all his life," Trippe noted. "He knew the problems of getting American capital to invest abroad in competition with government monopolies, that they would roll under one by one unless we funneled capital in."[40]

Thirty companies responded, then forty-six, bringing in a million dollars of capital. A new stock offering to the original shareholders brought in another million and a third. Pan Am absorbed West Indian Aerial Express, the airline that provided the plane for the contract-winning flight to Havana, capitalized at a third of a million dollars. An estimated four to five million dollars flowed in.[41] On June 20, 1928, Trippe placed an order for twelve Fokker F-10As, three Sikorsky S-38s, several Fords, and six Fairchild FC-2s. Eddie Musick was promoted Chief Pilot.[42]

By June 23, 1928, the Aviation Corp. of the Americas was reorganized in Delaware to acquire the assets of the Aviation Corp. of the Americas, the Atlantic, Gulf & Caribbean Airways holding company, and Pan American Airways.[43] "Pan American Airways" was officially adopted as the holding company name in 1931. "I remember the meeting when we decided that Pan American Airways was a better name than [Aviation Corporation of the Americas]," Trippe recalled. "It was just a feeling. I think ACA was too fussy and impersonal."[44]

## CHAPTER 6
# AN ACCUMULATION

*"The Caribbean operation gave us a break for the Pacific and that gave us a break for the Atlantic and that gave us a break for around-the-world. It was an accumulation. The experience and operating knowledge and . . . strength achieved in one route [got us] to the next route."*

—Juan Trippe[1]

Pan Am began expanding into countries with barriers to foreign companies, national airlines, and passionate resentment to Yankee interests—often all three. In response, Pan Am practically invented the "affiliated airline," a version of the American owned foreign airline Hambleton and Cooper once discussed. Pan Am controlled a country's airline behind-the-scenes, while its public face remained that of the home country.

Pan Am's first affiliate and model for such conquests was in Mexico, a grand prize to any U.S. airline with international ambitions—its northern border ran along Texas, New Mexico, Arizona, and California, its eastern coastline opened onto the Gulf, and it joined Guatemala in a natural link to Central America. Mexico also posed all the requisite obstacles—U.S. relations were tense, it had barriers against foreign investment, and a successful national airline was in operation, *Compañia Mexicana de Aviación*, known as "Mexicana" or "CMA."

Mexico's national airline was started by two U.S. entrepreneurs, George Rihl, a banker of Pennsylvania Dutch extraction, and W. L. "Slim" Mallory, an oil well driller, both partners drawn to the oil boom Gulf town of Tampico. In 1923, Mallory purchased a Standard Biplane so when the rainy season made dirt roads into oil fields muddy and impassable, they could fly to their claims and keep drill rigs going. A year later, Rihl, Mallory, and investors formed *Compañia Mexicana de Aviación* as a charter service for oil companies. By 1926, Mexicana expanded into aerial mapping of oil fields and its capital worth increased to $65,000. Investors included Sherman Fairchild, who owned 20 percent of the stock.[2]

In 1927, the government offered Rihl the nation's first airmail contract, a Tampico to Mexico City run. It was so successful the contract expanded to Matamoros, which was across the Rio Grande and close to Brownsville, Texas.[3] Brownsville, a town of simple clapboard houses bounded by lagoons, prairie, and borderland, became headquarters for Pan Am's Western Division. Pan Am had designs on Mexico, and its way in was to purchase Mexicana.

When negotiations began, the Mexican airline's capital soared to $125,000. Rihl and his counsel Basil O'Connor, law partner of Franklin Roosevelt, met Trippe in New York to discuss terms. Mexicana stock would be exchanged for Pan Am stock, plus warrants for purchasing more at its present price. Pan Am stock had skyrocketed from $15 to $40 a share, netting Mexicana's founders an estimated million dollars. Rihl was brought into the fold, Mexicana officially became a Pan Am subsidiary on February 16, 1929, and affiliate service connecting the Western hub at Brownsville began March 9.[4]

The planes were of Mexican registration, with the Mexicana name on the aircraft, but in the PAA style logo. A year later, new lettering declared Mexicana part of the "Pan American Airways System." In an unusual arrangement, the U.S. Post Office allowed Pan Am to "sublet" its foreign airmail contract to Mexicana. "Trippe must have done some persuasive talking in Washington," mused Pan Am's corporate history. What mattered was "the United States' need to get into the Latin American air before Europeans should take possession ... [and] the need to neutralize von Bauer."[5]

By the summer of 1930, Mexicana was providing sightseeing tours from Brownsville to Mexico City that included flyovers of the pyramids of San Juan Teotihuacan and the Floating Gardens of Xochimilco. Writing for *Aero Digest*, Pan Am insider Merian Cooper reported the tours helped make the airplane a familiar sight in Latin America: "With military, as well as commercial planes frequently flying overhead, the inhabitants of the small Indian village no longer fall upon their knees in prayer at the sight of a soaring plane."[6]

Mexicana planes, with U.S. pilots, were based and maintained at Brownsville. The flight schedule was so reliable that townspeople could set their clocks by it. Every morning at nine, a Ford Tri-Motor left for Mexico, and a plane that departed a week earlier returned by 4:15 that afternoon.[7]

The mountains and cloudy weather from Brownsville to Mexico City made it the ideal lab for the transition to "blind flying" or "instrument flying." "No description of [Pan Am's] Western Division is complete without saying that its pilots were beyond question the industry pioneers in the act of . . . 'instrument' flying,'" Pan Am's John Leslie notes. "The only possibility of maintaining regular service was to fly up through the clouds, go visually through the highest mountain passes, and then descend through the cloud layers into Mexico City and vice versa."[8]

Cloud cover and bad weather had been the bane of flying—it was easy to get disoriented and caught in a "graveyard spiral." Pilots had always flown around, above, or otherwise avoided clouds and storms. Pan Am's pioneers of instrument flying at Brownsville included chief pilot E.J. Snyder and George Kraigher, the latter a former Mexicana pilot and Serbian cavalry officer with the French Flying Corps in World War I. As Brownsville's chief pilot, Kraigher was a dedicated instruments man eager to take on clouds, bad weather, and recalcitrant pilots. He knew that if commercial aviation was to prosper, the barnstormer who flew by his own rules and "the seat of his pants" had to give way to instruments and uniform procedures.[9]

Harold Gray was the model for instrument flying. A pioneering airman and future Pan Am chairman, Gray was inspired by Lindbergh's transatlantic flight to study aeronautical engineering, became an Air Force cadet, and was only twenty-three when he came to Brownsville in March of 1929. "Gray was the exemplar of a new type of pilot—engineering minded, rational, analytical, a cause-and-effect man, a numbers man," observes Pan Am's corporate history. Gray divined the secrets of blind flying when it was still a mystery. Once, as he was climbing into clouds between Tampico and Mexico City, the air kept getting rougher. Gray saw a patch of blue that didn't seem "up" and felt the grip of a vertiginous graveyard spiral. He focused on his Turn Needle, re-centered, and checked his airspeed to read a safe eighty mph. He rose safely out of the clouds knowing he had to trust instruments.[10]

But the air was still a tricky place. Gray was flying a Ford Tri-Motor from Vera Cruz to Mexico City when he hit clouds at 13,000 feet. His airspeed indicator showed he didn't have enough speed. He pushed the wheel, but the indicator still had him flying too slowly. Gray listened to the over-revving engine and propeller, realized he was flying faster than the airspeed gauge indicated—he was in a steep dive—and pulled out. He learned ice on the wing had interfered with the sensing end of the airspeed indicator and affected his altimeter.[11] Gray's knowledge and instincts were so valuable that by October 1930, Priester dispatched him to Pan Am's new Miami airport for a few weeks of "missionary work."[12]

It was strange, even unnatural, for pilots accustomed to trusting their senses to put their faith in instrument gauges. In Florida, the transition was gradual and relatively comfortable, but Brownsville flyers "remember it as a mental operation that cut very deep," notes Pan Am's corporate history. "It was almost a change in personality—like making an easy-going, self-indulgent fellow over into a monk."[13] Brownsville pilots sent a telegram to Priester complaining about Kraigher's dictatorial manner in pushing the new methods—Priester's response was to give them a chance to resign.[14] Some pilots found the transition so difficult that as late as 1933, they let their co-pilots handle the instrument flying when needed.[15]

Instrument flying, radio communications, operational procedures—Pan Am led the way in what would be called "airline style."[16] "Safety and service are the guiding principles of all flights over Pan American Airways," notes the first Key West to Havana passenger timetable brochure.[17] The revolutionary airline policy can be traced to an airborne meeting between Trippe, Merian Cooper, and John Hambleton, who piloted the plane as they discussed a "safety first" policy.[18]

Priester developed the safety policy and was the rule maker when there were no rules. He also had an instinct for young talent. In 1928, John Leslie, then in his early twenties, was working at the Fokker plant in Hasbrouck Heights when he first saw Priester, who was inspecting the F-10 Tri-Motor under construction for Pan Am. "I saw him going down a corridor accompanied by some of the Fokker people and I wondered who that unusual little man was," Leslie recalled. "He was rather short and slightly built with a large, round bald head. He looked 'foreign' but not like all the Dutch and Germans who were manning the Fokker establishment at that time."[19]

Despite Leslie's youth and six months in the industry, Priester hired him as his assistant. On January 21, 1929, Leslie came to New York and "reported for duty" at Pan Am's new headquarters at 122 East 42nd Street. Leslie set the thirty-seven-year-old Priester "on a high pedestal" adding, "As with many others in Pan American who knew Priester in the early years, he never really came down from that pedestal."[20]

One of Priester's favorite expressions, recounted in his thick Dutch dialect, was "Ve freeze dat," meaning the point when research and development had to stop, and production go forward. It was the riskiest call—"frozen" too soon, the end result might not be good enough; frozen too late, one risked falling behind the competition. "Priester was very good at judgment," observed Pan Am engineer John G. Borger. "He was cautious but he had guts, too. . . . Priester kept needling the manufacturers, and kept setting them higher goals. One of his aims was to reduce the fuel thirst of engines. It would mean longer range . . . bigger payloads."[21] Leslie adds, "He waged an unremitting campaign for technological progress" and if a manufacturer failed to deliver, he "would descend upon them in mighty wrath." The phrase Priester reserved for such occasions: "Confidence is out!"[22]

Priester would create "Master of Ocean Flying Boats," a rank unique to Pan Am representing the highest echelon of pilots. One had to be a captain with at least twenty-five hundred flying hours, a master of instrument flying and celestial navigation, and versed in international regulations and foreign ports.[23] One who achieved the vaunted title was Eddie Musick, seemingly Priester's archetypal pilot and the personification of airline style. Musick was born to the air, happily married to his one and only sweetheart, Cleo, and without major vices (a hangover in his youth made him swear off alcohol; tea was his favorite beverage). But Eddie was a mold-breaker—he had been a daredevil pilot who allegedly flew outlaw booze between the U. S. and Canada, a lucrative sideline for Prohibition-era pilots.

★

Eddie Musick fell in love with flying when he was sixteen and growing up in Los Angeles. Musick and his pal, Harry Reynolds, attended one of the first major air shows in the country, the Los Angeles International Air Meet of January 10–20, 1910, at Dominguez Field, where French pilot Louis Paulhan set a new world's altitude record of 4,165 feet. Later that year, Musick and Reynolds returned to Dominquez Field for an exhibition by their hero, Arch Hoxsey, the "Beau Brummel of exhibition pilots." They saw Hoxsey crash and die, but Musick was still determined to fly.[24]

One of Musick's early aviation jobs was in the oceanfront town of Venice, California, home to several carnival companies showcasing daredevil flying. The twenty-one-year-old was hired as a plane mechanic and got it the hard way, replacing a mechanic who fatally stumbled into a whirling propeller. Musick was nicknamed "the jeweler" for polishing every plane part to a gleaming finish, even the glass coverings on instrument gauges. Older mechanics loved teasing the kid but quickly noticed that aircraft under his care never had forced landings.[25]

As weeks went by, Musick started having nightmares from seeing too many air show crashes—he even pulled one dead pilot from his wreckage. He believed pilot error was the cause. Musick discovered that when a plane went into a dive, it turned on its side before a spin. As the aircraft's "elevator" pointed up and down, it essentially took the place of a rudder. Pulling back on the stick only wrapped a pilot tighter into a tailspin—you had to push *forward* to get out of it. For months, Musick practiced controlled dives, hoping to show his stuff at an exhibition. But without a famous name, no one would put him on a program.

One Sunday, three flyers were finishing their show when a mystery plane zoomed past the crowded grandstand. There was a collective gasp—the plane flew straight up, stalled, fell into a tailspin. Just when it seemed about to crash, the pilot pulled out and leveled off. As he safely landed, the crowd rushed the field. A show manager got there first—Musick! With a flourish, the manager clasped the pilot's hand, turned to the gathering crowd, and shouted, "Meet Monseer Mussick, the great French flyer!" Thus began Musick's daredevil flying career.[26]

A near-tragedy during a summertime fireworks show focused Musick on a real aviation career. He was flying thousands of feet above Venice when an assistant in the rear cockpit released a rocket too soon, and it hit a wing that burst into flame. Musick began a dive, trying to land before the fiery wing burned off, but at a thousand feet the entire plane was ablaze. Musick aimed for a dark landing field, swooped down over the treetops, and pancaked on the ground. The flaming plane went up on its nose, the burnt wing collapsed, and Musick and his assistant dived out, hitting the ground running, their clothes trailing wisps of fire and smoke. They were clear when flames hit the gas tank and the plane exploded. As they looked back and watched the wreckage burn, the assistant apologized. The daredevil patted his shoulder and told him to forget it. "Shooting fireworks from a plane is monkey business," Musick concluded.[27]

By 1917, Musick was serving as an Army flight instructor at North Island, across the bay from San Diego, and became a commissioned lieutenant in the Marine Corps. After the war, he became Chief Pilot at Aeromarine Airways. Musick was made for "firsts," including the first delivery of an automobile by air, a Model-T Ford he flew from Detroit to Cleveland.

Musick was fearless. When Aeromarine pilot Wally Culbertson's flying boat went down in rough seas with three passengers aboard, Musick spotted them from the air, landed his seaplane on choppy waters, and safely took all aboard. When the roiling waters prevented liftoff, he taxied to safe harbor.

That rescue always stuck with Harry Bruno, the aviation publicist now working at Aeromarine. Bruno's nickname for Musick was "Cautious Ed," but "caution never hog-tied his courage." When Bruno thought of commercial air transport, Musick always came to mind. "Before he would start on a flight," Bruno noted, "he would warm up his motors and then turn the flying boat around and around until he thoroughly tested the engines and the controls a dozen times. 'Hell,' he said when we kidded him, 'we're not barnstorming. We're railroading, and when you carry passengers, you've got to think of them first.'"[28]

In 1924, Eddie married the former Cleo Livingston. When Aeromarine folded, Eddie moved on to Anthony Fokker's Philadelphia Rapid Transit Air Service, where he piloted a Fokker Tri-Motor to Washington at ninety miles per hour, landing before an awestruck crowd.[29] Fokker's airline went bust in 1927, dragged down by debt and failure to get an airmail contract renewed. Musick had a wife to support, but Bruno recommended him to Juan Trippe. Bruno noted Musick's "ideas for airline safety" fit in perfectly with Pan Am's safety-first philosophy.[30]

In November of 1928, Musick had the lead pilot's seat of a Sikorsky, with John Hambleton as co-pilot, on a three-week inspection tour of new Pan Am bases in Cuba, Haiti, the Dominican Republic, and Puerto Rico.[31] Musick emerged as a champion of radio communications, a personal crusade that began when he flew with Captain Wells on Pan Am's first official airmail flight to Havana. They had departed in blue sky, but it was storming when they reached Cuba and they had a struggle locating Camp Colombia Airdrome through the wet windshield.[32] Musick told Pan Am officials that flying would never be safe until installation of a communications system providing dependable weather reports.[33]

Leuteritz himself noted instances of pilots who thought they had landed at Havana, when actually, they were in Matanzas, nearly seventy miles away. Leuteritz proposed, and Priester agreed, that they build a direction finder (DF), a navigational device for determining the direction of radio transmissions.[34] A typical direction finder was too heavy and bulky for a plane, so it was decided to have a DF ground station and install a transmitter and receiver aboard aircraft. As with instrument flying, there was resistance. Pilot Robert Fatt told Leuteritz, "I've thrown better radio equipment off the airplane than you can build!"[35]

"The pilots thought radio in airplanes was silly," Leuteritz recalled. "Up to that time, the pilot had been king of the ship. Once you were air borne, you had to form your own judgments, make your own decisions. . . . A pilot in flight, before radio, was about as free . . . as man has ever been."[36]

Musick worked with Leuteritz on a test program for radio communications, a ground-based direction finding and radio-telegraphy system that would be used throughout Pan Am's operation. Leuteritz and his team developed a compact radio weighing only ten pounds, but powerful enough to send signals to Havana. A licensed radio operator became part of an airplane's crew. Leuteritz also worked on a meteorological service that transmitted weather updates across the System. Pan Amer William Grooch recalled that his friend Musick "insisted that trained weather observers be placed at the ground stations so that specialized information could be forwarded to pilots on the wing. When this was accomplished schedules were kept to the minute. Gone was the uncertainty of earlier days."[37]

Meanwhile, John Hambleton and Charles Lindbergh together were flying "the original epochal exploratory routes which were to open up Central America to commercial aviation," Merian Cooper wrote to Pan Am historian Wolfgang Langewiesche in 1961. "Lindbergh and Hambleton, taking turns piloting, layed [sic] out the possible routes and bases for Pan American in Central America in late 1927 or early 1928. . . . [They] laid the foundation for the commercial conquest by Air of Central America by Pan American."

That massive effort included ground exploration along potential flight paths and building infrastructure and supply routes, with native crews hacking trails through the jungle, filling swampland, building roads and bridges. "Few airports had ever been built in the tropics and little was known of the conditions that would be encountered," records a Pan Am historical document. "Construction parties at each airport had largely to live off the land until air service was established. Heat and dampness sapped the strength of engineers until the only driving force remaining was the determination that the airline should go through."[38] Trippe, speaking in 1934, added, "it was necessary to train natives, who had never heard a locomotive whistle, to whom an automobile was a rare curiosity, and who had never seen a steamer except on a distant horizon, to build airports for what they called 'thunder birds.'"[39]

In an internal report, Pan Am public relations head William Van Dusen chronicled the struggle, particularly the "four hundred threatening miles" from Havana to the Yucatan coast on the westward route to Panama. That distance was reduced by a third with an airport at Cuba's western tip and a landing field in British Honduras, with clear flying to Tela in eastern Honduras—but 800 miles of "heartbreak" across mountains, jungles, and swamps lay ahead.

"Existing charts proved worse than useless," Van Dusen wrote. "Even sketch maps made by explorers who penetrate the jungle . . . were found often fifty miles in error on the location of important landmarks. There were few roads, and many of those that did exist were impassable during the rains of the tropic summer. There were no available guides for much of the territory for the very good reason that no one had ventured into it. Death and malignant tropic disease lurked in every crocodile-infested stream through which the trail must lead.

"Nevertheless, by foot, by burro, by canoe, by airplane, the airline's pioneers took up the task. Survey planes, laden with sacks of white flour, flew back and forth across each section of the projected route. When pilot or observer would spot what seemed a likely site for an intermediate airport he fixed its location in latitude and longitude by a sextant's sight on the sun's position, then dropped one of the flour sacks which, striking the matted roof of the jungle, would break and filter down through the dense undergrowth to leave a splotch on the earth below. From the nearest town airport engineers would be dispatched to find it. . . . Mile by tedious mile the route thrust southward from Tela across Honduras, Nicaragua, Costa Rica and Panama to the Canal Zone. Still lacking, though, was the link between British Honduras and the tip of Yucatan, first land reached on the flight from Cuba.

"Low-lying, swamp-covered, matted with a jungle too dense even for the conquerors of the route from Tela southward. . . . Field scouts, scouring the area, found only one possible solution. Within the lonely island of Cozumel, off the coast of Yucatan, they discovered a jungle-bordered lagoon, protected by a high strand of beach from the heavy seas that roll through the Straits of Yucatan. But it was only a seaplane solution." There the advance halted until late 1928 when the first of the Sikorsky amphibian planes arrived.

Van Dusen described Sikorsky's amphibian as "a queer looking craft . . . a 'sesqui-plane' with a large upper wing and a stubby lower one. . . . But the ship mounted two engines and could stay aloft on one of them. What is more, its amphibian tests proved it the ideal solution for the land-and-water routes that must be crossed."[40] But Pan Am was about to be joined by an ambitious and supremely confident outfit that envisioned itself as the airline of the Americas.

---

In mid-March of 1928, passengers aboard a Munson liner bound for Rio included thirty-two-year-old Colonel Ralph O'Neill, a U.S. World War I combat ace whose decorations included the Distinguished Service Cross. O'Neill was Boeing's exclusive sales agent in Latin America and heading to Brazil to sell military airplanes. He also embarked upon a dream of creating a U.S. based airline linking the great cities along South America's east coast, and was armed with letters of introduction from the U.S. Secretaries of the Army, Navy, and State, the ambassadors of Brazil, Uruguay, Chile, and Argentina, and William P. MacCracken, Jr., Chief of the Bureau of Air Commerce at the Department of Commerce.

O'Neill, inspired by the New York, New Haven and Hartford Railroad, named his airline after the three principal cities in what would become the world's longest air route, the New York, Rio & Buenos Aires Line, known by its acronym, NYRBA. O'Neill felt his own triumvirate could out-do Trippe, Hambleton, and Whitney. He installed himself as president, Major

Reuben H. Fleet, founder and president of Consolidated Aircraft Corporation to provide the next generation flying boat, and James Rand, financier and president of the Remington Rand Company, who would pour $4,000,000 into the airline.[41]

NYRBA's survival depended on a U.S. airmail contract. O'Neill and a Boeing colleague met Assistant Postmaster General Glover to discuss NYRBA and the then-impending Foreign Air Mail Act. O'Neill bitterly recalled "Glover's cold and obviously disinterested reaction." Glover explained there were many problems at present, but when solved "we'll be putting in our own airline." An astonished O'Neill knew that meant Pan Am. But, O'Neill asked, wouldn't mail service be open to competitive bidding when the Foreign Air Mail Act became law? Glover allowed that "bids from qualified, competent contenders are always considered" and unceremoniously ushered them out.[42]

In 1929, in the final months of Coolidge's term, James Rand arranged a meeting at the White House between O'Neill and the president. Coolidge assured him there would be no favoritism in awarding contracts. O'Neill left feeling "considerably elated."

That autumn, NYRBA was flying Sikorsky aircraft to Argentina. During a stop in Miami, Eddie Musick met some of the rival pilots and listened to their plans for South America. "This NYRBA crowd will block us off from South America unless we move fast," he confessed to Cleo. "[N]o company can make a go of it down there without a mail contract from the United States post-office. If NYRBA gets one, we're licked." Another problem was Consolidated Aircraft was building big planes for them. "We haven't got the equipment," Eddie told Cleo. "Our Fokkers are no good beyond San Juan. We need big flying boats. Consolidated [is] the only firm building 'em, and NYRBA got them sewed up for a year."[43]

But in the summer of 1929, Pan Am began dreaming up its own giant plane. Sikorsky had many meetings in the Chanin Building with Pan Am's technical committee of Trippe, Priester, and its chair, Charles Lindbergh. "They set to work getting the sort of airplanes they needed, speeding up the coming of the Future," Pan Am's corporate history notes.[44]

Lindbergh officially became part of Pan Am in 1929. Lindbergh's general agreement letter on February 2, approved by counsel Henry Breckinridge, concluded, "Furthermore, I would suggest that if I am injured while acting for those companies, I will not make any claim for damages, and it is my wish, in case I should be killed, that my executors should make no claim for damages, and I request the beneficiaries of my estate to so authorize my executors by appropriate waiver." Trippe crossed out "suggest" and added, "state," making clear Pan Am would not be liable. Lindbergh agreed to the change.[45]

Having Lindbergh officially aboard was a highlight of what Matthew Josephson calls the airline's "miracle year." Pan Am's corporate history confirms the airline was enjoying the "enormous capital expansion at Hoover's behest . . . Pan Am was on the eve of that explosive expansion that came of early 1929."[46]

## CHAPTER 7
# THE MIRACLE YEAR

> *"It would have been pleasant to end the story of Pan-American and its Mr. Trippe with the circling of South America. But the end is not to be written. Mr. Trippe's work, perhaps, is never done. . . . The company is still expanding."*
>
> —FORTUNE, 1931 ARTICLE[1]

"Ladies and gentlemen of the radio audience, ten years ago the airplane was a novelty," Juan Trippe opened on the Gargoyle Mobil Oil sponsored "Aviation Activities Hour" on January 3, 1929. "Travel by air was hazardous. It was not thought of as an essential need—in fact, the aviator was regarded as a dare devil. The airplane was merely a war machine." Air travel was now safe, even routine, he said. Domestic airlines bridged the continent—the Palisades of the Hudson River were now within two flying days of San Francisco Bay.

The broadcast was a platform for Trippe's big news—the following Wednesday, January 9, U.S. aviation would "take to its wings internationally" with Pan Am's 1,400 mile air route linking Miami with San Juan in Puerto Rico via Havana, Port-au-Prince in Haiti, and Santo Domingo City in the Dominican Republic. The route would open in concert with Pan Am's new $100,000 terminal in Miami, a transit hub connecting with the Atlantic Coast Line Railroad, the Florida East Coast Railway, and six associated rail systems. Passengers disembarking from a train in Miami would be met by private motorcars and driven to the airport to enjoy breakfast on the observation terrace while uniformed attendants facilitated customs regulations.[2]

A huge crowd gathered for the official dedication of Pan American International Airport, popularly known as the "36th Street Airport," including such dignitaries as Lindbergh, aviator Amelia Earhart (often characterized as Lindbergh's daring female counterpart), Assistant Secretary of Commerce for Aviation William MacCracken, Miami's Mayor E.G. Sewell, and Postmaster General New. At 8:00 a.m., Captain Fatt left the Miami airport on the regularly scheduled departure for Havana. A half-hour later, an S-38 piloted by Marine Corps pilot Raymond Merritt was winging its way on Pan Am's first survey to Panama. A Fokker piloted by Captain Musick and co-pilot George Snow departed at 10:00 a.m. on the inaugural flight to San Juan with passengers Sewell, New, and Virgil Chenea, Pan Am's agent in Havana.[3]

The motivation behind Pan Am's creation—establishment of a commercial air presence in the strategic Panama Canal Zone—was realized with the start of airmail service there. "[T]he War Department and the Canal officials pushed forward the study of regulations applicable to all commercial planes, American or foreign," chronicled Francis White. "These regulations were ready the latter part of February [1929], at the time when the Pan American Airways was ready to start operations under its contract with the Post Office Department for the carrying of mails to the Canal Zone."[4]

That first airmail flight to the Canal Zone was announced with Lindbergh as pilot, Hambleton as co-pilot, and Henry Buskey as radio operator. There was no infrastructure along the route, but in January, under conditions of secrecy, Hambleton departed the Miami airport in an amphibian plane to arrange landing stops and fueling stations from the southwestern tip of Cuba to British Honduras, Nicaragua, and the Canal.[5]

The inaugural airmail flight was scheduled to depart Pan American International Airport on Monday, February 4, at 5:00 a.m. Because of the early hour, a celebrity-filled ceremony was held the previous Saturday. Flight day was rainy, but takeoff was only delayed an hour, with flashlights lighting the wet runway as Lindbergh, with Hambleton in the co-pilot's seat, lifted the amphibian Sikorsky S-38 into the darkness. Trippe was riding as far as Havana—it was Lindbergh's twenty-seventh birthday, and they would celebrate with cake in Cuba.

From Havana, the S-38 passed over the tobacco growing and cattle-grazing region of western Cuba. Lindbergh made the water landing at La Fe, the first refueling stop Hambleton prepared, with rowboats bringing them fifty-gallon drums of gasoline. The plane left Cuba, crossing the Yucatan Straits and the jungles of the east coast of Yucatan, and was ahead of schedule when Lindbergh landed in Belize City, capital of British Honduras. Hambleton's preparations included a hastily constructed ramp to allow the plane to put down its wheels and taxi to ground. But the ramp, Hambleton recalled, "had not been built quite far enough" and as the 10,000-pound aircraft rolled off, its wheels sank axle-deep in mud.

"We pretended it was nothing serious, and were cordially received by His Excellency, Sir John Burdon, Governor of the colony, and Lady Burdon," Hambleton recalled. "As soon as possible, I begged to be excused, and with the cooperation of several of the leading citizens, we quickly had a tractor, ropes and gangs furiously at work until the plane was back on the ramp again." Hambleton noticed the excitement at their arrival—the delivery to Panama gave British Honduras hope that they, too, might soon have air service.

At Managua, they landed at the U.S. Marine Corps airfield and were received by the American Minister and assembled Marine Corps. Hambleton later saluted the military cooperation that "did much to make our demonstration of the value of aircraft in commerce successful."

On February 6, they made another water landing at Puntarenas, Costa Rica, where Hambleton had a refueling stop. The harbor was so crowded in anticipation of their arrival—and superstar Lindbergh—that it took an hour to clear boats from ramming the S-38. "We carried no mail for this point, nor for any other point north of Cristóbal, but officials and citizens were beginning to realize what the possibilities of receiving mail were," Hambleton recalled.

As they entered Canal Zone airspace, a squadron of Navy pursuit planes escorted them to France Field, the U.S. military airfield in the seaport of Cristóbal. "It gave us quite a thrill to recognize some of our old friends as they came alongside," Hambleton recalled.[6] After landing, they were met by commanding officer Colonel Fisher, and a crowd assembled for a ceremony honoring the unloading of the mail. The next several days included secret meetings between Lindbergh, Hambleton, and officials of the government, Army, and Navy.[7]

The return airmail was so large that another S-38, piloted by Raymond Merritt and Frank Ormsbee, was dispatched to share the load. In the predawn hours of February 11, the flyers awaited the plane of the U.S. Postmaster for Cristóbal, Gerald D. Bliss, who was bringing mail. Bliss arrived in spectacular fashion, his plane's prop-wash scattering a mailbag's contents. Lindbergh and Hambleton joined the scramble to collect mail blown across the airfield.

The second S-38 reached Havana first, as rough seas delayed refueling of Lindbergh's plane at Cozumel. Lindbergh landed after dark on an airfield illuminated by automobile headlights. He made it to Miami the following day, a propitious one—Dwight Morrow announced his daughter's engagement to Lindbergh. Charles and Anne married on May 27, 1929.[8]

★

In 1929, *Fortune* hailed Ralph O'Neill's airline as "unembarrassed by situations angels might fear. It undertook, in one grand gesture, to operate a regular service the whole 8,000-mile length of both continents from New York to Rio and Buenos Aires[—]and did it." With James Rand's $4 million "[O'Neill's] pockets were soon stuffy with Argentine, Brazilian and Venezuelan mail contracts."[9]

NYRBA leased half the ninth floor of the Graybar Building in Manhattan, where James Rand had his company offices. Rand helped form the board of directors, and for counsel secured the attorney and Republican Party stalwart William J. "Wild Bill" Donovan, one of the most decorated American officers of the Great War. Donovan, reportedly considered for a cabinet position in Hoover's administration, was NYRBA's connection to the president. Richard Bevier and John Montgomery, who had started American International Airlines after being ousted by Pan Am, also joined the board. O'Neill had "qualms" about them, particularly their concept of airline operation (he noted their research seemed "limited to the study of a world atlas"). The saving grace was Lewis E. Pierson, Bevier's father-in-law and chair of the Irving Trust Company.[10]

O'Neill's confidence got a boost when he saw his signature Commodore aircraft during a visit to Consolidated Aircraft's assembly hangar in Buffalo—it was the flying boat of his dreams. Its hundred-foot wings were painted a bright coral, the hull a cream color down to the waterline. Mounted beneath the wings were two 550-hp. Hornet engines and each pontoon was big enough to make a six-person speedboat. O'Neill asked for an interior reminiscent of a plush Pullman rail car and got it. Three separate compartments, seating twenty-four passengers, were paneled in different waterproof pastel colors, with reading lamps and armchairs with thick cushions overlaid with silken fabric.

NYRBA pilot William Grooch flew the first Commodore to Anacostia. Taking a page from Pan Am's book, the first lady was scheduled to christen it the *Buenos Aires*. On the big day, O'Neill, Grooch, and an NYRBA group waited with a crowd by the ramp and reviewing stand where their docked Commodore floated on the water. They had been told to await Mrs. Hoover's motorcade, which included the chief of protocol, the Argentine ambassador and his wife, and Secret Service. O'Neill was admiring his glorious ship, its aft hull painted in large letters **NYRBALINE**, with *Buenos Aires* on the side of the bow. He mentally rehearsed—he would greet the first lady, escort her to the stand, make a few remarks about NYRBA's mission to link the Americas, and hand her a bottle of "fizz water" to break across the bow (the first family didn't want bootleg champagne).

The motorcade's arrival broke his reverie. Mrs. Hoover's limousine stopped, and the Secret Service began clearing a path. As he stepped back, he saw the first lady advance toward the platform with two men. The man on her right, O'Neill assumed, was chief of protocol; the smartly dressed man on her left—Juan Trippe! As newsmen, cameramen, and spectators rushed forward, O'Neill and his group were pushed back. Trippe made a speech extolling the virtues of Pan American Airways—in front of NYRBA's own aircraft. The shocked O'Neill was certain his nemesis, Assistant Postmaster General Irving Glover, asked Walter Brown, Hoover's new postmaster general, to call the president and State Department and arrange for Trippe to escort Mrs. Hoover. O'Neill put up a brave front, but, still burning decades later, recalled how "inwardly I was seething in an incandescent fury. My stomach felt heavy as lead. I had witnessed an unbelievable masquerade that would remain engraved in my memory for the rest of my life."[11]

⭐

Pan Am had come a long way from when Vic Chenea, whom Leuteritz called the "Traffic Man in Havana," hung around the bar near Pan Am's ticket office in Havana's Sevilla-Biltmore Arcade hotel plying Americans who arrived by boat with drinks in hopes of getting them tipsy enough to buy an air ticket home.[12] A 1939 Baltimore *Sunday Sun* article would salute the "happy combination, this trio" who started it all: "Whitney . . . was the financial man, staying behind [the scenes] to keep up the support. Trippe was the operations expert, matching practice with foresight . . . Hambleton was the trail-blazer, flying down the island route and then over the jungles of the southern continent, mapping airways, dropping flour bags from planes so his ground personnel could find the spots he chose for the carving of airports. . . . 'Organization and teamwork did it,' Mr. Whitney claims. 'But if you must mention individuals, do not forget Priester and Lindbergh.'"[13] *Fortune* hailed Bob Thatch's behind-the-scenes role as "the lawyer who put the company together. He plays roving center and acts as trouble shooter [sic] in Washington."

Insiders usually pointed to Trippe and Hambleton as setting the airline on its course of success. "In these years I found John Hambleton's practical, driving force, a very important supplement to Juan Trippe's perseverance," recalled Grover Loening, a founding director of Aviation Corporation of the

Americas. "It would be quite difficult to sort out exactly where Hambleton's vision and far-sightedness ended and where that of Trippe and others began."[14]

Hambleton's dynamic role as the Pan Am vice-president who flew with Lindbergh made him a major figure in aviation. In 1929, Hambleton began expanding his influence with his own company, Federal Aviation Corporation. On April 4, stock purchase warrants offering up to 400,000 shares were mailed under the cover letter of Hambleton & Company, Inc. Hambleton was president, and his board of directors included Merian Cooper, David Bruce, C. V. Whitney, Anthony Fokker, and R. K. Mellon. Federal Aviation Corporation would invest in companies such as Pan Am, purchase land to establish the first airport in Washington, D.C., conduct experiments in dirigibles and high-altitude photography, and "other affairs at that time viewed with considerable skepticism by [Hambleton's] less imaginative peers," David Bruce noted.[15]

On June 8, Cooper and Hambleton saw each other off on separate flights from New York. Cooper was piloting his Fleet airplane, and Hambleton was flying to meet his wife in Wilmington in the unaccustomed position of passenger on a plane belonging to Consolidated Instrument Company, a maker of aeronautics instruments. J. Von der Heyden, director of sales and promotions, was piloting, with his wife along for the flight. Von der Heyden was reportedly still in the pilot's seat during a stopover at Logan Field in Baltimore.

Margaret Hambleton, pregnant with their son George, was waiting at Bluethenthal Memorial Field when the aircraft arrived. As the plane circled it appeared to stall—then plummeted and crashed. Margaret's husband was pulled clear by the time she reached the wreckage. She held John in her arms and tried to revive him. It was too late for him and the others.[16]

"PAN AMERICAN AIRWAYS CHIEF DEAD IN CRASH," blared a June 9 headline, subheads adding: "Lieut. Col. Hambleton and Two Guests Die in North Carolina/ACCIDENT WITNESSED BY WIFE OF BANKER /Friend of Lindbergh Was War Flier and Noted in Air Circles."[17] Pallbearers at the funeral included Trippe, Cooper, and David Bruce.[18]

Hambleton's friends were adamant the aviator and air warrior, who usually only took a backseat to the likes of Lindbergh, could not have been in the pilot's seat. His old commander, Billy Mitchell, wrote, "Since the war Colonel Hambleton had devoted his time and given up his life to the development of commercial aviation in the United States. His loss is irreparable. . . . Few men have done more for their country, and none were better airmen." Mitchell noted reports that the plane appeared to stall on a turn before crashing: "Some day we shall build airplanes that cannot be stalled," his letter concluded.[19]

One condolence letter to Mrs. Hambleton was posted "Nairobi, Kenya Colony," where George Gibson Carey, a veteran of the British Royal Flying Corps and a big game hunter who bagged exotic animals for museum collections, was on expedition. Carey, a former suitor, had gracefully bowed out when she chose his friend, John Hambleton. He wrote, "It all seems so unjust and wrong and I've sat for hours at night in front of the tent, watching the great herds of game grazing out on the Plain below us under the full moon, trying to find some reason. . . . As you know, Peg, I loved John and admired him perhaps as much as you did, though in a different way, because he was everything a man should be and the kindest person in the world. He certainly loved life as much or more than most of us, probably because he had more to live for. But I know, because he told me, that if he had to die he would rather it be flying, the thing he loved best in the world, next to you."[20]

Merian Cooper, already active with Hambleton's Federal Aviation Corporation, was officially elected to the boards of both Pan Am and the Aviation Corporation of the Americas on February 10, 1932.[21] But without his fearless and visionary friend, Cooper lost his enthusiasm for life as an aviation executive.

In 1931, Merian had resumed his filmmaking career and within two years became production head at RKO Radio Pictures. His rise began with a story he had been writing during rare breaks from the demands of being an aviation executive. Sometime in February of 1930, Cooper left his midtown Manhattan office and heard the sound of a plane—he saw it, gleaming in the setting sun, as it passed over the New York Life Insurance Building. "Without any conscious effort of thought I immediately saw in my mind's eye a giant gorilla on top of the building," he recalled. Nature was personified by the gigantic gorilla and Civilization by a soaring skyscraper, with the rampaging primate brought down by the guns of "the most modern of weapons, the airplane." Cooper poured his experiences as a combat flyer, commercial aviator, and globetrotting filmmaker into the resulting movie he produced with Ernest Schoedsack—*King Kong*.[22]

In 1935, ill health compelled Coop to submit a letter of resignation from Pan Am's board—which Trippe returned. "Naturally I received this note with a great deal of regret for I have always considered your having 'carried on' on our Board in John Hambleton's place as one of his oldest friends," Trippe wrote. Cooper didn't change his mind, and his resignation became official on May 21, 1936. Merian's brother, John Cooper, Jr., an expert in international air law, became a vice president and one of Trippe's most able and trusted executives.[23]

Kathleen Clair, who worked for Trippe for decades, says she never heard "the Boss" mention John Hambleton's name in her presence. That was Trippe's outward manner, but he never forgot his friend and partner.[24] As if to demonstrate he was picking up the standard of his fallen comrade, three months after Hambleton's fatal crash, Trippe, Lindbergh, and their wives set off on a Caribbean survey, with Lindbergh flying a trimotor Fokker from Pan Am's Miami airport on September 29. Ahead were stops in Cuba, Haiti, Puerto Rico, Trinidad, Colombia, and the first airmail delivery as far as Paramaribo in Dutch Guiana. In Cuba, the couples were driven in an open car with a police escort to the governor's palace along a route teeming with crowds chanting, "Viva Lindbergh." Betty Trippe recalled Lindbergh's modesty when, at a palace reception, he was called to the balcony to be cheered by hundreds massed below and insisted Juan join him. He did, "much to Juan's reluctance," Betty added.[25]

Many stops ahead were without landing fields, so they switched to a Sikorsky S-38 amphibian—a life-saving decision. As they approached Barranquilla, the airfield was swarming with a crowd eager to greet Lindbergh. He circled for forty-five minutes, but the airfield remained mobbed. Suddenly, the engines quit. "It's all right, I have had my eye on a lagoon in the interior," Lindbergh coolly said, gliding to a water landing in the middle of thick jungle. Out of the gathering darkness, two canoes appeared, each full of naked children and steered by Indians in loincloths. The Indians took them to shore, where a waiting roadster drove a muddy jungle trail to a large open car that took them through the city gates, passing under a sign proclaiming, "Welcome Lindy," to encounter another cheering crowd.[26]

In early October, the couples parted. The Trippes for home; Charles and Anne to Belize to begin an aerial archeological reconnaissance of Mayan ruins and ancient sites in British Honduras, Guatemala, and southern Mexico. Lindbergh had planned it with Pan Am and the Carnegie Institution after sighting what looked like ruins when he and Hambleton took an inland detour off the Yucatan coast during their historic airmail flight. An article on the expedition in *The Geographical Review* explained that archeological research was hindered by slow ground travel, jungle, and rough terrain. "Such drawbacks are largely removed by the speed of the plane and its freedom from earthly barriers," the article noted. On October 10, near San Miguel, the Lindberghs visited an ancient ruin uncovered during construction of a Pan Am landing field. From there they flew back to New York, just in time for Wall Street's historic economic collapse.[27]

★

At the end of October, spirits were high at NYRBA's "bon-voyage" party in New York for the crews of two new S-38s, the *Pernambuco* and the *Bahia*. The next day, Ralph O'Neill wanted to talk with James Rand, but his partner was in the boardroom, behind closed doors, and didn't emerge until after seven o'clock that evening. "He walked stiffly, staring blankly ahead, his normal ruddy face the color of putty," O'Neill recalled. "I doubt that he saw me as he brushed past." O'Neill stuck his head in the boardroom where Jim

Reynolds, the airline's vice president and treasurer, stared blankly at a wall. O'Neill asked what was up with Jim; he looked like he had seen a ghost. "You would too if you'd lost two million dollars today," Reynolds snapped. "The bottom fell out of the market!"[28] That day, October 29, was "Black Tuesday."

The stock market crash shook NYRBA, but didn't topple it. The airline had a fleet of Commodores and was building a seaplane base at Dinner Key in Miami's Coconut Grove, with an inaugural flight scheduled for spring of 1930. "We could still succeed if we induced enough people to fly and if we were permitted to bid for [U.S.] air-mail contracts over our route," O'Neill recalled. "Bill Donovan, on horseback rides with President Hoover... continued to 'prepare the ground.'" NYRBA secured Hoover's old colleague at the Commerce Department, William P. MacCracken, Jr., as board chairman. "Despite the gloom in Wall Street, the progress of NYRBA continued full steam ahead," O'Neill noted.[29]

The problem was that elusive U.S. airmail contract. NYRBA kept lobbying, but it didn't help their cause that they charged Latin American governments half that of Pan Am's Post Office contracts with foreign governments. "Thus NYRBA disturbed plans that had been laid for foreign airmail routes and for setting up a standardized system of return payments from the foreign governments," historian Josephson notes. "Juan Trippe naturally exploited the ill will earned by NYRBA in the Post Office Department to the advantage of his own company."[30]

Within NYRBA, a coup to depose O'Neill was instigated by board chairman MacCracken and supported by Bevier and Montgomery. O'Neill was at their base in Belém, Brazil, when he got word a MacCracken emissary was waiting at his hotel with written orders from the chairman giving the man "a blank check to do damn near anything he wanted with my airline," O'Neill recalled. In a hard-boiled scene, O'Neill had "the punk" brought to him, tore up the orders, flung the pieces at the man and fired him on the spot. Back in New York, O'Neill asked for Montgomery's resignation. He ordered Bevier, "keep your mitts out of NYRBA operations," probably only giving fair warning because of his father-in-law, indispensable financier Lewis Pierson. MacCracken also "changed his tune," O'Neill noted, supporting the firing of his emissary and professing shock the airline president imagined he was party to a takeover plot.[31]

Good news finally came from Bill Donovan. During one of their horseback rides Hoover assured him there would be competitive bidding for the east coast mail route through South America. NYRBA's stock went up. But a day later, Postmaster General Brown stated airmail contracts would not be up for bid "until certain matters between competing airlines were settled," O'Neill recalled. NYRBA's stock sank.[32]

In July of 1930, Trippe began talks with William P. McCracken, Jr. "Trippe, of course, had kept the Executive Committee of Pan American informed concerning his negotiations with McCracken," Leslie recalled.[33] O'Neill claims MacCracken quietly met with Trippe and C. V. Whitney at Washington's Mayflower Hotel—Pan Am's power hub in the capital—to sell out his airline. O'Neill confronted MacCracken, who protested he only tried to ascertain news about the stalled airmail contract. MacCracken revealed that Postmaster Brown would consider NYRBA's airmail request—if it merged with Pan Am.[34]

Lewis Pierson invited Trippe onto his yacht to sail Long Island Sound and discuss a settlement. "I knew they were in financial trouble," Trippe recalled, "because it is a very expensive thing to run an airline over those countries."[35] The spoils included fourteen Commodores, the Dinner Key airport, and NYRBA's airways, which gave Pan Am a circuit of South America's east and west coasts. Musick assisted in the takeover of equipment, including the prized Commodores. "[Musick] was not a man to hold a grudge," recalled his friend, NYRBA pilot William Grooch. "Now that the feud was ended, he urged the company to employ the NYRBA crews."[36]

Many from NYRBA joined Pan Am, including Grooch, but not Colonel O'Neill. "I also imagine feelings were pretty raw by that time," recalled Humphrey W. Toomey, NYRBA's Rio-Buenos Aires division manager who also joined Pan Am. "I don't think [O'Neill] wanted to be anything except head man. Pan American took on most of the [NYRBA] pilots. If some of them were not taken on then and there, they were kept on a list and were soon hired."[37]

The purchase of NYRBA was made on August 20, 1930, assets transferred on September 15, and business wrapped up in New York that October.[38] O'Neill walked up Fifth Avenue to a luncheon preceding the final paperwork, raising his coat collar against the chill. His mood remained as gloomy as the autumn weather through what he remembers as "the sumptuous luncheon and gaiety of the Pan Am group."

After signing the papers, O'Neill left for his office in the Graybar Building to clean out his desk. Trippe followed, waved over a taxi, and offered a lift to 42nd Street. "I resisted a surly refusal," O'Neill recalled, but he took the ride. As O'Neill tells it, Trippe lit up a Havana cigar and offered him a management position in Pan Am's Latin American East Coast Division. "Listen, Juan, there's nothing more to say, except that you're the last man on earth I would work for," O'Neill replied. "I put too much of myself into NYRBA to ever think of running it for you. . . ."

The taxi arrived at their stop. Trippe paid the fare, and they walked off in opposite directions. O'Neill again turned his collar to the cold, recalling two sayings: "Who steals my purse steals trash" and "Think then you are today what yesterday/You were—tomorrow you shall not be less." He believed them both.[39]

★

Secretary of State Kellogg had renewed negotiations with the Colombian Foreign Minister and future president of Colombia, Enrique Olaya Herrera, and the result was the first bilateral air agreement in the Western hemisphere on February 23, 1929. The agreement stipulated a U.S. flag airline could fly over Colombia, land on its north and west coasts, and pick up commercial traffic, with the U.S. granting reciprocal rights to the Colombian-flag airline.

On March 27, an inaugural SCADTA flight landed in the Canal Zone, and regular service began that September.[40] The U.S. had not given in—a move was underway to give Pan Am control of the German-run airline. John Leslie notes that Dr. von Bauer insisted the arrangement be secret. "Nevertheless, the State Department was fully informed, both in the person of the Secretary, Mr. Kellogg, and the Assistant Secretary, Mr. Francis White," Leslie added.[41]

Francis White had written the American Minister in Bogotá on October 26, 1929, observing that von Bauer's ability to raise funds would put him in "a good strategic position to cause American companies a good deal of difficulty. . . . *If he will sell out to an American company a big thorn will be removed in the development of our airlines to South America* . . . [emphasis, Leslie manuscript]."[42]

SCADTA had begun losing money in 1928 and needed $200,000 to modernize and expand its fleet. But the stock market crash and on-going economic crisis ended von Bauer's fund-raising hopes. On February 15, 1930, he signed an agreement with Trippe's Aviation Corporation of the Americas (soon to be officially named Pan American Airways).[43] Much of the deal was public knowledge, including reciprocal agreements, such as exchanging equipment, and Pan Am purchasing 33 percent.

"But the second part of the deal—Pan Am's purchase of the substance and control of SCADTA—was not announced," Pan Am's corporate history notes.

Secrecy was the airline's policy with a number of politically sensitive or potentially volatile takeovers. In Colombia's case, government opposition to American aircraft and airmail "was terminated through the intercession of the Scadta Company" and negotiation of the reciprocal rights agreement, records a confidential Pan Am document. Public hearings regarding Pan Am's control of Colombia's airline might result in the government again barring U.S. aircraft and cutting off airmail service.

"At the time of the agreement . . . a very marked dislike among Colombians existed toward the type of U.S. investment represented by the agreement," notes aviation historian Wesley Phillips Newton. "The prestige Scadta had acquired as an entity independent of U.S. influences was in the company's favor." Trippe realized that, but there was also pressure from the U.S.

government—by 1934, with Hitler in power, the German threat to the Canal was "more than theoretical."

"It is no secret now that Juan Trippe and Peter Paul von Bauer made a singular bargain affecting PAA and Scadta," Newton continues. "A hypothesis suggests itself: almost from start to finish, Trippe and von Bauer staged a monumental charade, the one man having security-conscious official patrons looking over his shoulder, the other an intense national sentiment to placate." Colombian SCADTA executive Tomás Borrero later described the secret pact: "One fine day we went to bed enemies of the Pan American Airways and arose friends. . . . [The pact] gave to Pan American Airways an option to buy in a secret manner over a majority of Scadta's stock. . . ."[44]

There were suspicions about the extent of Pan Am's control, but for most of the 1930s, the deal was kept secret from the Colombian government and even SCADTA's board of directors. Outwardly, von Bauer remained majority owner, and the working language was German, with German pilots and mechanics. The lingering German connection would lead to the resurrection of the SCADTA threat.

★

Within fourteen months in business, Pan Am's Key West to Havana round-trip airway of 210 miles metamorphosed into a 12,000-mile system stretching from the Caribbean into Central and South America, including twenty-eight countries and colonies. Pan Am's growing fleet included the fourteen Commodores, thirteen Fokkers, fourteen Fords, fourteen Sikorsky amphibians, and other planes. In 1928 alone, the airline carried an estimated 15,000 passengers and 530,000 pounds of mail (at a net loss of $300,000). By the end of 1930, route mileage was 20,308 miles.[45]

Pan Am turned its sights on flying the oceans. In the autumn of 1929, plans were made to shorten the FAM-5 route, a 2,064-mile course from Florida through Havana to Mexico and on to Honduras, Nicaragua, and Costa Rica to the Canal. Chief Pilot Musick proposed a daring shortcut across the middle of the Caribbean Sea, an estimated 600 miles of open water. Musick flew the pioneering round-trip in a Commodore from Miami to Cuba, then Kingston, Jamaica, to Barranquilla. The new route was the longest nonstop flight over water in the world.[46]

By 1931, Pan Am promoted itself, "The World's Greatest Air Transportation System." The airline used Fokker and Ford Tri-Motors for land routes, and Sikorsky flying boats, produced to the airline's specifications. But its newly acquired Commodore seaplanes became integral to the Caribbean. "The first real transport seaplanes ever to be built in America, these 'Commodores' . . . proved the most efficient transport aircraft in existence at the time," publicity man Van Dusen observed. There were not enough seaplane pilots, he added, but talented land plane pilots and crews signed up "to learn the fine points of marine flying. . . . [S]tep by step an enthusiastic corps of flying seamen and a tested maritime ground organization, built up around the 'Commodores' was for the mastery of the over-seas routes. For two years the blue-bordered lines that indicated marine operations spread across the Pan American operating charts. Grown expert, these crews even negotiated, first in the brave little Sikorsky amphibians, then later in the 'Commodores,' aerial crossings of the Caribbean."[47]

Pan American turned its marine operating division into an "ocean flying laboratory." All six-person crews had to be "a complete airman—pilot, navigator, radio and engine man, meteorologist and executive," noted a 1937 Pan Am news release. "Not only would this line-up be beyond price in case of an emergency but it made possible a watch-relief system which permitted every member of the crew to spend at least one-fifth of his time in off-duty relaxation."[48]

Transoceanic flying ideas included "floating islands," runways built on hollow steel pillars set in steel tanks that could float or be submerged, although it quickly became clear that would be too costly. "We also studied the possibility of refueling in air, catapulted take-offs, aprons towed behind surface ships," Lindbergh wrote. "In the end, we concluded that Pan American transoceanic services should be started with flying boats and conventional operating procedures."[49]

Pan Am's communications network was ready to expand across the oceans. Leuteritz's team included David Grant, in charge of getting radio concessions and working with Leuteritz to formulate procedures, and Evan Young, a State Department veteran heading Pan Am's Foreign Department. "We would go to these countries and work out the concession for the radio and landing rights for the planes and for importing fuel," Leuteritz recalled. "The right to operate a radio was in some countries the most ambiguous."[50]

Throughout 1929, Pan Am had begun installing radio stations in Miami, Havana, Camaguey, Santiago, Port-au-Prince, Ciudad Trujillo, San Juan, and the Brownsville to Canal Zone airways. By the end of 1930, the network had thirty-six stations in operation.[51] By July of '29, Pan Am aircraft had been outfitted with radio equipment, designed and built by Leuteritz's department. For land-based equipment, Pan Am constructed its own 200 and 100-watt transmitters.[52]

"We didn't prefer to build and run the radio station ourselves," Leuteritz explained. "But we realized it was politically dangerous to ask the Mexican government, for instance, to put up money for those of an American company. So, in substance, we installed, furnished, and maintained and paid the salaries of the station [although] it was a government station . . . these services were solely for the use of PAA, and we could not render service to any other airline. . . . We felt we would have a better communications system if it was entirely under our control."[53]

In 1933, Trippe announced they were approaching the Atlantic in cooperation with England's Imperial Airways, Air France, Lufthansa, and KLM. "The careful study of conditions over the North Atlantic is obviously too big a job for any one airline to undertake," Trippe stated. "Hence the work has been divided among all five [nations] and the information gathered will be pooled for mutual study." He added, "America's part of this program is a survey in the far North, including Labrador, Greenland and Iceland."[54] By "America," Trippe meant, of course, Pan American Airways.

The Pacific Ocean was so vast the Atlantic was the realistic first transoceanic option, although it had special challenges. The north had shorter distances between land masses, but the weather was harsher; in the south, weather was milder but had greater expanses of water. In the early thirties, Pan Am mounted two North Atlantic meteorological and geographical research expeditions, the University of Michigan-Pan American Airways West Greenland Expedition, headed by Dr. Ralph Belknap, and the Pan American East Greenland Expedition, led by explorer H. C. Watkins (and, after Watkins' death, J. R. Rymill).[55] Both were two-year expeditions. Charles and Anne Lindbergh would undertake the follow-up in one of the most daring survey flights of all time.

Lindbergh, writing during the thirties, noted "great over-water distances constituted the last major barrier to the commerce of the air. The North Atlantic is the most important, and also the most difficult to fly. . . . Distance and climate have combined to place obstacles in the path of those who wish to fly over it."[56]

Lindbergh was preparing for the next stage of aviation. He retired the *Spirit of St. Louis* and, in that miracle year of 1929, provided engineers at the Lockheed Aircraft factory in Burbank, California, with specifications for a low-wing, full cantilever monoplane with a radial air-cooled engine. The result, designed by Jack Northrop and Gerard Vultee, was the first Lockheed 8 Sirius, a single engine prototype with a black fuselage and bright red painted wings, that would be used for Pan Am surveys in the Orient and the Atlantic.

The Atlantic survey was planned for six months of flying the ocean and frozen north, returning through Europe, Africa, and South America. Two months would be spent exploring the northern Greenland Route, the Azores Route, and the Great Circle Route. Despite Pan Am's recent expeditions, little was known of year-round weather conditions and terrain suitable for air bases. An invaluable consultant was Arctic explorer Vilhjalmur Stefansson, whose books recounting his adventures among the Inuit thrilled a teenaged Lindbergh.[57] Stefansson consulted on the northern route of the Orient survey, and for the Atlantic advised the Lindberghs take "amber glasses" to see through sun and snow glare.

By the summer of 1933, when the Atlantic survey was to begin, Pan Am had moved from the Chanin Building to new headquarters only a block away, still close to Grand Central Terminal—Trippe, ever the strategist, always wanted his base close by that vital transit hub.[58] Trippe could advance his expanding empire from an aerie high in the Chrysler Building, the new skyscraper whose lobby mural glorified American industry (including a giant image of a Ford Tri-Motor), while its heights were guarded by stainless steel eagles. Dominating Trippe's 58th-floor office was his father's gigantic Malby's Globe. Lindbergh once talked of "looking at the globe of the world so much," and it was probably that globe that he turned as he contemplated the Atlantic.

"It appeared to be such a marvelous route—all those nice pieces of land strung out right where you'd want to land," Lindbergh noted. "Stefansson kept saying a northern air route would be fine. Other explorers said it would be awful. I wanted to find out for myself."[59]

# Map I.
## LATIN AMERICA
### PAN AMERICAN AIRWAYS SYSTEM

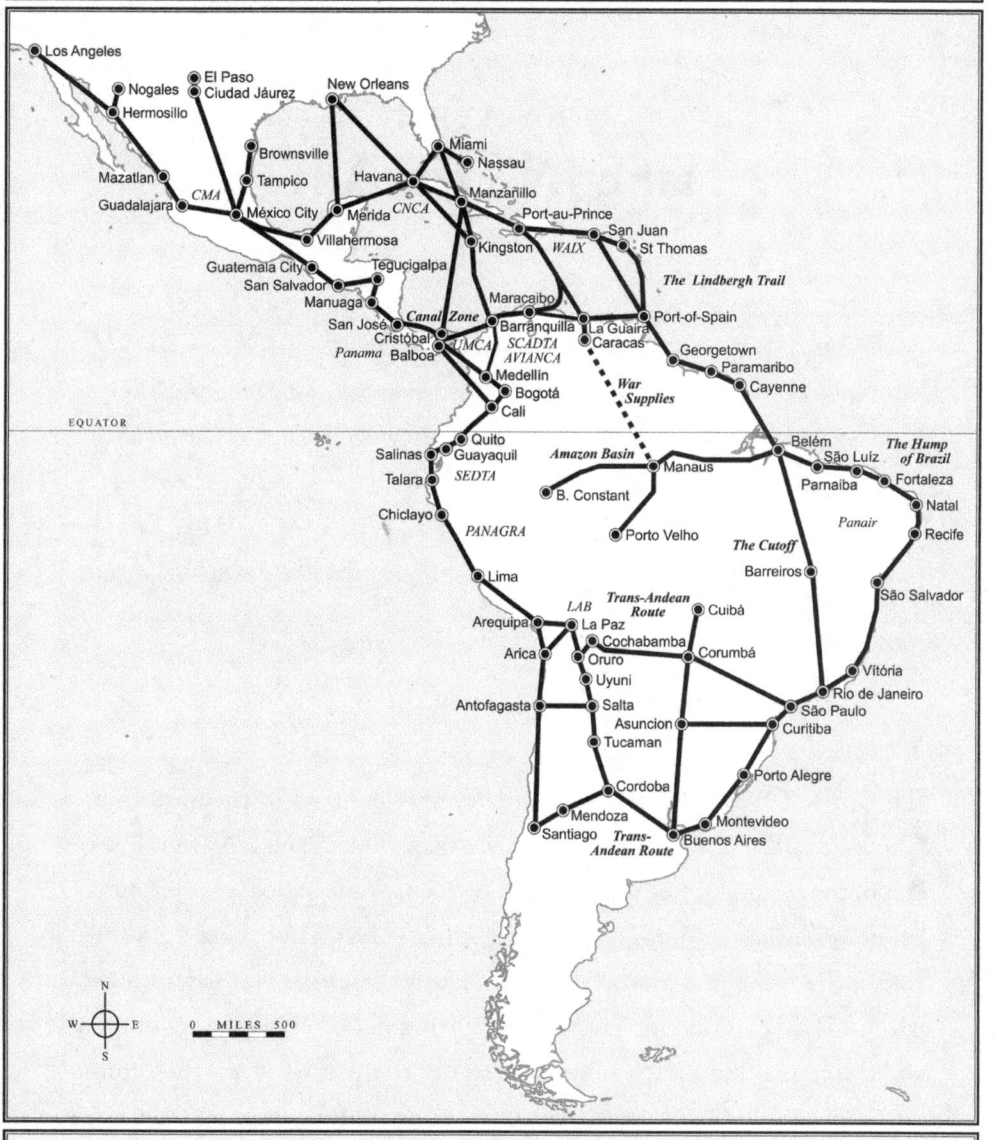

*Principal Routes & Destinations (composite)*
1927 – 1945

#### SUBSIDIARIES AND AFFILIATES

| | |
|---|---|
| *AVIANCA* – Aerovias Nacionales de Colombia (formerly SCADTA) | *PANAGRA* – Pan American-Grace Airways |
| *CMA* – Compañía Mexicana de Aviación | *Panair* – Panair do Brasil |
| *CNCA* – Compañía Aérea Cubana | *SEDTA* – Sociedad Ecuatoriana de Transportes Aéreos |
| *LAB* – Lloyd Aéreo Boliviano | *SCADTA* – Sociedad Colombo-Alemana de Transportes Aéreos |
| *Panama* – Panama Airways | *UMCA* – Urabá, Medellín and Central Airways |
| *WAIX* – West Indian Aerial Express | |

——— Scheduled service routes    ▪▪▪▪▪ Wartime raw materials route

## CHAPTER 8
# LIFE IN THE AIR

> "Sitting long hours in the back cockpit, operating the old-fashioned key radio and using a bubble sextant to check navigation, I did not realize we were part of the revolution in twentieth-century transportation. Life in the air was beautiful, limitless, and free."
>
> —ANNE LINDBERGH, RECALLING HER WORK FOR
> PAN AM SURVEY FLIGHTS[1]

In April of 1930, Charles and Anne Lindbergh broke in the Sirius with a transcontinental record flight of fewer than fifteen hours. Anne was seven months pregnant, but that did not keep her from high-flying adventures "of questionable wisdom," she later admitted. "No doubt, since I had difficulty believing I was married, I could hardly imagine I was having a baby. All that flying around in open cockpits, being pulled off a mountaintop in a glider, and making a transcontinental record flight at what was then considered high altitude (without oxygen) was, I now think, tempting providence. But I felt young and strong and invulnerable."[2] The baby, Charles Augustus, Jr., was born June 22, 1930.

The Lindberghs' first Pan Am survey, on a North Pacific route plotted by Trippe, was integral to plans for a Pacific airway and followed the Great Circle Route that skirted the Arctic Circle, the region Hambleton envisioned for future air travel. In preparation, the Sirius was retrofitted from a land plane to a seaplane, its wheels replaced with pontoons.[3] Charles and Anne trained in radio communications, with Anne serving as radio operator and Leuteritz supervising installation of Pan Am equipment and planning radio communications.

The "Orient survey" began with Charles lifting off from Flushing Bay in Long Island on July 27, 1931. They circled up from New York, flew across Canada and Alaska, crossed the Bering Strait to Russian Siberia, and on to the Kurile Islands, with stops in Japan including Hokkaido, Osaka, and Fukuoka. By September 19, they landed at Lotus Lake in Nanking, China. The lower Yangtze Valley was flooded, and from an anchorage at Lotus Lake, they spent nearly two weeks surveying and mapping on behalf of the relief effort.[4]

The day before their last flight over the flooded region, the river had risen too high to anchor the seaplane. The *Hermes*, a British carrier upon which the couple would depart the next morning, was equipped for launching amphibian planes and took the Sirius aboard, lifting it up from the water with harness and tackle. The next day, a derrick hoisted the plane up, along with Charles and Anne, and the plane glided down a rail to the water. But there wasn't enough slack in the cable, and it grew taut in the rushing currents. A wing dipped, and the plane tipped over. Charles and Anne jumped into the river and were pulled into a lifeboat, while a sampan full of passengers narrowly missed the cable. Anne had no fear for herself, but there was "one sickening moment I thought the Sirius was going to pieces before our eyes" and she thought of "all the infinite care that makes up a plane."[5]

On October 5, the *Hermes* was bound for Shanghai, where the Sirius would be shipped to the Lockheed factory in California for repairs. While on the carrier, Anne received a telegram from her older sister, Elisabeth. Their father had died of a cerebral hemorrhage.[6]

A few months later, Anne and Charles's curly-haired son, less than a year and a half old, was kidnapped from their estate in Hopewell, New Jersey. Anne never forgot the sound of the wind that howled that terrible night. Seventy-two days later on an overcast and drizzly afternoon the body of Charles Augustus Lindbergh, Jr., was discovered in woods two miles southeast of Hopewell. Anne was pregnant again and took solace when a baby boy, Jon, was born. The tragedy was the "climax," Anne noted, of the hell their public life had become. "[L]ife on the ground married to a public hero was a full-cry race between hunter and hunted. We were the quarry." Anne was an artist at heart who would express herself as a writer of popular books. Charles was naturally stoic and taciturn, but like any parent who lost a child he would never forget that tragedy. He bitterly resented being the hunted, despising the hordes of flash photographers and newsmen that pursued them. But for Charles and Anne there was always escape in the air, and they were bound for a primordial region of ice where the hunters would not follow. In the meantime, the couple had the solace of losing themselves in preparations for the Atlantic adventure.

Charles's personal policy as a consultant for various domestic airlines was to personally handle every detail and expense, and in that spirit outfitted the Sirius for the dangerous survey mission. "I wanted the freedom that personal ownership and operation gave me," he explained.[7] He ordered a powerful Cyclone engine, had a new two-position Hamilton Standard propeller installed, and added the latest directional gyro from the Sperry-Gyroscope Company.[8] Charles packed camera equipment but saved weight by foregoing parachutes. Emergency equipment included a tent, sleeping bag, waterproof matchbox, .38 and .22 caliber revolvers, and ammunition.

Lindbergh made an exception to his personal ownership rule in again accepting Pan Am radio communications and ground crew support at the airline's bases for the return through South America. Leuteritz organized communications, which included a Pan Am ship, the *Jelling*, as a floating base camp in the North Atlantic. A key objective was testing radio conditions in the North, seeing how frequencies might behave at various distances at different times of day or night.[9] Pan Am's proprietary radio system was designed to cut through static and humidity endemic to the tropics—now it would be tested in freezing weather. The radio set designed, built, and tested under Leuteritz's supervision weighed less than seventy pounds and used less current than a small light bulb.

Anne, again radio operator and copilot-navigator, described the adventure as "one of the best prepared and executed of all exploratory flights."[10]

She summed up her role as a link to Pan Am stations and "that outer world" that came through the static: "For to put on your earphones and tap into the radio waves is to open a window to another world, to have a peephole to the outside, an earhole."[11]

She welcomed the adventure, even though it meant leaving behind the new baby. "Flying was normal life for us, and the project lifted us out of the aftermath of crime and turned the publicity that surrounded us to a constructive end—the advance of air travel. For my husband there was the eternal fascination of adventure and exploration. For me, the trip was the nearest approximation to 'a life of our own' that could then be found."[12] Anne knew there would be long hours of intense work, risk, even "fear in the back cockpit." But she was determined to be an equal partner. "The feminist in me longed passionately to prove that I could hold my own and take the place of a man," she later wrote.[13]

---

The red-winged Sirius lifted off from Flushing Bay on July 9, 1933, at 19:37, Greenwich Mean Time, headed for Maine and Newfoundland. As they left Newfoundland for Cartwright in Labrador, Anne was in communication with the Pan Am ship. Nearing the coastal settlement that was their first stop, they saw three steamers, one with a band of blue and a white star painted on its smokestack—the *Jelling*. Charles circled as the Pan Am crew rushed to the deck to wave. "I get very excited as though we were coming home," Anne wrote on July 14. "That boat down there was for us. Here in this strange land, that was home. They had been watching us, hearing our radio, and now we were here."[14]

As they flew on into icy rain and fog, Anne worked hard to maintain radio contact with the *Jelling*. At Cartwright, Hopedale, and Hebron they flew over fog-shrouded icebergs. Further up the coast, fjords joined a sea covered with ice. They encountered Inuit villages and met missionaries who explained "heathen" natives killed clerics in the past but were not giving any more trouble. On July 22, they landed at Godthaab in Greenland, a settlement nestled in a harbor below frozen peaks. Local children gave the aircraft an Inuit name that stuck: *Tingmissartoq*—"The one that flies like a big bird."[15]

In early August, the *Tingmissartoq* landed at Ella Island in Greenland where Dr. Lauge Koch, head of a Danish expedition mapping the region by air, awaited them. The next day they flew to the Danish expedition's northern base at Clavering. Charles, the future conservationist, listened as Koch described the Arctic as "so easy to destroy," but it was easy to be destroyed in its unforgiving cold and ice. They recalled the deaths of Henry George Watkins, leader of the British Arctic Air Route Expedition, and Swedish balloonist Salomon August Andrée. But Koch loved the land and promised, "You will see the midnight sun."[16]

As the *Tingmissartoq* flew on into a realm of icebergs and glacial mountains, where polar bears and herds of musk ox roamed frozen landscapes, the plane's maintenance was vital to survival. When moored, a little water seeped into the pontoons and added weight, so they had to be regularly pumped dry. The fittings and wires, exposed to salt-water sprays during takeoffs and landings, had to be greased and the propeller blades oiled to protect against corrosion.[17]

The ice cap was foreboding, alien to life. Melting ice caused pools of an "intense and poisonous-looking blue" to form, Anne observed. At one point, Charles wrote a note on a map and handed it to Anne: "Every 5 minutes we save a day's walk."[18] As they penetrated the icy wilderness, there were times it became difficult to maintain their tenuous link to the outside world. "Bad radio," Anne wrote in an August 8 diary entry. It took an hour to reach Angmagssalik, and she couldn't contact Julianehaab or the *Jelling*. They finally landed at Julianehaab, an oasis where vegetables grew and sheep and cows grazed.

"It is strange, but Greenland affects people like an enchanted land," Anne wrote on August 11. "I think it is the intensity of the life, the intensity of one's impressions, the sharp outlines of the mountains, jagged, snow-streaked, the bare rocky hills, deeply shadowed in the evening light. . . . Isn't that thrilling—to drop into the ice age. I feel it up here, where there are no settlements and the great mountains and fjords are as though just finished by some god. Only a flimsy airplane between us and the ice age!"[19]

⭐

On August 18, during a stay in Reykjavik, Iceland, Charles wrote a twelve-page confidential rough draft survey report to Trippe. In a cover letter, Lindbergh praised Pan Am's *Jelling* crew, particularly commander Major Robert Logan ("I know of no one who we would rather have in charge of the ship expedition or to assist us under adverse conditions"), mechanic Homan ("one of the best mechanics I have ever had contact with"), and radio operator Wilson Turner Jarboe ("We were never out of radio communication when we needed it."). "All in all," Lindbergh concluded, "I feel that the Pan Am organization has been 101%."[20]

Lindbergh's "Dear Juan" letter opened: "In establishing a transatlantic route it is fully as important to decide which route will be most advantageous in the future as it is to decide which is best to operate over today. It must be remembered that the route which is best for our present equipment and experience will not necessarily be as good as some other route when we have more efficient aircraft and have learned more about transoceanic flying. It has always been my belief that with every advance in aviation the air routes will tend to follow more closely the great circle course [shortest distance between any two points on a sphere] between the localities they serve. I believe that in the future aircraft will detour bad weather areas by flying above them rather than around them."

Lindbergh recommended that Pan Am plan its transatlantic route "approximately" along the Great Circle Route. The downside was water distances and winter weather, but their exploration through Labrador, Greenland, and Iceland convinced him that reports of storms, extreme cold, and high winds "have been greatly exaggerated." Stefansson advised they would find agreeable weather far north of Julianehaab and so it was. Lindbergh warned that northern transatlantic service required high speed, long-range planes to overcome strong winds and distances. "A forced landing under these conditions would be very likely to cause the loss of both plane and personnell [sic]."

"It is not possible for me to over emphasize the necessity of a sufficient number of radio stations on a northern route to give reliable weather information and to give bearings," he noted. A lot of work was needed to prepare landing fields; otherwise it would be necessary to emulate the locals who used planes with flat bottom pontoons: "They make a regular practice of landing these either on snow or water. In fact, one pilot told us that he preferred flat bottom pontoons to skiis [sic] for either snow or ice landings. I believe that the first operation in the north should be with flying boats in summer and preferably with planes which can land either on snow or water in winter. After experience has been obtained the question of building landing fields can be decided."

Lindbergh felt any northern route should be over the relatively fog-free inland areas, not rugged coastlines. He preferred inland bases north of Newfoundland's Northwest River and south of the Hudson Strait fog area. During the short period of the year, when ice conditions permitted, Hafedale's large sheltered area and abundance of potential mooring spots made it a good base for flying boats. Hebron was probably better but was rarely ice-free. The mountainous coastlines of Hebron and Hopedale had no land area practical for constructing a landing field, although the Inuit informed them there was relatively flat country fifty miles west of the coast.

*Jelling* commander Robert Logan had suggested a base in Northern Maine, which Lindbergh felt deserved careful study. Pending study and future operations, a northern transatlantic route could stretch from Newfoundland's west coast to the town of Botwood, up to Godthaab, which was north of the foggiest areas, and across the icecaps. "We located several places where fields might be constructed close to water which is ice free in summer and accessible by boat. . . . From Godthaab I believe the route should go directly to Iceland via [Angmagssalik] but with the intention of passing over Angmagssalik when the weather prevents landing. From our observations and inquiries it seems that Angmagssalik has the worst weather of any point on the route I have outlined."

Lindbergh suggested Lake Ligord as an emergency base in case of stormy weather in Angmagssalik. Dr. Koch of the Danish expedition recommended Ella Island as a good location for flying boats, with plenty of land for constructing suitable landing fields. Although that seemed too far north, it could provide an emergency base for planes caught in bad weather between Godthaab and Iceland.[21]

Lindbergh emphasized his suggestions required more meteorological data. "However, I believe this is a good route to lay tentative plans around as a beginning," he concluded, adding that Greenland was wide open for airmail service as mail and boat schedules "are measured in months when there are any at all."

Lindbergh's report described the horizon over the icecap disappearing in overcast and whirling snow—a whiteout. Despite the bitter cold, Charles slid the canopy open to stare into the void through tinted goggles.[22] "Without the amber glasses which we had carried on Steffansons [sic] advice it was not possible to see the snow thru the haze and the light was very hard on our eyes. With the use of amber glasses, however, we were able to see thru the haze at all times."[23]

In the alien ice world they were exploring, Anne took pleasure in small comforts—layers of warm clothing, social time with the *Jelling* crew and local people, a cozy stop where she sipped a cup of hot coffee and listened as a Victrola played "The Swan" and "Ave Maria." She loved recounting how a Pan Am radio operator sent her a 150-word message through heavy static and exclaimed, "My God, she got it!" She described the focus required: "My head was down in the cockpit, my fingers on the transmitter key; and my ears, clamped by earphones, heard only radio code, maddeningly interrupted by crashes. There was little chance to observe the beauty of sea, sky, and mountains, or to think about my lost child or the new baby at home."[24]

But there were times Anne lifted her head and gazed upon glacial peaks, icebergs, and Inuit villages. And her thoughts always returned to that which could never be escaped. "From time to time, the inner process of reconciliation with the past broke through painfully in vivid dreams, or with the sound of a howling wind at night, or at the sight of a curly-headed child."

But the stark beauty of the icy wilderness and the warmth extended by Inuit and Danish settlers and explorers "washed us clear of memories. In those tiny, isolated outposts of the North the burden of fame fell from us and we achieved a measure of anonymity. We were strangers; we were guests; but we were not celebrities set apart from the human race. The daily round of the northern outposts flowed on regardless of our presence, and we enjoyed both watching it and sharing in its rhythm."[25]

As they headed for Europe, Anne realized how much she enjoyed docking with the *Jelling* and lamented they would have to leave the ship behind. "It has been fun to meet and compare notes," she wrote in Reykjavik on August 21. "Each time it was like coming home." Soon they would be in teeming cities, objects of curiosity and targets for reporters and photographers. Charles already anticipated the press, and Anne and Wilson Jarboe discussed their mutual concerns as to Charles's terse directive: "No schedules . . . I don't want people to know."

"But suppose I lose you—I'll have all of Pan Am down my neck," Jarboe told Anne. But "C.," as Anne referred to her husband, was right—it was "a nightmare to step into a newspaper-prepared hell of welcomes at different places."

The transition from ice age solitude to cosmopolitan cities was jolting to Anne, "somewhat unreal and arid." She later wrote, "With each new place my ability to absorb new impressions decreased and my longing to be home with my boy mounted."[26]

At the end of August, the Lindberghs met the King and Queen of Denmark. The first of September they attended a gala dinner and Anne described the glittering affair in her diary: "Mirrors and lights and white wine and nicely dressed women and not too obvious music, and strings of lights from the park out of the long windows. I want to dance—how I want to dance!" But C. declined because "there might be a story." Anne saw a "flashlight reporter" in the hall and woefully concluded, "C. was right."[27]

On September 15, Charles finished another handwritten "Dear Juan" letter, a six-page report written on the stationary of Stockholm's Automobilkubbens Hotel. "I believe that a transatlantic air route by way of Greenland and Iceland can be absolutely satisfactory during at least a part of the summer months," he opened. "Our survey this summer indicates that, even with existing equipment, it should be possible to compete advantageously with the Atlantic steamship schedules. . . . It is questionable whether an operation could be carried on during the winter with sufficient regularity to expedite the mails even to Northern European points."[28]

Lindbergh reiterated "the solution of Northern operation" lay in aircraft capable of flying day or night through, or above, bad weather. "When radio and other devices have been developed sufficiently to permit landing in fog and storm the problem of northern flying will, of course, be greatly simplified." Before they could locate air bases with confidence, better meteorological data was needed—Greenland had too many unknowns, and Iceland required further study. "Steffenson [sic] has already stated that one side of Iceland is frequently clear even tho the other is covered with fog. Our experiences tended to confirm this. . . . In fact, as I have already stated, it seems that the successful operation of the northern route will lie in the knowledge of where clear weather exists and the ability to reach these points under all intermediate conditions." With that, Lindbergh ended his report.

By October, the couple was in the British Isles. On the 16th, Charles wrote Trippe from Glamorganshire in southeastern Wales, reporting on their flyover of the coast of Norway between Bergen and Stavanger. An operation would be difficult in Bergen, with its coastline of glacial mountains, he reported. Stavanger was promising, with open areas for landing fields and abundant sheltered water areas for seaplanes. Lindbergh pinpointed the area between Stanger and the Southern Norwegian coast as best for a coastal base after "careful meteorological study."

In London, Lindbergh met Woods Humphrey of Imperial Airways, a competitor and potential partner. The British airline had nothing under construction to match the Martin aircraft Pan Am was developing for transoceanic flight, Lindbergh wrote. They were skeptical about "our ability to make the long water flights necessary on any but the far Northern route." Lindbergh concluded, "All in all I believe we are considerably ahead both in our planes and engines. Woods Humphrey told me that they had long ago written off the possibility of forced landings with their multi-engined planes and that they had no hesitation about flying land planes over water. With the possible exception of KLM, which I have not had the opportunity of seeing yet, Imperial is carrying on by far the best operation I believe . . . I do not know of anyone I would sooner work with in the Trans Atlantic development."[29]

★

By late October, Charles and Anne were in Paris. "It's impossible for C. ever to be in Paris inconspicuously," Anne wrote in a letter home. "They still regard him as a romantic young boy—the Fairy Prince. Women bang at the door of his car, crowds collect as he leaves the hotel. . . . And to Charles it was just bitter medicine. It was very sad. He talked about giving up Aviation, never going to any cities."[30]

By November the couple crossed Spain, Portugal, and the Azores. On the thirtieth of the month, they landed in Bathurst on the strategic Atlantic coast of Africa. Maintenance of aircraft in the tropics was "a constant battle," Anne recalled. She noted the steamy heat turned their plane's red-painted wings a dulled orange, giving it "the flat burnt-out look of an old car, left out in the desert, beaten by sun and dry winds."[31] Serious repairs were needed, and they found themselves grounded on the Gambia River. Charles stripped out all non-emergency equipment, and with metal shears cut off one of the gas tanks.

"On the last night that would have enough moonlight for our take-off, a light wind sprang up to help us," he recalled. As they got airborne, the engine began sputtering and choking. In her diary, Anne wrote, "My insides turn over. It's coming then—Death." But the engine smoothed out "like a long sigh," Anne happily noted. By moonlight and the glow of the radio receiver dials she recorded in the survey log: "Left Bathurst 02:00 GMT." Anne instantly made radio communications with Pan Am's Miami station; a transmission Trippe later offered as evidence that a Pan Am radio was unequaled by any other aeronautical radio.[32]

As they crossed the South Atlantic and neared Natal, on the tip of Brazil's eastern coastline, Anne radioed their imminent arrival to the Pan Am station. The couple welcomed the sight of the Pan Am house flag as they touched down at a barge on a river. By December 8, they flew up the northern coastline to Pará and another Pan Am base. During the two-day stopover, a Pan Am crew made the *Tingmissartoq* good as new, greasing and painting its pontoons, varnishing the floor, and giving the engine a thorough check. By now, Anne was ready for the journey to end, or at least see someplace familiar. But her husband's wanderlust was not satiated—Charles now wanted to fly to Manaus, a thousand miles up the Amazon.[33]

They flew over the fog-covered jungle to the Xingu River and Manaus, where they docked and were greeted by government officials. They spent the next day relaxing. "In the afternoon after a long hot rest C. and I go to the rubber factory," Anne recorded on December 11. "A stupid American blundered out excitedly, 'You know, we were the first to hear of the kidnapping here!' C. and I were so stunned. . . . It suddenly turned everything quite black. That thing—it happened, it happened here too. I had thought in this faraway place it had not happened."[34]

On December 12, they departed for Port-of-Spain, Trinidad's seaport capital, winging toward cloud-shrouded mountains in a torrential downpour—even stoic C. confessed the weather was terrible. They later learned that as the *Tingmissartoq* passed over a Waiwai village, the natives heard the engine buzz. As they glimpsed the outline of wings and fuselage through the storm, a lightning bolt struck the tribal chief's house, singeing his son and daughter, melting his prized hunting spear, and cracking open a log that was the chief's ceremonial seat. Word spread that the god Makanaima was angry and had sent a gigantic mosquito to sting them.[35]

By December 19, the *Tingmissartoq* ended its journey back in Flushing Bay. The flight log recorded their arrival at 19:37—the hour, to the second, they had departed. Speedboats crammed with reporters, photographers, and newsreel cameramen were waiting.[36]

A Pan Am historical report concluded the survey provided only "general knowledge" of conditions along segments of a potential transatlantic route.

In 1934, Pan Am lent support to artist and adventurer Rockwell Kent's year-long expedition to northern West Greenland that provided the airline with detailed weather reports.

But Lindbergh's confidential dispatches detailed a northern route for land and amphibian planes, pinpointed spots for flying boats and inland areas for building landing fields, tested radio communications, considered competition with steamships, and reported on Imperial Airways, while Bathurst and Natal would soon be key to Pan Am and American military strategists. Lindbergh anticipated high-speed and high-altitude land planes capable of crossing vast water distances—new airways would follow new technology. A few years after the survey, Lindbergh prophesied air travel would "insulate man from contact with the elements in which he lives. The 'stratosphere' planes of the future will cross the ocean without any sense of the water below."[37]

For the Lindberghs, the survey's aftermath was consumed by the arrest of a suspect in their child's death. Anne later recalled a tale of the Buddha's answer to a mother who lost her child: "According to the legend, he said that to be healed she needed only a mustard seed from a household that had never known sorrow. The woman journeyed from home to home over the world but never found a family ignorant of grief. Instead, in the paradoxical manner of myths and oracles, she found truth, understanding, compassion, and eventually, one feels sure, rebirth."[38]

⭐

Nineteen thirty-four began with Pan Am among the targets of a government investigation into sweetheart deals in the awarding of airmail contracts. The new administration of Democrat Franklin Roosevelt saw a chance for monopoly-busting reform, particularly since the alleged deal-making had taken place under Republican administrations. Pan Am was the nation's sole international airline, while Transcontinental and Western Airlines (TWA), United Air Lines, American Airways, Northwest Airlines, and Eastern Air Transport dominated domestic airways.[39]

It was left to Postmaster General Farley to recommend whether or not to cancel Pan Am's contracts. Farley's report concluded Pan Am had been shown favoritism—in virtually every contract, sufficient time was not allowed for competitive bidding, and Pan Am was high bidder in all but one winning contract. But apart from a $2,000,000 cost-saving adjustment to the government, Farley recommended the contracts be continued. Reportedly, Secretary of State Cordell Hull reminded him that canceling Pan Am's contracts would disrupt hundreds of international trade agreements and service in more than thirty countries. "Pan American had become entwined with half the nations of the world, like an ivy vine," *Fortune* concluded. "[Pan American] represents the rights of U.S. citizens upon the airways of the world. It alone acquired those rights and it alone holds them in the name of the American people."[40]

By year's end, Pan Am was ready to advance its transoceanic vision and would do so with the help of the government and a secret relationship with the Navy. It was at the December 1934 board meeting that Trippe calmly dropped a bombshell announcement before his shocked directors—Pan Am would fly the Pacific.

# PART II

# WAR CLOUDS

## CHAPTER 9
# ACROSS THE PACIFIC

*"The Atlantic was a lot easier than the Pacific, where we had a little island 2,400 miles away from nothing. On the Atlantic, you would hit somewhere along the coast on either side."*

—Hugo Leuteritz, Pan Am chief communications engineer[1]

Trippe and his inner circle settled on the Pacific as their first transoceanic challenge, but they were also preparing for the Atlantic. "At Pan American we never forgot that flying the Caribbean was a step toward flying the Atlantic and Pacific," Lindbergh recalled. As a Pan Am period document corroborates, "Utilizing the Caribbean service as a laboratory, Pan American looked ahead to transocean flight without regard to whether the Atlantic or the Pacific would be the first area for pioneer efforts. The dominant fact was that Pan American Airways accepted the concept of regular transoceanic air service as a goal susceptible of practical attainment at a relatively early date. Pan American Airways undertook to shape the progress of aviation to the uses of transocean flight through essential technical contributions based on experience, and to hasten the day when the equipment, the techniques and the trained personnel would be available to make sustained and safe over-ocean flight possible."[2]

The Pacific strategy included a Far East connection through China linking up with an airway across the ocean. William Grooch, the star NYRBA pilot now with Pan Am, was summoned to meet with Priester, who matter-of-factly told him that Pan Am was planning to fly the Pacific and that Grooch was to establish an airline in China. "The idea staggered me for a minute. How would we dodge the storms? Where would we refuel? . . . Priester's voice pulled me out of the clouds."

"You vill haf much to do," the chief engineer said in his thick accent.[3]

★

Trippe focused on a North Pacific route, thanks to the Lindberghs' 1931 Orient survey. "The reports submitted by Colonel Lindbergh upon the completion of his trip were generally favorable to the establishment of a route to the Orient by way of Alaska and Siberia," a Pan Am document recorded.[4] In 1932, with Alaska projected as the bridgehead of a Northern Pacific route, Pan Am purchased two American airlines in the territory, marking its "first tangible thrust at the Orient," *Fortune* reported.[5]

In 1933, Pan Am bought from an American company a 45 percent partnership interest with the Chinese government in China National Aviation Corporation (CNAC). The new affiliate was described as "anchoring the transpacific service," particularly its "Route No. 3," Shanghai to Canton route.[6]

By autumn of '34, talks with the Soviets about a base in Russia stalled, while tensions with Japan made a base there out of the question. Pan Am had to decide whether to develop the Northern Pacific route or recalibrate for the Central Pacific. "Urgent considerations of national interest made it desirable that transpacific service be inaugurated at the earliest possible date," a Pan Am historical document chronicles. "In view of the lack of progress in obtaining the necessary operating rights for the Northern route, Pan American determined early in 1935 to proceed with the development of the Central Pacific route."[7] That meant crossing at the Pacific's widest point, twice as far as the distance from the East Coast to Europe.

Thanks to the pioneering work of Captain Musick and four years flying regularly scheduled service across the Caribbean Sea, Pan Am was prepared.

It was the dawn of the Clipper ships, which began with the Sikorsky S-40 that went into production in the miracle year of '29. In 1931, the first S-40, dubbed the *American Clipper*, rolled out of a hangar for test flights and was christened by First Lady Lou Hoover that October. The *American Clipper* marked a new era, one focused on transoceanic travel. Trippe knew the historic challenge would require continual advancement and innovation—even as the S-40 was being launched, he had directed Franklin Gledhill, Pan Am's purchasing agent, to send a solicitation letter to U.S. manufacturers asking for a flying boat "which will eclipse anything ever built in long range performance characteristics and will be capable of flying either ocean on scheduled operation."[8]

"They don't want a flying boat, they want a miracle," one manufacturer reportedly commented. Only Igor Sikorsky and Glenn L. Martin attempted that miracle.[9] But before a contract was awarded, Lindbergh, Priester, and Trippe spent eighteen months in research and design for a flying boat initially projected for the Atlantic. Lindbergh, a no-frills flyer, favored speed over such heavy fuel burning "luxury" as lounges and dining rooms—he wondered why travelers would need accommodations typical of a luxury steamship when estimations were that by 1937 transatlantic air travel time would be a mere eighteen hours.[10]

Sikorsky worked with the committee and successfully argued for a big plane he could safely build. They were all leaping into the unknown and, potentially, the abyss. Trippe feared that failure would damage the cause of long-range aircraft. "Trippe hadn't mentioned the Oceans then publicly, but ocean flying was at stake," Pan Am's corporate history noted. "Sikorsky won the argument—and an order for three."[11] The S-42 Clipper that Pan Am ordered in 1932 had an anticipated gross weight of 38,000 pounds, a 114-foot wingspan, a height of seventeen feet and length of sixty-nine feet, and the power of four 750 hp. Pratt & Whitney Hornet engines. The price tag: $242,000 per plane.[12]

Pan Am also accepted the bid of the Glenn L. Martin Company of Maryland, ordering three of the even bigger Martin Model-130 at $417,000 each. When negotiations for an Atlantic airway bogged down, there were concerns the airline would be stuck with big expensive planes it wouldn't need, or cancel the order. Trippe greenlighting both was a prescient move. Sikorsky's aircraft was designed for the Atlantic, with its plentiful rest and refueling stops; the longer range Martin M-130 was perfect for the Pacific.

The Martin's gross weight was 52,000 pounds, its wingspan 130 feet, with a height of twenty-five feet, length of ninety-one feet, and four Pratt & Whitney Twin Wasp engines, each at 900 hp. The total 3,600 in horsepower equaled a cruising speed of 130 miles an hour.[13] The Martin could carry 2,600 gallons of fuel, enough to fly through thirty-mile per hour headwinds to Hawaii, even with a seven-person crew and a minimum 800-pounds of mail. The downside was the M-130 would not be ready for another year.

Priester's first choice for chief ocean flyer was Eddie Musick. The trailblazing pilot had concerns about big flying boats and asked Sikorsky to let him see the plane. Sikorsky led him to a hangar apron and "the ship of his dreams," Grooch recalled. Not a rivet head marred the silvery surface. Inside the soundproof cabin, Musick went straight for the lead pilot's seat. There were new instruments to learn, including one of the first automatic pilots on a transport. "Here's where I get back into coveralls," Musick said to Sikorsky with a grin. "Can you loan me a man who savvys this stuff?"[14]

Musick was reassured, but the tension was palpable in Pan Am's executive suites. The "Hawaii sector," as the military called the route from San Francisco to Hawaii, was the most daunting stretch of ocean. If an airline could establish scheduled service across it, then the whole world could be flown as no greater span of open water existed along a commercially viable air route. With the Martin still in the factory, the Sikorsky Clipper had to serve as the Pacific survey plane. By the summer of '34, the first S-42 was ready for a proving flight utilizing a 1,242-mile course over the Atlantic. On August 1, Lindbergh completed the course, averaging 157.5 miles an hour and setting eight world records. The S-42 was the most advanced aircraft in operation, but its absolute range was 2,540 miles, not a safe margin for the 2,400 miles of ocean between San Francisco and Honolulu.

The second S-42 became the designated survey plane and was sent back to the factory to be modified and retrofit for its mission, including stripping out passenger accommodations. The weight saving, even with a full crew, was a fuel capacity gain that translated into a flying time of over twenty-one hours and a range of nearly 3,000 miles. The plan was the survey plane's flying experience and operational data would be completed by the time the Martin Clipper was tested and ready to inaugurate regular Pacific service.[15]

Pan Am's new flying boats were inspired by the seafaring Clippers of old and in more than name. Flying an ocean required the same grasp of weather conditions as the "old 'weather-eyed' clipper shipmasters who made their living by knowledge of wind, cloud, and storm," Matthew Josephson wrote. "With their 'weather eye' always open, they recorded not only the weather 'habits' but even the height of cloud layers and storms as well as the areas of favoring winds in the remotest regions of the Pacific and in the neighborhood of the most forgotten desert islands. Trippe and his technical men gathered many navigational [clues] from the old clipper ship logs before they determined the future course of the Flying Clippers."[16]

Ships at sea steered by the stars, and so would transoceanic aircraft. Pan Am established a school in celestial navigation headed by merchant marine navigator Fred Noonan, considered the greatest of navigators. Musick was an enthusiastic student. "Night after night [Musick] sat on the roof of his house, with a star chart on his lap, until he could identify any constellation in the heavens," his friend Grooch recalled. "He almost wore out a bubble octant [a navigational measuring instrument], shooting the sun and the stars. The flight crews, realizing that he meant business, settled in for the long haul. Overnight the students of the 'Caribbean College' became nautical men, speaking the language of the sea."[17]

⭐

At the December 1934 board meeting, Trippe announced the company would fly from the West Coast to Hong Kong. The airway he outlined was 8,746 miles—the first leg alone, from San Francisco to Honolulu, was 2,400 nonstop miles over water.[18] In 1934 the technology *did not exist* to cross the oceans. But Trippe had the equation in his head and knew the pieces that were coming together. "There was a conviction on the part of some aviation engineers, one on our board, that the ocean distances were beyond the range of anything but lighter-than-air [dirigibles]," Trippe recalled.[19] That board critic was pioneering aviation engineer and aircraft manufacturer Grover Loening. "Earnings first and prestige of our system second, this is sound business," Loening reasoned. "More lines on the map of the world in PAA's colors do not necessarily mean larger net earnings."[20]

Loening resigned the board in protest, but others appreciated Trippe's almost mystical prescience. "Trippe might be a 'dreamer,' but Pan American was now the largest airway system in the world, embracing 32,000 route miles at the close of 1934," Matthew Josephson noted. "It had a surplus of $3,000,000, and actually began to pay dividends. Trippe's followers were willing to span either the Atlantic or the Pacific, at his word."[21]

In January of 1935, Pan Am opened a Pacific Division headquarters in Alameda, a waterfront town in the East Bay across from San Francisco. The Pacific Division manager was Colonel Clarence Young, a decorated officer and WW I pilot. Young was the first director of aeronautics in the U.S. Department of Commerce (he instituted the policy that all pilots be licensed), before joining Pan Am in September of 1934. Under Young's leadership, personnel experienced in over-water operations and seaplane maintenance, including Captain Musick, became part of the "migration" to the new headquarters.[22] John Leslie, who distinguished himself as Priester's assistant, joined as Pacific Division engineer.

Trippe and the board granted Leuteritz's department $10,000 in capital appropriation toward increasing the range and accuracy of the Adcock direction finder, along with funding for what Leuteritz called "very hushhush" practice flights. (The Adcock, named for British engineer Frank Adcock, replaced the early loop antennas with an antenna array that eliminated previous interference and distortions from atmospheric disturbances.)[23] The new technology was imperative if pilots flying thousands of ocean miles were to locate tiny islands in the dreaded "Hawaii sector" and beyond. After four months, with tests exceeding expectations, Leuteritz told Trippe they were ready for the Atlantic. The radio network was subsequently adjusted for the Pacific, with Leuteritz developing six to seven patents for the new DF.[24]

"The specialized development of Adcock direction finders for use in aviation, especially for operation in the higher frequencies, has been pioneered almost exclusively by the Radio Division at the Pan American Airways System under the direction of H. C. Leuteritz," Henry W. Roberts wrote in 1945. "[U]ntil 1939 when the Civil Aeronautics Authority began providing federally-owned Adcock direction finders for public transoceanic navigation, Leuteritz and his engineers were, for all practical purposes, the sole research agency in long-range Adcock direction finders."[25]

The Central Pacific route hinged on Pan Am securing rest and refueling stops. Potential airbases included Honolulu, a city rich in infrastructure and resources. The challenge lay in securing isles across "the intervening portion of the route" to Hong Kong, a Pan Am document explained.[26] Guam, a likely stop, had a large U.S. Navy base. The Navy claimed Midway, but had not developed it.[27] Midway, 1,300 miles northeast of Honolulu, was a lonely outpost, home to Laysan albatross and the Commercial Pacific Cable Company, a joint U.S.-British cable station staffed by a superintendent, his wife, and a small crew.

Pan Am needed a stop between Midway and Guam and found it in barren and virtually unknown Wake Island. Pan Am Captain Don Cooper recalls one story of Wake's discovery: "Trippe spent hours in the archives of the New York City Library searching through clipper ship log books and finally, in one ship's log, it made reference to an island that was located in the approximate location needed."[28] Wake, a coral atoll 1,185 miles west of Midway and 1,508 miles east of Guam, was surrounded by reefs and essentially three separate islands—Wake, Wilkes, and Peale—that formed a circle around a lagoon, an oasis of calm water perfect for flying boats. But did any nation claim it?

Trippe sent Captain Clarence "Dutch" Schildhauer, a Navy pilot and seaplane captain who knew the Navy's chief hydrographer, to Washington. Schildhauer spent three days discreetly studying charts and records of wind and weather conditions, and made inquiries as to Wake's status. In the autumn of 1934, Schildhauer set sail to "quietly" investigate potential bases. At Honolulu, he checked out the Navy base at Pearl Harbor. At Midway, he saw the lagoon was ideal for seaplanes. Another channel needed to be cut through the coral reefs, but that was fine by Rear Admiral Harry Yarnell and the Navy. They wanted a submarine channel, but such fortifications were denied because of concerns over Japan's reaction—so a commercial enterprise would be a way to do it. Schildhauer even showed Yarnell where to cut the channel.[29]

Trippe wrote Secretary of the Navy Claude Swanson to express the strategic urgency that a U.S. airline be the first to conquer the Pacific. He reported his technical committee "headed by Colonel Lindbergh, is now studying the question of terminal facilities in relation to local conditions, on the Pacific coast, as well as in Hawaii and the Philippines." Trippe explained that marine airports at Midway, Wake, and Guam were vital to Pan Am's Far East operations, but needed extensive work to make suitable commercial airbases. Even Guam, with its Navy presence, required fuel storage and fueling facilities, meteorological services, radio communications, a seaplane ramp, landing stage, and other infrastructure. Wake would be toughest, "in every respect a desert island," Trippe's explained. It was believed to be no more than sixty acres above sea level, an estimated twenty-one feet at its highest point. Wake needed facilities for technical operations, a hotel and living quarters for personnel, sanitary facilities, a power plant, and shoring operations to prevent erosion.

"The large amount of construction work to be done by the Company on Wake Island could be justified only if its capital there invested can be protected by an appropriate lease," Trippe concluded. He requested the Navy lease Wake to Pan Am for five years, with the right to renew for four additional periods of five years each, subject to the Navy's right to repossess the island at any time, at a fixed annual fee of $100. Trippe also requested authority to operate licensed aircraft of American registry through Wake, Guam, and Midway. "Because of the competitive international air transport situation in the Far East, the matter is of considerable urgency; and for this reason I beg the courtesy of your prompt consideration of the above request."[30]

Despite Japan's suspicions and British objections, on October 16, 1935, a confidential memo from Roosevelt to Secretary of State Hull endorsed the leasing of government territory to Pan Am. That year, Roosevelt transferred Wake from the Interior Department to the Navy. Rear Admiral Yarnell, whose command included the Hawaiian Islands, was a key supporter of Pan Am's use of the Pearl Harbor naval base at Honolulu. Yarnell was convinced the airline could serve their strategic objectives.[31]

Through the fall and winter of 1934, Priester's office worked out the logistics of the Central Pacific route. In January of 1935, Leroy L. Odell was named chief airport engineer in charge of planning and construction of the island bases. Everything required for living quarters, power stations, sewage systems, garbage disposal, and gardens had to be ordered and shipped; a small army of engineers, mechanics, carpenters, plumbers, stevedores, and laborers had to be hired. "What's amazing is that eight of us in the Chrysler Building in New York City planned this expedition in two months," recalled John Borger. "I was just out of college, and was chief clerk. I remember our request for Capital Appropriations was over a million dollars, one of the biggest . . . at the time; the Board okayed it immediately."[32]

The Sikorsky survey ship continued to be readied for its survey flights, with engineer John Leslie overseeing testing to determine best settings, altitude, and speeds. The survey preparations were tied into testing of the Martin-130, with both crews exchanging information and giving special attention to radio and navigation instruments.[33] Captain Musick would lead the first survey flights, with his crew of first officer Robert Oliver Daniel ("R.O.D.") Sullivan, navigator Fred Noonan, junior flight officer Harry Canaday, flight engineers Chauncey D. Wright and Victor D. Wright (no relation), and radio officer Wilson Jarboe, who contributed to the Lindberghs' 1933 Atlantic survey.

"Trippe's efforts in this regard were revolutionary: For the first time, long range flight was being scientifically analyzed, and the information tabulated and printed to show optimum engine settings for long range cruising," Captain Don Cooper noted. "Nothing was left to speculation."[34]

The final check flight over the Atlantic on March 23, 1935, was guided by Noonan's celestial fixes and radio bearings from Miami. The Sikorsky Clipper, dubbed the *Pan American Clipper*, successfully made it from Miami to the Bahamas, over the coastline of Florida, the Gulf of Mexico, back to Biscayne Bay—seventeen flight hours simulating the distance and estimated flight time between San Francisco and Honolulu.

The S-42 was scheduled to make its first Pacific survey flight on April 16. Because of a lack of seaplane facilities across the continent, the Clipper had to be ferried across the country to Acapulco on Mexico's Pacific coast, up to San Diego, and to Alameda. The flight departed Miami on March 27, and all went smoothly until Acapulco. Noonan, besides being a first-rate navigator, was a heavy drinker. "Captain Musick was aware of Noonan's hard-partying habit," Don Cooper recalled, "and made sure that he would share a room with him on all overnight stops. But that wasn't enough to stop Noonan in Acapulco; after all, that town was known to be a lively place after dark. Noonan decided to party all night."[35] Noonan returned at dawn, weaving and stumbling across the dock to board the Clipper—and fell in the water. Vic Wright and others pulled the soggy navigator out of the drink and kept him out of sight of Navy brass during the San Diego stop.[36]

Meanwhile, Odell secured a Maersk Line vessel to carry expedition cargo and crew to the islands. The S.S. *North Haven* was a 15,000-ton steam passenger and freight ship that usually carried cannery workers and products from Seattle to Alaska. Odell leased a warehouse at Pier 22 in San Francisco to store cargo before loading. Cargo included motor launches and barges for unloading, prefab housing, refrigerators, diesel electric generators, water storage and gasoline tanks, stills to extract fresh water from the sea, 250,000 gallons of fuel, food and water for months, and poles for building antenna masts.

With no radio facilities between Honolulu and Guam, the radio direction finding equipment from Leuteritz's department represented, in Pan Am's estimation, "Perhaps the most important item in her cargo."[37] William Grooch, fresh from his work for Pan Am's China affiliate, was named expedition leader and supervised renovations at Alameda base. George Kuhn would oversee loading and unloading, and much of the construction at Wake and Midway. Charles Russell was construction supervisor. Everything was marked and loaded in order of each stop—Honolulu, Midway, Wake, Guam, and finally, Cavite at Manila, which had a U.S. naval presence.

The rights to British-controlled Hong Kong were slow in coming, so Harold M. Bixby, Pan Am's Far East representative, had been directed to secure landing rights at Manila. The Philippines were under the American flag, but would become independent, so the franchise had to come from the new government. Bixby shuttled between Shanghai and Manila, negotiating with the support of the newly appointed military advisor to the Philippine Commonwealth, Major Dwight David Eisenhower.[38]

Japan was now alert to Pan Am's expansion in the Pacific. "Japan through diplomatic channels repeatedly made the most strenuous objections to the extension of the American company, which it described as a concealed military operation, a dress rehearsal for future aerial attack in the Pacific," Matthew Josephson reported. "Mr. Trippe, perhaps with much truth, let it be known that the designs of Pan American were entirely commercial. However, the Navy Department now gave vigorous support to Pan American's transpacific enterprise."[39]

On April 4, as the *Pan American Clipper* was undergoing final water taxiing tests in San Francisco Bay, the Navy issued a public denial of involvement in Pan Am's Pacific operations. "Attempting to dissipate foreign fears of 'hidden motives,' Secretary of Navy Claude Swanson reiterated today that the projected air line from California to China, planned by American interests, was strictly a commercial venture," United Press reported. "Much of the official objection was raised in Japan, although the Foreign Office emphasized that Japan did not oppose any venture of such nature that was strictly commercial."[40]

Despite his public disavowals, Swanson was privately discussing the strategic importance of Pan Am's Pacific airbases. "Pearl Harbor and Cavite [Manila], of course, are already established as important naval bases," Swanson wrote Trippe. "Midway, Wake, and Guam are so located as to possess potential possibilities for this purpose in time of war."[41]

Rear Admiral Ernest J. King noted "the requirements of Pan American Airways for a seaplane operating area is practically identical with the navy requirement for an auxiliary operating area. The two developments should go hand in hand."[42]

⭐

One of the eager new hires for the *North Haven* expedition was Alabama native George W. Taylor, the son of a suffragette. Better known as "Bill," he was one of those beguiled by Lindbergh's transatlantic flight—he first heard news of it while listening to Birmingham's one radio station on a crystal radio receiving set. He began subscribing to magazines like *Aviation* and *Aero Digest*, and bought a model kit of the *Spirit of St. Louis*. When Lindbergh's sensational air tour of the continent stopped in Birmingham in 1927, Taylor got to see the *Spirit of St. Louis* and attend the banquet at which his hero spoke.[43]

Taylor became an aeronautical engineer but never achieved his dream of becoming a pilot, having flunked two attempts to be a Navy Flying Cadet because of high blood pressure and other health factors. But he would travel widely with Pan Am. His first assignment was handling transit and radio work for the Pacific island expedition.[44]

Before departure, Taylor visited the *North Haven* at anchor and had his picture taken—visible in the background was the San Francisco-Oakland Bay Bridge, then under construction. Not pictured, but out by the confluence where bay met ocean, the mighty Golden Gate Bridge was also rising.[45] Ironically, despite the Great Depression putting millions out of work, monumental engineering and construction projects were still underway.

But just before the *North Haven* sailed on March 27, there was a waterfront scene that reflected the darker economic picture. Some of the crew were from the legions of unemployed and hired off the waterfront. One unnamed man, who appeared as the crew was boarding, was hired on the spot to replace a crewman who hadn't shown up. The nameless man got on the ship, Pan Am's corporate history notes, "without luggage, without goodbyes."[46]

## CHAPTER 10
# ISLAND STEPPING STONES

*"With reference to the proposed trans-Pacific air transport service which is to be initiated at an early date, it is requested that you issue necessary instructions to your personnel to insure security of information regarding the naval bases and reservations you are utilizing for airports . . . many efforts will be made by interested foreign powers to obtain a maximum of information regarding them."*

—Secretary of the Navy Claude Swanson,
1935 letter to Juan Trippe[1]

After the *North Haven* docked in Honolulu, Bill Taylor spent the layover on the north side of Oahu, at Mokapu, installing a radio station for the Pacific network.[2] The freighter took on more equipment, including a ton of dynamite and forty-two poles to make sixteen antenna masts for the new Adcock direction finding stations. John Borger had ordered thirty-five foot poles, not realizing an extra five feet was needed to root them below ground. The original poles would instead be used to build docks at Midway and Wake.

Additional crew boarded, including Chinese cooks and a young man who had grown up on the islands and been a star swimmer at Columbia University. Bill Mullahey was a surfer dude ahead of his time, and a sight to behold, coming aboard with a surfboard under his arm and dressed in his "Oahu hat" and swim trunks. He could swim like a fish, proved to be an ace dynamiter, and was Pan Am's future regional director for the Pacific.[3]

On April 12, the *North Haven* reached Midway. With no natural harbor or dock suitable for a 15,000-ton steamer, they had to anchor in the ocean. The crew crowded the deck to gaze upon the island and swells hitting the reefs. They would soon be loading barges on this open sea and taking precious cargo through those crashing waves to shore.

The first group ashore included Taylor, who had to lay out each air base according to plans from Pan Am's engineers in New York. Expedition leader William Grooch led the way, with John Steele, Priester's representative in the field (and a future Pan Am vice president), construction supervisor Charles Russell, Karl Lueder, engineer A.A. Mittag, and Junius Wood, a journalist chronicling the expedition.[4] Resident cable company staff greeted them at a small dock. The U.S. had declared Midway a refuge for the resident albatross population, and Grooch received instructions from the Navy about avoiding harming the birds. The "gooney bird," as they were nicknamed, became an instant icon, inspiring formation of the "Goofy Goonie Club of Midway."[5]

"The Navy worked closely with PAA in those days; in fact, PAA was practically an arm of the government," Taylor recalled. "There were two Navy officers with us on the expedition, one a Construction Corps officer, Mr. Porter, and the other, a flyer. I shared the engineering data I gathered with the former; he said this information would be very useful in their plans for the islands."[6]

Before unloading the *North Haven*, a boat boom with a Jacob's Ladder was rigged. A sounding of the water's depth was taken to mark off a safe channel through the maze of coral reefs. The water was deceptively clear—coral seemingly close enough to touch might actually be ten feet below the surface. Some sharks took an interest in the lead sinker as they took the sounding. "If you've never looked a ten-foot shark in the eye at close range, you've missed a thrill," Grooch recalled. "They gave every evidence of being hungry. We finally completed marking a satisfactory channel to the sand beach."[7]

Unloading was a dawn to dusk job. Each barge had a two-man crew, and it took skill, timing, and nerve to receive and stack each load as it came over the side while boat and barges swayed in the water. George Kuhn's advice: "When a load comes over and it looks dangerous, be sure to jump."[8]

"Many of our men had narrow escapes from being crushed under some heavy piece of equipment as it was lowered onto the lighter," Grooch recalled. "The crews on the lighters were not seamen. They had difficulty keeping their feet while the lighter did its dance—one moment straining away from the ship's sides until the securing lines were stretched taut as bow strings, returning on the next swell to dash against the ship's side with a jar hard enough to knock every man off his feet."[9]

"It was hairy," Borger agreed. "I watched one barge slide down a swell sideways. Strangely, we didn't lose a thing." Kuhn once sent an "express" delivery of a keg of nails by rowboat, but it capsized—Mullahey, the human fish, dove down and recovered it.[10]

Launches towed the loaded barges through the waves and reefs to shore, avoiding a deadly stretch of breakers the men dubbed "The Hook."[11] They slept on the island, eight to each sixteen by sixteen-foot tent. The first days were cold and rainy, but the "beach gang" discovered the lagoon was pleasantly warm and often jumped in. Once, Grooch discovered the crew taking a break, their grinning heads sticking out of the lagoon, looking "like pumpkins."[12]

On April 13, Taylor began laying out the base using a lighthouse at Midway's highest point as a guide. The last job before the freighter moved on to Wake was installing the radio direction finder that would provide radio compass bearings for the upcoming Clippers. To calibrate it the *North Haven* circled the island, sending radio signals every few minutes, making two circuits to ensure accuracy. Taylor kept the *North Haven* in sight of his transit from atop a forty-foot temporary platform built above the direction finder shack.[13]

When it was time for the *North Haven* to sail, a Midway crew stayed behind. Grooch, Taylor, Mullahey, and Borger were among those heading on, and they departed with a gift from the cable crew—a dozen hens and a rooster to found Wake's first chicken colony.[14] During the transition, they heard the *Pan American Clipper* had landed safely in Honolulu and was about to return to Alameda base. The first of four Pacific survey flights was halfway home.

★

"Some people felt the survey flight was suicidal; they would get lost and crash into the sea," Don Cooper recalled.[15] But it was a confident crew that departed Alameda at 6:50 p.m. on April 16. The *Pan American Clipper* was so loaded with fuel it smelled of gasoline. It was cold inside, so once aloft the crew got out of their blue uniforms and white caps and into warm and casual attire, which also kept their uniforms well-pressed and spotless to make a good impression on landing. Musick wore a ski-suit with "Reynold's Ski Club" lettered on the back; Vic Wright moved about in red flannel pajamas and slippers.[16]

By nightfall, they were at 6,000–7,000 feet and in perfect weather for correlating celestial fixes, dead reckoning, and radio direction-finding navigation. All the while, Jarboe was in contact with Pan Am radio stations by Morse code, as well as the *North Haven* and seven steamers stationed between Hawaii and the mainland. The radio was "remarkably dependable," Musick noted—Pan Am's stations in California and Hawaii followed them every mile.

Victor Wright was so busy operating equipment and reading instruments that he barely had time to share their midnight dinner. Fred Noonan was on his best behavior, and didn't even take his scheduled rest period. "Swathed in a heavy flying suit, face mask and goggles, he made more than a dozen trips down the long aisle to the aft observation hatch to take his periodic reading of the stars," Musick recalled. "[Noonan] also recorded a complete analysis of wind and weather conditions on the entire area we covered."[17]

Eighteen hours and forty minutes later, they landed at Pearl Harbor. It was a historic accomplishment—they crossed the Hawaii sector in less than a day.

Pacific Division Manager Clarence Young and Honolulu Manager J. Parker Van Zandt were waiting to greet them, and when the crew emerged in their fresh blue uniforms, it all seemed quite normal. "It was a routine job," Musick said. He later estimated they landed with almost 5,000 pounds of their original 16,000-pound fuel load, enough to have flown another 800 to 1,000 miles.[18] While those around them were in a celebratory mood, captain and crew knew better than to soak up the heady achievement—there was still the flight back.

The return proved to be everything the crew secretly dreaded. Fierce head and crosswinds sometimes slowed the Clipper to fifty to seventy miles an hour, all the while burning precious fuel. They were far out at sea when the estimated fuel capacity began running out. They could turn back, making for a rocky start and bad press for the operation's grand ambitions, or they could keep flying past the "Point of No Return," the threshold beyond which there would not be enough fuel to make it safely back. The decision belonged to the commander—Captain Musick chose to stay on course.

Trippe was at Pan Am's office in Washington, D.C., nervously following the Clipper's progress as it was hourly marked on a wall map. Dinnertime came and went, but Trippe and his employees had no appetite for anything but news of a safe landing.[19] The Clipper was now five very tense hours overdue. At Alameda, Pan Am personnel concealed their concerns, even as they reassured nervous wives.

Priester sent a message to the Clipper, asking how much fuel was left. "*He wants to know*," Musick mumbled. To Vic Wright it felt like the sea was reaching up to drag them into a watery grave: "You know how a wave sort of laps up and then tumbles over and makes a white cap? That time, I swear, the water seemed to leap up from both sides. The waves seemed to reach up for me."[20]

It was nearly half past 5:00 p.m. when the Northern California coastline appeared. "Musick kept a steady course and when the Bay was in sight, he slowly retarded the throttles and started descent for a straight in approach; he did not want to bank the aircraft for fear of starving the engines of fuel," Don Cooper wrote. "After landing he taxied to the ramp and cut the engines.

They had been airborne for twenty-three hours and forty-one minutes. For several minutes, they sat there in silence[,] relieved to be there and finally, they exited the aircraft and went ashore to be greeted by their wives. Back in Washington, Trippe was also relieved. He and the others could finally go out and enjoy their dinner." Vic Wright took a measure of the risk they had taken by dipping a stick gauge into the fuel tanks. It was "damp on the bottom," he noted. "I don't think we could have made it once around on the bay."[21]

★

As the *North Haven* neared Wake, Bill Taylor saw "a flat streak of land, not rising very high out of the water." It was the "only spot of land within a radius of twelve hundred miles," William Grooch noted.[22] Grooch led an exploratory team ashore and returned looking "forlorn," Taylor recalled. Of the three separate isles, the Navy authorized them to use Wilkes, but it was ravaged with deep gullies and storm debris. It was decided to take a rowboat ashore and investigate Peale and Wake. Taylor made a quick survey of Wilkes, the only place to unload cargo and where the construction crew had to build a dock. On Friday, May 10, Taylor went ashore to do his surveying. "Rough coral and stones make hard walking," Taylor wrote in his diary. "All kinds of fish around the island."[23]

Grooch and his team took a skiff that was sent to the boat landing and carried it overland to Wilkes Channel. They rowed the mile and a half to Peale, landed on the sloping beach, and started exploring. "It was at once apparent that Peale Island was a different place altogether from Wilkes Island," Grooch recalled. "There were no rocks and the soil was a rich brown loam . . . [and] no evidence whatever that the island had been under water."[24] Grooch was enthusiastic about Peale, and by Saturday he had Taylor running traverse and levels there. (The survey included sticking a tide gauge in the water. They discovered that the highest point on Peale was roughly twenty-six feet above sea level.) Such was Pan Am's symbiotic relationship with the Navy that approval was quickly granted to make Peale the commercial airbase. On Sunday, Taylor took soundings along the shore when a survey crewman named Tatum killed a nearly five-foot shark with a hatchet, a storied day in Wake Island lore.[25]

After a day's work, the crew headed to the freighter. By May 15, an island camp was established on Wilkes. Two days later, Taylor completed his survey. Grooch, Russell, and McKenzie approved his layout sketches, and Taylor started staking out buildings so construction could begin.[26]

Taylor surveyed a cross-section of the Wilkes channel to estimate the volume of coral to be blasted and how deep to make it for an ocean-going vessel—information also of interest to Mr. Porter, the Navy Construction Corps officer on the expedition. The coral had to be removed because it would rip the bottom off a flying boat, but was so thick the five tons of dynamite was used up within five months.[27]

Borger and Mullahey often worked as a dynamiting team. They rowed out to the buoys and Mullahey slipped on his homemade bamboo goggles, took a deep breath, and dived down with his bamboo spear to look for places to insert dynamite sticks. "The spear was in case he saw any fish that looked good for dinner while he was inspecting," Borger noted. Mullahey would surface, get dynamite sticks, and dive down to tie them to coral. After rowing a safe distance, a magneto button blew up the dynamite and they rowed back to collect the fish left floating.[28]

After clearing away loose coral, the crew tested to see if it was deep enough to float a barge. "The barge was lowered into the water from the *North Haven*, then towed to the entrance to Wilkes channel and held there until high tide," Taylor wrote. "At that point, everyone waded in to push the barge through. It was a struggle; it became stuck a couple of times, but we were able to get it done. We were all soaking wet from floundering around in the water. It was fascinating to see the varied growths of coral and the hundreds of brightly colored fish all around us."[29]

They delivered the cargo to Peale on what reporter Junius Wood hailed as "the shortest railroad in the world." Grooch noticed the beach sloped from the storage yard at Wilkes to the lagoon—they could roll loads down if tracks could be laid for some kind of rail car. The slope was slight enough that it wouldn't go too fast, and the emptied rail car could be easily pushed back up for the next load. "I remembered that we had brought along two sets of Ford automobile wheels and tires which were to be used in making up tracks to handle baggage on and off the planes, when regular transpacific flight service started," Grooch explained. "Inspecting the wheels I noticed a deep wide groove in the center of the rims. This suggested that the wheels would ride a rail. We found the proper-size rail among some iron stock brought along for use as braces, stringers or dead men. So we proceeded to build a railroad two hundred yards long. . . ."[30]

The railroad was soon doing brisk business while Wilkes became "a second-class neighborhood," Grooch observed. "Peale Island began to look quite important as the buildings went up. The station was laid out in the form of a crescent, looking down on the lagoon . . . soil on Peale Island proved fertile. We planted trees, gardens, vines and flowers."[31] In addition to the distillation plant, which had to be re-engineered, survival meant collecting rainwater—even tent flaps were fixed so rainwater would funnel into buckets. "Rained hard at noon, and all hands helped catch water in every available container," read Taylor's May 15 diary entry.[32]

Taylor staked out the radio direction-finder station using a magnetic bearing, finishing on May 29 and putting into place another piece of Pan Am's Pacific communications network. By afternoon, he was in the shark-infested waters of the northwest reef, surveying another possible channel. Taylor was at camp by 5:00 p.m. and returned to the *North Haven* for the five-day trip to Guam.[33] With its U.S. naval base, facilities, and a native population to draw on for labor, Guam would be a pleasant change from the primitive conditions at Midway and Wake.

There were reminders of the strategic nature of the new bases. "Through the radio came news of the elaborate maneuvers the Navy was holding that summer in the mid-Pacific," William Van Dusen recalled. "Maneuvers that included the visit of a large number of ships and aircraft to Midway."[34]

Dorothy Kaucher, an early traveler on the Pacific airway, had both a practical and romantic view of the island colonizing. "Wake Island was more than a coral atoll," she wrote. "She was an indispensable and strategic link in maintaining this American air lifeline to Asia. And she was a mysterious combination, too, of something that was opening the door of the new age of flying oceans and of something which belonged to the dead centuries of air, ocean, and coral."[35]

⭐

By June 12, the *Pan American Clipper* left Alameda on the second survey. Each succeeding survey ventured to the next stop along the route, so this flight went only as far as Midway. The Clipper made the round-trip without incident, and Taylor was heartened to hear that Midway's direction finder provided accurate navigation bearings.[36] With his second survey completed, Musick headed back to the Atlantic to get the Martin Clipper ready. The third survey was commanded by R.O.D. Sullivan with Jack Tilton second-in-command, and would fly as far as Wake.[37]

On August 9, the third survey left Alameda and landed in Honolulu. On August 16, it departed Midway for the eight-hour flight to Wake, where the eight-person crew was anxiously waiting. "Every day the wind blew from the southeast," recalled Wake crew member John Borger. "I recorded it. The first day it blew from the southwest was when Captain R.O.D. Sullivan and co-pilot Jack Tilton . . . flew an S-42 in on the survey flight. He discussed the cross-wind landing colorfully."[38]

*Time* reported the drone of the Clipper's four Hornet motors over Wake "was the climax of three months of arduous efforts . . . dynamiting a passage through the reef, building houses, preparing for the comfort of future passengers to the Orient." The newsweekly added, "To salute these eight men and their work, which it was the first to use, the Clipper circled twice, then slid into the lagoon."[39] Actually, Sullivan circled twice out of desperation. At Pacific Division HQ, Wake looked big enough on a map but was a flyspeck from the air, and the four-mile lagoon landing looked even smaller. Sullivan later grumbled he wouldn't have flown if he had known how small the channel was. The Wake crew had their own anxious moments as the S-42 descended—they had never seen an aircraft that huge.[40]

The fourth and final survey reached Guam on October 13 and safely returned to Alameda base. Manila, the last stop, was reserved for the Martin Clipper's inaugural flight. That August, even as island bases were being built and the third Pacific survey was underway, Postmaster General Farley advertised for bids on an airmail route to the Philippines. Pan Am was the one and only winning bid.[41]

By early October, three Martin Clippers were on the pre-delivery assembly line. On October 9, the day before the official ceremony at the Martin plant, Trippe flew in from New York with Lindbergh, who piloted his famed *Tingmissartoq*. Lindbergh dramatically circled the docked aircraft, christened *China Clipper*, before landing and taxiing to the Martin offices. Lindbergh's long strides took him through the office doors ahead of workers who recognized his plane and rushed to greet him. After inspecting the Clipper, Lindbergh retreated to the plant offices. He flew back to rejoin Anne in Maine, leaving the demonstration flight to Musick.[42]

The demonstration flight to Washington carried Trippe and forty-three passengers and crew. Musick circled the capital three times before returning to the Martin factory. Trippe served notice to a Baltimore newspaper reporter that this was only the beginning. "There are already boats on the drafting boards twice as large," Trippe revealed. "And the bigger they get the more efficient they are. Theoretically, almost any size flying boat is possible. And they will come."[43] Pan Am had already signed a contract with Boeing for a "Super Clipper."

On September 19, Bruno Richard Hauptmann, a suspect in the kidnapping and death of Charles and Anne's first-born, was arrested and the dark carnival of the "trial of the century" began. The Lindberghs soon departed for self-imposed exile in England. Lindbergh was always comfortable at Pan Am, but Trippe had seen the pressures of his fame. "I remember once in the elevator going up to our . . . offices in the Chrysler Building—the other passengers were caught up in a frenzy of wanting to touch him," Trippe recalled, "and by the time the elevator doors opened on the 58th floor, they had torn the left sleeve off his coat. He was polite, and good natured about it. He did not get angry. But all that day in the meetings as we went over technical matters, there was Slim, with the sleeve torn off his jacket."[44]

⭐

The inaugural Pacific flight and airmail-only delivery to Manila was scheduled for November 22, 1935, with Musick in command. By then, forty-one personnel had been transferred to Alameda from other parts of the System, building up the Pacific operation to 221 employees.[45]

Ten days before the flight, Secretary of the Navy Swanson wrote Trippe, emphasizing that the strategic locations of the civilian air bases made them potential military bases and outlined procedures "to ensure security of information." All views of Pearl Harbor had to be minimized and restricted air zones avoided. Photography was prohibited on approaches and departures at Pearl Harbor, Midway, Wake, Guam, and other areas. Photos already taken of sensitive areas required naval approval before being used for publicity purposes, and employees were not to discuss "hydrographic, topographic, or meteorological features of such ports with unauthorized persons."[46]

Musick ferried the *China Clipper* via the Miami to Acapulco route to Alameda, where an enthusiastic crowd greeted them and airplanes circling from nearby airports. Reporters and photographers were hungry for an angle, but Eddie gave them his usual—it had been "routine." Cleo was waiting at their car and cameras flashed as Musick kissed her. There were shouts to kiss her again—"kiss her like you meant it." Musick glared back before the couple drove away. "This publicity racket's getting me down," he confessed to Cleo. "Makes me feel like an ape in a cage."[47]

The week of the historic flight to Manila, Musick made the cover of *Time*. He was now, arguably, second only to Lindbergh as a celebrated pilot. "His desk at the airport was piled high with requests to sponsor cigarettes, liquor or shaving cream," Grooch recalled. "Musick tasted big-time publicity—and didn't like it."

Musick's colleagues knew the score. "Musick was our God," declared Captain John Hamilton.

Flight mechanic John Donohue added, "He had everything. You could see—this is a Captain. First thing, on getting into the airplane, he would wipe off the seat, the wheel and the throttles. He would neatly fold his coat and put it away. To stay clean and pressed in the Sikorsky S[-]38 was an especial feat because the airplane had to be closed for the take-off; it got very hot inside and everybody broke into a sweat . . . He [came] back from his trips always impeccable—much in contrast to others, some of whom 'always looked as if they had gone swimming.'" Pan Am's corporate history sums up Musick's success as "his adaptability to change his flying style for the new era of flight."[48]

On the eve of the inaugural transpacific flight, Juan Trippe flew into San Francisco. Once settled in at the St. Francis Hotel at Union Square, he held a preflight briefing and final check meeting in his room with Musick, mechanics, and engineers. Trippe warned that some reporter might ask whether the flight was a military operation—a few days before, a Japanese newspaper editorial declared the flight was "military preparations in the guise of civilian enterprise."

That night, two Japanese nationals reportedly slipped into the Alameda airbase to recalibrate the direction finder, which would leave the *China Clipper* hopelessly lost in the Pacific. The saboteurs were opening their tool case when FBI agents burst in and stopped them. "The attempted sabotage was not reported, historian Ronald Jackson wrote, "because it would have ruined both Pan American's and the [N]avy's plans in the Pacific."[49]

## CHAPTER 11
# CLIPPER GLORY

*"Until we had reached our destination, each officer had been too occupied with the innumerable tasks . . . to concern himself with affairs more than a minute ahead. But the actual sight of the Philippine coastline, hills, valleys, streams and villages, on the other side of the world we left such a short time ago, forced a new concept upon us. Manila meant the end of a long trail of preparation for this transpacific flight."*

—Captain Edwin C. Musick, wireless report to
*The New York Times*, inaugural Pacific flight[1]

The afternoon of November 22, an estimated 125,000 spectators waited, encamped around San Francisco Bay, to glimpse the flight of the *China Clipper* while the collective gaze of the 20,000 at Alameda base fixed upon the giant flying boat as it floated on the water, motors idling. Juan Trippe announced to the assembled, and listeners on a national radio hookup, that U.S. airmail was about to begin for the Philippines, 8,000 miles away. There were speeches from U.S. Senator William McAdoo, Governor Joseph P. Poindexter of the Territory of Hawaii, and California Governor Frank Merriam, who proclaimed this "Pan American Airways Day." Postmaster General Farley observed the fastest steamship connection from the mainland to Asia took seventeen days, but by air it would be five; Hawaii was five days by the speediest steamship, an overnighter by air. "Very soon the super-planes flying over this route will be transporting passengers and express," Farley added. "A person or letter will arrive in China within six days after leaving New York. This is, indeed, an epoch-marking achievement and one which rivals the vivid imagination of a Jules Verne."

Farley read a message from Roosevelt that recalled the president's naval background and observed that transpacific service coincided with the 100th anniversary of the first Clipper ship's arrival in San Francisco. "Please convey to the people of the Pacific Coast the deep interest and heart-felt congratulations of an air-minded sailor," Roosevelt wrote. "Even at this distance I thrill to the wonder of it all."[2] A wire from Philippines President Manuel Luis Quezon added, "Today we await impatiently the arrival of the flying Clipper Ships that will, with incredible swiftness, sweep away that barrier of time and space forever."[3]

The seven uniformed crew members were announced as they began boarding. Co-pilot R.O.D. Sullivan was first, followed by navigator Fred Noonan, Second Officer George King, engineering officers Chauncey Wright and Vic Wright, radio officer Wilson T. Jarboe, Jr., and Captain Musick. Code signals from Pan Am's bases at Honolulu, Midway, Wake, Guam, and Manila reported all was ready.[4]

Farley officially announced the inauguration of transpacific airway service. Trippe declared, "Captain Musick, you have your sailing orders. Cast off and depart for Manila in accordance therewith!" A band struck up the National Anthem, the crowd cheered, and Musick opened up the idling engines.

The 52,000-pound flying boat started moving across the water at 3:46 p.m., then began rising. Musick was supposed to fly over the San Francisco-Oakland Bay Bridge under construction, but the aircraft was climbing too slowly—Musick realized the massive plane wouldn't clear it and flew under the cables. "We all ducked," Vic Wright recalled. Trippe winced but the crowd cheered, assuming this was part of the show.[5] When the Clipper reached the uncompleted Golden Gate Bridge, it soared over its towers.

Among the thousands ringing the bay was a hardy group that had secured a prime vantage point that chilly morning at Land's End, a western bluff in

San Francisco overlooking the ocean with a view of the Golden Gate. The Land's End group included Dorothy Kaucher, who was sitting on the rock where she watched many glorious sunsets. In her early forties, Kaucher had a doctorate in English from Cornell University, was a teacher, and a pioneering female aviation reporter.

Kaucher's fascination with flight began in midsummer of 1924 when she sensed that beyond the sky was "this spirit of the metal wings," her mythic ideal of elemental forces and powered flight, something she further idealized as the "Old Man of the Air." The wonder of what was coming struck her that summer when she saw an airmail letterbox at the San Francisco Ferry Building. That a letter dropped in a box could fly to some faraway address was, she recalled, "the beginning of a world reborn because it began to look as if quite ordinary people like me, and not just heroes, would get into the air."[6]

As the Land's End group waited, freighters steamed out the gate, reminding Kaucher of the tall-masted clippers that sailed before them. "Then I heard a defiant symphony of motors, the like of which I did not know could ever be created this side of Gabriel's trumpet." Thus the *China Clipper* "sounded her magnificent entrance into history...

"Over the Golden Gate in all her might and beauty she sped, and over the packed humanity that watched with narrowed eyes as if what they saw through those diminutive optics could not be true. Some cheered, some waved, some wept, some ran along the high shore road above the ageless sea. Some stood as silent as stone in the wind... Like a vision from another world she came. And like a vision, majestic, uplifting, she was gone into the west."

"She'll never get to Manila in six days," a Land's End cynic muttered.

"She'll never get to Manila—period," replied another.

That night, Kaucher thought of the aircraft winging its way through the darkness. "I kept thinking, The ocean winds will race you, China Clipper..."[7]

Ocean winds did not race the Clipper—stiff head and crosswinds saw the projected seventeen-hour flight time come and go, and they were hours from Honolulu. The aircraft itself was heavy and loaded with fifty-eight bags of airmail for Manila, 1,837 pounds worth. The log recorded "every post requires relentless attention," although the flight was still "remarkably smooth." The Clipper was being tracked by Pan Am ground stations in the Bay Area, Los Angeles, Honolulu, and Midway, along with vessels at sea that included the U.S. Coast Guard cutter *Itasca*, the U.S.S. *Wright*, and the Norwegian ship, *Rogerville*.

By midnight, Jarboe acknowledged a return response to their message of greeting to the U.S.S. *Wright*. Noonan returned from the open aft hatch after taking a celestial sight through a hole in the cloud ceiling, still dressed in his fur flying suit and leather helmet as he bent over the chart table. They were piloting in "inky blackness," Musick recalled, his only light the glow of flight instruments. But by dawn, they saw volcanic mountains and Diamond Head.[8]

The flying boat glided to the channel at Pearl Harbor, twenty-one hours after leaving Alameda. They were welcomed as heroes, a heady atmosphere of press coverage, adulation from dignitaries and women, parties. "When we got to Honolulu, we were floored at the reception," Vic Wright said. "They gave us preferred treatment . . . it got Noonan."[9]

In Honolulu cargo was off-loaded and new cargo was taken on, along with fourteen Pan Am employees bound for Midway and Wake. The log likened the preparations to olden days when clipper ships had to be quickly loaded in time to sail with the tide. Among the cargo was more airmail and food for the "colonies," including twelve crates of turkeys for their first Thanksgiving dinner.

As the Clipper approached Midway, the log recorded, "There was a great commotion among the passengers, some of whom were seeing for the first time the place that was to be their home for the next six months. The island's appearance has changed greatly since the first flight was made by the 'Pan American Clipper.' The area has been largely landscaped, the buildings are brightly painted and everything is neat and orderly. Flags were flying and tiny figures in white uniforms were standing at their posts on the landing float.

"In salute we circled the base at 500 feet, then settled in for a landing and touched the water at 02:01 G.M.T. (2:01 p.m. Midway time). This one minute off schedule must have been due to that extra circle, but the noisy welcome from the Pan American and cable company colonists who crowded the little float more than justified it."[10]

On Monday, November 25, the Clipper began the 1,200-mile "jump" to Wake. It was the shortest stretch, but also, the log noted, the "most difficult span in the entire aerial bridge and calls for one of the most exacting feats of navigation on record—striking 'on the nose,' a tiny point smaller than a pinhead on the vast map of the Pacific Ocean." A sailing vessel could move a mile every two minutes, but they were flying more than 148 miles per hour while trying to locate, through cloud cover, that pinhead's worth of earth. They not only found it, but they also landed five minutes ahead of schedule. The log recorded: "5,242 miles of Pacific behind us."

By Wednesday, there were rough trade winds. Although they maintained "a good course" the altitude chart resembled "an erratic broker's graph, with a succession of peaks and valleys," the log reported. At times, the flight account sparkled with transcendence: "Climbing through a three thousand foot layer of clouds by instrument, we burst out on top in an empty world of dazzling sunshine, the cloud moisture on our wings flashing every color of the spectrum and the propellers describing great glistening arcs as we bore ahead in a world all to ourselves—except for nine radio stations, three radio compass stations." The last half hour they made up the time to Guam's Apra Harbor thanks to tailwinds boosting them to 170 mph, allowing the engines to rest on half their horsepower. When they landed at 3:05, local time, Bill Taylor was there to witness their arrival.[11]

At dawn, Taylor returned to watch the Clipper depart on the final 1,600-miles to Manila. "I was standing by the launch in the dark waiting for the car bringing the crew. When it arrived I was amazed to see that one of them couldn't walk and were [sic] being helped by two others. I suddenly realized that he was drunk; it was Fred Noonan. They departed on the launch as quickly as possible; it was fortunate that no local dignitaries were there. . . . That was the only time I ever saw Noonan in that condition; I was with him on the return [flight]."[12]

On November 29, under cloudy skies overlooking Manila Bay, a large sign for the Clipper crew spelled out in big letters the spirited Filipino word of welcome, *Mabuhay*. Two hundred thousand anxiously waited, watching a large signboard upon which a miniature Clipper was moved with each position update. When the plane was reported off the west coast of the island of Luzon, the whistle typically blown for typhoon warnings sounded.

As the *China Clipper* crew sighted the Philippines, the enormity of their achievement sunk in. "How many times we plotted in our classroom courses that port, until it became a symbol only for a tedious study problem through those five long years of preparation," the log recorded. "How many times that word [Manila] had driven on engineers, designers . . . when for a moment the magnitude of the problem had threatened to be insolvable. Yet in an hour we would be there."[13]

The crowd first heard the drone of the M-130 and an escort of U.S. Army aircraft. Among those waiting and watching was Pan Am's Far East representative, Harold Bixby. "Presently through a hole in the clouds the clipper suddenly burst into view, its silver wings shining in the bright afternoon sun," he described. "It seemed as though the crowd—strangely silent under the spell of this historic event—all spotted the plane at the same instant. There was a mighty murmur of voices followed by a din such as I have never heard before. Every automobile horn was sounded, all the factory whistles in town cut loose, and all the boats in the harbor emptied the steam from their boilers through their whistles. . . . Next to me a tough 'old timer,' who had come to Manila in 1899 toting a gun, was so choked up with emotion that he could not speak. His eyes filled with tears."[14]

The *China Clipper* made a perfect landing. Musick and his crew disembarked at a special enclosure to be greeted by officials and special guests as a band struck up "The Star-Spangled Banner." The thundering cheers cut short the welcoming committee's speech-making. Musick and his crew were driven with a police escort to Malacañang Palace, making it through the biggest traffic jam in Manila's history. At the Palace, President Quezon and his cabinet welcomed them, and Musick handed the Philippine leader a letter of greeting from President Roosevelt.[15]

On December 2, as the Clipper was flying home, that week's *Time*, with Musick on the cover, provided perspective: "Eight years ago, as Charles A. Lindbergh peered at the lights of France through the periscope of his *Spirit of St. Louis*, he dreamed of a huge airliner which would some day span oceans on regular commercial schedule. Last week such an airliner, final fruition of Lindbergh's dream, soared up from San Francisco Bay, droned westward on the first flight of a regular commercial schedule across the Pacific Ocean."[16] Lindbergh had spoken of crossing the Atlantic in "five or ten years." His timetable proved prophetic, although Pan Am had flown the most challenging ocean.

Bill Taylor awaited the homeward Clipper in Guam to board as a passenger, having earned a promotion to the Pacific engineering department. That night, Pan Am's weatherman tracked a "growing cyclone" 150 miles away. It was away from their flight path, but created unsettled weather over the protected berth at Guam's Apra Harbor. "No sooner had the mechanics completed servicing and fueling her when gathering black clouds poured down a squally rain, which was driven across the black waters of the harbor by a forty-mile gale," the log recorded.[17]

Departing at dawn on December 3, they flew into squalls left in the typhoon's wake. "We were having an unusual opportunity, flying in mid-ocean, to see the effects a typhoon exerts on weather in a large area of the globe," the log chronicled. "The squally winds momentarily disturbed the usual even balance of the great airliner. We cruised ahead, flying by instrument. The lighted dials of the radio instruments blinked as Radio Officer Jarboe switched from receiver to transmitter, acknowledging guiding bearings which pierced the thousand miles of air, rain, wind and clouds every ten minutes to check our course."[18]

Eight times that hour, rain lashed the aircraft before it burst into sunshine and rainbows, only to plunge back into the storm. Taylor noticed Noonan shaking his head as he plotted their position, grumbling, "Only 100 Knots."

It was night before they made Wake. "As we all watched, the lights of Wake appeared dead ahead; the DF brought us right to that tiny spot in the ocean," Taylor recalled. "After six months it was great to see a thriving community at Wake, with buildings completed and in operation where I had staked them out. It was good to see Borge, as Borger . . . was always called, and all the others who had put Wake into operation."[19]

It was sunshine and blue skies to Pearl Harbor, the Clipper averaging 141 mph. By Friday, December 6, the Clipper landed in Alameda, only a minute over the anticipated seventeen-hour mark. The unprecedented round-trip flight had taken one-hundred twenty-two hours and forty-two minutes total flying time, comfortably under the estimated one-hundred and thirty hours. The Clipper returned with 108,000 letters "to speed American trade and commerce to the Orient," the log noted.[20]

★

The *China Clipper* was still on its inaugural flight when the second Martin flying boat, called the *Philippine Clipper*, was delivered at Alameda. The third M-130, the *Hawaii Clipper*, arrived early in 1936. By then, Pan Am cargo service over the Pacific route was authorized and began in March of 1936. In preparation for passenger service, a second *North Haven* expedition steamed into the Pacific. This time, the manifest included solar water heaters, pillows in lots of fifty pairs, furniture, staff uniforms, beach umbrellas, and plans to bring tons of rich soil from Guam for the blooming gardens of Midway and Wake.[21]

In late October of '36, passenger service began. "When the first transpacific passengers arrived on these islands they found complete and attractive hotels amongst lawns and landscapes well supplied with shrubs," a Pan Am document reported. "The hotels had 24 double rooms of generous dimensions surrounded by broad, well-screened verandas. Each room was equipped with showerbath and electric lights."[22]

By 1936, Pan Am was the world's leading airline, boasting 40,000 route miles compared to 24,000 for Air France, 23,600 for Lufthansa, 21,000 for

Imperial, 11,700 for K.L.M., and 10,500 scheduled miles for Russia's Aeroflot. Pan Am led with $13,000,000 in gross revenue and $24,000,000 in assets, led in percentage of completed schedules, the effectiveness of its radio stations, and lowest fatal accidents.[23]

Pan Am based their advances on an "accumulation" of practical experience, but Pacific service was charting a steep and unprecedented new learning curve. The responsibility for releasing each Pacific flight belonged to Pacific Operations Manager "Dutch" Schildhauer. John Leslie, in charge of engineering and maintenance, was said to have gotten his prematurely white hair in the first nine months of maintaining far-flung bases, working out "bugs" in the Martins, and investigating engine failures. There was suspected sabotage, including a suspicious incident on January 5, 1936, when the *China Clipper* "scraped a submerged obstruction" while attempting a take-off from Alameda. Musick was at the controls and safely returned the plane to the dock for inspection and repairs.[24]

Bill Newport, who graduated from the Boeing School of Aeronautics as a licensed mechanic, started work at Midway on December 12, 1938, for "three squares and a flop, $152 a month." As power plant engineer, he took care of diesel engines, electricity, water tanks, and filtering systems. Labor and service work at Midway was generally staffed by Guam's indigenous Chamorro people, but in the early days "everybody had to help get the ship out again," Newport recalled of the weekly incoming flight. "They checked the engines, talked to the engineer, and found out what was bothering him. Sometimes the crew would have squawks. You gave the engine a thorough inspection each time. They had long check sheets. Usually, the airplane came in around just before dark, and they might be through by midnight. But sometimes they would have to work all night."[25] Once a month, aviation gas came to the islands on supply ships. Each fifty-gallon drum was floated to shore where everyone helped roll them onto the beach, where they moved via sleds and tractors.

Daily tasks, such as morning inspection of the three big food refrigerators, were vital to survival on Midway.[26] Using windmill power, rainwater was caught, filtered, and pumped into storage tanks. "It was a lot of work just to keep the island going," Newport said. "Big difference: you could not call in any help. You could not go down to the hardware store. Roofs leaked, rain troughs broke, and in the heavy rains the power cables [laid in the sand] would short out. You had the generator to run, and a light system. And the laundry—what headaches!"[27]

As transoceanic weather forecasting improved, a weather map was tied into flight plans. Initial forecasts became irrelevant if unexpected headwinds and storms slowed a plane and increased flight time and fuel consumption. Battling weather and winds across vast ocean distances "could get a little tense," Pan Am's corporate history admits: "Officially everybody kept smiling, cheerful, confident. But pilots' wives remember this as a time of great tension—those nights when the airplane was out there 1,000 miles at sea."[28] Harold Gray recalled piloting a return trip to San Francisco when he had passed the Point of No Return and the wind shifted against him. For the next twelve hours, Gray wondered if he would make it. He did, barely—the crew at Alameda could not even get a measure of fuel from his tanks.[29]

That drama of fearless pilots and crew braving the Pacific skyway became a part of Pan Am's mystique. In 1936, Warner Brothers released *China Clipper*, a feature-length dramatization produced with Pan Am's cooperation. Dave Logan, the airline leader, played by Pat O'Brien, was ostensibly a composite character based on Trippe and Priester; emerging star Humphrey Bogart was cast as Hap Stuart, the pilot who makes the daring inaugural Pacific flight.

To be a captain in the System was to live in the fast lane of an elite global operation. "Living was informal, helter-skelter, and always changing," Captain John Hamilton recalled. "You could be transferred overnight. You kept your suitcase packed, and tried not to accumulate possessions."[30]

The key to a Clipper flight was a captain's leadership and the efficiency of the flight crew. In one incident, Musick and Vic Wright were flying from San Francisco to Honolulu when the left outboard engine, No. 1, acted up and Captain Musick decided to shut it down. Wright pulled the dump valve, but gasoline poured in on the cabin's navigation table—a single spark would blow up the aircraft. Without hesitation, Wright pulled the master switch and turned off all electrical equipment, except for engine ignitions, and they opened windows and hatches to clear gas vapors.[31]

"PAA was the only airline in the world flying such long distances, and we were, therefore, originating techniques which had not been required before," Bill Taylor said.[32] As such, the government bonded with the airline, naval historian Justin Libby writes: "Whatever technical advances in navigation, meteorology, radio direction-finding equipment, and aircraft frame/engine reliability Pan Am developed were passed directly onto Washington for future use."[33]

★

By early 1937, Pan Am formed its Atlantic Division. "[T]hey needed an engineer with experience in trans-oceanic flight calculations, so Borger was transferred to New York," recalled Bill Taylor, who stayed with the Pacific operation. "It was at this time that Amelia Earhart was planning her around the world flight. Fred Noonan had left PAA to act as her navigator. He was still around Alameda making plans for the flight, and I remember seeing him assembling all of the navigation and emergency equipment."[34]

March 17, 1937, a rainy St. Patrick's Day, is noteworthy in the annals of Pacific flight—that day *three* airplanes flew into the Western sky, bound for Honolulu. The *Hawaii Clipper* departed Alameda on the regular Pacific route at 3:13 p.m. At 4:21, Musick left Alameda in a new Sikorsky S-42B, a plane with a slightly longer wingspan and greater fuel economy designed for survey flights to New Zealand. (The new Sikorsky was known as the *Pan American Clipper II*, but by December was given its final name, *Samoan Clipper*.) At 4:37 p.m., Earhart began her around-the-world flight from nearby Oakland.[35]

Earhart's departure required advance precautions because her speedy *Electra* would overtake Musick's Clipper en route to Honolulu. To avoid the chance of a mid-air collision, Earhart consulted with Pan Am and Coast Guard officials in Alameda. It was decided that Musick would fly no higher than 6,000 feet, Earhart no lower than 8,000. Earhart would stay in radio communication with the Clipper, with Musick responding in Morse code telegraphy.[36]

Dorothy Kaucher was among 3,000 on-lookers at the Oakland airport that rainy St. Patrick's Day. Crew members Harry Manning and Noonan were already in the cabin of the *Electra* when Earhart appeared. "She came, with touseled [sic] head and gallant smile, a tiny figure at the foot of the great doors of the navy hangar," Kaucher recalled. "She seemed even smaller when she came back through that huge, gaping doorway and smiled—smiled at the few there in drenching rain by the fence. It was this moment when she smiled at me in the rain that I knew I would have to fly out over the ocean soon."

Earhart sat in the cockpit, waiting for stormy clouds to blow away while ground crews with brooms swept excess water off the runway. "Then suddenly, off to the west, a path of white light shone above the gray and black," Kaucher recalled. "The sun burst through. Down the runway roared the plane, lifting—then settling for one breathless moment—then lifting again so surely into that path of white light."[37]

Kaucher marveled that two Clippers had already taken off for Honolulu: "Out there where [Earhart] goes between the Golden Gate and Diamond Head are just two other planes. Except for those three metal tubes the sky is empty of things."

The planes landed safely in Honolulu. But the next day Earhart cracked up on takeoff. "Rotten luck," Musick told her. "But don't let it whip you."

"We'll make it next time," Earhart replied, flashing her famous smile.[38]

After the *Electra* was repaired and tested, Earhart tried again. This time Noonan was the navigator and only crew member, and instead of flying west, they went east. On June 1, 1937, the Electra left Oakland for Burbank, then Miami, the northeastern coast of South America, Africa, and India. After a stop in Lae, New Guinea, Earhart was to cross near the Marshall Islands and other fortified Japanese territory. As part of its colonization effort, the U.S. built a land airport on Howland Island, and this was to be Earhart's last stop before Hawaii.[39] The morning of July 2, the Electra lifted off the grass runway at Lae, headed for Howland—and vanished. Pan Am's new long-distance radio direction finder was employed in the search.[40] But no trace of Earhart, Noonan, or the *Electra* was found. Some suspected Japan was behind the tragedy, suspicions less about evidence than a measure of increasing tensions in the Pacific.

Japan always suspected Pan Am was spearheading U.S. interests. Indeed, Pan Am had developed strategic Pacific bases in concert with the Navy and was working with Pacific intelligence operations. Previously, radio intelligence officers transmitted intelligence material or used commercial sailing ships, but Pan Am planes could swiftly deliver intelligence information between the Asiatic Fleet and Washington. As a Naval Historical Center report records, "After 1935, a small amount of [intelligence] mail could be sent via the Pan American Airways 'Clipper' using a strongbox built into the hull specifically for this purpose."[41]

Pan Am would face Japan directly when it staked a claim in a China airline as part of its strategy for transpacific expansion. China seemed a wide-open market for air service, a vast land of primitive roads where travelers were still carried by sedan chair. But the Republic of China, ruled from Nanking by the Nationalist government headed by Generalissimo Chiang Kai-shek, was contending with a Communist insurgency and powerful warlords who ruled entire provinces.

And over it all, the threat of war with Japan loomed.

## Map II.
# PACIFIC & ALASKA
### PAN AMERICAN AIRWAYS SYSTEM

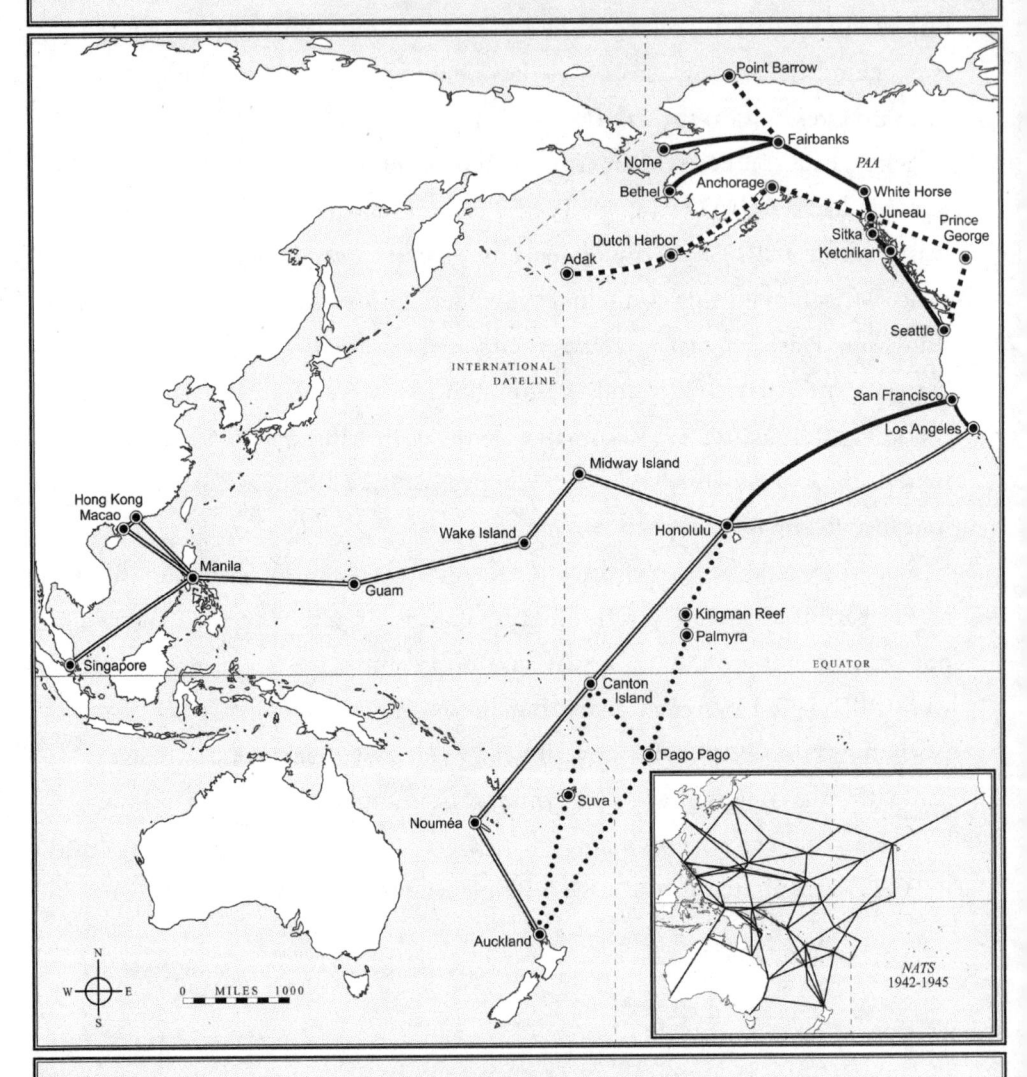

*Principal Routes & Destinations (composite)*
1935 – 1945

SUBSIDIARIES AND AFFILIATES

*PAA* – Pacific Alaska Airways
*NATS* – Naval Air Transport Service (contract 1942-1945)

— Scheduled service routes
•••••• South Pacific survey/alternative/temporary routes
= Scheduled service routes suspended December 7/8, 1941
▬ ▬ ▬ Alaska wartime routes

# CHAPTER 12
# WAR IN CHINA

*"I think CNAC was the most important of our efforts. When the Japanese [invaded] we had some hundreds of Americans spread throughout China. And instead of an isolated country, one part from the other, where the warlords were running things as they pleased . . . the airline could bring people together . . . this was welding a whole new nation."*

—Juan Trippe[1]

Harold M. Bixby did not fit the image of a swashbuckling adventurer, but as a leader of Pan Am's efforts in China he "became a veritable Marco Polo on wings," Matthew Josephson wrote.[2] Bixby was a St. Louis banker and Lindbergh's principal backer, helping finance construction of the *Spirit of St. Louis*. But in 1932, like millions of Americans, the economic disaster left him jobless, broke, and in debt. He came to New York, hoping to land a job at Pan Am with the support of his friend "Slim" Lindbergh. An interview was arranged with Trippe, who had a job to offer—he needed a foothold in China.[3]

The problem was the Nine Power Treaty, and Open Door Policy compelled China to extend commercial opportunities to all foreign signatories, including archenemy Japan. Pan Am's way in was the affiliate strategy, but the Nationalist government in Nanking already had a majority stake in Eurasia, an airline with a minority interest held by Lufthansa, and the China

National Aviation Corporation, with a 45 percent partnership interest ostensibly held by the American company, Curtiss-Wright. The CNAC charter clearly stated that neither partner could sell their shares without the other's consent.[4]

The China National Aviation Corporation was founded in 1929 by Clement M. Keys, president of Curtiss-Wright Aircraft, in partnership with the Nationalist government and used American planes and pilots for flights along the Yangtse River and between Shanghai and Hankow. By 1933, the airline was feeling the global Depression, and Florida businessman William Douglas Pawley became president. CNAC became a magic box of linked pieces: The American interest of 45 percent was actually held by China Airways Federal, Inc., a subsidiary of Intercontinent Aviation, Inc., a Pawley company. Pawley had a previous Pan Am connection—in 1928, he organized and was president of *Compañía Nacional de Aviación Curtiss* airline in Cuba, which he sold to Pan Am in 1932.[5] Trippe felt the CNAC could serve as a trunk line on the mainland of Asia—and be had for a bargain.[6] Bixby was to go to China and initiate negotiations.

In January of 1933, Bixby left for China by steamer. He expected to be gone three months—his China adventure lasted five years. It did not begin auspiciously. Bixby's company codebook, essential to Pacific operations, went missing and was presumed stolen. It cost the airline thousands of dollars to draw up a new one.[7]

Bixby arrived, unannounced, to look at CNAC planes and attend a board meeting where the Chinese directors were discussing bankruptcy. "Buying of the company was on Bixby's say-so," Pan Am's corporate history notes. "Bixby sent back his personal analysis of what Trippe could get it for." On March 31, 1933, Pan Am did an end run around the Chinese partners by purchasing China Airways Federal, along with its sole asset—the 45 percent CNAC share. "Technically, the founding contract hadn't been violated, but its spirit of partnership most definitely had, and the airline's Chinese officials were furious. . . . They'd lost face," historian Gregory Crouch notes.[8] Assets included a small hangar at the Lunghwa Airport at Shanghai Municipal

Field, seven Loening Amphibians, and five single-motored Stinsons, four of which were out of service and under reconstruction.[9]

"The commercial and administrative departments of the company are to be directed by the Chinese, while the flying operations will be managed by Pan-American, who will draw on their vast experience," *Scientific American* reported. "It is understood that Pan-American will introduce larger and more efficient equipment and will greatly extend the services between Shanghai and Peiping and develop the coast line towards Hong Kong." The purchase was also part of the airline's vision for a trans-Pacific network, the article noted: "It is an open secret that Pan-American has been conducting technical surveys in the Far East since 1929."[10]

The American leaders at CNAC included William Langhorne Bond, an operations manager, and chief pilot Ernest "Allie" Allison. In 1931, Bond was working for a Curtiss-Wright subsidiary in Baltimore when George Westervelt, the plant's general manager, sent him to Shanghai to manage the affiliate airline. "Bond, who had never been in China before, wended his way day by day through the Chinese labyrinth," Robert Daley writes. "Indeed, he seems to have fallen in love with China and its people, and of course, he was already in love with 'his' airline."[11]

CNAC pilots included six Americans and one German, along with Chinese co-pilots. Chief pilot Allison was "a weather-beaten tousle-haired old veteran of the first [United] States airmail routes," Bixby noted.[12] Moon Fun Chin was an American born in China who would master the most dangerous air route in the world, the mighty Himalayas. Charles "Chili" Vaughn, based at Hankow, flew two round trips per week to Chungking and was so dependable the laborers at Chungking cried, "Here Comes Chili," instead of "Airmail."[13]

The German pilot, Erik Just, became good friends with Cecil G. Sellers, the seventh American flyer to join CNAC. Both were veterans of the Great War, Sellers as commander of an American bomber squadron, Just as one of von Richtofen's Flying Circus. "One day they got out their respective logs and a comparative study disclosed the startling fact that [during] one of

Seller's sorties over the German lines, Erik chased him for a long way and probably failed to [shoot] him down only through the jamming of his machine gun," Bixby recalled. "Erik said that he was mad as H . . . when that gun jammed, but now he saw that it was all for the best."[14]

William Grooch, newly arrived to his China assignment as Pan Am's operations manager worked closely with Bixby. "For four years I had flown over the jungles, rivers, coasts, and mountains of most of the countries in South America," Grooch recalled of his NYRBA experience. "I was due for a change of scenery. China sounded good to me."[15] Grooch and a party that included pilots Bob Gast and George Rummel reached Shanghai by steamer, maneuvering past junks, sampans, steamers, and warships to berth. As they disembarked, the steaming heat, the singsong chanting of the dockworkers, and a grinning Bixby dressed in cool whites and wearing a pith helmet, greeted them.

The key to launching Pan Am's new affiliate was reviving CNAC's airmail franchise, Route No. 3 between Shanghai and Canton that included stops at Wenchow, Foochow, Amoy, and Swatow. The reorganized CNAC was obligated to deliver mail on the route by July 8, 1933, or forfeit. Powerful forces favored Eurasia and were conspiring against CNAC. "Had CNAC's option on 'Route No. 3' been allowed to lapse, it might have passed to the German-Chinese company Eurasia," a Pan Am period document observes.[16]

With no land airports in Canton, the route had to be flown by seaplane. A Sikorsky Amphibion was shipped from the U.S., arriving just in time.[17] But when the S-38 was to depart, post office officials refused to provide airmail. Bixby wired the Minister of Communications, who was in charge of aviation, and discovered new conditions were imposed. "They've got us over a barrel and they know it," Bixby confessed to Grooch. "They tricked us into bringing our equipment and personnel over here."[18]

But Bixby had an epiphany. The contract did not designate official airmail, but "carry mail by air." Bixby convinced the postmaster in Canton, an Englishman he met at a party in Shanghai, to give him an unlocked bag of regular mail to deliver to Shanghai. During the overnight flight, Bixby wrote down each letter's sender and address as proof, if needed, that the letters had been delivered.

Bixby visited Mr. Wah, Minister of Communications, to announce they had fulfilled the obligation. The minister and his assistant betrayed no emotions as Wah replied that official airmail had not been delivered and the franchise was forfeit. Bixby read him the terms, noting the contract did not stipulate "airmail." Wah and his assistant suddenly burst into laughter. Bixby laughed too. "You win," Wah chuckled, admiring Bixby's maneuver. Airmail Route No. 3 was later described as vital to anchoring Pan Am's projected Pacific service.[19]

The biggest fear in Pan Am's New York headquarters was the likelihood that CNAC would be caught in a war between China and Japan. Such a scenario nearly happened in 1932, when Japan bombed Shanghai. Westervelt ordered CNAC to suspend operations, but William Bond wired back: "Consider it imperative we keep this line running . . . I'm not being insubordinate but believe your decision was merely for our safety." Westervelt relented. Even when the Chinese military demanded the airline fly machine gun ammo from Shanghai to Peking, Bond refused, arguing CNAC must maintain neutrality as a civilian enterprise.[20] Bond won his point and even at the height of Japan's aggression the enemy left his planes alone.

CNAC's new American leadership learned the Nanking government was not all-powerful. "Actually, various political subdivisions are practically independent, and maintain independent aeronautical organizations," reported a 1933 *Aviation* article. "In addition to the South China Government at Canton, there is some activity at Peiping in the north, Chungking in the mountainous interior at the end of the Yangtze Gorge, and at Yunnan, a mile-high city further to the south. Each of these is a potential market for American aircraft and must be contacted separately."[21]

Warlords ruled the interior, and one of the most powerful was General Liu Hsiang, who controlled Szechwan province above the Gorges of the Yangtze River and reportedly had a standing army of more than 200,000 men.[22] Liu Hsiang had subjected other warlords to his will, making Szechwan a network of "semifeudal alliances" that he controlled from Chungking.[23]

Bixby decided to venture into warlord country to prepare the way for a new CNAC line from Chungking to the ancient city of Chengtu. It was dangerous—the warlord ruling Chengtu was Hsiang's uncle, and the two were at war.[24] A relay of radio messages notified an emissary of Hsiang that Bixby was coming to Chungking, a thousand mile journey following the river. Joining him was Bond, chief pilot Allison, American co-pilot Burton Hall, and A. M. Chapelain, Shanghai's postal commissioner. On May 26, 1933, they left Shanghai in a Stinson Detroiter, with Bixby bringing a leather briefcase of mail for Chengtu.[25]

It was a flight into China's wonders, from a fortified city on cliffs with steps carved into the rock, to Yangtze River trackers—"the hardest working men on earth," Bixby marveled. "These Yangtze River trackers, tied to long bamboo ropes and stripped of all clothing, fight upstream along the narrow tow pattern cut in the side of precipitous mountain ledges, towing behind them the junks which dare to challenge the swift waters of the upper Yangtze. Big junks will have fifty or sixty of these naked, sweating trackers straining at the long ropes . . . clawing, swearing under the relentless lash of the head man who drive them on with a large whip. . . ."[26]

Arriving at Chungking, the group met another emissary of General Liu Hsiang, who reported they could meet him early next morning. There seemed little hope they would be permitted to fly to warring Chengtu. Bixby considered postponing the trip when Chapelain explained, "A Szechuan war was not too serious an affair." Chapelain had been similarly advised to cancel his first trip to Chengtu because of clashing warlords. He pressed on, arriving at a string of small white flags marking the front line for one of the armies. Chapelain saw no soldiers and learned they were away having lunch. Further on, he came to a line of blue flags marking the opposing general's line—they, too, were at lunch. "He had been right through a war without seeing a single soldier or even being challenged!" Bixby recounted. "Naturally such a tale was reassuring. . . ."[27]

The next morning, Bixby and his party arrived at Hsiang's headquarters. "There we met the warlord who controlled the lives and destinies of the seventy million residents of Szechwan Province," Bixby recalled. "He was a man of average height and weight dressed in a severe dark blue silk robe. He held his hands together Chinese fashion and bowed his shaved head slightly while his face lit up with a smile of cordial welcome." Bixby noticed bodyguards in every corner of the room. After sipping glasses of warm champagne and exchanging small talk through an interpreter, they got down to business.

The warlord explained that he appreciated CNAC service between Hankow and Chungking, but Chengtu was different—his uncle might commandeer their planes and use them against his air force. Bixby countered that his aircraft were commercial, of no military value. Besides, they had airmail for Chengtu, and the Nanking authorities were anxious to have it delivered. The warlord agreed to wire Chengtu that Americans were coming with mail, adding that he wouldn't be responsible for what might happen to them.[28]

Allison flew the group to Chengtu, where the appointed stop was a landing strip on a parade ground full of obstacles—high walls fronted the field, telephone wires slanted across, and a mob gathered. Allison kept circling, finally landing between a double-row of soldiers with fixed bayonets. The soldiers formed a ring around the plane, standing so close that when Bixby's party emerged and they presented arms, a bayonet pierced a wing.

Chengtu's postal commissioner greeted them, along with "Big John," the warlord's personal Chinese pilot and a former CNAC pilot fired for cracking up a plane. As they were led to a limousine, the crowd pressed in, and a lowly laborer snatched Bixby's briefcase, running off with its letters and first flight covers. The limo door was opened—Bixby saw a human thumb stuck inside. Someone flicked it out. They slid in and the chauffeur cleared the crowds by leaning on his horn all the way to the old Manchu Governor's yamen, which had been converted into a military headquarters.[29]

The military headquarters was packed, with General Liu Wenhui, warlord uncle of Liu Hsiang, inducting a new mayor. The Americans were introduced to the warlord and Bixby was given a chance to speak to the assembly, a translator conveying his words in Chinese. "Apparently I made a good speech by proxy for the applause was long and enthusiastic," Bixby recalled.

A few days later, during a pleasant conversation with a general, Bixby mentioned his stolen briefcase. The general replied that Chengtu's mayor had actually seen the thief who stole Bixby's briefcase. The man was caught and the briefcase and letters were retrieved, but the stamps were gone. The general explained the thief had been "appropriately punished." Bixby asked what that meant. The general coolly replied that they had separated the man from his head.[30]

"Suspicious though they might be at the start, the provincial war lords usually ended by yielding to air power's advance, as happened at Chengtu," historian Josephson reports. "The development of China National Aviation proceeded rapidly, and distant cities that were several weeks apart by riverboat or oxcart were brought within a day's travel of each other. High National Government officials . . . now moved about the country over the airlines to bring together the provincial rulers into a common front as war with Japan threatened."[31]

★

It wasn't smooth flying for Pan Am in China, especially at the start and especially on Route No. 3. "The Pan Am people were cocksure and confident, certain they were the best, most experienced aviation men in the world at over-water and coastal operations," Gregory Crouch notes, "and they didn't feel they had much to learn from a bush-league foreign outfit like the China National Aviation Corporation." But on November 24, 1933, CNAC's first passenger flight on Route No. 3 from Shanghai to Canton crashed in foggy weather. The S-38 was destroyed and there were injuries, but, miraculously, no one was killed. On April 10, 1934, pilot Bob Gast took off in an S-38 on the Shanghai to Canton run with two other crew and one passenger, reported he was returning because of fog in Hangchow Bay—and vanished. The wreckage of the S-38 was subsequently found. Several months later, Gast's decomposed body was discovered, floating in Hangchow Bay.[32]

In late January of 1934, there had been another tragedy. Eyewitnesses saw William Grooch's wife leap from the rooftop of their Shanghai apartment building, firmly holding the hands of their two young sons. Bond remembers it as a horrible accident, with the boys playing too close to the edge of the rooftop, and falling as their mother jumped after them "in blind despair." Bond found Grooch "in the most awful state of shock that a person can be in and survive . . . Grooch lived with me for four or five weeks. The first week was a nightmare. It was hell on earth for Bill."

Grooch went back to work. When Gast's plane went missing, Grooch joined in the search along with Bond and Allison, Captain Cecil Sellers and Pan Am co-pilot Hugh Woods. During a water landing at Hangchow Bay, Grooch's S-38 became battered by rough waters and was drifting toward a deadly shoal of rocks; a towline from a steamship didn't help as a wingtip impaled the prow of the anchored ship, forcing the crew to chop off the wing's end to free their ship. Bond did "damage control for Pan American," Gregory Crouch notes. "In six months, Pan Am had wrecked two airplanes, killed four, injured nine, and its vaunted air service was at a complete standstill." Grooch went home, where he was reassigned to the colonization effort for the Pacific island bases.

Instead of Pan Am operating as an independent entity, they effectively integrated operations and personnel into CNAC, with Bond in control of all operations. The CNAC established additional radio and weather reporting stations along the Shanghai to Canton route. To deal with fog and bad weather, Chief Pilot Allison set up an instrument training program for pilots. "Following careful preparations, service reopened on November 2, 1934, and it was to operate successfully and profitably for the next two years," notes William Leary, Jr. "Had it not been for the outbreak of the Sino-Japanese war in 1937, Pan American probably would have recovered its entire developmental costs. . . ."[33]

Grooch assumed foreigners would comprise most of their passenger service, but was pleasantly surprised that 90 percent, by his estimates, were Chinese. Rich and poor preferred air travel that crossed the 600 miles between Hankow and Chungking in seven hours, as compared to a steamer journey up the Yangtse that took eight-to-ten days and was vulnerable to pirate raids.[34]

At its 31st meeting, CNAC's board abolished China's complicated airmail zone system in favor of a uniform postage rate, with a unanimous agreement for "an intensive advertising campaign" to bring the change to the public's attention. CNAC's Shanghai stop benefited Pan Am's transpacific effort, while Pan Am's meteorological operations in Shanghai and elsewhere provided forecasts for Manila and the eventual Guam to Hong Kong route. In addition to new radio stations and direction finders, by the close of 1934 modern flying equipment was ready for delivery to the Shanghai-Peiping and Yangtze River routes. CNAC's Chungking to Yunnan run was inaugurated, and by September of 1936, the popular Shanghai to Canton flight was increased to three times a week.[35]

By April of '37, Pan Am extended regular service to the British colony of Hong Kong, which had been secured thanks to a typical Trippe maneuver. When Great Britain made it difficult to get into Hong Kong, Trippe looked to nearby Macao, a Portuguese possession and island seaport at the mouth of the Canton River. John Cooper, Jr., while in Lisbon negotiating landing rights in the Azores for the Atlantic airway, brought up Macao. The Hong Kong business community, notably Sir Elly Kadoorie and his sons Lawrence and Horace, knew they would suffer if American trade, led by Pan Am, set up shop in Macao. They convinced the government to let Pan Am in. But Trippe ended up with both Macao and Hong Kong. And because Pan Am negotiated the agreement, the U.S. did not have to grant reciprocal concessions to Britain.[36]

★

The nightmare scenario—war with Japan—arrived on July 7, 1937, when an unknown gunman shot at Japanese troops on maneuvers at the Marco Polo Bridge near Peking. No one was killed, but that gunshot was the excuse Japanese hardliners needed—the "China incident" has been called the "true beginning of the Second World War." On August 14, the undeclared Sino-Japanese war accelerated when the Chinese air force struck Japanese warships in Shanghai's harbor.[37]

That August 14, the war came to the CNAC when T. V. Soong, Chiang Kai-shek's brother-in-law and a leading economic expert, asked CNAC to pick up a load of currency. A DC-3 piloted by Charles Sharp arrived, but instead of bankers or government officials, armed soldiers were waiting. They commandeered the plane, ordering Sharp to deliver a load of bombs to Hangchow. The pilot calmly radioed company headquarters and got Bixby, who told him not to fly the ammunition. Buying time, Bixby phoned Soong, who gave him the news—China's Air Force had just attacked Japanese ships in Shanghai harbor. "Mr. Bixby, the thing is out of my hands, the military have taken over," Soong lamented.

Sharp reluctantly flew what was essentially Pan Am's first military transport operation, departing Hanshaw just before Japanese planes bombed the airfield. Bixby telephoned Soong and declared CNAC planes would not fly until the Generalissimo ordered the military not to interfere with its operations. Several days later, Chiang Kai-shek issued the order. Japan bombed CNAC's hangar in Shanghai, but the planes were flyable, and Bixby had them flown into China's interior.[38]

From his office rooftop, Bixby watched the aerial assault of Shanghai. It was a grim walk home, seeing the devastating aftermath. "The streets were absolutely covered with blood," he recalled. "Did you know that it's impossible to walk through blood? It is extremely slippery. I had to make a detour. Pieces of people were hanging on the telephone wires. After that CNAC was never far from the shooting. The war that was to become America's war at Pearl Harbor—Pan American was in it from that day on."[39]

⭐

The Cloud Club atop the Chrysler Building was reserved for the likes of E. F. Hutton, Henry Luce, Condé Nast, and Juan Trippe. The club formed three linked levels at the base of the skyscraper's dome and included a Tudor style lounge and Bavarian theme bar. In the main dining room, where marble columns rose into a vaulted ceiling painted with clouds, William Bond was lunching with Juan Trippe and discussing CNAC's future. The conversation grew contentious. Bond wanted to continue operations until the full ramifications of the war was known, even if that meant years; Trippe wanted to close the affiliate and have Bond take charge of the airway to New

Zealand. The heated talk continued into Trippe's office where Bond declared, "[M]y job is in China and I must go back." With a wave of the hand, Trippe reportedly muttered, "Go on, go on." Bond took that vague dismissal as permission to catch the next domestic flight to San Francisco, where he boarded a Clipper for Hong Kong.[40]

The Chinese Air Force had taken control of CNAC. Bond went to Hankow and confronted the new director, Air Force Colonel Lem Wei-shing, who declared the airline was now a military transport system. He invited Bond to stay as operations manager. Bond declined, and the two parted with a bow. Meanwhile, Bixby was trying to place his pilots elsewhere in the Pan Am System. Chili Vaughn, for one, began flying the Manila–Hong Kong route.[41]

Bond kept pushing to remove the Air Force, install a Chinese civilian as managing director, and have Americans again operating the airline as a Pan Am affiliate. He traveled to the government seat in besieged Nanking to lobby W. H. Donald, an Australian and financial advisor to Chiang Kai-shek. Bond left in one of the last riverboats out, narrowly escaping the fall of Nanking.

Bond met Bixby in Hankow, another city under siege. Bixby had their escape planned—they would fly to Chungking, then Chengtu, and travel by rail to Hanoi. Bond explained he was staying in Hankow to await Donald's reply. Bixby left for Chungking alone, but Bond's tenacity was rewarded. Donald contacted him, asking that he submit three Chinese candidates for consideration as managing director. A few days later, Bond got everything he asked for. The military was out, P.Y. Wong, CNAC's former business manager and one of Bond's candidates, was managing director, and the airline was back in control of the Americans.

Bond flew to Manila to tell Bixby the good news. Now they had to win over Trippe. Bond had a plan—he would resign from Pan Am to work for the CNAC. In a transpacific telephone call, Trippe agreed to let Bond "resign" and stay on to safeguard Pan Am's stake for as long as China could survive.[42]

Bond brought back most of the pilots who had left or been reassigned. CNAC routes changed as Japan continued taking territory. Former stops in

Peking, Shanghai, and Hangchow were lost, leaving Hong Kong the only seaport not in Japanese control. The government moved west, into the mountainous interior to Chungking, a centralized city that allowed Chiang Kai-shek to reach battlefronts with supplies and reinforcements, had cliffs for natural air raid shelters, and winter fog to provide cover from Japanese planes.[43]

After Canton fell, the escape from Hankow began. From October 22–25, CNAC pilots flying mostly DC-2s evacuated nearly 300 government officials. Oil lamps lit fields for night flying, with takeoffs and landings on mined runways. Charles Sharp flew Chiang Kai-shek to safety.[44] Captain Moon Chin's Commodore seaplane was the last out, and he flew to Lake Wuhan, east of Hankow, where CNAC kept planes overnight. That airfield was deserted, so Chin flew back to Hankow, where he saw bodies and wreckage floating down river and fires burning in the distance. "There was so much stuff floating in the river, I decided we'd better take off while there was still daylight," he recalled.[45]

On August 24, 1938, CNAC American pilot Hugh Woods departed Hong Kong for Chungking in the DC-2 *Kweilin*. He was flying with a two-man crew and a passenger list that included two influential Chinese bankers and Dr. Fun So, a former Chinese finance minister who canceled his reservation at the last minute. The Kweilin was 40 miles out when Woods sighted a patrol of five Japanese fighter planes. CNAC pilots had seen such patrols and flown without incident.

Woods was radioing Hong Kong that they were being followed by Japanese planes when, suddenly, they opened fire. Woods climbed into the clouds as bullets pierced the hull and entered the cockpit, smashing the instrument panel. The *Kweilin* went into a spiral as the fighters followed and kept firing. Woods aimed for the Pearl River, shut off the engines, and hit the water on the plane's belly. He shouted for his crew to get the passengers out, pushed open an overhead emergency escape hatch, pulled himself up and dropped into the river. Passengers trying to swim to shore were cut down by machine gun fire. Woods avoided being killed by diving underwater, resurfacing to catch a breath, and diving below as he dodged bullets.

When the Japanese departed, fourteen were dead, and only three survived the first recorded air attack on an unarmed commercial plane.

Bond had the river dragged, and the *Kweilin* was lifted out, repaired, and put back in service. Japan ignored U.S. State Department protests.[46]

CNAC went to ingenious lengths to keep planes in the air, but the resurrected *Kweilin* seemed cursed. Walter Kent, a thirty-two-year-old pilot from Louisiana, was flying passengers and crew on the *Kweilin* from Chungking to Hong Kong, where he planned to say goodbye to his wife and three-year-old son before they evacuated to the United States. Japanese fighters suddenly attacked, but Kent found an emergency field near Changyi. Kent was taxiing toward tree cover when the *Kweilin* was hit with a 20-millimeter shell that instantly killed him. Thirteen passengers and crew leapt from the burning plane, but strafing runs gunned them down, leaving only three survivors.

The incident shook even Bond's indomitable spirit—could CNAC survive?[47]

## Map III.
## ASIA
### PAN AMERICAN AIRWAYS SYSTEM

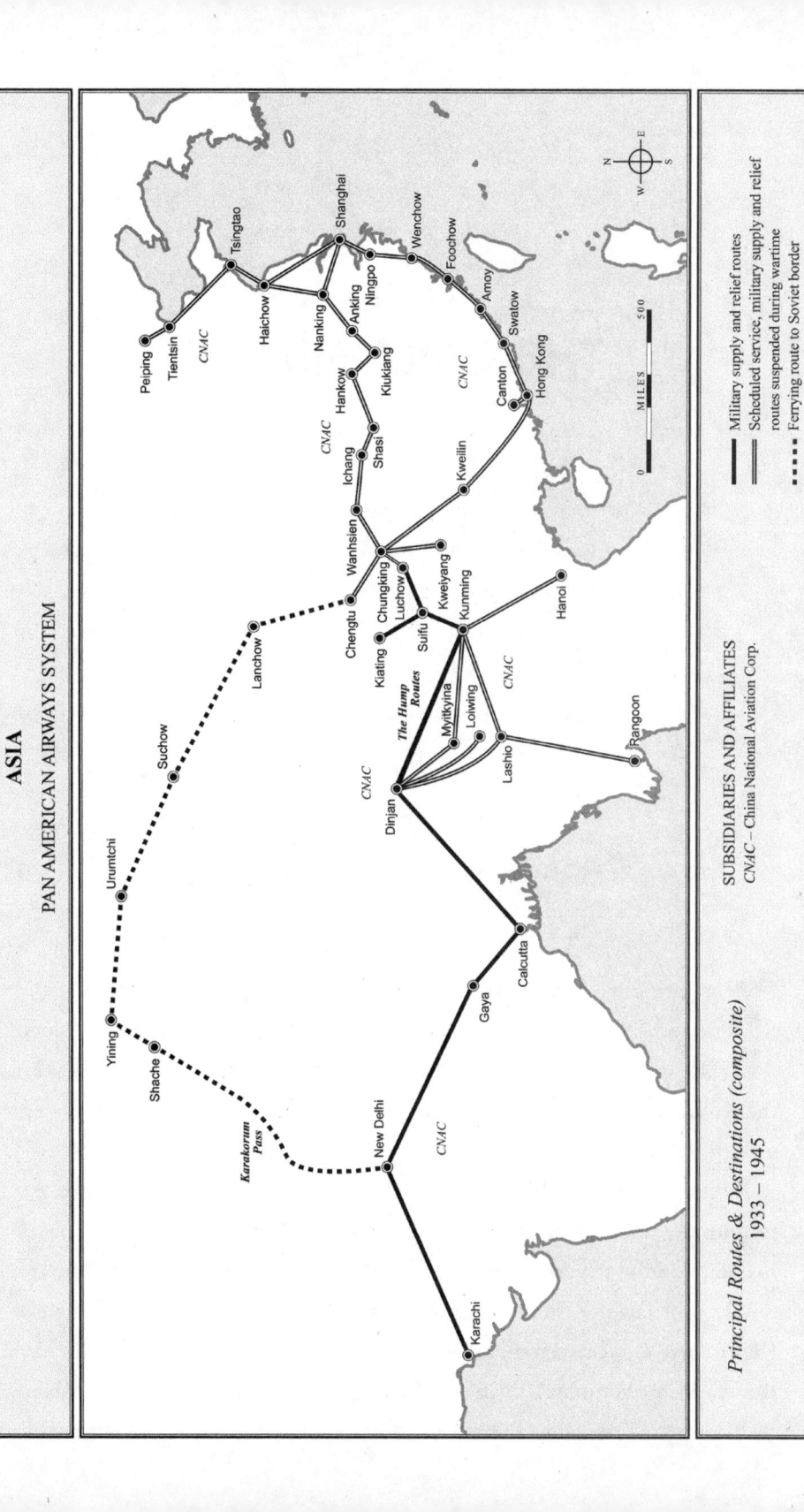

*Principal Routes & Destinations (composite)*
*1933 – 1945*

**SUBSIDIARIES AND AFFILIATES**
CNAC – China National Aviation Corp.

— Military supply and relief routes
= Scheduled service, military supply and relief routes suspended during wartime
····· Ferrying route to Soviet border

## CHAPTER 13
# THE COLONIZERS

*"Civil aviation is a bulwark to our national defense... Next year America will be the first to span the Atlantic with over-night passenger service to Europe... America's security, America's economic welfare, can best be assured by full development of America's military and civil air power."*

—Juan Trippe, 1938 speech, "Trying to Keep the Peace Through The Power of Wings"[1]

### "Shanghai Has Been Bombed"

The headline from the typed radio newssheet greeted Dorothy Kaucher along with eggs and toast during her first breakfast on Wake Island. The war in China pricked the bubble of her idyll on a Pacific isle, but she would never regret being among the first wave of commercial air passengers to fly the Pacific.

Kaucher and other pioneering air travelers took to heart such Pan Am promotions as its "Transpacific" brochure that declared, "Here is a travel-magic Aladdin never dreamed of... the opportunity to experience this new-day miracle of travel while the wonder is still fresh upon it—while the flight across an ocean is still looked upon as reserved for only those who have the world to command. While those unbelievable little mid-ocean islands of Midway, Wake and Guam are still unknown to tourist's tours... The thrilling experience of being among the first to ever set foot upon the newfound island colonies of the age-old Pacific, which fewer than a score of men had ever seen before the coming of these flying clipper ships. . . ."[2]

When the weekly westbound flight left Alameda every Wednesday at 3:00 p.m. Kaucher and other "air pilgrims" faithfully walked a dirt trail to the water to watch a Clipper depart, while lucky passengers passed them in a limo. In the summer of 1937, Dorothy was the one in the limo, having raised funds to defray the considerable $1,845 airfare, and planned to write a book about her experience.

The day of Kaucher's departure was glorious, all sun and blue sky. The big bulletin board, in bold black letters against white, announced: "Trans-Pacific Crossing No. 135. Hawaii Clipper . . . Captain Musick . . . Departing Alameda 3 p.m." Kaucher remembered the *Hawaii Clipper* was christened in Honolulu with coconut milk and the blessing, "May the Hawaii Clipper forever sail the air of the universe without mishap." It was a beautiful thing, that flying boat straining at the ropes as it floated on the water. She wished it were the pioneering *China Clipper*, but it was special to fly with Captain Musick.[3]

As the Clipper went airborne, Kaucher thought: "My country gone, nothing but sea, but sky, and this little metal bird nosing into infinity." They were served tea and treats, but then came the "empty, cold, clammy moment" when the sun had set and they were in darkness—darkness that disappeared when the steward snapped on electric lights. She gazed out at the "cold country of clouds" and the ocean, a rarefied view few humans had ever seen.[4]

Midway was wonderful, but Wake was "the island of my special dreams," Kaucher wrote.[5] One could enjoy a four-course dinner in a modern dining room, then walk into a starry night as frothy waves swept over white sands. Two years earlier Wake was a barren and unknown isle where only trade winds blew; now it was a settlement powered by generators and lit by electric lights. "To us in 1937 Wake Island was a puzzling mixture of a modern air base and of something that belonged to the dim, silent centuries," Kaucher wrote.[6] Wake had a history, some of it uncovered by Pan Am's colonizers of '35, notably a rusty anchor that was all that remained of an 1866 shipwreck, along with a legend the castaways buried $300,000 in silver somewhere on the isle.[7]

The news of the attack on Shanghai, and reports that the Cathay and Palace hotels had been bombed changed Dorothy's itinerary—she tore up her reservation for the Cathay Hotel and began rethinking her plans to connect with a CNAC flight to Peking and a visit to the Great Wall. Kaucher did fly to Hong Kong, but the city was full of war fears and she decided to spend the balance of her travel time back on her island of dreams. That decision was rewarded with a glorious vision upon her return: "That night there was moonlight on Wake Island such as I have never seen in my life. On the silver lagoon, the Clipper shone like silver."[8]

One night, she and another traveler followed the whispers of Wake's history to where hermit crabs scuttled around an old iron kettle, rusty barrel hoops, fragments of rice bowls, and a sampan's remains. Night clouds drifted across the stars, waves rhythmically washed ashore, and she felt the ghostly presence of the people who once camped here. By a gray pole were the remains of a Shinto shrine and an empty grave. "All they know is that in 1900 the Japanese had come here to Wake and in 1908 they had left. . . . They had really sat here on Wake Island and talked in the evenings where now we stood beside the old battered boards of the sampan. . . . That grave! That shinto! It haunted me."[9]

On this speck of earth and coral, "a person could have strange, distorted images of impending doom in 1937," Kaucher wrote. During a conversation with fellow visitors, a man mentioned Amelia Earhart's disappearance, declaring the radio on Wake received her distress signal and that Earhart was shot down while on a secret government mission to appraise the strategic importance of Pacific islands. At that moment, Kaucher recalled the woman who inspired her to come to Wake and that rainy St. Patrick's Day when she watched brave Amelia lift her *Electra* into the path of white light that broke through the clouds.

Fears of a world hell-bent for war was voiced by another visitor to Wake who mused, "Maybe this rock pile won't slide under the water. But the day'll come when that wind will be blowing through empty windows of the Inn yonder, and shutters will be clapping their hands like ghosts, and booby birds will be making their nests on the floor of the lobby and croaking in what used to be [the] kitchen."[10]

Even as press and public attention were drawn to Pan Am's Central Pacific surveys, the airline was expanding into the South Pacific. In the fall of 1935, Trippe's man in the South Seas was Harold Gatty, of Tasmanian descent and famed as navigator for Wiley Post when they flew around the world in eight days. Australia was a problem—Imperial Airways and the Air Ministry did not want air service until a British flag airline was ready. But that October, P. C. Coates, New Zealand's minister of public works, announced Pan Am would carry mail and passengers between his country and the U.S., complete with a flying boat terminal at Auckland. However, projected service by August of 1936 proved optimistic.[11]

Pan Am needed island stepping stones to Auckland—many potential bases were controlled by the British—and Gatty suggested Kingman Reef and the U.S. possession of American Samoa, an island network that included Tutuila Island and Pago Pago harbor. The problem was that Pago Pago had looming cliffs around a tight harbor. Only at the end of a long flight, when fuel loads were low, would a flying boat be light enough to make the tricky landing. But Pan Am had to begin survey flights or lose the franchise, and New Zealand had already extended its deadline. Trippe's reaction was, "Let's go," notes Pan Am historian Jon E. Krupnick. The Central Pacific islands worked perfectly, why wouldn't a route from Honolulu to Kingman Reef, Pago Pago, and Auckland? "So they have to start service by the end of '37; they've got to do three survey flights before they start there. Because of the difficulty, they send Ed Musick," Krupnick noted.[12]

Musick departed Honolulu on the first survey flight on March 23, 1937. The first stop was Kingman Reef, a 1,100-mile trip that took eight hours and five minutes. They arrived in a storm, and it was still raining the following morning when they left for American Samoa and Pago Pago. Ten hours and thirty-five minutes later, Musick was unhappy to see the S-curve shaped harbor over which loomed "Rainmaker," a 1,700-foot cliff. Musick had to come in on a curve, but his first approach was too high and fast. He pulled away, coming in slower—reportedly, palm trees brushed the plane's belly, but landed safely.

During the five-day stopover, Musick obsessed about the takeoff. When it was time to leave he ordered all excess equipment and luggage off the plane. The departure was recalled as "hairy," but they made it to Auckland, where Vic Wright and John Stickrod worked on an oil leak they discovered back in Honolulu. They continued on the inbound course and safely arrived in Hawaii.[13]

Musick was in his early forties, but starting to show the physical wear of his pioneering and relentless responsibilities. That October, Cleo dragged Eddie away on a rare vacation, a drive from San Francisco to Los Angeles. They visited Eddie's mother and brother, and old friends like Harry Reynolds, with whom he first shared his passion for flying. Cleo had Eddie promise he wouldn't keep doing the work of two men. But it was not to be.[14] "His company was engaged in a world-wide struggle for supremacy in ocean air transport," Grooch noted. "They were planning, in the near future, to start transatlantic schedules. Six super airliners, half again the size of the *China Clipper*, would soon be ready for test at the Boeing plant in Seattle. There was too much at stake to risk putting a new man in Musick's job. He shrugged and carried on."[15]

On January 9, 1938, Musick flew the *Samoan Clipper* for the third survey to New Zealand. At Pago Pago the Clipper was fueled, the forecast was excellent.[16] On January 11, at dawn, the Clipper took off with Musick and his crew of former CNAC pilot and First Officer Captain Cecil Sellers, Junior Officer Paul Brunk, Navigation Officer Fred MacLean, Radio Officer Tom Findlay, and Flight Engineer Officers Jack Brooks and John Stickrod. They were carrying 900 pounds of mail.

A little over an hour out, an oil leak was discovered. Musick decided to turn back, but with his aircraft fully fueled he didn't want to attempt a landing at Pago Pago until he lightened the load. Dumping fuel was standard practice, although Sellers always felt discharging gasoline near hot engines was never routine. It was past 8:00 a.m. when the Clipper was reported over Apia Harbor in British Samoa, a seventy-four-mile westerly detour from Pago Pago. At 8:27, the Clipper radioed they were finally dumping fuel and expected to land shortly. But the Clipper didn't arrive. There were no further radio transmissions. Within the hour a search began.[17]

An oil slick and debris were sighted, fourteen miles northwest of Pago Pago. Bobbing atop oil smeared waters were charred pieces of aircraft, a pair of Brooks's trousers, Findley's tie clip and coat, navigation papers, other detritus. "[The Clipper] was then only six minutes away from the base.... Apparently an explosion ripped the Clipper apart an [sic] she plummeted into the sea killing everyone aboard," *Midway News* reported. Soundings established the water depth at the crash site at 6,000 feet, making it virtually impossible that bodies or aircraft could be recovered.

The tragic news was radioed to the Chrysler Building—André Priester wept. Condolences poured in, including from Australia's prime minister and Auckland's mayor, where flags were flown at half-mast. There was criticism from former board member Loening, who declared, "This accident brings into focus the monopolistic aims of this one company in a tragic blunder of overexpansion."

Trippe released a statement: "I feel that Captain Musick and his crew were entirely blameless. Radio reports from the Samoa Clipper prove . . . [Musick] carefully followed the most conservative technique possible. Needless to say, everyone connected with Pan American Airways is grieved beyond expression at the untimely fate of Captain Musick and his splendid crew. It is an irreparable blow to our company and will be a distinct loss to American aviation."[18]

"The dump valves on the S-42 were just flush openings on the bottom surface of the wings," Bill Taylor later explained. "During previous use of these valves it was noticed that some of the fuel tended to run along the bottom of the wing. Evidently some of the fuel had worked its way into the engine nacelles and been ignited. As a result of this accident strict federal regulations were adopted governing the design and testing of dump valves."[19]

Some argued that Musick should have tried landing at Pago Pago, but his old flying partner, Victor Wright, dismissed such second-guessing. "With the full load the landing would have overshot the short protected area of Pago Pago harbor and the airplane would have made its first contact in the heavy seas outside," Wright said. "The crack-up would have been terrible. Anyone with any experience in landing this type aircraft at sea knows that. Perhaps [Musick] should have made a crash landing at sea. Maybe he would have gotten out of it. When he finally pulled the dump gas valve it blew them out of the sky."[20]

On January 24 a memorial was held in the grand rotunda of San Francisco City Hall, with Mayor Angelo Rossi presiding. "There is no death" was sung, a bugler played taps. Cleo was left with the solace of Eddie's last words to her: "I'll be loving you every minute."[21] Trippe did not fly in from New York for the funeral and garnered criticism for the perceived slight.

Trippe's secretary, Kathleen Clair, recalled an incident in the 1960s when she entered the Boss's office. Trippe was standing and gazing out the window, lost in thought. When Trippe turned around, his reverie interrupted, he had an unsettled look on his face.

"Eddie made a mistake," he said.[22]

★

In late July of 1938, Captain Leo Terletzky was piloting the *Hawaii Clipper* westward with a full crew and a passenger list that included Edward Wyman, Trippe's personal assistant. At a layover in Wake, Captain Joe Barrows, who had flown in the opposite direction, told Terletzky about rough weather around the Philippines, confessing that even with a 200-mile detour it was the closest he had come to breaking up. He advised Terletzky not to go; the rough weather would still be there. Reportedly, that night in the Wake hotel dining room, Terletzky said a prayer thanking the Lord for putting him in America and Pan Am.[23]

The *Hawaii Clipper* continued and was off the coast of Guam on July 29 and in routine communication with Pan Am's weather station in the

Philippines. At noon, Manila time, the Clipper's radio operator, in Morse code, reported: "Flying in rough air at 9100 feet. . . . Rain. During past hour cloud conditions have varied." The operator at the Panay station acknowledged and was about to provide routine weather reports when the Clipper operator requested the report be held for a minute because of rain static.[24] That was the last ever heard from the *Hawaii Clipper.* The biggest thing flying simply disappeared.

The presumed crash, the first casualties for transpacific service, were a tragic end to the christening prayer that the *Hawaii Clipper* "sail the air of the universe without mishap." On August 17, the Secretary of Commerce, as directed by the Air Commerce Act, appointed a three-person board to investigate. They considered various unidentified theories, the final report stating they could not include conjecture. The official conclusion: "[T]here was a failure of communication between the ground and the Clipper; that communication was not thereafter reestablished; and that no trace of the aircraft has since been discovered."[25]

"Was the Clipper hi-jacked by the Japanese?" Pan Am's corporate history mused over the Number One theory. "Some in Pan Am have always thought so."[26] The engine was the most powerful in American aviation and would have saved Japan years of research and development. Conspiracy theorists noted that Wyman was reportedly carrying a million dollars of "Rice Bowl Fund" collected by San Francisco's Chinese community to help Chiang Kai-shek's government. The theory gained traction the next month when Japanese fighters shot down CNAC's *Kweilin.*

With the tragic losses of the *Samoan Clipper* and *Hawaii Clipper,* Pan Am was suddenly short on Pacific aircraft. The search was also on for a better airbase than Pago Pago. Canton Island, 1,900 miles south of Hawaii and 400 miles from Samoa, had been discovered by a New Bedford whaler, worked by Americans digging nitrogen-rich guano, and annexed by Great Britain in 1890, but had since been deserted. In 1917, Rear Admiral Albert P. Niblack, commander of Navy forces at Gibraltar, suggested the Navy take disposition of the Pacific's "guano islands" to protect sea lanes to Asia. "It is not a question of fortifying, but of providing stepping stones, and lines of communication which may, in case of war, turn out to be the lines of operations or which can be converted into such," Niblack wrote.[27]

The Guano Islands Act of 1856 stipulated the Navy had to protect U.S. nationals mining guano on deserted islands, provided the guano was shipped and sold in the United States. Pan Am's lawyers felt they could use the old law to claim islands and demand government protection. The Navy supported the plan, but the State Department had reservations, and won a major concession—Pan Am had to establish an actual guano digging company to qualify for protection. Trippe and C. V. Whitney set up the American Nitrates Corporation, complete with an office and storage facility under the Brooklyn Bridge.[28]

By the end of February of 1938, Harold Gatty learned the British *Essex* was preparing to sail from New Zealand to occupy Canton Island. He cabled Trippe in secret company code—if they wanted it, they better move fast. To get guano diggers there in time, they needed to send them to American Samoa and have the Navy ferry them to Canton, about 400 miles away. Trippe discussed the situation with Sumner Welles, acting Secretary of State in Cordell Hull's absence. Welles and the Cabinet were against it, so Trippe met with the Navy and with Roosevelt.[29] The guano diggers were in place, awaiting instructions, when Cordell Hull returned to Washington—the answer was yes. A cable authorized the go-ahead, with a State Department proviso for the removal of the Navy gunboat's guns.[30]

On March 7, 1938, the Americans arrived at the eastern anchorage, the narrow entrance to Canton. A day later, the *Essex* arrived, but with the Americans blocking the main harbor, the British ship had to drop anchor on the north side. The British Captain ordered the Americans out, but the Navy man in charge retorted that they were there to get guano and protect workers. The British established what claim they could by erecting a shack on the north side to serve as a British Post Office, leaving a Mr. Fleming to run up the British flag and serve as postmaster.[31]

Trippe met with Hull to make a presentation on the situation, which included poring over Pan Am's survey maps. "He's a real brigand at heart and a great American," Hull exclaimed, admiring Trippe's style. The administration put Canton and Enderbury Islands under Interior Department control.[32] A new expedition was mounted that included veterans of the Midway and Wake expeditions, with George Kuhn leading construction operations.

The freighter arrived in the rain, which Mr. Fleming considered providential—no rain for six months but the skies opened for the Americans. The freighter stayed two weeks, putting five tons of cargo ashore, while underwater dynamiting cleared a runway channel for flying boats. They were working so hard Kuhn told his crew that if the supply plane did not arrive by July 15, they would take a day off and get drunk. Good as his word, when the plane didn't appear Kuhn called for all hands to knock off and roll out the beer. Fleming, now practically one of the crew, contributed two precious bottles of scotch.[33]

The British lodged a formal protest and Hull invited Trippe and the British ambassador to his office. Trippe explained, matter-of-factly, that he had the protection of the law. "A British Ambassador in 1938 had larger concerns to worry about than this little game," Pan Am's corporate history notes. "For one thing, Great Britain relied on the United States for the defense of the Pacific against possible Japanese aggression. She could not really view with indignation anything that increased American capability in this regard."[34]

With Canton Island secured, Pan Am needed another island accessible to New Zealand and Australia. In November of 1938, Harold Bixby went to Paris and successfully negotiated landing rights for Nouméa, on French-held New Caledonia. Pan Am still needed entry to Australia, so it bought a yacht once owned by the late publisher Cyrus Curtis, renamed it the *Southern Seas*, and used it as a floating hotel when moored at Nouméa and as a ferry to Australia. "Australia couldn't block PAA from ferrying passengers from Nouméa to Australia in the yacht," explains Pan Am's corporate history, as the *Southern Seas* had legal access to any port in the world. Australia finally relented, granting Pan Am air rights.[35]

On October 26, 1938, the *New York Herald Tribune* held a forum on the potential for war in Europe. It was broadcast coast-to-coast over the N.B.C. radio network from New York's Waldorf-Astoria hotel and included the Trippe speech titled, "Trying to Keep the Peace Through the Power of Wings." Trippe, sounding like an air power advocate, said the nation had to prepare for a foreign air attack, although civil aviation had given the country the capacity to prepare. "Civil aviation is a bulwark to our national defense," he declared, adding that Pan Am was in the vanguard of America's global role. "Next year America will be the first to span the Atlantic with overnight passenger service to Europe."[36]

The loss of the *Hawaii* and *Samoan* Clippers stretched the transpacific service capacity of the *China Clipper* and *Philippine Clipper*, lowering the completed schedule rate to 58 percent—in 1937, the first full year of Pacific service, the rate was 92 percent. The annual report for the fiscal year ending December 31, 1938, had other glaring negatives. The $46,671.87 in reported profits was a big drop from $510,416.68 in 1937. Operating costs of Latin American operations had increased from $11,240,000 to $12,899,000.[37]

There were positives. CNAC was maintaining operations in Nationalist territory, from the provisional capital of Chungking eastward down the Yangtze to Ichang, northwestward to Chengtu, and southward to Yunnan-fu. In the South Pacific, Canton Island was secured. On the Atlantic, discussions for establishing ground facilities and operating arrangements were ongoing, with delayed service now planned for 1939. The U.S. and Bermuda route carried 1,829 passengers on what was "an invaluable proving ground for future transatlantic operations." The System boasted 5,000 employees and total route mileage was 53,548 miles. Challenges included, in rank of importance, the Civil Aeronautics Act of 1938 and "the aggressive growth" of foreign airline competition.

The report acknowledged the large investment in transoceanic service, but the combined revenues from transpacific and transatlantic service in the near future meant "a more profitable operation." The message to board and stockholders was patience. "It is believed by your management that the next few years will demonstrate the wisdom of this policy," the report stated. The policy hinged on a super seaplane, six of which were on order.

Pan Am's technical team always knew their transoceanic operation required a bigger aircraft than even the Martin Clippers. Pan Am had approached Boeing with the challenge, and designs for Model-314 Super Clippers were accepted and a contract signed on July 21, 1936, months before Martin Clippers began Pacific passenger service. The innovations requested or developed by Pan Am included the Wright Cyclone No. 14, the largest aircraft engine ever built, specifications for reduction of fuel consumption on long-range flights, the first use of high octane fuels, first fireproofing of all cabin furnishings, and first fuel meter showing the rate of flow, a Pan Am development that became a standard instrument.

The contract stipulated the first Boeing be delivered on December 21, 1937, with the final five on the 21st of February, April, June, August, and October of 1938.[38] *Life* magazine's August 1937 issue celebrated impending Atlantic service and showcased the Super Clippers with a photo spread of construction underway at Boeing's Seattle plant, spotlighting lightweight Duralumin furniture, plastic window panes, porous sound-proofed fabrics— "as befits anything so modern as a transatlantic passenger plane." *Life* added, "Next year unless all present signs fail you will be able to fly from New York to London in twenty-four hours for $500."[39]

Unfortunately for the fiscal year 1938, Boeing missed its due dates—its first Clipper would not be delivered until January 27, 1939. The remaining aircraft would arrive throughout the year, with the last Super Clipper coming into the Pan Am system on June 16, 1939. (Four of the planes would be assigned the new Atlantic Division, two to the Pacific.)[40] Before the 1938 annual report went to press, Trippe managed to slip in a mention that the first Boeing Clipper was received and testing had begun.

The Civil Aeronautics Act of 1938 also empowered a Civil Aeronautics Board (CAB) with new regulatory and oversight powers. With many ten-year airmail contracts coming up for renewal, it seemed certain the CAB would revise Pan Am's lucrative Latin American contracts downward, yet another revenue loss at a time of diminishing profit margins.[41]

In open revolt, Pan Am's board voted to depose Juan Trippe. The coup's leader was the board chairman, Juan's friend, and one of the airline's founders, C. V. Whitney. He had not shaken his image as a polo-playing playboy, but dreamed of being a captain of industry. C. V.'s wealth was monumental—he had just inherited $20,000,000 to go with the 156,032 shares of Pan Am stock that made him the airline's largest shareholder. (In contrast, Trippe had 7,056 shares, with 10,000 shares in trust for his children.)[42] C. V.'s move took advantage of growing resentment against Trippe's fondness for secrecy, belief in his absolute vision, and his use of the board as a rubber stamp. Trippe had also lost trusted board members, including Richard Mellon, Merian Cooper, and David Bruce, who helped open doors for the young airline but sold his Pan Am stock at a loss.[43]

The board voted Whitney in on March 15, 1939, twelve days before Pan Am's first transatlantic flight.

## CHAPTER 14
# THE WORLD OF TOMORROW

> *"We as a nation are appreciating more and more the position our country must occupy in the World of Tomorrow. Through aviation America, the land in which the airplane was born, can lead the World of Tomorrow to greater progress, prosperity and, I hope—peace."*
>
> —JUAN TRIPPE, ADDRESSING THE NEW YORK WORLD'S FAIR "BANQUET OF THE WORLD OF TOMORROW"[1]

In 1936, Charles and Anne Lindbergh were living at Long Barn, a rustic cottage in the countryside of Kent, an hour outside London. William Caxton, England's first printer, was born at Long Barn, and his ghost was said to work a spectral printing press during nocturnal manifestations. But the only night sounds the Lindberghs heard were the rustling of mice and bats. Other than an occasional visit from a protective local chief constable, they were mercifully left alone.[2]

Long Barn was among the special places where the famous couple found "private peace and happiness," Anne recalled.[3] Their growing family included another boy, Land, born in 1937. Anne had begun writing a book about their 1933 survey; Charles was working with rocket scientist Robert Goddard and heart specialist Dr. Alexis Carrel. Charles refused entreaties from Pan Am and TWA to come home, but had not severed connections. "If anything, his correspondence about aviation increased while he was in

Europe—especially with Pan Am, whose officers he kept apprised of the latest European developments in aircraft, air routes, and airports," Scott Berg writes.[4]

The Lindberghs were witnesses to Europe's march to war. Anne later pinpointed the start of the Spanish Civil War in 1936 as when they became aware of "the cloud of danger looming over Europe." That year a new role for Charles began when Major Truman Smith, U.S. Military Attaché in Berlin, asked him to visit Germany to assess its air power.[5] Smith made inquiries and the architects of German air power—Field Marshal Milch and Reichmarschall Göering, commander of the Luftwaffe and Hitler's appointed successor—consented. "The Nazis were delighted to show off their air strength, and they even let my husband fly their newest planes," Anne noted.[6] Officially, the Lindberghs visited as guests of Lufthansa. Charles visited air installations and factories no American had seen, saw the latest bombers and fighters and spent a day with the Luftwaffe's elite fighting group.[7]

In March of 1938, Germany annexed Austria. Hitler then turned a covetous eye toward the Sudetenland, a largely Germanic area of Czechoslovakia, the young nation created in 1919. The Czechs appealed to England and France to intercede on their behalf.[8] When Charles and Anne visited London on September 21 of '38, war fears were as thick as the misty overcast and coal smoke. Prime Minister Neville Chamberlain was shuttling between England and Germany to resolve the crisis diplomatically, but talk on the streets was of war. Around the corner from their hotel in Piccadilly, Charles was startled to see an Air Raid Precautions station handing out gas masks. Charles met Ambassador Joseph Kennedy at the U.S. embassy and, at Kennedy's request, turned in a brief report that concluded German air power was too great for any European nation—only the U.S. was capable of competing. The ambassador cabled Lindbergh's report to the Secretary of State.[9]

On September 29, Chamberlain and France's prime minister, Edouard Daladier, joined Hitler and Mussolini in Munich to sign a pact giving Germany the Sudetenland and sparing Czechoslovakia. Chamberlain announced the agreement meant "peace for our time." General Hap Arnold dismissed "the appeasement pact," later declaring, "[W]ithout firing a shot, dropping a bomb, or even starting an engine, Hitler's Luftwaffe and his armored forces won for him his first major victory of World War II."

The day of the Munich pact, Arnold was appointed Chief of the Army Air Corps, succeeding his boss, General Oscar Westover, who died in a September 21st air crash while approaching Lockheed's runway in Burbank. Westover had been flying his plane around the country, sounding the alarm about America's lack of air power, pushing himself hard: "Too hard," Arnold reflected. "It was too much for any man his age whose flying reflexes were being sapped day after day the way Oscar's were at that nerve-racking task." Now the full weight of America's air crisis was on Arnold's shoulders.[10]

As Arnold and others anticipated, the Munich accord was wasted paper—in March of '39, Hitler invaded and occupied Czechoslovakia. That year Winston Spencer Churchill became First Lord of the Admiralty at age sixty-four; by May 10, 1940, he would be installed as a wartime prime minister.

"After Hitler's annexation of Czechoslovakia," Anne Lindbergh wrote, "my husband felt he should return to his own country in order to contribute to the critical expansion of U.S. army aviation installations, which alone, he felt, could match German air strength."[11]

For the new Army Air Corps chief, Lindbergh couldn't get home fast enough. "I think one of the most wasteful weaknesses in our whole setup was our lack of a proper Air Intelligence Organization," Arnold recalled. "Nobody gave us much useful information about Hitler's air force until Lindbergh came home in 1939."[12]

In April of '39, Charles Lindbergh was aboard the *Aquitania* and sailing to New York, with Anne and their boys to follow. On the 13th, a day out from New York, Lindbergh received an urgent radiogram from General Arnold asking him to telephone upon arrival.

When the ship docked and customs officials boarded, a mob of reporters and cameramen followed. Lindbergh let the other passengers disembark before he took the plunge, with dozens of police and plainclothes officers forming a wedge. "All the way along the deck the photographers ran in front of us and behind us, jamming the way, being pushed aside by the police, yelling, falling over each other on the deck," Lindbergh recalled. "There must have been over a hundred of them, and the planks were covered with the broken glass of the flashlight bulbs they threw away. I have never seen as many at one time before, even in 1927, I think." The disgusted ex-exile confessed: "It was a barbaric way to enter a civilized country."[13]

On Monday, Lindbergh met Arnold. "Lindbergh gave me the most accurate picture of the Luftwaffe . . . that I had so far received," Arnold noted. He asked Lindbergh to go on active duty, Lindbergh accepted, and was immediately activated as a colonel in the Army Air Corps. Arnold asked the aviator to help determine the development of military aircraft on a board that included General W. G. Kilner and then-Colonel Carl Spaatz. What Arnold called the "Kilner-Lindbergh Board" began on May 5, 1939. "The value of the findings of that Board was inestimable," Arnold later stated. "I can still see poor stolid Lindbergh being trailed though the halls . . . by excited clerks and predatory newspapermen as he did his job."[14]

Lindbergh also returned to Pan American Airways. On May 23, he drove to New York to lunch with Trippe at the Cloud Club. "There has been a reorganization in Pan American and 'Sonny' Whitney is now apparently in control," Lindbergh noted in his journal. "He has Juan Trippe's office, and Juan has moved to the other corner of the building. I do not yet fully understand all of the details . . . Juan continues as president, but with much less influence. In many ways I am sorry to see this, for I like Juan and have always felt he had great ability."[15]

Trippe kept his inscrutable façade in place, but a chill of Arctic proportions descended upon the company. It was, Matthew Josephson wrote, "a house divided." Thomas Morgan, a recently arrived directorate who was president of the Sperry Corp and chairman of the board of Sperry-Gyroscope Company, was selected to head a three-person committee to bridge the chasm.[16]

Trippe seemed to be biding his time. When Whitney moved into Trippe's big corner office on the fifty-eighth floor, he allowed Juan's iconic world globe to go to his now smaller office. "[Trippe's] famous . . . globe—he had been photographed beside it for dozens of newspaper and magazine articles—was then wheeled out of Whitney's office down the hall to Trippe's," Robert Daley records. "Many of the other executives stood in their doorways watching—and musing perhaps on the vagaries of power—until the globe rolled by and disappeared into the small new office and the door closed behind it."[17]

★

At the start of 1939, Trippe could not imagine he would be ousted from power. He was empire building, his plans including an airway across Africa. "He foresaw the strategic importance of Africa long before others did," Josephson observed. "And in the Far East, as he had pressed the British to give Pan American entrance to Hong Kong, so he pressed them further for entry to Singapore, one of the great natural junction points of the world's air routes. He had, it has been said, a passion to girdle the globe."[18]

The corporate coup happened as the transatlantic triumph was at hand—indeed, Pan Am vice president John Cooper felt they should have already been flying the Atlantic. "When transoceanic aircraft, ordered by Pan American Airways, became available in 1935, a transatlantic service could have been made immediately available to the world," Cooper wrote in 1947. "But the United States did not have the political right to fly into and out of British-controlled Newfoundland or Bermuda or the Portuguese-controlled Azores, or into the countries on the European Atlantic coast. . . . National airspace control is absolute. . . . On the Atlantic, the greatest over-ocean trade route of all, airspace control definitely delayed the opening of service." The United States was also at fault, Cooper added. The Civil Aeronautics Act of 1938 stipulated no American air carrier could lawfully engage in interstate or overseas and foreign air commerce unless the new Civil Aeronautics Board granted a certificate authorizing it to do so, and the same rule applied to foreign air carriers wanting reciprocal rights.[19]

A big break was the pre-CAB rivalry between America (represented by Pan Am), and Britain (represented by Imperial), had developed into a cooperative venture. In 1935, British air policy clarified that Pan Am would not be barred from Newfoundland—it was to be an Anglo-American airway. Imperial formed a new company, Imperial Atlantic Airways, to share a flight-for-flight transatlantic schedule with Pan Am.[20] Representatives of Britain, Ireland, and Canada met in Washington in 1936 to discuss mutual landing rights. Pan Am was permitted to land in Nova Scotia, Newfoundland or Bermuda, and Ireland, with the United States granting reciprocal rights. Negotiations lasted into spring of 1937, but a fifteen-year contract was hammered out for two British and two American flights per week. The catch was a clause mandating both services open simultaneously.[21]

Trippe picked John Leslie to head the new Atlantic Division. The guiding principle was to draw from throughout the System, particularly Pacific Division employees now experienced in transoceanic service.[22] In 1933, Pan Am had acquired a seaplane base at Port Washington, Long Island, which now served as a temporary base for Atlantic survey flights and the start of Bermuda service, while they developed new airports in Baltimore and New York.

By 1937, the Atlantic Division moved its base of operations and Bermuda service to the new $600,000 municipal airport in Baltimore. The first Bermuda flight departed November 14.[23] Operating experience in Bermuda included successful installation of "de-icer" equipment, a first for an aircraft the size of the S-42, and the reciprocal use of foreign-owned maintenance facilities and radio stations, "a condition that would inevitably be encountered in the operation of a transatlantic service," notes a Pan Am document.[24] Pan Am was ready to begin transatlantic service—but Imperial was not, forcing a delay.

Trippe was busy negotiating with Portugal for rights to fly the strategic Azores and Portuguese Guinea on Africa's bulging west coast. On April 3, 1937, Trippe won a twenty-five-year monopoly of landing rights in Horta in the Azores, and a franchise to Lisbon that excluded other American companies. In turn, the British obtained similar rights from Portugal. "It was a diplomatic triumph for Trippe which, however, was not appreciated by the

Roosevelt administration, and in the end hardened its desire to control such affairs," noted historian Josephson.[25]

By 1939, the British were still not ready to start Atlantic commercial service but granted Pan Am permission to start.[26] "Shortly before this British consent was received, arrangements had been made with France for transatlantic landing privileges," Cooper reflected. "Whether this influenced the British decision to authorize the opening of United States service to Britain before Britain was ready to start its reciprocal service I have never known."[27]

Pan Am had its own delays in the contracted Boeing Clippers, but was otherwise ready, pending approval from the new Civil Aeronautics Board. Harold Gray, now chief pilot of the Atlantic Division, spent almost a year in Seattle for test flights at Boeing and knew the challenges of building the whale-like 314-class. "Problems included the vertical tail had to be tripled to make the plane fly right; another problem was 'porpoising [up and down pitching] on take-off,'" Gray noted. "In short, all was not known about very large airplanes. Boeing was pushing into new territory . . . Pan Am's selecting Boeing had been an act of faith. . . ."[28]

Finally, on January 27, 1939, the first Boeing 314, called the *California Clipper*, was delivered at Astoria, Oregon. It would be added to the Pacific Fleet, crippled by the mysterious loss of the *Hawaii Clipper* the previous summer. The first Super Clipper delivered to the Atlantic Division was the Boeing 314 NC-18603, which arrived at Baltimore on February 24. First Lady Eleanor Roosevelt christened it the *Yankee Clipper* at a March 3 ceremony at the Naval Air Station at Anacostia, Washington, D.C., where notables included Army Air Corps Chief Arnold. The *Yankee Clipper* was selected to make the first transatlantic commercial flight.[29]

Despite his ouster, Trippe remained the visionary voice for Pan Am and international aviation. In a 1939 radio address titled "America Unlimited," he returned to his favorite theme—aviation as a continuum of the nation's pioneering past and engine of its promising future. He hailed the *California Clipper*, which on August 22 took off from its new base, a manmade island in San Francisco Bay, on an 8,000-mile survey to New Zealand by way of

Hawaii, Canton Island, and New Caledonia. Unmentioned was aviation's resiliency—the survey was revisiting the airway where the *Samoan Clipper* exploded, killing Captain Musick and crew.[30]

Pan Am applied for a Certificate of Public Convenience and Necessity to engage in scheduled air transport of passengers, freight, and mail between the U.S. and Europe on February 13.[31] The Certificate was granted on May 19, and the next day, the twelfth anniversary of Lindbergh's transatlantic flight, Pan Am launched its first commercial flight to Europe. Both historic events were celebrated during Aviation Day at the New York World's Fair, the highlight being a flyover of the Europe-bound Super Clipper.

On the other side of the continent, another world's fair was showcasing Pan Am's Pacific operation.

★

The Golden Gate International Exposition of 1939–1940 celebrated completion of twin "spans of steel," the San Francisco-Oakland Bay Bridge and Golden Gate Bridge. The Exposition site represented a third engineering wonder—a virtually manmade island adjacent to Yerba Buena Island christened "Treasure Island," its name inspired by Robert Louis Stevenson's classic adventure tale.[32]

"At about the time the two bridges were being woven into the bay region's design of living, Treasure Island was rising from the rocky shoals just north of Yerba Buena Island," chronicled a Federal Writers Project report. "When the job was completed a 400-acre island . . . had replaced the shoals once feared by seamen. Built to support the $50,000,000 Golden Gate International Exposition, Treasure Island is destined to become, when the Exposition closes, a terminal for the graceful Pacific Clippers that fly to Hawaii, the Philippines and the Orient."[33]

The plans included a seaplane and land plane airport. Treasure Island was also built for immediate occupancy by PAA's Pacific Division, with flying boats arriving and departing on schedule from the Port of Trade Winds, the protected lagoon that became known as Clipper Cove. The Exposition opened February 18, 1939, and five days later the *California Clipper* left Treasure Island on its inaugural flight, and the New Zealand survey departed that August.[34]

A causeway from Yerba Buena Island to Treasure Island connected automobile traffic coming off the new Bay Bridge. A Federal Writers Project reporter romantically described the first view driving off the causeway "like a 'stately pleasure dome,' conjured up by the magic of modern science from Kublai Khan's Xanadu. By night this unearthly effect is enhanced by panchromatic floodlighting which transforms the exposition's towers and pavilions into a floating city of emerald and vermilion palaces."[35]

There were national pavilions from France, Italy, and Norway, but the Exposition had a special Pacific and Latin American flavor. Japan was represented in its Samurai House and Temple pavilion that featured feudal period architecture, a meditative garden, and a traditional bridge over a serene lagoon.[36] *Pacifica*, a gigantic Amazonian figure sculpted by Ralph Stackpole, symbolized peaceful cooperation between the Americas and her Pacific neighbors.

The pavilions would be taken down after the Exposition ended, but the hangars and airport infrastructure would remain. The Exposition Company managing the Fair operated out of the four-story semicircular Administration Building, which also headquartered Pan Am's Pacific operation on the first, third, and fourth floors of the south wing.[37]

One hangar housed the Hall of Air Transportation where the "complete Trans-Pacific base of Pan-American Airways is presented to public view as an 'airline under glass,'" noted the official guidebook. An overhead platform provided a spectacular view of Clippers being serviced, refueled, and readied for flight.[38] Every Monday, the scheduled outbound Clipper made a four-hour test flight. On Tuesday mornings, fairgoers could watch a returning Clipper dock at Clipper Cove, and that afternoon the outbound flying boat would wing westward over Treasure Island and the Golden Gate.[39] The sight of Clippers over Treasure Island became an iconic image of the era.

On the other side of the continent, Pan Am's start of transatlantic service neatly coincided with the New York World's Fair set to open on 1,200 acres of the reclaimed ash heaps of Flushing Meadows on April 30, 1939. Fifty-eight nations were participating, Germany not among them. The fair's symbols were the 610-foot spire dubbed the Trylon, and the Perisphere, a 180-foot diameter sphere housing a diorama of a utopian city.

On April 20, four days after the *Yankee Clipper* completed a survey flight of the Northern transatlantic route, Trippe addressed the Merchants Association of New York's pre-fair "Banquet of the World of Tomorrow." Trippe's speech, "Aviation in the World of Tomorrow," acknowledged war clouds gathering and the reality of four-engine bombers capable of flying 20,000 feet, far beyond "the small, lumbering bombers" of World War I. But aviation's peaceful potential outweighed military purposes, he declared—in fact, aviation was the incarnation of the glorious future the fair was anticipating. In tomorrow's world, there would be no limits to the size of aircraft and research indicated airplanes of the future would fly "as swift as the speed of sound."

"Today, as the World of Tomorrow dawns, America's Yankee Clippers are ready to cross the last frontier of aviation—the spanning of the Atlantic Ocean, in regular service to link the new world and the old in twenty-four hours of travel time," Trippe told his audience. "New York, through the efforts of so many of you here this evening, will serve, with Baltimore, as the North Atlantic terminal for the Transatlantic service. At the very doorstep of the World's Fair [there] will shortly be opened, a great air terminal for the World of Tomorrow—a fifty million dollar project which will give to New York City—and to America—the honor of having the greatest air terminal in the world."[40]

Trippe's World of Tomorrow was manifest on May 20. The morning began with a pre-departure ceremony at Port Washington, where Harllee Branch, representing the CAB, officially presented the certificate to Trippe. By 1:08 p.m., the *Yankee Clipper* departed with airmail for Europe. As it circled above the Aviation Day festivities, Captain A. E. LaPorte was in radio communication with distinguished guests and, through loudspeaker connections, the crowd. Speakers included New York Mayor Fiorello La

Guardia, future admiral Captain John H. Towers, Major General D.C. Emmons of the Army Air Corps, and Aviation Day chairman, Pan Am director Thomas Morgan. As with the Pacific opening, Roosevelt saluted the occasion via telegram: "Pan American Airways deserves great credit for bringing about this new era in Transatlantic communications. . . . Hearty congratulations and wishes for an endless succession of happy landings."[41]

A day after departure the Clipper landed in Lisbon and the day after that was in Marseilles, where it picked up mail for the U.S., returning to Port Washington on May 27. The Clipper carried 1,804 pounds of mail to Europe, returning with 2,025 pounds.[42] On June 28, passenger service began. Pan Am's twice-weekly flights took two separate routes: North Atlantic through Nova Scotia, Newfoundland, and Ireland to Southampton, England; the mid-Atlantic through Bermuda and the Azores to Lisbon and Marseilles. When winter weather arrived, both biweekly schedules would fly the mid-Atlantic route.[43]

★

Decades later, New York fairgoer Gilda Snow recalled the day—September 1, 1939—when the happy façade of the World of Tomorrow came tumbling down. "We were going up this huge, beautiful walkway, with flowers all around us," Snow recalled as she and her father approached the Polish pavilion. "But as soon as we got up to the building, the lights went out. My father, he figured they had an electrical short, because the rest of the fair was all lit up. And then we heard over a loudspeaker that Germany had just invaded Poland, and that they were closing down that pavilion. And that, of course, was the beginning of the war."[44]

Roosevelt called Congress to a special session to amend the Neutrality Act. In a blow to the growing isolationist movement, new legislation passed on November 4 allowed England and France to purchase arms on a "cash and carry" basis. The spirit of neutrality remained in other aspects, including U.S. ships having to dock with neutral nations and not enter combat zones, as defined by the president. There were further changes later that month when an amendment allowed armed U.S. merchant ships bound for the U.K. to sail through war zones.[45]

Less than four months into transatlantic service, Pan Am's stops at Southampton and Marseilles were now war zones and immediately canceled. In October, service to Foynes, Ireland, was suspended according to the original cold weather plan to shift to the mid-Atlantic, but Foynes's subsequent designation as a combat zone made it off-limits. From October 3 on, the schedule operated along the mid-Atlantic route to Lisbon.[46]

Rather than cripple transatlantic air service, the war created an unexpected demand for it. John Cooper later expressed incredulity the Atlantic began with such limited service. "When I look back over the long and tortuous course of those negotiations and recall that everyone was quite satisfied with an exchange of landing rights for only two British and two United States flights per week, I realize how little we understood . . . the tremendous increases in the volume of air commerce soon to come," he wrote.[47]

With the war in Europe, competition with domestic carriers wanting to fly the Atlantic, and the need for innovation—the era of land planes was upon them—Pan Am's board returned to the architect of its success. Juan Trippe was voted back into power as chief executive officer on January 23, 1940. His indispensability became obvious in the months following the coup—almost any significant question or problem had the same response: "Ask Trippe." *Time* noted that when those "ask Trippe" questions were posed to the man himself, the answers kept getting shorter. Industry gossip was Trippe would quit unless restored to power.[48]

Trippe picked up where he left off. Pan Am, investigating an alternate westbound South Atlantic route to avoid daunting headwinds, was considering an African base in Bolama on the coast of Portuguese Guinea. Negotiations with Portugal stretched from July 4 through September 13, 1940, but were successful. On January 22, 1941, Roosevelt signed a CAB-approved temporary amendment to Pan Am's transatlantic certification allowing a stop in Africa. By November of 1941, Natal, on Brazil's Atlantic coastline, became a stop. "America's merchant marine of the air, for the first time, was in the position to become an operating factor in the South Atlantic," reported Pan Am's in-house *New Horizons* magazine.[49]

On May 25, 1940, the New York World's Fair marked another black day when the tricolor flag of France atop its national pavilion was lowered to half-staff—France had fallen. Although more than twenty-five million visited the fair, when it closed in 1940 (strangely, on Halloween), the promise of Tomorrow had been snuffed out. The spirit of war was in the air—when the great symbols of the Trylon and Perisphere were torn down, the three thousand tons of steel wreckage was donated to the military.[50]

In San Francisco Bay, the wondrous island Exposition that had been illuminated each night shone for the last time on September 29, 1940.

"[W]e have been joyously tending our garden while all around us the world has been bent on destruction," Exposition President Marshall Dill said in the last speech of the closing ceremonies. "I like to think that all the peaceful legions that have trouped through this fair have had their spiritual wells deepened and are now prepared for whatever Fate may have in store . . . 'The feast is over and the lamps expire.'"[51]

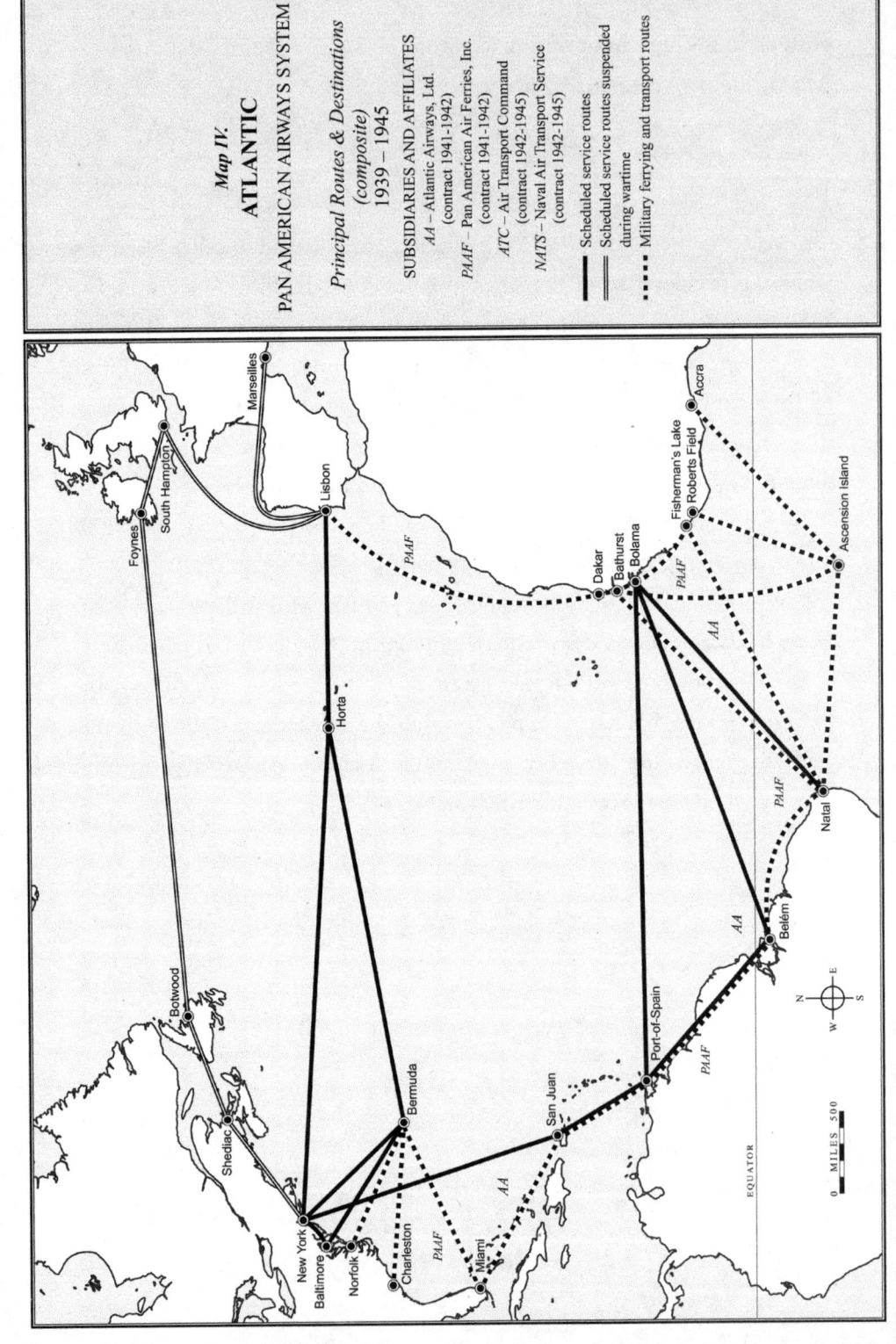

*Map IV.*
ATLANTIC
PAN AMERICAN AIRWAYS SYSTEM

*Principal Routes & Destinations*
*(composite)*
1939 – 1945

SUBSIDIARIES AND AFFILIATES

AA – Atlantic Airways, Ltd.
(contract 1941-1942)
PAAF – Pan American Air Ferries, Inc.
(contract 1941-1942)
ATC – Air Transport Command
(contract 1942-1945)
NATS – Naval Air Transport Service
(contract 1942-1945)

▬▬ Scheduled service routes
═══ Scheduled service routes suspended during wartime
▪▪▪▪ Military ferrying and transport routes

# PART III

# WARTIME MISSIONS

## CHAPTER 15
# THE SECRET PLAN

*"The Secretary of War classified the contract SECRET. . . . The conditions and developments in Europe necessitated speed if we were to be prepared to defend this hemisphere or to move aircraft rapidly for the defense of Panama, Alaska or the South American bulge. . . . Airdromes could not have been built in foreign countries as a U.S. Government project. They could only be constructed in the time available by utilizing agreements in existence between Pan American Airways and the Governments concerned. . . ."*

—Major General Clayton Bissell, reporting on the secret Airport Development Program between the U.S. and Pan Am[1]

Nazi Germany and Fascist Italy exhibited their air prowess on American soil during the 1933–'34 Chicago World's Fair. Warmly received was a fleet of twenty-four Italian flying boats commanded by Italo Balbo that had flown from Italy. But the *Graf Zeppelin* that traveled to the "Century of Progress Exhibition" and hovered over Chicago was, for many, a disquieting reminder of the new Germany. A few years later, Juan and Betty Trippe took a trip around the world, stopping at Seven Oaks to visit the Lindberghs before traveling to Berlin, where Juan met with Lufthansa officials and air power leader Erhard Milch at the Air Ministry. The open talk of military aviation and war startled Trippe.

Juan Trippe would remember Erhard Milch as "a personal friend." But Trippe wasn't expecting the letter signed by Milch that arrived at his New York office via Clipper from Lisbon around the summer of '39 that proposed dividing up the world's airways. The letter suggested Milch was ordered directly by Hitler to see if Trippe might find out if the U.S. government "would be interested in an arrangement in having the western hemisphere be our zone and the Germans would consider Europe and Russia as their zone and the question of Africa would be settled later," Trippe recalled. "[T]hey didn't want to take this up in government channels, but would a senior member of our government be interested?" Representatives would meet in neutral Lisbon for talks; if there were no response, Germany would know there was no interest. Trippe turned the letter over to Secretary of State Hull.[2]

Germany established its foreign aviation interests under its government-owned monopoly, Deutsche Lufthansa. In Latin America, the cartel included Condor, which expanded into Argentina and Chile in 1934 and 1935. In 1937, Deutsche Lufthansa was in Buenos Aires, where there was linkage with Air France and the airline of Fascist Italy, *Linee Aeree Transcontinentali Italiane* (LATI).[3] In June of 1939, LATI began semi-monthly passenger service from Rome to Rio through Natal and Recife. By December, LATI was a cover for a Fascist espionage ring in Brazil and served German airlines in South America, including *Sociedad Colombo-Alemana de Transportes Aéreos*.[4] Despite Pan Am's secret control, SCADTA was infiltrated by Nazi zealots.

In March of 1939, Condor and LATI's presence on Brazil's coastline triggered hemispheric security talks between the State Department, War Department, Navy, and Civil Aeronautics Board. The problem was the U.S. could not make overt moves against foreign companies operating under the laws of other governments. "It was almost impossible for the United States, a neutral country, to cut off the fuel supplies to [Condor and LATI] without some provocation, and both Condor and LATI were meticulously careful not to give the United States such an opportunity," chronicles the U.S. Air Force's official South Atlantic history. The "German airlines cartel... had the final effect of consolidating all of the principal non-American enterprises, so that at the beginning of the war the lines were clearly drawn. There was one Axis combine, easy to identify. Nor, as it turned out, was it difficult to fight. For against it there was our own monopoly [Pan Am]."[5]

Pan Am and its Latin American affiliates were perfect surrogates for "delousing" or "de-Germanization," as the campaign against Axis-airlines in the Americas was called. One tactic was to work with sympathetic governments to nationalize commercial air service, as happened with Bolivia's airline, *Lloyd Aéreo Boliviano* (LAB), founded in 1925 by German interests. By early 1941, Deutsche Lufthansa had offered the Bolivians a newly upgraded fleet of planes in exchange for a stock swap, which would have put the airline under complete pro-Nazi control. Panagra, the Pan American-Grace Airways partnership, came up with an alternative agreement in coordination with the Bolivian government and the U.S. State Department. The highest levels of Panagra—president Harold J. Roig, vice presidents Harold R. Harris, Douglas Campbell, and Gustavo Vidal—were directly involved in negotiations with Secretary of State Cordell Hull, Douglas Jenkins, State's representative in Bolivia, and the Bolivian Cabinet. Vidal, who was company controller, took point in implementing the "reorganization." On May 6, the Bolivian government issued a decree nationalizing LAB.[6] The outstanding privately held stock, mostly in the hands of German shareholders, was purchased at a fair market price. Panagra was contracted to manage the airline and run its operations system-wide—immediately, all Germans employees were dismissed. The U.S. Defense Supplies Corporation provided the new operator with three Lockheed Lodestars, and capital advances that would reach $600,000.[7]

Competition was another means—Pan American-Grace's expansion served the interests of the U.S., and the Allies, "thus eliminating an additional 2,800 miles of Axis-controlled air lines in South America," notes a period Pan Am document. In addition to Bolivia, this included Ecuador, where expansion targeted the German-controlled airline *Sociedad Ecuatoriana de Transportes Aéreos* (SEDTA), effectively driving them out of business.[8]

SCADTA, the perennial antagonist, was atop the "delousing" list. That effort began in 1938, when Trippe informed the State Department that

Hitler's government wanted complete control of SCADTA and was pressuring Dr. von Bauer. Ironically, von Bauer and some of his German colleagues were out of step with Hitler's regime. "In retrospect, the founders, pioneers, and senior personnel of SCADTA were strongly German but not of a class prone to enchantment by Nazi doctrines—quite the contrary," John Leslie noted. "Nevertheless, the Nazi Party apparently did penetrate the German community in Bogotá and the true power in the Embassy was said to be a representative of the Nazi Party who sat in the back room. By 1937, also, the Nazis had begun infiltrating the SCADTA pilot group. The company had always found its pilots in Germany, most of them graduates of the German Government Transport Pilots School . . . young men of good family and education. Then the first classes of Nazi-selected, Nazi-indoctrinated pilots began to come out of Colombia. . . . They wanted a voice in the management . . . they attacked von Bauer as a Jew."[9]

Herbert Boy, a German pilot in the Great War and one of SCADTA's founders and a colonel in Colombia's Air Force, confirmed the threat: "The Reich exerted its influence throughout the world, relying on Germans outside the country and, therefore, the Ministry of Aviation endeavored to intervene in the internal affairs of SCADTA. . . . Pilots newly arrived in Colombia were imbued with the [Nazi] ideology then prevailing in Germany."[10]

Pan Am's secret ownership made it tricky to purge SCADTA. In Colombia, only former president Enrique Olaya Herrera knew about the deal, Colonel Boy recalled. Trippe always claimed U.S. State Department officials knew, including former Secretary of State Frank Kellogg and former Assistant Secretary of State Francis White. And Pan Am's 1931 annual report recorded acquisition of "a substantial interest in SCADTA." By 1939 and the start of the de-Germanization campaign, the State Department began inquiring about the extent of that "substantial interest."[11] Trippe finally revealed the secret arrangement, which was a shock to Colombia's current president, Eduardo Santos.

SCADTA was a crusade for Spruille Braden, a Yale man and former mining engineer appointed U.S. ambassador to Colombia in 1938. Braden, noticing the national airline's abundance of German pilots and personnel, was convinced that somewhere, probably the lonely prairies outside Bogotá, Germans were secretly building air bases to attack the Panama Canal. When it was finally revealed that Pan Am owned the foreign airline that Braden considered a Trojan Horse, he accused Trippe and his airline of being Nazi sympathizers.[12]

Meanwhile, the Nazi Air Ministry, on the pretext of defining Colonel Herbert Boy's military status, summoned him to Berlin where "high officials" (Boy does not name them), declared Dr. von Bauer, as a private citizen, could not be a majority stockholder in SCADTA. Boy was to order him to turn over his shares to the German government immediately.

Boy visited von Bauer at his villa in Klagenfurt, Austria, and delivered the Reich's message. He seemed "visibly concerned," Boy noticed, although he did not then know von Bauer's holdings were in escrow and his secret commitments prevented him from delivering his shares. "I must admit that I was then under the impression that von Bauer was sole owner of a majority of SCADTA stock, being completely unaware of his obligations under the terms of the gentleman's agreement . . . with Pan American Airways," Boy wrote. "For this reason, I did not hide from von Bauer my concern for the measures which the German Government would doubtless take against him if he did not put at their disposal his block of SCADTA shares." Von Bauer asked Boy to inform the Air Ministry that obligations to his airline prevented him from immediately fulfilling their command. He was only buying time to escape Europe.

"On returning to Berlin to render account of my conversation with von Bauer," Boy adds, "I found the attitude in the Ministry much more severe than on my first visit and I was coldly informed that von Bauer would be summoned directly to discuss the situation. Von Bauer succeeded in leaving Europe, not without certain difficulties."[13]

Pan Am's de-Germanization campaign in Colombia started slowly, not only because of the secret ownership issue but because this was the period during which Whitney replaced Trippe. After the disclosure of Pan Am's control, the U.S. insisted that Colombian military officials ride as observers on all flights commanded by German pilots and that navigation and radio direction-finding systems be "Americanized" so Pan Am could monitor the true bearing of all flights. President Santos acquiesced on such points, but maintained that Colombia was neutral and could not forcibly remove personnel because of their German heritage—many, in fact, were Colombian citizens.[14]

By 1940, with Trippe back in power, Pan Am moved ahead with the purge, stressing secrecy and surprise. At times, the operation had the cloak and dagger trappings of a spy novel. Bill Del Valle, Pan Am's representative at Boeing, was secretly sent to the American embassy in Bogotá and a meeting with Ambassador Braden, Pan Am vice president George Rihl, and Captain "Hank" Shea. In a room darkened by drawn curtains and lit by flickering candles on a concert piano, Braden described a German plot to blow up the Canal. Del Valle was to be slipped into SCADTA as assistant superintendent of maintenance and, under the guise of inspection tours, evaluate essential, and expendable, German employees. Reportedly, Del Valle found no evidence of Nazi plots.

But the U.S. could no longer wait on removing Germans, given Nazi victories were coming with brutal regularity—the occupation of France finally compelled President Santos to back off from protecting German crews.[15] Trippe was upgrading SCADTA's fleet, and new planes provided cover for bringing in American personnel. A preview of commercial aviation's future was the four-engine Boeing 307 Stratoliner land plane, the world's first pressurized commercial airliner that could fly above bad weather. "High Road to Rio" would be a Pan Am slogan—and when it made its inaugural landing in Barranquilla to fanfare and speeches, Pan Am employees disguised as tourists quietly off-boarded. Spanish-speaking girls comprising a covert secretarial pool were flown into Barranquilla and ensconced at the Del Prado Hotel, where they spent two days typing dismissal letters for an estimated 170 German employees. By June 12, a Friday afternoon, Rihl gave the go-ahead—the Germans were summarily fired, with Del Valle handing out dismissal letters to the shocked assembly.[16]

After escaping to New York, von Bauer met with Trippe, "who endorsed and agreed to back the idea of nationalizing the SCADTA company, thereby demonstrating his breadth of judgment and understanding of the problems being faced in Colombia," Boy recalled.[17] They changed the name to Avianca and effected a merger with Saco, another Colombian airline. Pan Am's interest was reduced to 64 percent, while a 1938 law provided that Colombians would ultimately own a majority of stock.[18]

The year 1940 marked a turning point for the neutral United States. The Military Appropriation Act passed on June 13 allowed the president to authorize and fund wartime projects secretly. On September 2, Roosevelt and Churchill announced that in exchange for fifty American destroyers, Great Britain would grant America leases of ninety-nine years on sites from British Guiana to Newfoundland. On September 16, Roosevelt signed the Selective Service Act, the first peacetime draft in the nation's history.[19]

Pan Am opened the way for the strategic use of American air power in South America. A September 1940 *Time* article said it all in its headline: "Two Days Less to Rio." Previously, Pan Am flights from Miami were a five-day, 5,777-mile trip, with flying boats hugging Brazil's Atlantic coastline, that stretch alone counting for two days and 2,525-miles. But a modern Pan Am land plane airport was being carved out of the jungle in Barreiras, in Central Brazil, to facilitate a new "cut-off" route that abandoned the seacoast schedule. *Time* reported: "Next week Douglas DC-3s will take over from Belém, fly 1,530 miles across country to Rio in nine hours, pausing briefly halfway at the new forest-shrouded airport at Barreiras." It was a big step for "seagoing Pan Am," which would feature the high-altitude Excalibur land plane under construction at Lockheed's factory in Burbank. On the drawing board was a 300-mile-per-hour "plane of the future" capable of departing Rio in the morning and reaching Miami by evening. *Time* added a prescient note about the new airport: "It is also an excellent potential base for U.S. Army planes."[20]

The first week in July of 1940, the U.S. asked Pan Am to undertake an even bigger mission than the on-going de-Germanization campaign.

Curiously, when Trippe was called to Washington to meet with the president on an urgent matter of national security, Pan Am was fighting off the challenge of American Export Airlines (AEA), an Atlantic rival the administration strongly supported. In meetings that included Roosevelt and Secretary of War Stimson, Trippe was asked if Pan Am and its Latin American subsidiaries would secretly build a chain of land airports and seaplane bases, financed with 12 million dollars under the Military Appropriation Act.[21]

Plans for the Airport Development Program (ADP) had been coalescing since the previous year's high-level hemispheric defense discussions. The program, first considered as a means for solidifying defense of the Panama Canal as the conduit for American sea power, changed with the fall of France. Germany now had a foothold in French-controlled territory in West Africa, notably Dakar.[22] Brazil, the strategic jumping off place for Africa, was key to the ADP and its next phase—a ferrying and trans-Africa airway to deliver airplanes and war materials to British forces in North Africa. The State Department, part of the chorus wanting to break Pan Am's international air monopoly, initially opposed the plan. But Neutrality Act restraints made secrecy paramount and other options, such as creating a new government agency or contracting directly with South American governments, were too time consuming or unworkable.[23]

Major General Clayton Bissell, then a member of the War Plans Division of the War Department General Staff in Washington, recalled, "Pan American Airways was the only American owned foreign airline in existence and the only American aviation enterprise operating in the countries concerned. . . . The reason for entering into the construction and maintenance program was military in anticipation [the U.S. would get in the war]. . . . The conditions and developments in Europe necessitated speed if we were to be prepared to defend this hemisphere or to move aircraft rapidly for the defense of Panama, Alaska or the South American bulge." Although American construction crews would be used, and Pan Am was given freedom to do so, "on a large scale, it would have been obvious immediately that the program was not a commercial airline aviation undertaking and the countries involved would possibly not have permitted the work to proceed."[24]

From the government's viewpoint, the ADP was legal. Unlike the normal appropriations process, the financing tapped into emergency funds designed for just such a discretionary—and secret—program. General of the Army George C. Marshall called the proposed contract with Pan Am "more essential to our national defense than any other single matter."[25]

Trippe said no.

"Considerable difficulties were encountered in securing Pan American Airways acceptance of the contract," Bissell noted. "They risked their rights in the Latin American countries concerned and prejudicing their status as a commercial airline."[26]

Pan Am's Brazilian affiliate, *Panair do Brasil* feared postwar reprisals if it became known they were complicit in "American imperialist expansion."[27] Trippe characterized the ADP as "very awkward . . . we lost some Directors and it caused great concern. . . . Pan Am didn't want to be known as an agent of the U.S. military and government."[28]

But Trippe wanted to serve his country, and that was the telling argument. "It was the patriotic thing to do . . . there are certain things done abroad by us and our government that can't be done under government auspices," he explained. "American companies have historically done this and Pan Am was no slacker."

Trippe concluded his airline had the legal right to undertake the ADP. Pan Am subsidiaries were always working with their national governments on expanding airline infrastructure and the new long-range, heavier aircraft required stronger runways, while the growing popularity of air travel necessitated airport expansion and modernization. "The U.S. Government need not be invoked," Trippe concluded. "[If] the U.S. wanted to subsidize us, there was no reason for them not to. There was nothing legally wrong, as long as we did it as a Pan Am project. There was no change in the local laws. We had the authority. We had to get permission for new airports. This is the same as with the first airports we built."[29]

But the ADP was not business as usual. "The territorial rights were being pre-empted," Trippe later acknowledged, even placing it in context—how would America feel if Canada began building air bases in the U.S.? "Nobody was being fooled," Trippe concluded.[30]

The ADP became an open secret among Latin American governments. "That this [the Amapa airfield] . . . the real sponsor was not Panair was thoroughly understood in the capital, too," the Air Force South Atlantic history notes. "On June 16, 1941, an official of the Brazilian embassy in Washington admitted that air bases had been negotiated. . . ."[31]

To run the secret operation, Pan Am incorporated a "dummy subsidiary" in Delaware called "Pan American Airports Corporation." "Then the parent company, in turn, would arrange with its foreign subsidiaries, *Panair do Brasil, Compana Mexicana* and *Compania Nacional Cubana*, for the construction work," records the Air Force's history. "The arrangement would please the military because necessary wartime preparation could begin; and the Department of State would approve because the position of the United States as a neutral would not be weakened; the device of a succession of agencies put the government, which was paying for the fields, so far away from the Airport Development Program which would build them, that the connection could not be proven, no matter how apparent it was."[32]

The "Contract between the United States of America and Pan American Airports Corporation" was secretly entered into on November 2, 1940, for "the purpose of developing and assisting in the development of airfields and other facilities for the defense of the Western hemisphere," the contract stipulated. Henry L. Stimson, Secretary of War, signed for the government, and Vice President John C. Cooper signed for the airline. As the agreement explained, the president, on the advice of the Chief of Staff of the Army and the Chief of Naval Operations of the Navy, determined that national security required the construction of new land airports and seaplane bases, improvement of existing bases, and additional construction of buildings and infrastructure, such as radio and meteorological facilities "with all practicable speed."[33]

The new and improved bases and facilities were to be made available to the U.S. Army, Navy, Marine Corps, and Coast Guard (providing authorization from the respective governments, of course). Work sites included Amapa, Belém, São Luíz, Fortaleza, Natal, Recife, Maceió—all on Brazil's strategic Atlantic coast. But despite the contractual urgency, the work was as hard a slog as the rainy season in which it began. The airfield at Amapa, as with "jungle airports" at Belém and São Luíz, "had to be built practically from scratch," with native labor hacking through the jungle with machetes and hoes. At São Luíz teams of oxen hauled uprooted trees in rough-hewn carts while a thousand burros carried dirt away in raffia panniers. There were delays in survey and construction permits, even the search for suitable landing fields.[34] Axis interests were aware of ADP, putting the program on guard against sabotage.

But Pan Am was winning the hemispheric de-Germanization campaign. By their estimates, in September of 1939, German airlines in Bolivia, Colombia, Ecuador, Peru, Chile, and a Trans-Andean operation in Chile-Argentina controlled 12,273 miles, compared to 5,734 miles of U.S. airways; by September of '41 Axis airlines had only 870 miles, compared to 15,928 for the U.S.[35]

But along the coast of Brazil, LATI and Condor remained entrenched, each with airbases and facilities near ADP sites and sometimes at them. At Recife, LATI maintained a radio station and shared the old Air France airfield where ADP was enlarging the runway—the Italian planes operating there were reportedly "almost grazing the heads of A.D.P. workmen."[36]

Juan Trippe was concerned about pro-Nazi infiltration within Pan Am's own operations in Brazil. He asked the War Department, Military Intelligence Division, to investigate and on August 28, 1940, Brigadier General Sherman Miles reported they had identified six suspects. Miles also suggested the chief of Pan Am's map section in Rio, an Austrian refugee believed to be anti-Nazi, "might be of service in your investigation." Trippe passed the information to Vice President Evan Young, whose purview included the Brazilian operations. In a follow-up letter to Miles, Trippe conveyed his appreciation for the help "in weeding out undesirable alien elements among our personnel."

The favor was returned the following month when the Navy Department Office of Naval Intelligence, in a confidential letter to Trippe, reported that Commander Yositane Kisaka was retiring as Assistant Naval Attaché in Washington and planning to return to Japan from San Francisco by Clipper on September 24. "For official and confidential reasons affecting the national interest, it is desirable that neither this officer nor any Japanese naval or military officer be permitted to take passage on this route," the letter advised. On September 30, Trippe received a letter from the Under Secretary at the State Department in thanks for "apprising me of cancellation of a transpacific flight reservation."[37]

★

By 1941, LATI and Condor were openly working for Axis interests. LATI's passenger lists were made up of Lufthansa pilots who were naturalized Brazilian citizens but returning to Germany for Luftwaffe duty. The Italian line also flew off-course over the ocean to inspect targets for German submarines.[38] Reports conveyed that if LATI's fuel supply were cut off, the Germans would deliver a cargo of gasoline drums to them from Dakar, the French colony on the African coast.[39] It was suspected that Condor's seaplane base at Natal was radioing Berlin about ship and plane movements, but no evidence was found. The search even led to a seminary where five German Catholic priests lived—again, no clandestine spy station. Frustrated local authorities simply padlocked Condor's radio facilities.[40]

Natal was a hotbed of intrigue, particularly after an American military survey mission in July of 1941 concluded it was a likely landing place in an Axis invasion.[41] Harold Sims, U.S. vice counsel at Natal, was always on the lookout for potential threats. In a March 22, 1941, report to Jefferson Caffery, U.S. ambassador to Brazil stationed in Rio, Sims reported that LATI appeared to be storing fuel "in small lots throughout the interior or along the coast, either for use by airplanes or thirsty submarines."[42] In a confidential May 5,

1941, memo to Caffery, Sims reported his suspicions that Panair's manager was "definitely detrimental to our work here . . . by virtue of the fact that he has some business relations with LATI, CONDOR and AIR FRANCE, and full access to Parnamarin [sic] field where Panair is to build a base, he might be slowing down the activity."[43] On August 14, Sims reported to the U.S. Secretary of State that a flammable bomb was ignited in a Standard Oil warehouse near the ADP base, but an alert night watchman extinguished the fire. In November, Sims reported to Caffery that a Japanese diplomat named Masakatsu Nosaki spent three days in Natal taking photographs of ADP work and was inexplicably left alone by police, although assumptions were that it was due to his diplomatic status.[44]

U.S. Military Intelligence Division reports were concerned about the ambiguity of Brazil President Getúlio Vargas' allegiance. Ambassador Caffery later reflected, confidentially, "had President Vargas not come over to our side, we would have been compelled, I assume, to occupy Northeast Brazil by force of arms."[45]

The prevailing sentiment was that the U.S. not impose its will militarily—it didn't need to. It was determined that General Gomes, Brazil's air commander of the Natal-Recife area, was in control of Brazil's strategic northeast and his good will would facilitate the U.S. military presence. Colonel Robert Olds, commander of the Ferrying Command, successfully cultivated Gomes' friendship and cooperation.[46]

---

On May 6, 1940, Roosevelt, speaking before both houses of Congress and, with a bank of radio microphones before him, to the nation, issued a clarion call to meet Germany's air threat. Roosevelt called for production of 50,000 planes a year, an aerial armada that would outstrip current production capacity ten times over. The address celebrated the "toughness of moral and physical fiber" that were "the characteristics of a free people, a people devoted to the institutions they themselves have built." At his conclusion, the joint session echoed with a standing ovation.

In response, a nationwide May 18 radio speech by Colonel Charles Lindbergh decried Roosevelt and his administration for stoking the fires of "defense hysteria," darkly referring to the "small minority of the American people . . . [that] control much of the machinery of influence and propaganda." Lindbergh, who had worked shoulder-to-shoulder with General Arnold and U.S. air power advocates, was now leader of the isolationist America First movement. Roosevelt was a charismatic and garrulous figure, but as first lady Eleanor Roosevelt once remarked, when FDR got angry with someone "he was like an iceberg . . . he could say things that would finish a relationship forever." And Roosevelt was angry with Lindbergh.[47]

In late December 1940, a Roosevelt "fireside chat" radio address declared that America should be the "arsenal of Democracy." The resulting "lend-lease" bill was introduced in the House as H.R. 1776. Lindbergh called the legislation "another step away from democracy and another step closer to war." Senator Robert Taft argued H.R. 1776 would grant the president dictatorial power to conduct wars on a whim and thrust the U.S. into the current conflict in Europe. The counter-argument was that helping America's allies would keep the country out of the war.

Roosevelt used two key emissaries to help the legislation. In early January, Roosevelt sent the first, his trusted special representative Harry Hopkins, via Clipper to England to meet Churchill. During his visit, Hopkins rose during a small dinner party with Churchill and declared, "I suppose you wish to know what I am going to say to President Roosevelt on my return. Well, I'm going to quote you one verse from that Book of Books . . . 'Whither thou goest, I will go and where thou lodgest, I will lodge, thy people shall be my people, and thy God my God!'" Hopkins paused and added his own words: "Even to the end." Tears streamed down Churchill's face.

Historian Doris Kearns Goodwin writes, "With their friendship sealed, Hopkins moved to elicit Churchill's help in the lend-lease debate. In early February, Churchill was working on a major speech to be broadcast throughout the world. At Roosevelt's request, Hopkins asked Churchill to skew the speech to American public opinion by promising that lend-lease was the best means to keep the Americans out of the war."

The second emissary was Wendell L. Willkie, the recently defeated Republican presidential candidate and now Roosevelt's ally, who flew by Clipper to London. Willkie's visit included handing Churchill a letter from Roosevelt that included a Longfellow verse. Willkie was flying home on a historic Clipper flight when Churchill used it in his February 9 radio broadcast in support of H.R. 1776:

"Sail On, O Ship of State!

Sail On, O Union Strong and great!

Humanity with all its fears,

With all the hopes of future years,

Is hanging breathless on thy fate."

"Here is the answer I give to Mr. Roosevelt," the prime minister continued. "Put your confidence in us. . . . Give us the tools and we will finish the job."[48]

## CHAPTER 16
# AIR CARRIER OF THE ARSENAL OF DEMOCRACY

*"Agreements have been concluded under which the Pan American Airways System will ferry aircraft from the United States to West Africa and then will ferry those planes on to the Middle East.*

*"In connection with the ferry system, Pan American Airways is establishing an air transport service from West Africa to the Middle East and plans are underway for a transport service from the United States to West Africa. . . . The ferry system and the transport service provide direct and speedy delivery of aircraft from the 'Arsenal of Democracy' to a critical point in the front against aggression. The importance of this direct line of communication between our country and strategic outposts in Africa cannot be over-estimated."*

—PRESIDENT FRANKLIN ROOSEVELT,
OFFICIAL WHITE HOUSE ANNOUNCEMENT, AUGUST 18, 1941[1]

On February 6, 1941, the shoreline of Bolama in Portuguese Guinea was crowded with 3,000 members of various tribes. They had been amassing for days, the collective excitement and expectation mounting until they finally saw the wonder they awaited—a plane coming in for a landing. "That's not an airplane; it's a steamboat," one tribesman exclaimed in Portuguese as the silver hulled Pan Am flying boat landed.[2]

Pan Am's Boeing 314 *Dixie Clipper* was arriving from Lisbon on a round-trip route proving flight and homeward bound to La Guardia Field. Bolama marked the first time commercial aircraft of U.S. registry had landed in Africa. It was also the first stop on the planned South Atlantic airway across to Port-of-Spain, Trinidad, up to San Juan, Puerto Rico, and on to New York. It was longer, and 2,000 miles farther south of the Lisbon-to-New York route the airline had been flying for two years, but the mid-Atlantic had tough 50-to-60-mile-an-hour headwinds. Reports indicated a westbound South Atlantic course had calmer trade winds, potentially allowing a doubling of payloads.[3]

The flight began on February 1 from La Guardia Field with Captain Marius "Lodi" Lodeesen in command and carrying Civil Aeronautics Board inspectors, Juan Trippe, Harold Bixby, now a PAA vice president, and Captain LaPorte to help evaluate the route's potential. After landing in Lisbon for a two-day layover, Trippe and Bixby inspected the *Aero Porto de Lisboa*, Pan Am's land plane base under construction and scheduled to open by 1942.

Captain Harold Gray, who piloted the regularly scheduled *Yankee Clipper* to Lisbon, took command for the flight home, with three of his earlier passengers boarding the *Dixie*—one was Willkie, returning from London. At the end of the proving flight, Gray and LaPorte confirmed the route's benefits, noting easterly headwinds did not prevail at 8,000 feet or higher. It provided a strategic "aerial Atlantic world," notes historian Jenifer Van Vleck. "Pan Am's *Dixie Clipper* had flown the first commercial air route linking North America, South America, Europe, and Africa."[4]

Upon landing on Bowery Bay at La Guardia Field, Willkie told assembled reporters that Britain stood resolute and united: "Nowhere did I find any trace of defeatism." Trippe told reporters he hoped the Civil Aeronautics Board would grant Pan Am the new route (they did, within forty-eight hours). When reporters asked Gray how the flight went, he replied in the laconic tradition: "Routine."[5]

"When Willkie returned to the States on February 11, he went directly to the Hill to testify in behalf of the lend-lease bill," Goodwin notes. "It was the most important testimony in six weeks of hearings. In a blue suit rumpled from the plane ride, with his hair drooping over one eye and his voice as hoarse as ever, Willkie declared that if we sat back and withdrew within ourselves there was no telling where 'the madmen who are loose in the world' might strike next." In the marble halls of the standing-room-only chamber, with news photographer flashbulbs bursting, Willkie warned fellow Republicans against being "the isolationist party." When committee members brought up his critical comments about Roosevelt during the 1940 presidential campaign, Willkie replied, "He was elected president. He is my president now."[6]

The legislation passed on March 11, 1941. The Office of Lend-Lease Administration was established that August, with Roosevelt appointing Harry Hopkins to head it. The new law allowed the U.S. to maintain neutrality and still provide whatever aid and materials the president deemed "in the interest of national defense."[7]

★

Clippers played a vital role in wartime diplomacy—never before had nations separated by oceans been able to facilitate face-to-face communications so swiftly. Practically overnight, Pan Am became a lifeline. An October 1941 *Life* article observed: "World War II vastly increased the U.S. need for, and diminished its means of, crossing the oceans fast. Pan American Clippers, opportunely installed, put Lisbon within twenty-seven hours and Manila within six days of Washington at the precise juncture in history when this improvement was most essential."[8]

The war created an "astronomical increase" in passengers. "At one time it was estimated that there were 40,000 refugees in Portugal and it seemed that practically every one of them desire to arrange Clipper transportation to the United States," a period Pan Am document chronicles.[9] Two years after transatlantic passenger service began, Clippers had carried 3,600 passengers and flown 14,500,000 revenue passenger miles.[10]

Transatlantic mail service exceeded all expectations. In April of 1939, the Post Office Department estimated Pan Am's annual mail loads to Europe at

136,760 pounds and 50,960 pounds to the United States. Pan Am's projections were more modest: 132,000 outbound, 26,280 pounds homeward. But its first year, Atlantic Clippers flew 242,223 pounds of mail to Europe, returning with 192,540 pounds. Mail loads on individual flights were as high as 13,000 pounds.[11]

Pan Am had the planes and bases, the experience and technical know-how to fly the Pacific, the North, and mid-Atlantic, and had opened the South Atlantic from Brazil to Africa. Pan Am was the obvious partner in the next step of a transatlantic ferrying and transport service to and across Africa.

Arnold pinpointed 1940 as the year it became clear that "a real, honest-to-God air ferry line, and perhaps an air transport line, must be built across the North Atlantic." The Royal Air Force and the Royal Canadian Air Force were trying to operate such service between Newfoundland and England, but combat duty was a priority. "They asked President Roosevelt for help," Arnold noted. "He, in turn, asked me what we could do to assist the British in ferrying the American-built planes to the United Kingdom . . . I suggested that it might be possible for some of our civilian agencies, preferably for one of the air lines, to tackle the job. The President agreed to this plan, which was the start of our overseas Transport Service."[12]

Arnold commissioned the president's son, Elliott, as a captain in the Air Corps. He was criticized for seemingly currying favor, but it was Elliott Roosevelt who proposed and undertook an aerial survey of Greenland's ice cap. The survey would be vital to the survival of pilots and crews making forced landings there. Elliott Roosevelt next made a photographic survey flight over Africa. French colonial outposts had effectively turned over their governments to the Germans and were holding a line of airports from Dakar eastward, almost to Khartoum in the Anglo-Egyptian Sudan.[13] Those bases paralleled the airway Imperial Airways began in 1936, a weekly run from the British base at Takoradi, on Africa's Gold Coast, to Lagos in nearby Nigeria, and Khartoum. The British were attempting a South Atlantic ferrying operation along their old route that fed the stratagems of U.S. military planners who wanted to set up a U.S. supply line from Brazil to Takoradi.[14]

In 1940, ferrying began across the "Takoradi Route" to the Western Desert campaigns in Libya and Egypt.[15] Shipments, notably crated warplanes, were flown to the Takoradi airfield, reassembled, and flown to Egypt by the Royal Air Force. But the operation had problems, including the hardscrabble old Imperial airway itself—"a low-capacity, bush-type operation," Pan Am's corporate history called it.[16]

Solutions were debated between the U.S. and Britain, as well as internally between the British government and its Air Ministry. *Time* subsequently provided an assessment: "The R.A.F., which has for at least six months been ferrying planes from Freetown to Cairo, has lost about 20% of its planes for lack of gadgets and getup necessary for steady, lossless shuttling."[17]

The Air Corps Ferrying Command was created on May 28, 1941, when Roosevelt directed Secretary of War Stimson to have Army seaplanes ferry planes and supplies from U.S. factories to the North Atlantic coast, where the British would take over and ferry them across the ocean. The South Atlantic was also in play—on May 13 Arnold sent Commander Tomlinson a memo titled "Ferry Plan—Takoradi-Cairo," while another memo that day, "Transport Airplane Movement to Africa," was sent by the Air Corps Liaison Office to Assistant Secretary of State Dean Acheson. "There was no established southern ferry route, but the commercial stops and the defense outposts provided one for the asking," the Air Force's history notes. "As the U.S. Air Corps mapped it out, it would go from Tampa or Miami to Trinidad, Belém, Natal, Bathurst and Takoradi."[18]

Having the British operate along the North Atlantic coast would protect American neutrality, but there was a lack of trained personnel. When the depleted forces of Field Marshal Sir Archibald Wavell, British commander-in-chief of the Western Desert campaigns, was routed by a *panzer* counter-offensive by Field Marshal Rommel, and the British suffered defeats in Greece and Crete, it became obvious "the war, whose winning was so much in our interest, would not be won by the British Empire alone—then the direction reversed, and we were in the ferrying business," records the Air Force's South Atlantic history.[19]

Pan Am, called upon to assist the U.S. Army in a South Atlantic ferrying operation, formed another subsidiary, Atlantic Airways, Limited. It began with a State Department call asking Trippe to have twenty Lockheed and Douglas planes flown to the British in Egypt, and to arrange with Robert Cross, president of Lockheed Aircraft, to assemble the necessary crews. Trippe telephoned Cross at his Burbank office, told him of the assignment, and asked if crews could report to Miami in a few days. "Okay," Cross replied. "They will be there."

The Army would ferry warplanes from Los Angeles to Miami, where Atlantic Airways would take over with a crew that included Army personnel. After landing in Natal, Army personnel disembarked, and Pan Am's subsidiary continued to Bathurst. "The presence of the Army crews was significant," the Air Force's South Atlantic history notes, "for it indicated that the Air Corps strongly desired to train its men 'in flights of this nature, and to familiarize them with the terrain over this route,'" quoting an Arnold memo. Seventeen planes were delivered on the first mission.[20] The Air Force's history records it as "a pioneering success. Indisputably, it may be said to have opened the South Atlantic ferrying route. . . . When it was flown, who could have said that planes, crews, parts, supplies computed in thousands would be following? The airports were unbuilt; the United States was not at war; the Ferrying Command was in its infancy and the Air Corps had not yet come to be the Air Forces. . . . But out on the unacknowledged frontiers of the nation an unacknowledged change of mission was already taking place."[21]

★

The day after his May 28 order to Stimson about an air-ferrying operation, Roosevelt reported to Churchill, "I am prepared to direct the Army and Navy to assume full responsibility for the transfer of American-built aircraft from factory to the point of ultimate takeoff and to supply maintenance and servicing facilities along the way and at the ultimate staging field."

On June 3, Churchill's correspondence with Roosevelt emphasized a larger support organization to sustain forces in the Nile Valley. Captain Elliott Roosevelt, who had been in London, suggested Port Sudan or Massawa near Asmara in the Sudan as a potential point for "reception of American materials which you are sending to us in increasing quantities," Churchill reported. "American tanks and American aircraft require a good sprinkling of American civilian volunteer personnel to instruct us in their use and help keep them serviceable."[22]

Roosevelt's June 17 correspondence reported the Army was studying a ferry operation from Natal to potential Africa stops in Bathurst and Freetown in Sierra Leone. He proposed the U.S. would build "any necessary servicing facilities," adding, "I feel there should be three possible landing places because of proximity of Bathurst to [Vichy dominated] Dakar.... I find a feeling here that up to recently there has been a good deal of delay in delivery between Takoradi and lower Egypt, chiefly through difficulty in servicing the small hopping stones on the way across the Continent. Please let me know how you regard the working out of this problem." Roosevelt concluded, "I have a distinct feeling in my bones that things are looking up with you and with us. After freezing the German and Italian assets on Saturday, I closed the German consulates and agencies yesterday, and the reaction here is, I should say, 90% favorable."[23]

The day of Roosevelt's June 17 correspondence, Trippe was in London to deliver his Wilbur Wright Memorial Lecture on "Ocean Air Transport" before the Royal Aeronautical Society. He took pride they had assembled for a lecture on civil aviation "amid the chaos of a war-torn world.... It is, I think, graphic proof of the fact that all of us in aviation are looking forward to the day when the airplane can lay aside its duties of destruction and once more assume its truly great role as a constructive force in world civilization.... Yet the war has left only the United States in a position to carry on with scheduled trans-oceanic air transportation. Upon us, therefore, has rested the task of maintaining essential overseas air communications, as well as the responsibility for continuing the development of this vitally important phase of the air transport art."[24]

The intrigues following Trippe's talk—his invitation by Air Ministry officials into their inner sanctum, Trippe's suggestion of a ferrying operation to North Africa, his ensuing midnight meeting with Churchill—unfolded, as if preordained.

In July, Harold Bixby sent an "off-the-record letter" informing John Steele, Pan Am's leader at Atlantic Airways, of negotiations underway regarding a new service "to and within Africa." The British, Bixby reported, had brought planes by freighter to Takoradi, but there was a lack of pilots to fly them. In 1940, Imperial Airways had merged into a new national airline, the British Overseas Airways Corporation (BOAC), that was supposed to be operating the old airway between Takoradi and Khartoum. But reports from Atlantic Airways' own pilots underlined the conclusion "that BOAC has been entirely unable to cope with the situation and that the service has broken down completely. For this reason, the British and American Governments have called us to organize a transport service . . . [and] requested us to continue and expand the present South Atlantic ferry service and the contract which is now under consideration will call for the winding up of Atlantic Airways and the organization of a new company." (Bixby added that Pan Am wanted Steele to stay on with the new ferrying operation.)

"The two governments turned logically to Pan American Airways," notes the Office of Air Force's Official History of World War II. "Preliminary plans were drawn up at a conference in General Arnold's office on 26 June 1941, with representatives of the British Air Commission and the Pan American organization in attendance. At that time, it was expected that some 400 Glenn Martin medium bombers . . . purchased by the British prior to the passage of the Lend-Lease Act, would be ready within a few months to start moving from the factory to the Middle East front and that these would be followed by a steadily increasing flow of lend-lease aircraft."[25]

The contract between the United States of America and Pan American Airways, Inc., dated August 12, 1941, was produced pursuant to the Lend-Lease Act and encompassed Pan Am and two new companies incorporated in Delaware: Pan American Air Ferries (shortened to "Ferries" in contractual references) and Pan American Airways-Africa, Ltd. ("African").

The contract declared "the President has authorized the Secretary of War to provide HIS MAJESTY'S GOVERNMENT IN THE UNITED KINGDOM . . . with aircraft and parts therefor which are to be delivered to the British Government in Africa. . . ."

Pan Am and its new subsidiaries would ferry "aircraft and parts" between the U.S. and the west coast of Africa, and take over British ferrying and transport operations from Takoradi to Khartoum "or another point to be agreed upon." The "Transafrican Agreement" clause directed PAA-Africa to organize and operate the "Transafrica route" between Bathurst and Khartoum, or another agreed terminal point.[26]

Pan Am and its new subsidiaries would conduct proving flights, recruit personnel, maintain bases, and construct and maintain ground operations and meteorological and navigational communications facilities in San Juan, Port-of-Spain, Belém, and Natal. The U.S. financed the services with $20,588,528, almost $18 million of which would be charged to Lend-Lease, the rest from emergency funds.[27]

On August 18, the president publicly announced Pan Am's ferrying and transport mission would "provide direct and speedy delivery of aircraft from the 'Arsenal of Democracy' to a critical point in the front against aggression. The importance of this direct line of communications between our country and strategic outposts in Africa cannot be over-estimated." Roosevelt noted transport would "supplement the ferry system by returning ferry personnel and carrying spare plane parts and items essential to effective delivery of aircraft to the Middle East."[28]

The plan had to be approved by the Civil Aeronautics Board, and the trans-Africa route itself had to adhere to the Neutrality Act and avoid designated war zones.[29] But these were formalities. Pan Am made its formal CAB application on August 22. A secret CAB session on September 8 was followed by an open session, with chairman Harllee Branch declaring the president's support "indicates that the national defense is the paramount basis" for the proposal.[30]

*Time* concluded, "This was a job for pros" adding that Pan Am expected to have service ready "before snow flies in the U.S." With the Civil

Aeronautics Board having permitted an extension of Pan Am service to Singapore that April, *Time* observed the assignment served the airline's ambitions: "It pleased Pan Am, which now needed only a Cairo-to-Singapore link to have the basis of the sole round-the-world postwar airline."[31]

Pan Am-Africa's operations took over the 44th floor at the Chrysler Building headquarters. Trippe later recalled with pride, "A great many people who started the Yale-Harvard game in 1940 helped build the route across Africa."[32] Trippe tapped Dave Ingalls, a veteran of the "Millionaires' Unit" of WW I flyboys who had become assistant secretary of war, to head Pan Air Ferries in Miami; Franklin Gledhill, Pan Am's president of purchasing, was a stranger to Africa but now boss of Pan American Airways-Africa, Ltd.

A month before the contract was signed Pan Am was on the job, laying the groundwork in Africa. By August 18, when Roosevelt made his official announcement, the route had been surveyed, and equipment and building materials were on the way.[33] This reported exchange between Trippe and Gledhill illustrates the wartime urgency:

"Frank, I think you ought to go to Africa and get this going."

"When do you think I ought to go?" Gledhill asked.

"Well, I have checked, and we could get an airplane out tonight."[34]

The U.S. Army Air Corps believed the trans-Africa route was key to future Allied military operations. In August of 1941, Lt. Colonel Caleb V. Haynes and Major Curtis E. LeMay flew a B-24 from Washington, D.C. to the South Atlantic and across Africa to Cairo over Imperial's old airway. The pioneering military survey flight confirmed its potential as a year-round airway to the Middle East and European theaters of war. All that was needed was upgrading primitive landing fields to accommodate larger aircraft and install radio and navigational facilities and infrastructure—all the pieces Pan Am had been contracted to put in place.[35]

## CHAPTER 17
# THE PAN-AFRICA CORPS

*"At times when employees in Teheran were shivering in the bitter cold of Caucasian winter, employees at Accra were sweltering under the heat of Africa's mid-summer sun. While employees at Cairo were night-clubbing, employees at El Gebeina were playing checkers under gas lamps in the heart of black man's Africa. While employees were witnessing civil riots in Karachi, employees at Fisherman's Lake were watching preparations for the election of a new President in Africa's only republic. While employees in Lagos crept cautiously through the nightly blackouts, employees at Khartoum drove by company bus to theaters and amusement spots down brightly lighted streets."*

—Voit Gilmore, PAA-Africa personnel director[1]

Franklin Gledhill was of the new breed of power player operating on a global stage. A friendly onlooker once described Gledhill "wrapped in a bathrobe, sprawled on an easy chair in a hotel room somewhere in the world. In one hand, a Bourbon-and-water, in the other the telephone, he negotiates with as little apparent effort as if he were arranging tomorrow's sight seeing trip."[2] Gledhill had the right stuff for Africa—in one month of crisscrossing the continent by air he reportedly amassed 75,000 miles, or 2,500 miles a day.[3]

Other key personnel included Pan Am veterans John Yeomans as assistant manager, with George Kraigher and Karl Lueder as operations managers. Gledhill expanded his administrative staff by naming Navy man Jim Smith his "political anchor" in Cairo (Smith eventually became Assistant Secretary of the Navy for President Eisenhower), and picked Voit Gilmore to head personnel.

In July of 1941, less than a month after Trippe's midnight meeting with Churchill, a special Clipper flight piloted by Captain Harold Gray landed in Bathurst with Gledhill (along with Douglas aircraft factory men headed to Asmara to set up an assembly plant to build bombers for Russia). Awaiting Gledhill was Lucius Clay, who was in Africa for the Airport Development Program, which was building strategic Roberts Field in Liberia.[4]

Gray was supposed to fly a group of pilots, co-pilots, and radio operators back to Miami, but was instead ordered to make a secret aerial survey of potential seaplane and land plane sites along Liberia's coast—of special interest was a place called Fisherman's Lake. Gray stopped for fuel at Pan Am's new Bolama facility, contacting the governor upon arrival and requesting formal clearance to depart. Gray was told he could "proceed at will" and that there would be no formal recognition of the plane having been there. "This was interpreted as a friendly effort on the part of the governor to unofficially cooperate with Pan American Airways," Colonel Frederick Sharp explained in a report to the War Department. "The Governor was not advised of the purpose of the flight."[5]

Gray flew south to Liberia and circled over Fisherman's Lake, Monrovia, and Marshall. Fisherman's Lake looked promising. Gray estimated six by three miles of seaplane space, flat terrain for land planes, and he observed huts—to empire builders with a wilderness to conquer that meant potential labor. Monrovia had similar conditions. Marshall had a Firestone Company base with seaplane runways.

Back at Bathurst, Gledhill was satisfied with Fisherman's Lake's potential and directed Karl Lueder to make an on-the-ground survey. In Colonel Sharp's War Department report on Gray's survey mission, Pan Am expressed security concerns: "Mr. Leslie, manager, Atlantic Division of P.A.A. states that if G-2 wishes specific observations made, these should be requested from Washington in order that the pilot in command be confidentially instructed to make such observations 'unofficially,' in order to take full advantage of these 'off record' flights."[6]

Gledhill's survey of the trans-Africa route began at Takoradi, where he was greeted by his British liaison, Vernon Crudge, director of African affairs for the British Overseas Airways Corporation. Crudge had just arrived, having been at his office in Nairobi when directed to meet Gledhill and "extend maximum co-operation." Both men set off in Crudge's light De Havilland 86 biplane on a whirlwind itinerary: August 8: Kano; August 11: Khartoum; August 13: Cairo, with a side trip to the desert battlefields of the Western Campaign; August 16: Asmara. On the ground, the stations were barely a sketch for modern airfields and not big enough for modern bombers.[7] At each stop, Gledhill calculated construction needs and at night cabled New York for equipment to immediately begin shipping.

Pan Am's corporate history singles out Vernon Crudge for "bridging the gap between the very British Governors . . . Colonial Secretaries, etc., and the very American Americans."[8] It didn't hurt Anglo-American relations that Gledhill and Crudge became instant friends. Crudge tried to placate his suspicious countrymen who felt Pan Am was setting up for postwar dominance in their backyard. "Pan Am and BOAC kept right on jockeying for good starting positions for the post-war race, a silent and fairly grim struggle," Pan Am's corporate history records.[9]

★

It took the native boatmen a day and a half to deliver Karl Lueder from Monrovia, on the shores of West Africa, to Fisherman's Lake, a world of jungle and waterways where natives steered dugout canoes and fished like their ancient ancestors. He met Father Simmons, a missionary who assisted in recruiting native workers. Lueder checked the lake as a potential seaplane channel, noting the depth and marking off the channel with buoys. "Fish

Lake," as it was nicknamed, was perfect for flying boats and a land plane base. Lueder, who would supervise construction, sent a positive report to Gledhill, who diverted supply ships already steaming up the coast of West Africa to Bathurst.[10]

A War Department document summed up Lueder's report: "The clipper base at Fisherman's Lake is vital to the Ferry Command as it is the only place between Bolama, Portuguese Guinea, and Lagos, Nigeria, where the clippers can land supplies and freight necessary to maintain Roberts Field as a service and maintenance base for planes being ferried to Africa and the Middle East. . . . Roberts Field is vital to the war efforts, as it is the only airfield in Africa, large and near enough that is, at present, available to the United States as a ferry base for B-24s and B-25s." Lueder noted even the primitive conditions provided a strategic advantage, including jungle hills between beach and base where invaders could be spotted and fired upon from high ground.[11]

The construction at Fish Lake was not unlike the bases Pan Am built upon the cleared jungles of Central and South America, or the sands of Wake and Midway. Hundreds of native laborers worked alongside American construction crews, with work continuing into 1942. By May 7 of '42, a Military Intelligence Division Attaché Report delivered by Colonel Frederick Sharp reported, "The airfield being constructed by Pan American Airways Africa Ltd., on the northeast corner of Fisherman's lake will be completed in about two weeks. There is no runway, but the field is packed with gravel sand, is well drained, and can be used throughout for taxiing and taking off. The length of the field is about 4,000' and the width about 400.' There are no hangars or lighting equipment. There are no obstructions as all high trees have been cut down."[12]

Fisherman's Lake and its new Benson Field would replace Bathurst as the regular port of call. The final facility included a radio station to provide navigational and communications support for future military flights by the U.S., Naval Air Transport Service, and Royal Air Force.[13] PAA-Africa Personnel Manager Voit Gilmore marveled how "within a few months international travellers who visited this former tract of uninhabitable jungle were casually taking shower baths, sending their clothes to the modern laundry and eating frozen foods from the United States and freshly made ice cream."[14]

Captain Frank Briggs was one of the Pan Am pilots who became a veteran of the South Atlantic run from Natal to Fisherman's Lake. "To take off from Natal we would taxi up-river, around a curve to a bridge," Briggs explained. "Our takeoff point was around the bend of the river, the big boat finally separating from the water's surface in time to cross the beach with the ocean surf lapping at our hull. We carried very heavy loads and flew a steep-climb to conserve fuel."

Although a Boeing 314 could fly the 1,876 nautical miles nonstop, they weren't pressurized. They couldn't fly above storms, and it wasted fuel going around—they flew through. "Generally, as we neared the line of cumulonimbus storms we selected a penetration course between the lightning flashes at night, or between the tallest clouds in daytime," Briggs recalls. "This was to avoid the powerful updrafts in the core of each thunderstorm."

At night, they navigated celestially and in overcast took "drift sights" from a drift meter in the starboard wing. Approaching Africa, an amorphous mass of jungle from the air, they followed the coastline. "Pan Am had carved a base out of the jungle on the shores of Fisherman's Lake, and we landed the flying boats on this large body of water," Briggs said. "We slept in large tents there. During off-duty hours we hunted in the jungle and fished for large edible barracuda in the lake. We once found two motherless leopard cubs and raised them at our camp. . . . At this base, malaria was endemic and we faithfully took atabrine or chloroquine. Of course, a more pleasant way to take quinine was in a few gin and tonics."[15]

⭐

Accra, on Africa's Gold Coast, was headquarters for the trans-Africa line. Although there was no protected harbor to accommodate Clippers, there was an existing airport, with ideal dry weather and cool sea breezes. The work there included widening and extending an existing paved runway for one mile, paving two rougher runways, building two steel hangars to go with an existing British hangar, paving the two-and-a-half-mile road to the airport, and installing underground cables for power and telephone service.[16]

The whole of Pan Am's Africa operation recruited and employed a thousand Americans and 10,000 Africans. On the American side, applications required British approval as well as letters to draft boards, contracts, briefings, travel orders, inoculations, passports—Pan Am assistant vice president and Washington fixture Anne Archibald was skilled at cutting bureaucratic tangles.[17] The vetting considered potential espionage and sabotage—the Federal Bureau of Investigation, the British Security Office, and even private detective agencies scrutinized everyone. "There were numerous instances of technically qualified individuals who were refused employment on the basis of irregularities in their personal or family background," Gilmore reported. It was "probably the most intensive recruiting program for aviation technicians yet to occur in aviation history." Some 150 administrative and supervisory personnel were borrowed from throughout Pan Am's divisions, Gilmore estimated, and an arrangement with the Army Air Corps facilitated the release from active duty of pilots and cadets to form the core of the flight group.[18]

The average age of PAA-Africa personnel was twenty-seven, with the youngest eighteen and the oldest sixty. Incoming Americans were issued six pairs of trousers, twelve shirts, two khaki coats, a raincoat, and tropical helmet. Each employee was given one bed-sized mosquito net, along with citronella and quinine to prevent malaria. Field equipment included flashlights and pocketknives. All personnel were provided cloth and metal insignia labels marked "Pan American Airways-Africa, Ltd."[19]

The number of American personnel at each station varied. Fisherman's Lake usually was staffed with fifteen, Roberts Field twenty-one, El Fasher six, Khartoum twenty-six. Accra had the lion's share, with 347. The six-day workweek began at 7:30 a.m., with an hour lunch break at noon and quitting time at 4:30 p.m.[20]

Each station had its unique character. Fort Lamy, in French Equatorial Africa, cut through the rainforest and tribal villages and was an outpost of French resistance to German incursions in North Africa. It was where a

French army officer, who went by the pseudonym Lt-General Philipe Leclerc, marched to strike at Rommel from the south and where, early in '42, a German bomber attacked, trying to disrupt the operation. Its one bad road was a washout in the rainy season, and almost every employee endured at least one bout of malaria and dysentery.[21]

Kano was a walled city and beyond its gates were a mosque and a sultan's palace. For crews laboring on the airport runway, a local chief posted a tribal man astride a camel who carried a long horn and kept watch for incoming planes. When he spotted one, he raised his horn and sounded the warning for work crews to move back. Pan Am's corporate history recalls how thousands of travelers never forgot "the strange, plaintive, haunting note of that horn."[22]

Throughout the Line, basic necessities were often unavailable. Aircraft could be grounded for lack of parts that could fit in one's pocket, such as a DC-3 brake bladder. At one point, the soft brass safety wires for securing nuts so a plane's vibration wouldn't back them off the bolts were not to be had in the whole continent—they used telephone wires or flew without. "I hope Priester doesn't come over here," one Africa hand reportedly said. "It would kill him."[23]

A particular need was fueling equipment. British flyers previously used natives to pump petrol by hand, a tedious and time-consuming process. Camel caravans had been transporting gasoline, which took days to deliver a single load of thirty-five gallons, only enough to keep a DC-3 in the air for half an hour. Later, truck convoys transported gasoline in fifty-gallon barrels.

There were inevitable culture clashes. One that was quickly resolved came in Basra, where a newly arrived Pan Am carpenter was giving a pep talk to a workforce of local Muslims. When he finished, the workers turned and walked away. Shocked and thinking they had quit, he suddenly realized it was holy hour, and they were walking a short distance away to pray. The relieved carpenter joined them.[24]

There were weather extremes—the hottest day along the Line, which passed into Pan Am legend, was measured in El Fasher, where the temperature reportedly hit 155 degrees Fahrenheit in the shade.

Malaria was a threat and miles of drainage ditches were dug in a futile effort to curtail the disease. Pan Am brought in specialist Dr. Chester Coggeshall, a professor at Northwestern University, who discovered that hundreds of gasoline barrels stored outdoors at airports and refueling sites were collecting rainwater on the barrelheads, a perfect breeding ground for mosquitoes. Painting the barrels with a mixture of paint and engine oil created a film that kept mosquito larva from taking hold, dramatically reducing incidents of malaria around airports.[25]

Despite challenges and hardships, the "Clipper Glory" spirit transplanted well to Africa. Pan Am's mostly young Africa Corps knew they were engaged in a vital wartime project. Many saw the River Jordan, Jerusalem, and other wonders, and at stopovers in Accra often asked personnel manager Gilmore if they could borrow a Bible to look up ancient landmarks.[26] Gilmore fondly recalled two "young shavetails," freshly arrived from the U.S., who hadn't known their destination until they opened sealed orders after takeoff. "What adventure to rip open an envelope and find tomorrow you will be flying over camel caravans and giraffes!" Gilmore said. "They wanted to know everything: about the mosquitoes and where the lions were and what Rommel was doing."[27]

Accra headquarters was a bustling base, home to hundreds of employees, native Africans, and a steady stream of visitors, pilots, and crews. There were fraternal, social, and religious groups along the Line, but they flourished at Accra, from Protestant and Catholic societies to drinking clubs, the latter including the Snafu Club ("Snafu" being military shorthand for "Situation Normal, All Fouled Up," politely stated). The inevitable contingent of Yale alums formed the Yale-Accra Club or "Yaccra Club." For a taste of home, everyone headed to the Gold Coast Grill, which was as famous for its two-fisted cook and counterman, Cookie Lidz—a "spectacular character," Gilmore recounted, right out of the Popeye "Thimble Theatre" comic strip—as it was for Cookie's American-style hamburgers and "cackleburger," a hamburger with a fried egg.[28]

In its first weeks, the trans-Africa operation started with only five DC-3s, borrowed from domestic airlines. "In the next 12 months, it grew into the biggest air transport operation the world had seen up to that time," Pan Am's corporate history notes. The Line would stretch through Africa and the Middle East to Karachi, India. At Khartoum the route branched—one to Cairo, with extensions to Palestine, Basra, Abadan, and Teheran; the other split from Khartoum to Asmara, Aden, Arabia's southern coast, and on to India.[29]

⭐

Trippe and Pan Am's role in hemispheric defense and the overseas war effort was featured in the October 20, 1941, *Life* cover article that included a full-page photo of the forty-two-year-old airline president in his master-of-the-world pose, with a pipe clenched in his mouth and papers held in his right hand, standing beside his gigantic world globe and scrutinizing the continents. An accompanying map showed Pan Am's lines stretching from both U.S. coastlines, south to Latin America, west to China, east to Europe and Africa, the latter now marked with stops at Bolama, Bathurst, Lagos, Leopoldville, Khartoum. The only gap in a world-encircling airway was the Indian Ocean between East Africa and Singapore. *Life*, already anticipating the postwar world, reported the airline was planning to increase the frequency of flights and supplement its main lines, with England's airline looming as the main competitor. As for the transatlantic and trans-Africa ferrying assignment the president announced in August, Trippe had hoped to have it operational within ninety days; he was ahead of schedule—the first flight was departing Miami that week.[30]

Trippe "realized that he was being handed a chance to penetrate Africa," Robert Daley observes. But Trippe needed more than military air routes; he needed "commercial penetration," Daley adds. "Trippe applied to the Civil Aeronautics Board for a certificate of convenience and necessity for a route to Leopoldville in the Belgian Congo; if he could get this far, then after the war the whole of the rich southern portion of Africa would lie open to him. The CAB held hearings, but it was difficult by now to tell which projects had the War Department behind them, and which had only Trippe. The

CAB hearings were partly open, partly secret . . . and the certificate was awarded with unusual haste."[31]

The airline's secret ADP work had begun filtering into the press. In November of '41, *Time* reported airbases being built in Brazil "at U.S. Government behest. . . . The vulnerable eastern hump of Brazil, which sticks out sore-thumb like on all maps of U.S. grand strategy, is for one U.S. corporation already an active fighting front. The corporation: Pan American Airways. On the hump, Pan Am lines parallel Axis airlines. . . . The difficulties in Pan Am's way are as real as war and not unlike it. Pan Am men confront Axis agents, spies and businessmen every day." ADP work had intensified at Natal, a bustling city of 56,165 that was now a boomtown overflowing with "engineers, ferry pilots, tractor drivers, Axis spies," *Time* noted.[32]

LATI and Condor were hanging on. "Axis espionage and sabotage will be lessened if & when Lati and Condor pack up and leave, as other Axis lines in South America have already," *Time* reported that November. "This week Lati, at last, seemed to be on its last legs in Brazil. When Pan Am starts its South Atlantic Clipper service, there will be no more reason for Brazil to tolerate Lati." Indeed, a week before the *Time* report, the *Capetown Clipper* passed Natal on its 18,290-mile proving flight from New York City to Leopoldville and within a few weeks was scheduled to inaugurate the first airmail flight to the Belgian Congo.[33]

The United States solidified relations with Brazil, and the bogged-down ADP program got moving when it severed relations with the Axis. In April of '41, the Brazilian government seized three Axis vessels and warned LATI for an unauthorized flight. By July 25, *Panair do Brasil* successfully lobbied for Brazilian Decree-Law #3462, giving the ADP official sanction by Brazil's government. *Panair do Brasil* was officially authorized to "construct, improve, or equip" airports at Amapa, Belém, São Luíz, Fortaleza, Natal, Recife, Maceió, and San Salvador in Bahia. From July through October of 1941, American technical experts began staffing key positions.[34]

A Lend Lease agreement between the U.S. and Brazil was signed in October of 1941. The hemispheric authority of the Ferry Command was also expanding. On October 3, 1941, a communication from Roosevelt to the Secretary of War declared, "I hereby extend such authority to empower you to deliver aircraft to any territory subject to the jurisdiction of the United States, to any territory within the Western hemisphere, the Netherlands, East Indies and Australia, on behalf of any country to which I shall have authorized the delivery of defense articles under the Lend-Lease Act." The directive included staffing, supplying, and improving all staging fields and weather and communications facilities.[35]

First up was the South Atlantic and trans-Africa airway, and by December of '41 the U.S. wrapped up an agreement in which Brazil agreed to allow the U.S. Army unlimited use of the north coast of Brazil, as far south as Recife, for the movement of military aircraft. "The severance of relations with the Axis by Brazil . . . helped pave the way for the granting of such request," noted the Air Force's South Atlantic Division history. "Operations in both the Pacific and North Africa were far from encouraging at this time. Rommel was advancing in Libya against the British, and Allied warships were sustaining heavy losses in the Pacific. Thus, the passage of planes through Brazil and their arrival at the scene of hostilities was considered of vital importance in the course of the war."[36]

The likelihood of America entering the war compelled a reorganization of military aviation, fulfilling a dream of air power advocates. In June 1941, the Army Air Corps was given a measure of autonomy as the U.S. Army Air Forces.

Pan Am was also preparing—if and when war came in the Pacific, all aircraft and stations would be alerted by a prearranged signal: "Case 7: Condition A."

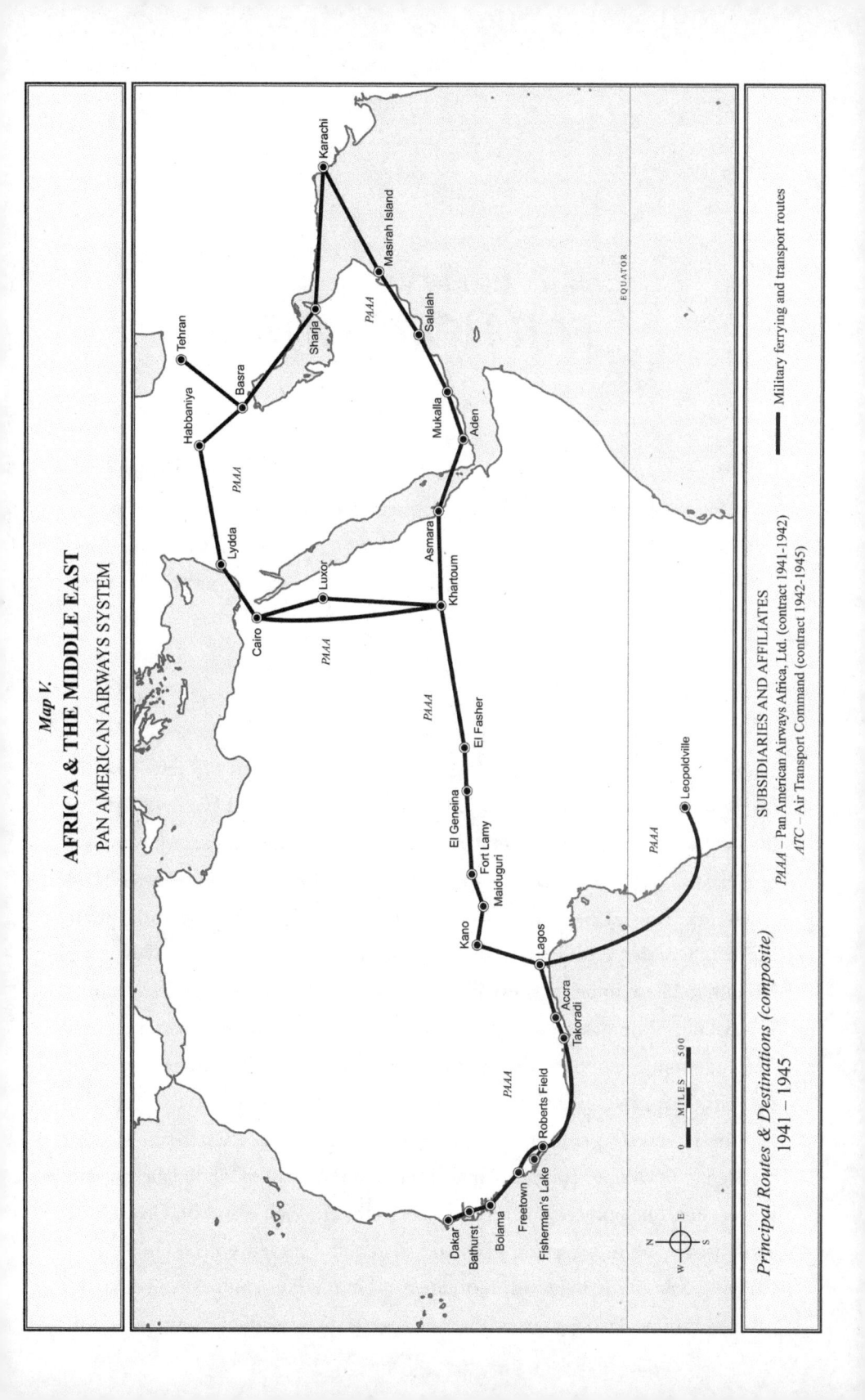

*Map V.*
## AFRICA & THE MIDDLE EAST
PAN AMERICAN AIRWAYS SYSTEM

*Principal Routes & Destinations (composite)*
1941 – 1945

SUBSIDIARIES AND AFFILIATES
*PAAA* – Pan American Airways Africa, Ltd. (contract 1941-1942)
*ATC* – Air Transport Command (contract 1942-1945)

— Military ferrying and transport routes

## CHAPTER 18
# FAR HORIZONS

*"Fifty years from now people will look back upon a Pan American Clipper flight of today as the most romantic voyage of history."*

—Clare Boothe Luce,
first-person account of a Pacific flight[1]

A typical Pan Am Clipper flight from Treasure Island to New Zealand departed at noon, 11:30 a.m. in winter. As the usual twenty to thirty passengers boarded, stewards greeted and seated them, allowed for proper weight distribution, made sure all had their seatbelts securely fastened, and stowed hats and coats. The route included a nearly three-hour flight down the California coast to Los Angeles and an hour layover for refueling. The Clipper was usually westbound to Hawaii by cocktail hour.

Cocktail hour had become a tradition on the Pacific airways. The New Zealand–bound Clippers boasted the "South Seas cocktail," a concoction of two-fifths gin, two-fifths orange juice, one-fifth curacao, cracked ice, shaken vigorously and strained into cocktail glasses. The North Pacific run recommended the "Clipper cocktail," one "pony" (small glass) of white label Puerto Rican rum, one pony of dry French vermouth, one-half teaspoon Grenadine, poured over ice in a mixing glass and stirred and served with a cherry in a Clipper cocktail glass, its rim moistened with a lemon rind. After cocktails, passengers moved to the lounge that had been transformed into a dining room, where dinner was served on bone china and flatware. At midnight, a supper of sandwiches and cold cuts served with milk or hot chocolate was available.[2]

Pan Am's China affiliate could only dream of cocktails and midnight suppers. CNAC was in the middle of war and, despite its civilian status, enemy crosshairs. After Japan bombed CNAC's home base at Shanghai, the airline was on the move. "As the Japs moved west CNAC slipped west, played a grim game of geographical hide and seek as the Japs bombed CNAC airports days before their infantry moved in," *New Horizons* reported. Or, as William Bond put it, "After the hell broke loose we did our best to save the pieces."[3]

In 1940, Japan moved into Indo-China, forcing CNAC to abandon its Hanoi base, although they had already run much of the maintenance equipment, spare parts, and other material to Hankow. When Hankow fell, CNAC moved further into the western interior to Chungking, capital of Chiang Kai-shek's Nationalist government. Flight operations were staged in a river at the foot of Chungking, with the maintenance and equipment facility maintained in a deep cave above the city.[4]

Ever since Japanese fighters shot down the *Kweilin*, CNAC pilots flew in stormy weather and cloud cover where the enemy would not follow—there was bitter truth to the joke that CNAC was the only airline in the world that cancelled flights because of good weather.[5] CNAC kept flying passengers and mail, businessmen, refugees, Red Cross medical personnel, diplomats and military personnel. The airline connected Hong Kong with Chungking and Rangoon, Burma's capital city, and complemented the more than 700-mile Burma Road from Lashio, Burma to Kunming, China.

CNAC would work closely with an American who came to China to help the beleaguered national air force. Claire Chennault was a child of the northeastern Louisiana wilderness beyond the cultivated cotton fields, a place of swamps and oak woods and wolves, bear, and other wild animals. Growing up, he learned combat strategy by studying the ancient wars of Rome and Greece. Chennault learned to fly in the Army Air Service during World War I, became an instructor at the Air Corps Tactical School at Langley Field, flew with an Air Corps aerobatic team and had risen to colonel. But his independent personality and air power theories—Chennault believed heavy bombers weren't enough, that fighters flying in tactical groups could turn the tide of battle and even win a war—was not a comfortable fit for the straitlaced military command.

By early 1937 hearing problems pushed Chennault into unhappy retirement. But he began getting news from friends in China about the invasion and the inevitability that America would be fighting Japan. And then Roy Holbrook, advisor to the Central Trust Company of China and a confidant of the Nationalist government, extended an offer on behalf of Madame Chiang Kai-shek—would Chennault consider coming to China for three months to make "a confidential survey" of China's Air Force for $1,000 a month plus expenses, a car and chauffeur, interpreter, and the right to fly any plane in the Air Force? Chennault ended his brief retirement on the morning of May 1, 1937, departing San Francisco by boat to a new mission in China.[6]

Chennault traveled to Yunnan, a province of high plateaus and jade-green lakes surrounded by snowy peaks connecting with the mighty mountain ranges of Tibet, Burma, and India. The old Jade Road that Marco Polo traveled centuries before went through Yunnan, and in its lower plains Burmese kings once unleashed armored elephants to battle the mounted archers of Kublai Khan. The region was now known for copper and tin, spicy ham, illegal export of opium, and ferocious Lolo tribesmen who lived, unconquered, in the mountains. Chennault settled in Kunming, what he called "a sleepy, backwoods Oriental town." Kunming would be Chennault's base of operations for the next seven years.[7]

Chennault recruited a small group of American Air Corps reserve officers to staff his training school—a "lusty crew," Chennault recalled. Some were future CNAC pilots, including Emil Scott, who later died piloting a CNAC transport through an electrical storm over Kunming, and Frank "Dude" Higgs, who was in his early thirties and hailed from Columbus, Ohio. Higgs even inspired the swashbuckling cartoon character of Dude Hennick, a daring American pilot in China created by fellow Ohio State University classmate Milton Caniff for his hugely popular *Terry and the Pirates* syndicated newspaper comics strip.[8]

Higgs had been a U.S. Army Fighter pilot who resigned his commission to join Chennault and train Chinese air force cadets in dive-bombing, dog-fighting, and aerial gunnery. Higgs often spoke with Madame Chiang Kai-shek and shared with *New Horizons* her observation that CNAC was "a fine outfit whose work could not be done without its U.S. personnel."[9]

Higgs described his first CNAC flight as his most harrowing, a round-trip between Hong Kong and Chungking in a perfect storm of rain, snow, sleet, and lightning over Japanese-held territory—if he descended below the storm his unarmed transport was prey for Japanese fighters. "When it was all over I felt as though I'd been through a meat grinder," he admitted.[10]

Chennault settled into "the endless grind of training" and came to know and respect the risks taken by not just the China Air Force (CAF), but the China National Aviation Corporation. In addition to Chennault's air travels—"I learned to know the face of China as only an airman can"—there were, he wrote, "occasional trips by car and mule into the mountains to reclaim the bodies of C.N.A.C. or Eurasia air-line pilots who had blundered into cloud-screened Yunnan peaks."[11]

By 1940, planes and aviation equipment were scarce, making CAF operations virtually impossible. Chennault later wrote that in the first two years of the war, "China had suffered losses that by conventional standards would have forced a nation to surrender." By Chennault's reckoning, losses included eleven provinces, all key railroads, the major water arteries of the Yangtze and Pearl Rivers, 95 percent of industry, and a decimated army and air force. "Yet China kept on fighting and only a few even thought of surrender," he noted.[12]

Chennault wanted to take the next step and engage the enemy. Americans would be recruited as paid volunteers—detractors called them mercenaries—to help China fight its air war. Besides piloting skills and stratagems, Chennault instilled ferocity in his American Volunteer Group (AVG). "My ideas about fighting," he once told an interviewer, "was never give the enemy a chance and kill him as quick as you could." The AVG painted the fuselages of their P-40 Tomahawk fighters with snarling shark fangs, inspired by similar war paint in a photo of an RAF squadron in the Libyan desert. It was always a mystery to Chennault why his fighting squadron got the nickname that stuck: "Flying Tigers."[13]

The American Volunteer Group began during a May 1939 business policy meeting between Finance Minister H. H. Kung and William Pawley, who was briefly CNAC president, represented Curtiss aircraft in China, and was president of the Intercontinent Corporation. The Kung meeting included Intercontinent vice presidents Edward Pawley (William's brother), and Captain B. C. Leighton, USN. The meeting was wrapping up when Pawley asked what America might provide China's embattled air force. Kung asked for volunteers in the tradition of the Lafayette Escadrille, American airmen who helped France in World War I.

An ensuing partnership between Pawley and Chiang Kai-shek's government included Intercontinent and the Central Aircraft Manufacturing Company (CAMCO), of which Pawley was president and sole stockholder, the latter to build aircraft in China and the vehicle by which Pawley and China formed the volunteer group. Pawley was empowered to employ 350 men and purchase and ship the necessary aircraft for assembly in Rangoon. "Thus the AVG was born," Pawley later explained.[14]

Pawley reached out to British Air Vice Marshal Sir John Slessor for support in securing airfields and hiring RAF pilots and ground crews. With the U.S. neutral, and fearing a Japanese attack on Singapore and other British possessions in the Far East, Sir Slessor was "enthusiastically cooperative," Pawley recalled. "Therefore, he visualized the American Volunteer Group as the possible nucleus for an international Lafayette Escadrille, to which the United States could stealthily continue to contribute men, arms and support facilities. This international fighting force would be able to back up the thin RAF contingents in Southeast Asia and could be developed into a powerful enough element to counterattack by bombarding Japanese cities [from bases in China]."

Sir Slessor later wrote, "I suggested to the Air Ministry that we should . . . take a gamble on it by sending some pilots from India but, no doubt for very good reasons, they felt we had already enough on our hands. So we had no share in a romantic venture which later developed into that extraordinary force under General Chennault, the world's greatest expert at running an Air Force on a shoestring."

Sir Slessor's advocacy helped and "British authorities did everything within their power to provide us with our needs," Pawley noted, including an airfield in Burma. By April of '42, CAMCO facilities in Burma and Loiwing were working exclusively for the AVG, from recruitment to processing paperwork and helping volunteers adjust to life in Asia. Pawley's memoirs estimated CAMCO performed 95 percent of AVG repairs, but Chennault claimed the opposite—as damaged planes began "to pile up" during training, CAMCO did not perform needed repairs. "I have always suspected that Pawley, like the Japanese, thoroughly believed the British and American intelligence reports that the A.V.G. would not last three weeks in combat," Chennault charged.

Pawley admitted he feared "difficulties" between himself and the fiery Tigers commander, particularly in staff and recruitment. "It was impossible to get only the cream of the crop," Pawley recalled. "The subsequent combat record of the Flying Tigers is both a tribute to Claire Chennault as a combat leader of genius and a refutation of the charge that . . . CAMCO engaged in haphazard or irresponsible recruitment."[15]

In wartime China, a bond formed between Chennault's American volunteers, CNAC airmen from China and America, and Chinese air force pilots. Olga S. Greenlaw, whose husband, Harvey Greenlaw was representing the North American Aviation Company then assembling and testing planes in China, was another American who knew China and its brotherhood of airmen. In 1938, after years in China, the Greenlaws were in Hong Kong and ready to sail home to America, but as she was packing the phone rang—it was CNAC pilot Little Mac for Harvey. When her husband came to the phone, Olga heard him say "Chennault," and she knew to start unpacking. They had known Colonel Chennault "almost from the day he first stepped off the boat" in China, and they were about to be swept up into the world of his Flying Tigers, with Harvey serving as Chennault's executive officer.

The last time Olga had seen the "Old Man," as Chennault was affectionately called, her husband had been in Hong Kong, and she was returning to their home in Hengyang by troop train at night, arriving in time for an enemy bomber attack. After crossing a river in pitch-black darkness and narrowly missing being shot by a guard, she made it home, only to be told by an apologetic servant that the house was full—her own bed was taken by a "Colonel Chen-Chao-ult." Thinking it was some Chinese officer she stormed up the stairs to the bedroom, muttering profanities. When she threw open the door, the man leaning against the bedpost said, in a low Louisiana drawl, "Only an American girl could swear so picturesquely, Olga. Makes me homesick."

"The Colonel had stopped over on his way from somewhere to somewhere else and knew he was always welcome," Greenlaw shrugged. "So was everyone else. It was like that wherever we were—house full, beds full, extra people for meals, Chinese officers, American officers, the C.N.A.C. boys and almost anyone who happened to be in town. . . . Anyway, that was us—Hotel Greenlaw—comfortable beds and good meals at all hours."[16]

The Flying Tigers were a godsend to the beleaguered China Air Force, and CNAC did its best to keep them supplied. "I don't know what we would have done without C.N.A.C. as we had no transport planes except the old decrepit Beechcraft," Greenlaw wrote in a 1943 memoir. "C.N.A.C. was always moving men and equipment from one place to another, sometimes making as many as three round trips a day. Their pilots were never too busy to do something for the A. V.G. Their office in Calcutta was of inestimable value in slashing customs and other red tape, to get the important spare parts and equipment so sorely needed, and never would C.N.A.C. land at Kunming without a load for us. This airline has had a great influence in the lives of the Chinese people as it has been the only means of communication and transport from the interior."[17]

As the Japanese advance pushed the CNAC westward toward the Himalayas, the airline pioneered an airway, and future military supply route, over the "Hump" of the monumental mountains between Kunming and Assam, India. The Pan Am affiliate became veterans of the high altitudes and dangerous mountain passes and would lead the way for future American air operations. "Mastery of the Hump was one of the great epics of the war," Chennault declared. "However, it posed no great problem for experienced personnel of commercial-air-line caliber. American pilots of C.N.A.C., who made the first Hump survey flight in November 1941, proved that."[18]

Although Captain Moon Chin was one of the first CNAC pilots to fly the Hump—and would eventually make more than 400 flights over it—he credits the initial surveys over the eastern Himalayas to CNAC flyer Charles Sharp. "The Hump was all high mountains, at least 15,000 feet," noted Chin.[19]

CNAC Captain Harold Chinn, a native Canadian who learned how to fly and came to China looking for work (he reasoned China had the greatest need for pilots) also became a veteran of the Hump. Chinn's flying career began in the air force of warlord General Chanchi Tong. In 1936, he joined the CNAC, attained the rank of senior pilot, and became Chiang Kai-shek's personal pilot. As Chinn got familiar with the Himalayas, the challenges made the peaks they navigated from Kunming to Chungking "seem like little hills."[20]

⭐

John Kinney once recalled he had an "inborn instinct" to be an aviator. In 1936, he accepted a commission as second lieutenant in the U.S. Army Reserve and became a mechanic for Pan Am's Pacific fleet. Kinney drove to work in a 1929 Model A Ford coupe and brought his own tools, a $50 set from Sears, Roebuck. His "initiation," as he called it, involved using two-foot long screwdrivers to remove the covers on a Martin Clipper's lower wing fuel tanks to clean out saltwater corrosion and repaint with zinc chromate, cover with a rubberized solution, then reinstall the covers. And he kept dreaming of becoming a flyer.[21]

Kinney finally arranged for a leave of absence from Pan Am, resigned his Army Reserve Commission, and reported to the U.S. Marine Corps base at Oakland, California. He entered the Marine Corps Reserve commission as a private first class for the weeding out phase in May of 1938. He passed muster, and John Leslie granted him further furlough to begin flight training in Pensacola, Florida. "My dream would come true," Kinney recalled, earning his wings and becoming a marine pilot.[22]

Kinney was assigned to Wake Island, which Pan Am now shared with the military, arriving the morning of December 4, 1941.[23] Of the three isles—Wake, Wilkes, and Peale—the western tip of Wake comprised Camp 1, home to a tent city of the marine defense battalion. Camp 2 on Wake was home to construction workers, while Peale remained Pan Am's center of operations. The Navy's air station had an estimated 1,200 civilian construction crew building airstrips and underground ammunition storage bunkers, seaplane facilities, water purification plants, and other infrastructure. The military leadership included Wake commander Lieutenant Commander Winfield Scott Cunningham, Major Paul Putnam commanding (Marine Fighter Attack Squadron) VMF-211, and Major James P. Devereux in charge of the Marine defense battalion.

But Kinney felt the island was vulnerable—its entire air force was a dozen Wildcats. "There were shortages everywhere . . . spare parts were almost nonexistent and there was an extreme shortage of mechanics who had any experience working on Wildcats," he recalled. "In spite of the shortages the patrol flights began as scheduled on the morning of December 5, and even though we were not yet at war they still had an element of danger to them. With the lack of up-to-date radio equipment in the Wildcats, I found myself constantly plotting my speed, bearing, and time on course so that I could find my way back to the island again. I could not relax my vigilance for a minute during these flights because scattered clouds cast shadows on the ocean that, from the air, look like so many islands."[24]

Kinney visited Peale to watch the *Philippine Clipper* make its scheduled stop on its way to Manila. He was happy to see an old friend among the crew, Flight Engineer Ed Barnett, and learn that one of the modifications he made as a Pan Am mechanic on this very plane was working perfectly. Barnett also had sobering news—Pan Am was evacuating its female dependents from Manila before war began. "As I headed back to my quarters I thought about what Ed had said," Kinney recalled. "I sure hoped that the war would wait a little longer before it got to Wake. None of us in VMF-211 had ever even fired the machine guns in the Wildcats yet. This was about to change."[25]

Around the time Kinney arrived at Wake, the B 314 *Pacific Clipper* (originally the *California Clipper*), commanded by Captain R.O.D. Sullivan, left La Guardia Marine Air Terminal on the first secret Clipper war mission. The top-secret flight to supply Chennault's Flying Tigers with tons of ammo and supplies, known as "Special Mission No. 1," was a rugged 11,500 miles from New York to Miami, to Natal, across the South Atlantic to Lagos, Leopoldville, Khartoum, Aden, Karachi, and Calcutta, ending in Rangoon, Burma. While using dead reckoning navigation during a heavy dust storm between Port Bell and Khartoum, the Clipper almost hit a mountain—Sullivan instinctively made a sharp turn with a "wing-on-end tilt" that caused some of the secured cargo to spill, but otherwise averted disaster. When the B 314 returned to anchor in La Guardia's Bowery Bay on January 6, 1942, America's wartime role had dramatically changed.[26]

In November of '41, Japan's special envoy, Saburo Kurusu, and his aide, Shiroji Yuki, journeyed to Washington to meet with Secretary of State Hull. Despite Pan Am's collusion with Washington to prevent Clipper passage for Japanese military personnel, an exception was made for this last-ditch diplomatic mission. Kurusu and an aide were extended the courtesy of flying from Tokyo to Hong Kong, which had also been closed to Japanese aviation, to catch the *Hong Kong Clipper*. The Flying Boat was held to allow a Clipper connection at Manila to take them to Honolulu where Kurusu and Yuki flew by *California Clipper* to the mainland. They flew all three types of Clipper—Sikorsky, Martin, Boeing—and completed in nine days a trip that ten years before would have taken a month.[27]

That month's *Life* magazine featured a report on a Pacific Clipper flight by Clare Boothe Luce, wife of Henry Luce, magazine magnate behind *Time* and *Life*. Her voyage began with passengers and crew gathered in the early afternoon at Treasure Island's Clipper Cove. An "unusual friendliness" was expressed in glances and smiles as they waited to board. To Luce, it was the recognition "that we are to share for six long days a common danger and a high adventure through the skies."

The United States was being irresistibly pulled into a world war, and the passengers embodied wartime efforts already underway. There was the "tough-looking, heavy-jawed" Army engineer bound for Chungking to help build a railroad to parallel the Burma Road. The "good-looking, curly haired boy" was an ex-lawyer and naval reservist headed to Manila to help the Philippines and Hong Kong smooth out financial difficulties regarding their freezing of Japanese assets. Two clergymen were embarked on a six-month trip to encourage missionaries "to hold the Christian front in all the Asiatic hot spots." There were motormen whose job was to see that trucks and cars were delivered to the Burma Road. A group of Army and Navy men were off to missions in the Straits Settlement and Moscow, and one passenger would be operating a giant shovel to build bomber runways at Cavite, the U.S. Navy base on Manila Bay's southern shore they shared with Pan Am. There was Alfred and Lady Diana Duff-Cooper, on their way to Singapore to coordinate "the Far East Defenses of the Empire." Luce later asked Alfred Duff-Cooper about the world situation and reported, "[He] speaks quietly of the hell over London, the inferno that is Africa." Of course, in the proper British manner, he was confident "it will be quite all right, you know."

The first stop at Honolulu had the outward trappings of the Pacific paradise, as advertised, but Luce detected tension among native Hawaiians that resented the influx of mainland soldiers, sailors, contractors, and laborers. "The Army men go to Forts Schofield or Shafter, the Navy men visit Pearl Harbor where there is a high fever of activity, where building is going on faster than during any peacetime boom, where the bulk of the Pacific Fleet lies," Luce wrote. "How much? A lay-man can ask but isn't told. What there is of the Pacific Fleet in the harbor is painted a deep gray, almost black now . . . lowers the visibility from the air."

Midway was next, where Pan Am's base was shared with Marines who were deep into war preparations under the command of the "red-faced, hard-jawed, capable looking" Colonel Pepper. "Big pain in the neck to Colonel Pepper is how the mainland laborers imported to build the runways for bombers, the barracks, (arsenals), gun emplacements, breakwaters, oil storage tanks, which are beginning to network and cover the little island, get as much as $600 a month and won't 'stick' at Midway for more than three months," Luce noted. The Marines were getting $21 a month and likely there "for the duration."

When they arrived at Manila, the "Geneva of the Pacific," as Luce called it, she checked into the "swanky" Manila Hotel. But even in this cosmopolitan city, the political climate was feverish with war fears. Manila was "clearinghouse for the rumors of all the Orient, the hothouse of many of its intrigues," Luce observed.

That evening, a few blocks from the Manila Hotel, there was a party for the city elite at the estate of the High Commissioner. Luce changed into an evening gown and joined them. It was a typically hot and humid night, so the heart of the party was out on a wide portico lush with orchids and colorful macaws. There was a stunning view of the city and a sunset over Manila Bay that Luce described as "kaleidoscopic." But the conversation was all about next week's air raid drills and chances of war. Would Japan by-pass the Philippines and make a thrust at Singapore and the Dutch East Indies? If so, how could they leave a vulnerable flank to America? Manila, like Tokyo, was built of "tinderbox stuff" and wouldn't the city go up in flames if bombed?

And then the sunset was gone. The guests began heading out into the night, but Clare stayed on the high terrace, gazing over the city. "Now, the neon lights are flaming over the Jai-Alai Club, Manila's most glamorous and fashionable nightclub-café-restaurant-and bar. Everywhere in the hot, crowded, streets you see [Douglas] MacArthur's soldiers, [Admiral Thomas C.] Hart's sailors, a khaki-and-white stream flowing through the heart of the town, red corpuscles in the great civilian lymph." She thought of how the

U.S. flag would fly over this "Ameurasian city" until 1946 and concluded the city "is preparing for war. Here at last, there can be no question—that the 'bombs that fall will fall on American soil.'"

Luce headed back to the Manila Hotel.

"I fall into a fitful sleep. Through it comes the drone of the Clipper winging on to Singapore. If it were not a Clipper? If it were a Japanese bomber? Well, you can't expect to hold even in escrow an Island Empire like the Philippines and not get bombed . . . or can you?"[28]

## CHAPTER 19
# CASE 7: CONDITION A

> "The Pearl Harbor attack, of course, abruptly terminated the PAA Pacific Division operation. Things were much confused. The [Pan Am] aircraft were chartered to the Navy and Army Air Force for special missions around the world. All of us waited for plans to be sorted out."
>
> "I can remember giving [my baby] her 2:00 AM feeding and then turning on the radio to get the latest war news. There were blackouts along the west coast because of the possibility of air attacks. The news from the Philippines, Malaya and the Dutch East Indies was all bad as the Japanese advances continued. With such momentous events, I can't recall that we had much of a Christmas."
>
> —BILL TAYLOR, PAN AM PACIFIC DIVISION[1]

Early in November of 1941, a Japanese strike force of carriers and cruisers for launching fighter planes and bombers steamed out of the Japanese naval base at Kure. They arrived, undetected, within 275 miles of Pearl Harbor on Sunday morning, December 7. The commander, Vice-Admiral Chuichi Nagumo, launched the first attack wave from the carrier decks—forty-nine bombers, forty torpedo bombers, fifty-one dive-bombers, and forty-three fighter planes. A second wave unleashed fifty-four bombers, seventy-eight dive-bombers, and thirty-six fighters. Reportedly, as the first wave approached Oahu, a shroud of clouds parted for a clear view of Pearl Harbor—an omen, to the attackers, of divine intervention.[2]

The surprise attack killed 2,403 military personnel and civilians, wounded 1,178, and damage to the fleet included six sunken battleships and three destroyers and two battleships damaged. The airfield was shot up, with 164 airplanes destroyed and an additional 128 in need of repair. Only Nagumo's fear of a counter-attack prevented a third strike against fuel installations and other facilities.[3]

Caught by surprise, the Navy and Pan Am personnel at Pearl Harbor and nearby Pearl City worked to contain the damage. Two launches equipped with firefighting equipment and manned by Pan Am maintenance men helped fight the flames along the bombed-out waterfront. Pan Am communications personnel kept the system open and within ten minutes relayed the coded warning—"Case 7, Condition A"—to PAA aircraft and Pacific stations.[4]

Simultaneously, it was Monday morning, December 8, at Pan Am bases across the International Date Line. The morning at Wake Island began for pilot John Kinney as one of four Wildcat pilots taking off for dawn patrol. The *Philippine Clipper*, commanded by Captain John Hamilton, departed on schedule from the Peale Isle lagoon to begin the 1,500-mile flight to Guam with passengers, mail, and 200 airplane tires and supplies for the Flying Tigers.

The Clipper's radio operator received the alert—"Case 7, Condition A," followed by Wake Island Commander W. Scott Cunningham's message for Hamilton to return. The Clipper landed at the lagoon, passengers off-boarded, mail and freight were unloaded. Captain Hamilton and Pan Am airport manager John B. Cooke had their driver, Tommy, take them to the commander's office to discuss the emergency. Cunningham's Wildcats did not have a Clipper's flying range, and he asked Hamilton to take the Clipper up for a reconnaissance of potential Japanese air forces.

John Kinney and the morning patrol also returned, but Major Paul A. Putnam and Commander Cunningham ordered them to stay aloft until it was confirmed if they were at war. The four planes on patrol paired up, with

Kinney flying alongside Sergeant Bill Hamilton (no relation to the PAA pilot).

Tommy was driving Hamilton and Cooke back to Peale when they heard the drone of engines—a squadron of thirty-six planes was overhead. Tommy pulled over, and the men scrambled out, diving into the gaping hole dug for a foundation just as a bomb exploded, showering them with sand and debris. Hamilton jumped out and ran for cover, but machine gun fire kept Cooke and Tommy pinned. Cooke saw a bomb hit his house, blowing it up. Pan Am's hotel and radio installation were soon in ruins, while other living quarters and facilities were being blasted by machine-gun fire. A bomb exploded close enough to rock the moored Clipper, followed by a gunner ripping dozens of machine gun holes along its fuselage.[5]

The patrol was sixty miles from Wake and flying in stormy weather. "We still had not received confirmation of the Japanese attack at Oahu, and nerves were on edge," recalled Kinney. He and Hamilton were in radio silence but maintaining visual contact with each other. Sixty miles was the allowable limit to safely find their way back to the tiny island, given their lack of homing devices, and they decided to return to base. Kinney was coming through the clouds when he saw two bomber formations far below—he later learned they were the new Mitsubishi Navy attack bombers. Kinney then saw columns of smoke rising from the island.[6]

With no radar, the low-flying Mitsubishi fighters had not been detected when they attacked at 9:30 a.m. Batteries D and E responded with anti-aircraft guns, but to no effect. The attack left seven of the eight Wildcats sitting on the airfield "completely unsalvageable," Kinney recalled, and severely damaged the other. Two above-ground fuel tanks were hit, and black clouds from 25,000 gallons of burning gasoline were billowing into the air. Kinney estimated that of the fifty-five men of the VMF-211, twenty-three were dead, eleven wounded. "By the time I landed, the military and civilian medical staffs had begun to treat the wounded at the hospital at Camp 2, and able-bodied survivors had taken all the dead to the refrigerated storage facility until proper burials could be arranged," Kinney noted.[7] Nine of sixty-four Pan Am employees were among the dead. The only good news was the bullet-riddled Clipper could still fly.

The dazed islanders assumed there would be another attack, although the enemy would probably not risk approaching at night. They dug foxholes, rigged gun emplacements with camouflage screens, cleaned empty gasoline jugs and filled them with fresh water in case the next attack put the distillation plant out of commission. The island's air force was reduced to the four patrol planes. With the only experienced mechanic in the island hospital with dysentery, Major Putnam put Kinney in charge of keeping those Wildcats flying.[8]

Captain Hamilton loaded seventy passengers and Pan Am employees into the *Philippine Clipper* to fly to San Francisco. The plane boarded without Pan Am employee Waldo Raugust, who was so busy driving an ambulance across the hard-hit island and helping wounded Chamorro hotel staff, that he told a fellow-employee that if he wasn't back in time to go ahead without him. The plane did leave without Raugust and, shockingly, purposely left without its Chamorro staff. Despite having stripped out all extra equipment and cargo, including supplies for the Flying Tigers, the Clipper was dangerously overloaded with passengers and two takeoff attempts failed.[9] On its third try, the ship got airborne, and as it gained speed the cabin filled with sounds of air whistling through the bullet holes.

The *Philippine Clipper* was on its way to Midway when Hamilton saw two Japanese warships and relayed that information to military authorities. Hamilton received news that it was safe to land on Midway to refuel, which had been shelled that morning by the warships. Although the attack demolished the facility for Pan Am's direction-finding equipment, no personnel died, and they would be evacuated by surface ship.[10] Hamilton continued to Pearl Harbor, now a fiery disaster zone but also reported safe for landing. On December 10, flying under radio silence, Hamilton brought the *Philippine Clipper* home to Treasure Island.[11]

In addition to Wake and Midway, Pan Am personnel were evacuated from Canton, Suva, Nouméa, and Auckland. Pan Am's island bases wouldn't reopen until September of 1942 when Pan Am personnel returned to participate in the Naval Air Transport Service.[12]

⭐

In Hong Kong, the morning of December 8, William Bond learned that Captain Fred S. Ralph had, strangely, been told not to take off on his scheduled flight to Manila, while the government in Hong Kong told him to depart immediately. Bond, who was across the bay from the Kai Tak Airport in Kowloon, phoned Ralph and told him to fly the *Hong Kong Clipper II* to Manila. Ten minutes later, Ralph phoned back—Japan was at war against the U.S. and Britain. Bond knew they needed to get all their planes out of Hong Kong, and told Ralph to fly the Clipper to Kunming. After hanging up, Bond drove to Victoria Harbour to catch a ferry to the Hong Kong side, arriving just as an air raid closed the ferry.[13] But with the help of some soldiers, Bond commandeered a sampan to get across the bay.

Captain Moon Chin was still in bed at his home overlooking the waterfront and seaplane dock at Kai Tak Airport when he glanced out his window and saw an approaching formation of fighter planes. "I thought they were practicing," Chin recalled. "From my bed, I could see the American Clipper in the water. I saw the tail of the DC-2 in front of the hangar. All of a sudden I saw water spraying up. They were machine-gunning that Clipper. That Clipper had been waiting to go to Manila, so it had a lot of gas in its tank, and it caught fire right away."

Captain Ralph and his six-person crew were at the dock, waist-deep in water and discussing how to get the Clipper to safety when the attack came. They shielded themselves behind a concrete post, repeatedly diving underwater as their flying boat was ripped with bullets and became engulfed in flames.[14]

By the time Bond arrived at the airport, eight CNAC transports on the airfield were destroyed. But there were five unscathed planes in the hangar. A battle-tested group that included shop superintendent Soldinski, communications man Price, and pilots Sharp, Angle, Schuler, Kessler, and Scott were pushing planes off the field, spacing them hundreds of yards apart in vegetable patches and camouflaging them with mud and straw.

Night and heavy overcast settled in and under what *New Horizons* called a "double cloak of darkness," CNAC began evacuating U.S. citizens, government leaders, and others into China's interior. Frank Higgs, at the controls of a DC-3, was first to leave on the 200-mile flight to Namyung, departing with CNAC staff and families. Harold Sweet followed fifteen minutes later in another DC-3, and Kessler took off a half hour after that in a DC-2.

Later that night, the drone of an approaching plane galvanized Kai Tak Airport, with searchlights sweeping the sky and British anti-aircraft guns ready to fire—they stood down when the plane was recognized as Frank Higgs' transport, completing the first round-trip. By 4:00 a.m. the others returned for the next 400-mile round-trip.

All through the night and into the following evening planes departed and returned. "Every man was in the place where he was needed most, and there he stayed," Bond described. "We had to assign pilots to each flight to stop arguments; each pilot wanted to fly every flight." Sixteen reported trips evacuated 275 adults and more than a hundred children.[15]

★

The morning of December 8, Rush S. Clark, acting section operations superintendent and airport manager at Pan Am's Cavite base in Manila, arrived to make scheduled flight dispatches for Wake to Guam and Hong Kong to Manila. But he discovered "inexplicable messages." He called the Navy and learned Pearl Harbor was bombed. Clark sent out the emergency code to Wake and Guam; Hong Kong had eliminated the use of Pan Am's code, so he sent a direct message to Captain Ralph recommending he not fly as scheduled to Manila, the call that caused the confusion for Bond.

Clark felt the Navy was not accurately monitoring and relaying information of incoming aircraft to Army and Air Force stations. Pan Am had twenty-six weather observation stations throughout the Philippines connected by telegraphic cables to Cavite airport, and Clark used the network to monitor enemy aircraft. The weather station at Lingayen Gulf was especially valuable, the operator reporting Japanese planes that usually left Formosa each day at dawn, hitting Manila at precisely 1:00 p.m.

For the next month, Manila was under attack. On December 10, Clark was at a meeting at the Manila Hotel, when a Japanese bombing run headed for Cavite. He took a naval barge back to base, arriving just after the bombers passed over the naval yard, leaving behind sunken ships and shattered buildings. Clark learned that 1,600 had died. He had seen no U.S. planes meet the onslaught and ground fire hadn't even disrupted the attack formation.

The adjacent Pan Am base was not hit, although several days later bombs fell near the terminal and seaplane docks as airline personnel dug in. "From our small air raid shelter we blessed our sandbags and watched the bombs falling and heard the distinctive chilling whistle and flutter of the bombs as they seemed to be coming in to each of us personally!" Clark recalled. "They did not hit any of the Pan Am installations."

The Navy left Cavite, General MacArthur moved his forces to Bataan, and Pan Am ordered all local employees dismissed. By December 24, Navy representatives arrived and told Clark that Japan had begun its invasion of the Philippines—they wanted Pan Am's facility destroyed, along with the naval base, before it fell to the enemy. Clark argued that Pan Am was a civilian company and its facility should remain open. If official word from the Navy felt the facility was of no further use, Clark argued, he would take responsibility for destroying it. He got that order on December 31.

On January 1, Japanese ground forces were within hours of Manila. Clark drove to Cavite and, with the help of nearby employees, began rolling gasoline drums into the supply and shop areas. Pan Am's wooden terminal building, other than its iron roof, burned easily. Clark rolled several oil drums to the docks, opened them to let the oil run out, and used a lighted broom as a match. "Right then I realized there is a science in making destruction safely—and almost got blown off from the floating dock when the drum [exploded]," Clark recalled. "However, it went a different way and missed me. I was unable to destroy the concrete ramp but was able to do considerable damage to it and also to the boats and gear. As I left there were towering flames and huge black smoke." Clark raced back to Manila, which was occupied by sundown.

Strangely, the next day was the wedding of Pan Am operations representative Ken Huebsch. Clark and two friends showed up for the 11:00 a.m. ceremony at a Catholic Church in Manila's center. They noticed a Japanese guard post was seemingly letting people through. Unfortunately, Clark later realized it was only "dark skinned locals," and Clark and his friends were held at bayonet point. "We were put on the back of a truck together with a drunken merchant sailor who had been collected [along with several other Americans]," Clark recalled. "I felt that probably the merchant sailor had the right idea and rather envied him. He could barely stand up as he had so much to drink, but he was not really concerned as we were. So we were bundled in this truck and off we went [past] the church and waved to Ken's fiancée and drove away."[16]

★

Japanese warplanes returned to Wake by midday, December 9. Wildcats met them in the air, along with fire from the anti-aircraft batteries—this time the guns blew up a Japanese fighter to the cheers of the battery crew and islanders. The attack was repulsed, but dozens of the civilian construction crews were killed. Peale was struck again, and Camp 2 hospital took a direct bomb hit.

The enemy attacked on schedule, with bombing raids coming at predawn and midday. December 11 was a big day for island defenders, with two Japanese destroyers sunk and Wildcats and antiaircraft guns again holding their own. All the while, Wake prayed for American reinforcements. The battle was in its second week when the Japanese began attacking with a new type of fighter plane, one that would be synonymous with Japanese air power—the Zero.

By December 22, Kinney was suffering from dysentery and reluctantly checked into the hospital. That night two converted Japanese destroyers landed at Wake's south shore, and one thousand troops poured out. Communications between the atolls were cut off, but Commander Cunningham managed to radio Pearl Harbor: "Enemy on island. Issue in doubt." Cunningham also sent a message "in the clear" to alert American submarines. The reply from Pearl Harbor was devastating. "[The message] simply said that the subs were not there anymore and that, in fact, there were no friendly ships within twenty-four hours' steaming time of Wake," Kinney recalled. "The relief force had been recalled!"

Kinney, stuck in the hospital without even a sidearm, heard automatic weapons fire heralding the arrival of Japanese soldiers. Dr. Gustave Kahn, the Navy surgeon, answered a field phone and learned the island was overrun. Although there was spirited resistance, Commander Cunningham realized they were postponing the inevitable and surrendered.

"About an hour and a half after we learned of the surrender order Japanese soldiers finally arrived at our part of the island and began banging on the steel door of the hospital bunker with their rifle butts," Kinney recalled. "Dr. Kahn opened the door, and all of us who were able to do so raised our hands above our heads. We were unarmed and completely at their mercy, and we did not want them to think that they had stumbled into a fighting bunker and come in shooting. It did not matter. They fired a few random shots from inside the doorway anyway. As bullets ricocheted around the room several patients were hit. Two men near my bed were killed, and a few others were so badly re-wounded that they died soon after... They did show at least a small shred of humanity by allowing Dr. Kahn to remain with those hospital patients unable to move."

By January 12, Japanese troopships arrived. Some prisoners remained on the island as slave labor; others were herded into the troopships and headed for prison camps, among them John Kinney and stranded Pan Am employee Waldo Raugust. "We spent most of the time merely trying to survive, both physically and emotionally," Kinney recalled. "Early hope that the war would be short and we would all soon be free faded by then."[17]

# CHAPTER 20
# CLIPPERS AT WAR

*"[Japan's] occupation of Wake, Guam and the Philippines cut the trans-Pacific line to the Orient. But the alternative military air route to China via the South Atlantic was available, serving Africa, the Middle East, Russia and India as well. Bombers and military supplies were en route to our allies. Critical materials from the Orient, the Middle East, Africa and South America necessary for our munitions plants at home were soon on their way. World-wide communications for vital mails and important passengers were maintained."*

—Juan Trippe[1]

Japan hit Pan Am hard—nine employees dead, thirty-three missing, forty-nine interned, nearly a million dollars in equipment losses. The Pacific Division was reduced to the San Francisco–Honolulu route, crews dropped from sixteen to nine, and two Martin M-130s and one Boeing 314 were flying the world's longest scheduled airway in radio silence and without normal meteorological support. "At the same time it was considered expedient to hold a nucleus of the pre-war organization in the Pacific Division to permit its rapid expansion later into full wartime operations," a Pan Am period document records.[2]

After the attack—"Pearl Harbor" was all that needed to be said—Pan Am flights from Honolulu evacuated the wounded and women and children to

Treasure Island, returning with blood plasma, vaccines, serums, and other medical supplies. The route shuttled military and government officials and mail loads as high as 7,818 pounds a trip.[3]

Air traffic to the Far East was rerouted through South America and Africa. The trans-Africa airway was always key—four days before Pearl Harbor, the Army Air Force and Pan Am were working on a Supplemental Contract extending operations from Africa to the U.S.S.R., with new service from Khartoum to Basra.

In Latin America, ADP had gotten off to a slow start—in September of '41, the War Department officially complained to Pan Am that it was "unsatisfactory." But the day after Pearl Harbor, John Cooper alerted Secretary of War Stimson that ADP head Graham Grosvenor was being replaced by Samuel Pryor, a Pan Am vice president and assistant to Trippe. Pryor, a Yale man and Republican Party insider, took charge and the turn-around began. As Pryor got results, ADP's budget grew from twelve to ninety million dollars. Fifty airports would be built, with the workforce peaking at a thousand Americans and 25,000 native laborers. For his leadership, Pryor would be decorated with the Medal of Merit, the nation's highest civilian honor. "Pryor himself proved a brilliant manager, and as success followed success the morale and efficiency of his men reached incredible heights," historian Robert Daley notes. "No job stopped these people."[4]

December 13, 1941, was a landmark day in the integration of civilian airlines into wartime operations, including recommendation and approval of a "Secret" Supplemental Contract to the original August 12 agreement between the War Department and Pan Am and its subsidiaries, Pan Am Air Ferries and Pan Am-Africa. Provisions included delivering planes and parts to the British, the Republic of China, the Union of Soviet Socialist Republics, Port Sudan on the Red Sea, and "other points to which such routes may hereafter be extended."[5] With no provision for war risk insurance, the government on December 13 also purchased eight of Pan Am's Boeing Clippers, concentrated in the Atlantic Division, for certified operations and what was called "special missions."[6]

On that busy December 13th, Roosevelt delegated control of all civilian airlines to the Secretary of War. "American aircraft assembly lines could not hope to fill all these needs on short notice, and it became necessary to call upon civilian airlines for assistance by utilizing aircraft already in their possession to help overcome the lack of sufficient military transport planes," the Air Force's South Atlantic history records. "The War Department contracted with Pan American, Trans-continental and Western Air and American Airlines to transport strategic air cargo, chiefly to foreign destinations."[7] On December 29, representatives from all U.S. airlines were called to Washington to hear War Department, Army Air Force, and Ferrying Command presentations concerning national security policy, including wartime release of information to the press.[8]

It was already clear that international air operations in wartime would not be a one-airline show. The day after Pearl Harbor, a CAB public hearing included competing applications by Pan Am and Export Airlines for temporary certification of air service to Foynes, Ireland. Major Eugene Gillespie testified for the War Department that "in the interests of National Defense" both applications "be favorably acted upon." An internal War Department memo to General Arnold from Lieutenant Colonel Harold George of the Air Staff summarized the testimony: "The War Department stated that in view of recent events and with permission of the Civil Aeronautics Board, it would like to state to the present applicants as well as all commercial air carriers that the War Department would not further tolerate the subordination of National Defense interests to the commercial agitations of air carriers. It was expressed that this statement might engender complete cooperation essential to the great task in which we are all presently engaged."[9]

Pan Am's importance was manifest in the many PAA-Africa, Ltd. schedules in operation, with over 500 American employees either in Africa or on their way when war began. "[L]onely Pan Am boys in the desert Coast of Arabia pumping gasoline into a Bomber cannot be cast as heroes; But they were something that was rare in those first off-balance weeks after Pearl Harbor: Americans in the right spot with the right equipment," Pan Am's corporate history records.[10] Service between Brazil and Africa, primarily established to return ferry pilots from Africa, now transported critical war supplies.[11]

The massive Boeing Clippers, with their huge load-carrying capacity, were indispensable. Of the eight purchased by the government, four would continue commercial operations, including "anti-LATI" service. The remainder were assigned special missions by the government and War Department. "In the first year of the war there was a large element of pioneering about many of these special missions," a Pan Am document reports. "An aircraft might be dispatched on two or three days' notice on a flight covering as many as four continents. . . . Security restrictions were so rigid that at times the flight plan and destination could be disclosed in advance only to the Atlantic Division Manager and Operations Manager."[12]

Clippers were gray camouflaged and flew "blacked-out" and without radio and weather reports.[13] One of the most dramatic pioneering missions was the flight of the *Pacific Clipper*, its transition to military service coming as the Clipper was in the air and bombs and bullets were hitting Pearl Harbor.

★

On December 10, 1941, a handwritten letter addressed "Gentlemen," in care of La Guardia Field, arrived from J. D. Ford, chairman of Harvard's Department of Romance Languages and Literatures. His son, Clipper Captain Robert Ford, was last heard from on December 4, on his way from Honolulu to Auckland. "Can you give me definite word about my son[?]," he inquired. "We suppose that he concluded his trip unaffected by the Japanese. We trust that he can follow a return course that will mean safety. I shall greatly appreciate a reply from you."

Bixby gave John Leslie the go-ahead to contact Ford's parents. Leslie telephoned their Cambridge home, got Mrs. Ford on the line, and assured her that Robert was in New Zealand and would return by a safe route; he would just be out of touch for a few days.[14] It was an understatement—Captain Ford was about to embark on one of the great air odysseys.

The morning of December 8, Robert Ford, his crew, and three Pan Am employees flew from Nouméa, New Caledonia, in the *Pacific Clipper*. They were two hours from Honolulu when one of the employees, radio operator

Eugene Leach from Nouméa, while experimenting with new DF and receiving equipment, began picking up radio broadcast signals. Suddenly, a news announcer from Auckland boomed in with unconfirmed reports that waves of Japanese bombers had struck the Pearl Harbor naval base and other targets. Captain Ford was told, and even as he requested confirmation, Leach received it over his headphones via Morse code from the Nouméa ground station.

Ford got his flight bag and took out the sealed envelope. The "Top Secret" emergency orders included getting to a safe harbor as quickly as possible, offloading passengers, and camouflaging aircraft. Ford announced they were in wartime mode and would continue to Auckland to await further instructions.[15] Fourth officer John Steers wrote in his diary: "At first no one believed it true. The Captain silenced the radio, then posted watches in the blister [the observation dome], then altered his course about fifty miles." Steers saw Ford get out a .38 caliber pistol.[16]

On December 12, Ford's crew was camouflaging their plane when they received orders to return to the U.S. via Australia and India. They were to first fly back to Nouméa, pick up twenty-two Pan Am employees and fly them to Gladstone, Australia, and dissemble two engines and bring them as spares to Karachi and Bahrain, off the coast of Saudi Arabia. That was the first milestone—first flight between Nouméa and Gladstone. Ford continued in radio silence and had to forego company protocol for weather forecasting and other preflight preparations.[17]

The day Ford got his orders, Trippe reported to Arnold that the *Pacific Clipper* was flying home by way of Australia and India, "utilizing our emergency fuel caches along the route," and transporting personnel and war supplies.[18]

One of the tensest incidents came when the Clipper flew to Surabaya, Java, to refuel, a stop Ford thought was cleared by the American consul in Port Darwin, their previous stop. It appeared the notification was never made—as the camouflaged aircraft approached the harbor, a RAF Brewster F2A Buffalo fighter was on its tail. The fighter radioed the control tower and asked, "Shall I let them have it?"

The pilot did not know if the aircraft was German or Japanese, but by chance spotted part of the U.S. flag that had not been fully camouflaged. "That doesn't mean anything," the controller replied after the pilot's report. "Anyone can paint on an American flag." The pilot asked for air support, and four fighters were scrambled. "Stay on her tail," the controller ordered. "If she gets even a little way off the normal course for landing, shoot her down."

But that glimpse of an American flag bought Ford time to land. "They were still suspicious and followed us right into the bay," First Radio Operator John Poindexter recalled. "When we hit the water they sailed right over us and on into the airport. As we slowed down, a speedboat zigzagged out to our position. Captain Ford put the Clipper in a tight turn to stop our forward progress. The boat approached and we were instructed by bullhorn to follow close behind to our mooring. Then the voice told us why: 'The harbor is mined.'"[19]

"The skipper decided to stay in Surabaya until he could proceed with assurance that there would be no repetition of this incident," Steers noted. "We chatted with the fighter pilots in the officers' mess, and they agreed that we were very lucky indeed. They had had several air raids and were not only keyed up but were eager for it."[20]

There was not enough 100-octane fuel available in Java, so the *Pacific Clipper* had to use automobile fuel, leaving the four engines popping all the way to Trincomalee, Ceylon. On Christmas Eve, bound for Karachi, cylinder head studs snapped, forcing repairs back in Trincomalee.[21] They made Khartoum, but an engine blew an exhaust tank en route to the Belgian Congo. Ford landed in Leopoldville, where Pan Am had recently opened airmail service. There were no exhaust parts available, and despite a fire risk, Ford decided to press on in the morning. There was aviation fuel, and Ford ordered more than 5,100 gallons for the ocean crossing to Natal.[22] The withering heat during takeoff pushed the four Wright Cyclone 14-cylinder engines beyond limits—the average for holding engines at full throttle was forty-five seconds; Ford had to maintain it for more than three minutes. The "grueling take-off subsequently dumbfounded aeronautical engineers who heard of it, represented a bright feather in the cap of the Wright Aeronautical Corp., makers of the Clipper's engines," *New Horizons* reported.[23]

The leg to Natal was the longest nonstop flight by a Pan Am aircraft—3,583 miles in nearly twenty-four hours. Natal was only a respite for refueling and makeshift repair of the blown exhaust stack. On January 3, they left Natal for Port-of-Spain, but the exhaust stack blew during takeoff, the engine hammering all the way to Trinidad.[24]

Before dawn on January 6, 1942, the La Guardia Airport control tower received the message: "*Pacific Clipper*, inbound from Auckland, New Zealand, Captain Ford reporting. Due arrive Pan American Marine Air Terminal La Guardia seven minutes." There was no flight plan for a Clipper from New Zealand, and with America on high alert, La Guardia wondered if Nazis commandeered an American plane. Landing a seaplane at night in Bowery Bay was not allowed, so as the Clipper circled until dawn, military personnel were on the way, along with Atlantic Division Manager John Leslie, Public Relations Director William Van Dusen, and others.

The Clipper landed, and Ford led his crew wrapped in blankets against the freezing weather. "The water splashed up on the sea wings and froze solid," Steers recalled. "The hawser on the buoy was like a chunk of ice." Division engineer Edward W. McVitty came aboard for a look. Apart from a washroom sign written in red crayon about conserving water, and a dirty white shirt hung in the tail compartment, there was no evidence of the marathon 31,500-mile flight.

Ford described it as a "routine operation," but *New Horizons* provided the proper perspective: "As a test of ingenuity, self-reliance and resourcefulness, the flight . . . proved sensationally Pan American's Multiple Crews, operating techniques & technicians could meet any possible situation that might arise in long distance flying."[25]

Meanwhile, on December 20, the Air Force Ferrying Command ordered "special operation order No. 6," its cargo including 129 urgently needed plane parts for the Flying Tigers' grounded P-40s. The route from New York to Natal, Leopoldville, Khartoum, Karachi, to Calcutta would become familiar to Pan Am's future "Cannonball" and other transport operations. In command was Captain Harold Gray, at the controls of the *Capetown Clipper*, the same captain and aircraft that inaugurated mail service to Leopoldville a few weeks before, on December 6.[26]

Gray's mission covered the initial stages of his historic airmail flight, but the day after Christmas "swung from the Congo River to begin the farthest island penetration ever attempted by an ocean flying boat," notes an internal Pan Am report. Nine hours later, the Clipper landed at Port Bell in Uganda. The next day it made the Khartoum seaplane base maintained by the British Overseas Airways Corp. At Aden, Saudi Arabia, mechanical problems caused a day's loss, but an overnight push covered the 1,470 miles to Karachi. The final 1,230-miles crossed desert and plain, with Gray setting down on the Hooghly Channel of the Ganges Delta. It was a hand-off, with CNAC taking the supplies the rest of the way.[27]

Chennault later wrote it was the Tigers' first supplies since the designated AVG shipment dumped on Wake became "booty" for the Japanese. "C.N.A.C. planes rushed the precious cargo from Calcutta to Kunming in one of the first large-scale deliveries of air cargo across the Hump between India and China," he noted.[28]

Clipper supplies for fighting fronts included 12,000 pounds of engine dust filters for the Western Desert Campaign. One desert flight returned with the barrel and breech of a German 88-millimeter anti-tank cannon that was studied by ordinance experts at the Army Proving Grounds in Aberdeen, Maryland. Between May and December of 1942, special mission cargo to Africa amounted to 2,239,500 pounds, with westbound shuttles carrying 54,000 pounds of crude rubber for retreading. From September of 1941 through September 1943, Pan Am completed ninety-nine special missions for the Army, Navy, and State Department, racking up a staggering 2,232,047 miles.[29]

★

Bad weather battered the B-24 over the northern coast of Brazil on July 13, 1942, blowing it off course and knocking out radio and compass bearings.

Pilot Felix W. Kershner, forced to make an emergency landing, miraculously found a jungle clearing and set down on an ancient lake bed thick with waist-high scrub. The only damage was the landing gear and a cracked bombardier's window, but a half-million-dollar bomber was out of the fight. Kershner and crew trekked out, the nearest outpost of civilization being 150 miles away. On their ninth night, while drifting on life rafts, they successfully signaled a steamer with a cigarette lighter.

The U.S. Army Engineering Corps called on Pan Am's Airport Development Program to help find the bomber and get a work crew there to clear a runway. The operation was led by ADP engineer Mario de la Torre, ADP labor foreman William Moulton, and civilian engineer Donald Smith of the Army Engineering Corps. The B-24 crew provided a rough location and U.S. Captain Robert Payne and Mario de la Torre began a survey flight on July 28. On the fourth day, they spotted the stranded bomber, seventy-one miles inland from Belém.

Work crews moved in. Torre, a thirty-three-year-old self-described "Tropical tramp" from Ecuador with five years experience as a construction engineer in South America, forged by motor launch up the Acara Grande River with a team of ten porters and crew. "On such jobs, he learned practically all there was to know about preserving one's life in an atmosphere of hot tempers, quick triggers, fast blades and tropical fevers," reported *New Horizons*.

After 150 miles, Torre's crew switched to native canoes at a smaller tributary, paddling fifteen miles upstream until it narrowed. They left the canoes and began a grueling four-day hike, Torre setting a pace that drew incredulous stares from natives they passed. On the trail a venomous bushmaster snake bit Torre on his left index finger—"had to shoot the end of the finger off to avoid dying," he wrote in his diary. The next day, the group stepped out of the jungle and into a clearing—and under the shadow of the B-24s left wing.

While Torre got the work started, Moulton and a construction team, engineer Smith, and the bomber pilot and crew followed the way to the stranded plane, arriving on August 20. In fierce heat, foreman Moulton and fifty-four workers began clearing brush. The labor force quickly increased to 104. Water was brought from a creek two miles away and boiled and sprinkled with iodine, although native workers cut long vines to drain for water. In twenty-two days, 100,000 square yards of jungle was cleared and 2,000 cubic yards of earth moved. On September 12, ten days ahead of schedule, a 5,000-foot airstrip was ready. The bomber roared down it, taking to the air at the 3,300-foot mark to the cheers of engineers and workers.

"Shade in their eyes in the white heat of the tropical sun, the weary but triumphant salvage crewmen watched the B-24 waggle its wings, turn its nose north toward Belem—and active duty against the Axis," *New Horizons* reported. "Then they gathered up their meager tools—machetes, hoes, picks, shovels and home-made dirt carrying platforms—folded their tents, started the long trek back to civilization."[30]

With ADP on track, Pan Am also finished its de-Germanization campaign in Brazil. Pan Am applied to amend its certification to take over Axis airways and the U.S., unshackled from Neutrality Act restraints, cut off gasoline supplies, putting Axis airlines out of business. LATI had gasoline reserves and could have kept flying, but when the U.S. promised Brazil a replacement service to Europe LATI's fate was sealed, and it ceased operations on December 24, freeing 10,500 route miles.[31]

"LATI has ceased operation and the replacement service promised Brazil must now be installed," William Burden, vice president of Defense Supplies Corporation in Washington, reported to Major Gillespie in early January. Burden requested that a War Department representative testify to the "military necessity" of LATI's immediate replacement at a January 9 Civil Aeronautics Board executive session regarding Pan Am's certification amendment. Gillespie represented the War Department, State Department and Navy representatives appeared in support, and Burden testified to his company's agreement to supply Pan Am with a Boeing 314 for operations between Brazil and Portugal, and two DC-3 transports between Natal and Buenos Aires.[32]

Brazil's demand for replacement service before fully supporting LATI's termination had left U.S. military officials wary. Indeed, in March of '41,

Brazil authorized LATI to import, free of duty, 400,000 kilos of aviation gasoline from Aruba, and 15,000 kilos of aviation oil from New York.[33] "The fact that we had just signed the Lend-Lease agreement with Brazil did not mean that Brazil was completely pro-Ally," the Air Force South Atlantic history observes. "A shift in the war situation might easily have caused a break in Brazilian-American relations. The military situation continued to be very black. In the battle of the Java Sea thirteen United States warships had been sunk, while the Japanese lost only two; on February 23, at Santa Barbara, California, oil tanks had been shelled by Japanese submarines; and the loss of all East Asia was imminent."[34]

Brazil was the linchpin of hemispheric security and anchor of the transatlantic and trans-Africa operation, and while it was cooperating it wasn't working fast enough for Brigadier General Leland W. Miller, military attaché in Rio. That February, Ferrying Command leader, Brigadier General Olds (he was promoted in January) was called upon to help with the "rather delicate situation," as Miller called it. Key to Brazilian-American relations was Olds's friendship with General Gomes, air commander of the Natal-Recife region. Olds notified Washington on March 19 of a plan that included the U.S. keeping its own commitments, including fifty promised planes so Gomes could fulfill his end of their joint security responsibilities. Olds visited Brazil for discussions with General Gomes and President Vargas, inviting Gomes to return with him to the U.S. for more high-level talks and tours of military installations. The two nations began drawing up a comprehensive military and political accord. When shown the draft, Gomes replied, "Put some teeth in it."

"His immediate reaction was that it lacked strength . . . and teeth went in, concessions which a decade ago would have been unthinkable," notes the Air Force's South Atlantic history. Negotiations were completed by May of 1942. The U.S. agreed to assist Brazil if attacked by an "extra-continental power" or Axis-controlled "American republic," and to speed delivery of planes and war materials. Brazil agreed to cooperate in hemispheric defense, mobilize its war industry to build airplanes and naval craft, and guard against internal threats and sabotage.

There was a lingering pro-Nazi sentiment in Brazil, along with enemy submarines prowling its coastal waters—three ships were sunk that April with no public outrage. But pro-Allied sentiment had taken root. On May 1, 1942, President Vargas announced the pact with the United States "was an important obligation based on continental solidarity."[35]

⭒

Pan Am's trans-Africa operation boasted twenty-six airports and forty-eight transports. Cargo and supplies were flown from the U.S. to Brazil, across the ocean by Clipper to Benson Field at Fisherman's Lake, and loaded onto PAA-Africa C-53s or C-47s for delivery. The operation began in October of 1941 with twenty-nine flights and 15,190 miles; by September of '42, it was 1,667 flights and 907,692 miles.[36]

"We are really beginning to hum!" an enthusiastic Harold Whiteman in Accra reported to PR director William Van Dusen. "A half dozen of the American Volunteer pilots who have been fighting in China and along the Burma Road have been here recently to ferry a convoy of P40s across the continent. What flyers! They put on shows for a couple of days that stopped work for everyone and panicked the natives, who have been talking about nothing since." Whiteman's next report observed, "I got a distinct thrill the other night when a British officer in Accra said to me, 'You fellows certainly have gingered this place up a bit.'"[37]

"The route continued to evolve rapidly as the tide of battle changed in the Africa, Europe, and the China-Burma theaters of war," write Pan-Africa historians Tom Culbert and Andy Dawson. "By April 1942, Pan Am-Africa had aircraft and air crews ranging out as far east as Kunming, China, and as far north as Kuybyshev, in the Soviet Union. Thus, PAA-Africa's mission had expanded greatly from the operational concept that was first developed in July 1941."[38]

By the summer of '42, Ascension Island became a South Atlantic stopover between Natal and Africa's Gold Coast. "The enemy submarines often used the same radio frequency as that of the Island and caused confusion and danger for flight crews," recalls Pan Am's Ernest Colant. "This is mentioned from personal experience."[39]

U.S. entry into the war did not alter the uneasy alliance between British and American air interests in Africa. The Royal Air Force delegation in Washington complained to Arnold when Pan Am opened a booking office in Cairo. Britain had also agreed that Pan Am take over communications operated by the BOAC, but bristled at General Olds's request for diplomatic arrangements allowing Pan Am to install radio transmitters for Ferrying Command use between Cairo and Bangalore. "[T]he existing facilities on the far east route on the sections in question are, in our view, adequate to deal with all the traffic for which provision is necessary," A. T. Harris, of the RAF delegation, wrote Arnold. "These sections form part of the peacetime Imperial Airways route, and in such circumstances, the installation of a separate communications system seems unnecessary, introduces possibilities of dislocation and confusion to both parties, and jeopardises [sic] security."[40]

In a secret memo to the Air War Plans Division, Olds explained that a contract extension with Pan Am was signed with British knowledge and without opposition. The extension granted full commercial rights to Pan American Airways-Africa, Ltd. to carry cargos, passengers, and mail because BOAC's route was to be discontinued, given its planes and personnel were urgently needed elsewhere. Olds noted Pan Am's service was in operation and financed through Lend-Lease funds "strictly for the benefit of the British Government."

Olds addressed the radio network in words that would not warm the hearts of the British aviation industry: "[B]y contract with Pan American, point-to-point radio facilities are being initiated and placed in operation as rapidly as possible to meet, not only the air transportation requirement over this route from Miami to Calcutta, but to permit the movement of United States Army Air Force combat echelons as well as the flight delivery of Lend-Lease aircraft with American crews. . . . The experience of every American pilot flying over the route from West Africa to Bangalore to date has been identical. That is, the existing Royal Air Force or BOAC communications net is totally inadequate, inefficient and non-operative at times when needed most. We can neither depend on such inadequate communications to accomplish the gigantic task with which we are confronted, nor attempt to operate with characteristic American efficiency when vital dependence upon the success of operations must be placed on inefficient communications nets operated under the control of other agencies."[41]

⭐

In April of '42 Captain Moon Chin and his CNAC crew made their scheduled landing at Chungking, but the takeoff for Kunming was delayed—Chin knew something was up when he spotted the American ambassador and other high officials. Finally, with ten passengers aboard his DC-3, Chin got the go-ahead. They were en route when an air raid warning forced an emergency landing on a mountain airstrip (alerts ranged from daytime signage to flashing lights at night). Chin scrambled into a ditch and was joined by a passenger he now recognized—Colonel Jimmy Doolittle, inexplicably dressed in "pretty dirty" clothes. Chin last saw him in 1933, while working as a mechanic at a Shanghai airfield where Doolittle performed a dangerous stunt in his Curtiss-Hawk—a vertical approach with both hands up and waving at the crowd and then a sudden barrel roll before climbing back up into the sky. Chin didn't know the old daredevil had just escaped a riskier flight—leading a bombing mission over Japan.

"Then when we got clearance, I got all the passengers on the plane, but [Doolittle] didn't get on the plane," Chin recalled. "He just stood there near the wing tip [to] talk to me." Doolittle was concerned because the mountaintop airfield wasn't level and the plane was parked on an incline. "Then of course there was some telephone wires on a bamboo pole in a ditch or something. . . . So he said, 'What about those?' I said, 'Gee, if we don't make it we'll just take the wire with us.' [laughing] He got on the plane."

In Kunming, Chennault awaited Doolittle. Chin saw them drive off, but when he was ready to depart for Dinjan, India, Doolittle returned to reboard. Chin had new orders to fly to Myitkyina in northern Burma and pick up a radio operator and his equipment; a risky assignment given Burma was under siege.

When Chin landed at Myitkyina, a desperate crowd pressed around the plane. "They all wanted to go," Chin remembered. "We tried to take as many as we could. . . . Doolittle helped. We had to take the ladder away because we didn't want people climbing up. We picked the older people and the ladies with kids. . . . When we were nearly packed, Doolittle wanted to know what the hell I was doing. I said, 'We do this quite often.'" Seventy passengers crowded into a transport that normally carried twenty-eight passengers and a three-person crew.

With not enough fuel for Dinjan, Chin landed in Calcutta, where American Embassy officials were waiting. As they ushered Doolittle away, he waved goodbye to Chin. "He didn't go through customs," Chin recalled. "He didn't go through immigration." The airline knew Doolittle was aboard, "but they didn't know he had bombed Tokyo," Chin added. "Nobody [knew]. See the news didn't come out until after he left Calcutta." Chin later found "plane pieces" from the "Doolittle raid."

Preparations for Doolittle's strike included an Army Air Force officer visiting Pan Am in New York—they needed a safe place in China to land after the mission. Harold Bixby directed the officer to talk to William Bond, who was then in Washington. Bond recommended Namyung, the remote area that was CNAC's destination when it flew evacuation missions when Hong Kong was attacked. "I was very much surprised that they did not swear me to secrecy," Bond recalled. "They did not tell me who would be in command of the raid, but they did tell me the raid would take place between April 10 and April 20, 1942."[42]

The Doolittle raid began April 18, with sixteen B-25 bombers manned by eighty volunteers launching from the *Hornet* aircraft carrier to hit targets in Japan, including Tokyo. But reported detection by Japanese patrol boats resulted in a premature launch—there wouldn't be enough fuel to get to safe haven in China.

After targets were hit, with gas gauges low and a stormy night ahead, the raiders bailed out over eastern China, close to Japanese lines. Gunnery

Sergeant Edward Horton answered the order by calling out to his pilot, "Thanks for a swell ride," before stepping out into blackness lashed with rain. That night abandoned planes crashed and burned along the mountainsides as parachutes bloomed and floated to earth. The men shivered through the cold, wet night wrapped in their thin, silken parachutes. By morning, they were taken in at villages and word spread to get them to safety.[43]

Doolittle barely escaped and nine Raiders died, but the mission was a psychological boost in the United States. China bore the brunt of Japan's vengeance, what Chennault characterized as the "bloody spear," a three-month scorched earth campaign driven through the heart of Eastern China. "The Chinese paid a terrible price for the Doolittle raid, but they never complained," he wrote. Chennault was incensed mission commander Clayton Bissell did not notify anyone connected with the "vast warning net of East China. If I had been notified, a single A.V.G. command ground radio station plugged into the East China net could have talked most of the raiders into a friendly field. . . . My bitterness over that bit of bungling has not eased with the passing years."[44]

## CHAPTER 21
# HELL RIDERS OF THE HIMALAYAS

*"Hell-riding pilots of China National Aviation Corp. had one of the toughest assignments of their bullet-spattered careers last week: to fly out officials, soldiers, wives, children and loyal Burmese from Burma to India through skyways thick with Jap planes."*

—*Time*, May 18, 1942[1]

The China-Burma-India (CBI) theatre of operations began in spring of 1942. "The CBI command was the stuff of legends; Americans used to say that you needed a crystal ball and a copy of Alice in Wonderland to understand it," Theodore H. White and Annalee Jacoby wrote soon after the war. "It had everything—maharajas, dancing girls, war lords, head-hunters, jungles, deserts, racketeers, secret agents."[2] General Joseph Stilwell was assigned the command, a political maze with free China led by Nationalist leader Chiang Kai-shek but contending with a Communist insurgency, Burma controlled by the British, and combative Chennault and his Flying Tigers in the mix.

There was the strategic Burma Road, which followed the old trading route between China and India, a mountainous region where missionaries recollected elderly Chinese who once watched elephants majestically lumbering from Burma, bearing tribute to the throne at Peking. But what a 1941

*Fortune* article recalled as the "romantic fidelity" of the past didn't square with on-the-ground reality: "From Lashio at one end . . . to Kunming . . . the Burma Road runs through 726 miles of the foulest driving country in the world, twisting and contorting through some of the deepest gashes on the wrinkled face of the earth." But, the article added, "The glistening silver-winged Douglas transports of China National Aviation Corp. can make the flight in two hours."[3]

With Japan on the offensive the Burma Road was in danger, T. V. Soong warned President Roosevelt in a memo on January 31, 1942. Soong, who was appointed China's Minister of Foreign Affairs, proposed what would be called the "aerial Burma Road," although that airway was not quite the "comparatively level" stretch between Sadiya, India, and Kunming the memo described. "This was the famous Hump, as villainous and forbidding a stretch of terrain as there was in the world," records a work by the Office of the Chief of Military History. "One hundred DC-3's on this route, Soong assured Roosevelt, could fly 12,000 tons a month into China." The president approved and assured Chiang Kai-shek that aerial supply to China via India could be maintained "even though there should be a further set back in Rangoon." Roosevelt ordered Stilwell to get the Hump going.[4]

In late January, an air route between Sadiya and Myitkyina was deemed flyable throughout the year. In early February, General Arnold gave verbal instructions to Colonel Clayton Bissell for an air force headquarters to be activated to handle China aviation issues and plan air transport connecting the terminus of the Indian railroad system to the Burma Road.[5]

The "Calcutta-China Ferry Service" designated Calcutta as debarkation point and Sadiya, where the railroad ended, as a starting point for a straight flight to Kunming, or Bhamo on the Burma Road. Arnold, outlining routes in a February 4 memo to Roosevelt, echoed warnings that worsening conditions in Burma necessitated a new supply route to China other than through Rangoon. Arnold explained the Takoradi-Cairo-Ceylon Ferry Service "is the main system and must be built up as rapidly as possible," first priority being supplying British forces in North Africa. "In view of slow delivery of Army cargo planes and the urgency of putting this plan into effect, any aid which can be received by securing cargo planes from airlines will be of tremendous value," Arnold's memo concluded.[6]

On February 6, Roosevelt forwarded Arnold's request to the Secretary of War, with a cover letter giving presidential authorization to requisition a minimum twenty-five airline aircraft using Lend-Lease funds if necessary "with China particularly in mind." An Air Transport Command wartime report declares this directive "historically significant beyond the field of service to China, as being the first authorization of any large-scale requisition of airline equipment."[7]

The proposal for China was for a hundred DC-3s (or similar transport), with seventy-five allocated to the 10th Air Force and twenty-five to the CNAC, delivered by June of '42—a plan that proved wildly optimistic. CNAC was integral to the operation as stressed in a February 22 memo to Arnold from Assistant Secretary of War for Air Robert A. Lovett. ATC's report adds, "[CNAC] pilots are noted for their skill, and taking into consideration their activities at the fall of Hongkong [sic] . . . and in the interior of China while the Japanese advanced, it is doubtful if any pilots in history have seen more adventurous flying."[8]

★

In March of '42, Roosevelt activated the Assam-Burma-China Ferry Command to forge a military supply airway over the Hump. Its base was Dinjan, a tea growing area in the Indian state of Assam, with Colonel Caleb V. Haynes in command and Colonel Robert Scott as operations manager and executive officer. It was an airfield bustling with CNAC transports and RAF and Flying Tigers fighters. "It was our assignment to open up the Hump route across the Himalayas from Dinjan to Kunming," Scott recalled. "We'd take off from Dinjan in the big loop of the Brahmaputra and climb across the Naga Hills on a course of 119 degrees for Kunming, China, 500 miles away. Most of the way we barely topped the clutching mountains."[9]

In April, the Assam-Burma-China Ferry was joined by a detachment from PAA-Africa, Ltd., of thirteen captains, eight first officers, two flight engineers, four radio operators, and ten DC-3 transports. The joint operation orders were for PAA-Africa to fly 30,000 gallons of high-octane gasoline. But the "Dinjan Mission" turned into an extended military operation lasting from April 7 through May 15. PAA-Africa's cargo included Army jeeps and Ryan airplane parts, P-40 parts for Kunming, 525,000 rounds of Bren Gun ammo, 450,415 rounds of .30 ammo, four AVG officers and a thousand pounds of equipment, and twelve U.S. Army Signal men with 3,000 pounds of equipment.

Captain Dallas Sherman, a leader of the Africa Group who hailed from Houston, Texas, used the military term "fog of war" to describe the uncertainty of civilians undertaking military missions in combat conditions. "It is impossible to separate PAA-Africa and the Army as to these operations," Sherman wrote in a subsequent report. "There was a complete fusion and interchange of tasks. . . . The legal and contract status of our personnel was not established for such conditions. The insurance clauses of contracts was uncertain. It was not established whether there existed a difference between those personnel who held military rank and those who were strictly civilians." The Chief of Staff of the 10th Air Force, which had jurisdiction over U.S. Air Force combat operations in the CBI theater under Stilwell, did convey his "personal appreciation to the PAA-Africa crews for a tough job well done," Sherman added.[10]

PAA-Africa's joint operation was concluding on May 9, when the Japanese arrived in Burma with the monsoon. The main air supply terminus at Myitkyina was nearly completed—tonnage estimates were as high as 7,500 tons monthly—when the airfield was taken on May 12.[11]

A *Time* report singled out the "Hell-riding pilots of China National Aviation Corp" whose stripped-down transports evacuated 1,200 in a three-day period.[12] But the RAF, Assam-Burma-China Ferry Command, the Army Ferrying Command, and PAA-Africa also flew the Burma airlift. An estimated 10,000 were flown to safety, including defeated British soldiers escaping the Malay Peninsula, Englishmen from the Burma Oil Company, American families working for Standard Oil and Coca-Cola, and intrepid newsmen (including future television news journalist Eric Sevareid). Seven hundred and fifty thousand refugees fled by car, cart, horse, or foot, an exodus that "streamed through mountain passes so treacherous that probably not more than half . . . were likely to get through, and many already lay dead of cholera," *Time* reported.[13]

Some pilots competed to see who could carry the most. PAA-Africa Captain John Passage and First Officer Sam Belieff got the nod from *New Horizons* for seventy-four passengers and one Scottish terrier. "A Britisher had shown up at the last minute as I was closing the cargo door," Passage recalled. "He had a Scottie with him. He asked if he could ride on top of the luggage. I said: 'It will be very cold.' He said: 'Better than staying here.' So I made a stirrup with my hands and lifted him in. The dog was begging to get in with his master, so I threw him in too."[14]

"Pilots were fully aware of the fact that the extreme aft center of gravity of the aircraft caused by the excessive overloading was way beyond any reasonable limits and presented an exceedingly dangerous flight condition," adds PAA-Africa pilot Don Stoeger. "In the face of the advancing enemy troops, each flight became more of a desperate attempt by skilled and responsible pilots to help these unfortunate people without killing them, or ourselves, in the process." Incredibly, only one PAA-Africa transport was damaged by enemy fire during operations between India, Burma, and China. That unlucky aircraft was sitting on the runway of Loiwing airfield when hit during an enemy bombing strike on April 28, an attack that missed five other exposed planes—Don Stoeger managed to board and get one airborne, even as bombs were dropping around him.[15]

PAA-Africa airlifted 3,564 evacuees, 480 wounded British and Indian troops, and one corpse (an evacuee died in flight).[16] Sherman listed challenges that included "head hunters" and fierce Chinese and Burmese tribes, lack of advance meteorological reports, "fifth column" instigators disrupting airlifts, and enemy fire. Many refugees were wounded, sick, or both—transports were often rank with the odor of vomit and gangrene. "Loading went from weighed and listed passengers to wild mobs pushing their way aboard in uncertain numbers and weight," Sherman reported. "There was one instance of a man forcing his way aboard with a gun. He was later removed by gun threat before takeoff. Many injustices were done in rejection of certain refugees and in the acceptance aboard of others, but this was to a large degree unavoidable under the circumstances."[17]

Decades later, Merian Cooper wrote his friend, now Brigadier General Robert Scott, inquiring how Pan Am performed in Assam. "I remember the Pan-American boys well back there at Dinjan," Scott replied. "Just imagine trying to fly the Hump and not even being privileged to wear the uniform of our country . . . which they did. Neither fish nor fowl they did their best. Having been ordered in one fell swoop to pack up aboard their rickety old castoff airline DC-3s and fly to a lost place called Assam. But they came and without even their insurance being [valid] and having no government insurance they pioneered the Hump run. . . . They did evacuate a good many refugees from places like Myitkyina, Lashio and Loiwing. In fact I was with some of them out of Myitkyina."[18]

PAA-Africa Assistant Manager John Yeomans forwarded Sherman's report to Franklin Gledhill with a cover letter recommending the men be decorated. He noted Sherman gave credit to the Army and "sticks to the factual side," but understated their challenges. "Many unusual feats were performed . . . such as, flying for two hours at 21,000 feet without any oxygen equipment," Yeomans explained. "This is the type of mission that has been performed so successfully by CNAC in the past. However, I doubt if any civilian organization has performed a mission of such magnitude in the same amount of time under combat conditions. . . ." Yeomans argued that soldiers were trained for combat "whereas our men who had been assured by us in good faith that they would not normally be required to fly in combat areas, were thrown into this without any 'by your leave' or prior warning." Army personnel were armed, civilian airmen only had emergency arms that might be on an aircraft; captured soldiers expected humane treatment under international law, captured civilians could be shot as spies, he added.[19]

The Dinjan Mission was an eye-opener to Yeomans. To Gledhill's frustration, Yeomans would support the militarization of Pan Am's trans-Africa operation.

★

Billy Mitchell died in a New York hospital on February 19, 1936, at the age of 56. It was the end of an era, but Mitchell's disciples, air power advocates all, were in power. The group, led by Hap Arnold, included Major General Lewis H. Brereton, commander of Air Forces in the Middle East, Major General Carl Spaatz, who commanded Air Forces in England, and Colonel Harold George, assistant chief for War Plans for the Air Staff in Washington.

The militarization of civilian air operations began with the early presidential directive putting U.S. airlines under War Department control. By January, an Air Corps memo added: "It is considered feasible and proper for the Army Air Forces to take over Air Transport and Ferrying in the theater where this type of operation is now being conducted by civilians."[20] Militarization was phased in throughout 1942, claiming even China's freewheeling AVG.

One April morning, Olga Greenlaw was in the Adjutant's office when a decoded message reported fifty enemy planes raided Loiwing, but four Tigers shot down twenty-two, without losses. The pilots came in later, and conversation turned to "the Tenth Air Force officers who were continuously arriving from India," Olga recalled. "They sat around, drank coffee and talked about resignation; getting back to the United States; joining the Ferry Command. . . . The place was not the same. The Army was moving in." Olga was moving out—Chennault was stationing her husband in Calcutta.[21]

"The A.V.G. was not enthusiastic about rejoining the services," Chennault noted. "All of them were reservists, and most of them joined the A.V.G. as an escape from rigid discipline and discrimination by regulars against the reserve. By April when the induction terms were published at Loiwing and Kunming, they were war weary and bitter about the failure of the United States to provide spare parts and replacement planes while Air Forces DC-3s shuttled about China carrying high-ranking staff officers, complete with swagger sticks and briefcases. They viewed every 'brass'-loaded transport as so many potential spark plugs, oxygen bottles, tires, and carburetors. When they saw comrades crash and die for lack of these things, their bitterness was understandable."[22]

Militarization arrived during what Chennault called "the gloomy summer of '42." The American Volunteer Group ended, and the China Air Task Force (CATF) of the Fourteenth Air Force was born at midnight, July 4, 1942. That day, Chennault officially returned to active duty with the U.S. Army as a brigadier general in command of the CATF. The mythical Tigers aura remained—a 1943 *Time* cover portrait of Chennault included a snarling winged tiger, the cover copy saluting CATF as "Dragons" for China and ferocious "Tigers" to Japan.[23]

Militarization did not change China's supply situation. That summer CNAC delivered more tonnage than the Assam-Burma-China Ferry Command, Chennault noted. Pan Am executive Fife Symington hailed Clipper special missions to the Far East for providing a "lifeline" for the AVG. But the new CATF largely survived off hoarded supplies. "As the stepchild of the Tenth Army Air Force [headquartered] in distant Delhi the C.A.T.F. had to fight, scream, and scrape for every man, plane, spark plug, and gallon of gas," Chennault lamented. "The C.A.T.F. lived off the land like a pack of hungry mastiffs. China was completely cut off from the rest of the world—sealed in a military vacuum between the Japanese, the Gobi Desert, and the frozen Himalayan peaks. Only an occasional Army plane crossed the Hump from India. The idea of an aerial supply line was still fantastic to orthodox military minds although DC-3's of C.N.A.C. were showing what could be done with a small but steady trickle of airborne supplies into China."[24]

The Hump was known as "Hell on Earth." In January of 1944, CNAC pilot Donald McBride, a veteran of the Hump, had one of his worst flights, fighting snow, ice, freezing rain, and high winds all the way to Dinjan—of four planes, his was the only one that made it.

McBride kept a wartime diary, and his February 27, 1944, entry describes a hidden realm, timeless and awe-inspiring, where mortals piloting fragile aircraft were intruders: "There are places in the Himalayas where we fly over dense tropical jungles and a few seconds later are over regions of eternal ice and snow. There are gorgeous waterfalls from the melting snow and beautiful sea-green rivers winding through canyons with vertical sides two and three miles high. I have seen mountains split in two by earthquakes, and freaks of nature like the 'Devil's Slide' in Nevada have been duplicated on a scale that makes the original look like something in miniature. There are valleys in which the Creator could easily have lost the Grand Canyon. I found a valley west of Likiang that is an excellent replica of the 'Garden of the Gods' in Colorado, only much larger. Between Likiang and Sichang there is a range of mountains that have tipped over on their side, completely revealing the layers deposited during the various geological ages. In a small valley on the west side of the Salween Range west of Paochan are three newly formed volcano craters, so recent that no vegetation has grown. High up on the west bank of the Mekong River west of Weishi, stands a tremendous natural stone arch. There are hundreds of crystal blue lakes hidden in watersheds slightly below the snow line. Sometimes there are native huts and villages on the shores of those lakes and I often think how peaceful their existence must be."[25]

CNAC flew cargo and passengers over the Hump. William Bond was on one rough passenger flight—"solid soup" at 14,000 feet, the heater gave out, and frost formed inside the aircraft. "The passengers stood it remarkably well," Bond wrote China colleague Harold Bixby. "It really is amazing, almost pathetic, the licking CNAC passengers will take without complaint." He praised his pilots and crews: "You know Bix[,] I take my hat off to these boys. I really am proud of them. If there is any worse flying it is difficult to imagine it. Their morale is absolute tops."[26]

★

Captain C. Joseph Rosbert was one of many former Flying Tigers who joined the CNAC and became a veteran of the Hump. His co-pilot, Charles "Ridge" Hammel, was a master of desert flying who came from PAA-Africa and distrusted this region of icy storms and jagged peaks soaring three miles into the sky. Both knew flying the Hump was a calculated risk.

One mission, Rosbert, Ridge, and radio operator Li Wong took off from Dinjan in their loaded C-47. At 12,000 feet they were in thick fog and torrential rain was turning to snow—perfect CNAC flying weather. When they were within a thousand feet of clearing the Hump, Ridge grinned and declared they'd soon be home free. Rosbert sums up what happened next: "But we couldn't get that last thousand feet."

Ridge had his back to the pilot and didn't see what Rosbert was seeing—a thin layer of ice spreading over the windshield was suddenly six-inches thick. All windows were icing over, and the aircraft was dropping. Rosbert rubbed the palms of his bare hands on the windshield to clear a spot when the clouds opened—a peak was dead ahead. Rosbert swung the transport into a bank, yelling they were about to hit the mountain . . . they seemed to miss it by inches.

"Then my heart stopped," Rosbert recalled. "A huge dark object swept by. A terrible scraping noise tore under the cabin; an explosive crash struck right behind me; the engines raced into a violent roar. Something stabbed my ankle; an intense pain shot through my left leg. Then, suddenly, we were not moving."

. . . After a time, Rosbert heard Ridge call, "Get out of that thing before it catches fire!" He realized Ridge was outside the plane, but it wasn't going to burn—both engines were torn off.

"Come on back in," Rosbert shouted. "You'll freeze to death out there." The cabin was intact, but Wong lay behind the cockpit—dead, from a broken neck.

Rosbert looked up and saw Ridge by the rear bulkhead, holding his left ankle, his right eye swollen shut, blood dripping from hands and facial cuts. "Nothing seemed very real," Rosbert recalled. "I tried to take a step, but my left ankle turned under me. The pain almost took my breath away. I looked down. I seemed to be standing on my leg bone, and my foot was lying at a right angle to it. Holding on to the roof supports, I swung myself down beside Ridge."

There was a long silence before the co-pilot murmured, "What happened?"

"We hit a mountain."

Night was coming with freezing winds driving snow flurries, and they huddled together to keep warm.

They awoke to bright sunshine. It had stopped snowing, although the plane was almost buried in it. Snowy peaks surrounded them, including the jagged slope they hit at an angle—another fifty feet and they would have smashed to pieces. They figured they were somewhere on the Tibetan frontier, 16,000 feet up in the Mishmi Mountains, and a thousand feet above the timberline.

They waited three days, gathering strength to hike out. They set splints for their injured ankles, tearing parachutes into strips and bandaging and wrapping the silk around them. They ripped up floorboards for makeshift sleds. They left Wong's body behind and stumbled, slid, and rolled to the tree line. After eight days they reached the dead end of a canyon. Long heavy vines hung from the vertical walls, and they used them to climb to the top, where notched saplings seemed to mark a trail—first sign of "civilization."

The thirteenth day, at the limits of endurance, they came upon a smoky hut inhabited by six naked children and two old women, one blind and the other nearly so. They wore ragged cloths draped over one shoulder that went around their waists; their hair was long and coarse, each had a metal band around their heads. At first, they were frightened by the strangers but served them corn and spice soup from a steaming iron kettle. After eating, Rosbert and Ridge fell asleep for eighteen hours.

Three days later, the two oldest children disappeared, returning with "three men who stepped out of the Stone Age," Rosbert recalled. They had matted hair past their shoulders and were barefoot and naked except for loincloths. Each wore a knife on one hip and a fur-covered pouch on the other, and animal teeth ornaments dangled from their ears. Using sign language, the airmen communicated that they were from the sky and wanted to return to the world beyond the mountains. To the people of this hidden land they were from another world—their watches, zippered jackets, and boots fascinated the men; a flashlight dazzled the children.

Rosbert and Ridge were led to the main village and ushered into the biggest hut. "There in that primitive smoke-filled hut, deep in the heart of the Himalayas, Ridge and I held court for two incredible weeks, receiving scores of these long-haired, leather-jerkined, bare-legged men of the Stone Age. Their implements were cut from wood or stone and, from what we could learn, they had never heard of Chinese or Indians, let alone Americans. After days on the trail and in their smoke-filled huts, we were as dark-skinned as they." They met an elderly trader who had seen white people and sent his son to bring them chicken, tea, and rice. Rosbert tore off a corner of their flying map and with a pencil wrote a note for the boy, hoping his father could get the message to the outside world: "We are two American pilots. We crashed into the mountain. We will come to your camp in five days."

By noon of the fourth day, the boy returned with an envelope—an India telegraph form, sealed with wax. The flyers excitedly broke the seal. The letter was from Lieutenant W. Hutchings, commanding officer of a British scouting column that was a four days march away. They were sending rations by messenger, along with a medical officer. Rosbert and Ridge hugged each other and cried, as the boy explained to everyone what had happened. Wood was heaped on the fire, alcohol was brought out, and there was dancing. In an hour, porters dispatched by Hutchings arrived with the promised supplies that the airmen happily shared.

Captain C.E. Lax, the British medical officer, took two days longer to make the trip "but never was anyone made more welcome," Rosbert recalled. "He told us that no white man had ever set foot in this country before and, had it not been that the British column, because of the war, had penetrated even as close as four days' march, we might never have been found. It was one chance in a million, and we had hit it. Another of our miracles." The doctor had good news. Ridge's ankle was badly sprained but healing; Rosbert's ankle was fractured but also healing.

The next day, at dawn, they left the village for what would be a sixteen-day hike out of the mountains. "Such a swift change of fortune had unsettled us a bit," Rosbert recalled, "and we both confessed to a heavy tug at leaving these strange people who had been so kind and hospitable to a couple of strangers who, dropping suddenly out of another world, had been taken into their family and treated as brothers through these many days. We divided among them everything we had—the pencil, the flashlight, everything out of our pockets—and then borrowed all the silver coins the captain had, in an effort to express our appreciation. They, too, seemed to regret our going, and accompanied us to the edge of the clearing as Ridge and I, leaning on the shoulders of the two native messengers, followed the doctor down the rocky wall.

"Over the tough places, our little native helpers, who weighed fifty pounds less than either Ridge or I, carried us, resting in a sling swung from their foreheads. Up the sides of cliffs, along boulder-strewn river beds, on cable-slung bridges that Gurkha engineers built ahead of us over monsoon-fed raging torrents, these little men led us until, finally, we reached the crest of the last mountain range. There, below us, in a lovely green valley on the banks of a great river, lay a little British frontier station, Sadiya, a sight as welcome as the skyline of New York."

Within a month, Ridge was back flying CNAC transports. Pan Am flew Rosbert home, and within five days a specialist in Seattle was tending his ankle. The doctors, mystified how two injured men survived weeks of trekking the Himalayas, called it a miracle. Rosbert felt the entire adventure was a miracle.

"You hit a mountain at 180 miles an hour, and that's that," Rosbert said. "Together, we thanked God for being alive, and all my life I will make deep and humble acknowledgment to God that I do not take any credit for our rescue. The fact that we were the first white men to come out of that unknown section of the Himalayas has little to do with it; it is partly the knowledge that in any one of a hundred different instances death awaited a wrong decision . . . and partly the marvelous chain of coincidences—or 'miracles,' as Ridge and I called them—that led us through forty-seven days and nights, into and out of another world and back to civilization again."[27]

## CHAPTER 22
# MILITARIZATION

> "It has been the Air Forces' intention since our entry into the war, to completely militarize all of our overseas operations, and I have issued such instructions. Our method, however, will have to be one of infiltration rather than drawing a deadline that can not be met. Until the time when we have a sufficient number of skilled technical personnel, and personnel of the services, available, it will be necessary to use whatever personnel we can find who are ready right now to perform the task. . . . Our present plans call for militarization as soon as it can be accomplished."
>
> —H. H. ARNOLD, LIEUTENANT GENERAL, U.S.A., DEPUTY CHIEF OF STAFF FOR AIR, FEBRUARY 20, 1942, MEMO[1]

The Selective Training and Service Act of 1940 required men between twenty-one and thirty-five to register for the draft, but America's declaration of war inspired a patriotic surge of citizens wanting to do their part, regardless of age or sex. Two such men wanted to answer the war effort at Pan Am—thirty-nine-year-old Charles Lindbergh, and forty-four-year-old Wall Street broker Howard B. Dean.

To join the airline, Dean stepped down as a governor of the New York Stock Exchange and took a year's leave from his partnership in the brokerage firm of Struthers & Dean. A Yale man, Dean was brought aboard by schoolmate and friend Juan Trippe, and neatly slipped into the fast pace of airline life. Dean worked under vice president Evan E. Young, and his assignments included managerial duties in the Latin American Division, special missions, and projects at the 36th Street Airport, which had him bouncing between the Chrysler Building headquarters, the Mayflower Hotel and PAA office in Washington, and the Miami hub. Dean schooled himself on far-flung divisions and subsidiaries, particularly in South America, and the strategic Miami to Rio run ("four trips per week," he noted in his diary on May 1). He worked closely with military officials, such as Harold George. Dean's professional and social circle at Pan Am included Harold Bixby, John Cooper, George Rihl, and Franklin Gledhill. His friendship with Trippe often featured golf and tennis outings.

Dean got a taste of what he signed up for in July of '42. He was in Miami and arrived at Dinner Key airport to catch the scheduled 12:30 a.m. *African Clipper* connection to New York, but bad weather delayed its arrival. It was 2:00 a.m. when Dean, who had fallen asleep on a bench alongside the radio operator, was roused by the arrival of the Clipper piloted by Captain Marius "Lodi" Lodeesen. Dean boarded with the wives of two Pan Am employees, two boys, and two cocker spaniels. Most of the seats had been removed to haul crude rubber from Brazil.

"Fell asleep at once and in an hour was awakened by a fierce storm," Dean wrote in his diary on July 2, "which continued all the way to N.Y.—a really terrific ride—20 miles south of Sandy Hook ship came down to within few hundred feet of the ocean to get its bearing. Thru a hole in the clouds we saw a tanker sinking stern first with two life boats alongside. Then up and over Long Island in a dense fog and rain storm[,] no visibility at all. Flew around and around over La Guardia for almost two hours and finally made a perfect blind landing in the middle of the sound . . . taxied up sound to La Guardia . . . Damn glad to be alive and very proud of the Clipper crew. To the apartment to change clothes, bath etc. as one of the kids had thrown up all over my suit. Then to Union Club for a quick lunch—first meal in forty-two hours. Then to PAA office + reported to EEY [Evan Young]. Was told to catch the Congressional Ltd. for Wash D.C. + meet VP Cooper at Tracy Square house at 9 p.m.—some life."

One time in Miami, Dean got a call alerting him to a serious accident involving two planes, one a bomber, at 36th Street Airport. "[I] saw the remains of wreck—it was really awful—arms, legs, bodies in pieces + both planes burnt and exploded to bits," he wrote on September 22. "The fault was entirely with the Bomber Command."

Toward the end of 1942, Dean heard Wall Street's siren call. "They want me to return at once to Struthers & Dean & I don't feel like it," he confessed to his journal on November 15. But the firm "agreed to let things ride until my leave of absence expired," he noted the next day. "This is more than fair & I am glad it is settled." Dean remained with Pan Am for the rest of his life.[2]

For Lindbergh, the America First movement ended with Pearl Harbor. Lindbergh's isolationist crusade, which earned Roosevelt's anger, forced him to resign his Air Corps commission, and his offer to contribute to the war effort was rebuffed in face-to-face meetings with Secretary Stimson and with General Arnold and Robert Lovett, special assistant to the Secretary of War. At least Arnold was optimistic: "I think you can find some way to straighten all this out."[3]

Lindbergh next met with Trippe. "[S]ince it seemed best for me to make my contribution to the war through the aviation industry, my first choice would be Pan American," he said, advising Trippe to make sure Roosevelt had no objections. Trippe felt there was many things Lindbergh could do for Pan Am, and would probably have a chance to talk to the president later that week.[4] But in a subsequent phone call, Trippe told Lindbergh "obstacles had been put in the way." Sensing Juan did not want to go into details on the phone, Lindbergh agreed to meet him the following week.[5]

Lindbergh's follow-up with Trippe had some good news—the War Department was supportive of his involvement with Pan Am. "*But* [emphasis Lindbergh's] he said, when he talked to the White House, 'they' were very angry with him for even bringing up the subject and told him 'they' did not want me to be connected with Pan American in any capacity," he recorded in his journal. "He said the feeling at the White House toward me was extremely bitter. Juan seemed very much chagrined about the entire situation. He agreed with me that it would be inadvisable for me to make any active connection with the company at present but suggested that the door be left open because attitude and conditions might change later on."[6]

Lindbergh eventually got in the war as a technical consultant at Ford Motor Company's Willow Run Plant outside Detroit, the largest aircraft factory in the world that was turning out bombers like autos off the assembly line. Lindbergh also served as a technical advisor for the U.S. Navy's Bureau of Aeronautics and flew fifty combat missions in the Pacific.[7]

On March 10 of '42, while Lindbergh was still in limbo, he lunched with his old friend Harold Bixby. "[Bixby] says the government may take over Pan American Airways," Lindbergh recorded in his journal. "If they do, it will certainly reduce the efficiency of the organization, and I do not see what would be gained. The company is doing everything the government requests, as it is, and a commercial organization cannot be turned into a military organization overnight."[8]

★

In March of '42, Brigadier General Olds helped facilitate an accord between the U.S. and Brazil, but by the 26th of that month a heart attack forced him to step down from the Ferrying Command. Arnold offered the command to Colonel Harold George. (Olds was promoted to Major General and given command of the Second Air Force, but never recovered his health and died in Tucson, Arizona, on April 28, 1943.)[9] George initially turned it down. "I had devoted my entire service, almost twenty-four years, to the potentialities of Air Power in modern war and had expected an overseas command after the Pearl Harbor disaster," George wrote.

Arnold was insistent, but George confessed he had no idea how to run a ferry and transport system. "There are some exceptionally broad-visioned people in our airlines who could make substantial contributions to the solving of our problem," Arnold replied, recommending George meet C. R. Smith, president of American Airlines.[10] When George and "Mr. C. R.," as Smith was known, huddled in a Washington hotel suite a wartime partnership was born. The Air Ferrying Command shifted into a "world-wide Air

Transport organization," the phrase Arnold used to explain his vision to George and Smith.[11]

In July of '42, the operation got a new name: Air Transport Command (ATC). It began with Commander George and Chief of Staff Smith (promoted to Brigadier General and General, respectively), and a clerk in "a small room," Arnold recalled; within two years it numbered 85,000, with transports crisscrossing the planet. "The growth of the Air Transport Command paralleled closely the expansion of the whole Air Force," Arnold added.[12]

Roosevelt and Arnold wanted Trippe to head the ATC, explains Kathleen Clair: "[Trippe] didn't want to go into the military, he wanted to stay with his company and keep it going until after the war. And Roosevelt and Hap Arnold got a little sore at him because he wouldn't do that. But he thought he could do more good right where he was sitting. And, actually, he did. . . . So then they asked C. R. Smith, and he took it."[13]

Militarization was a rough adjustment for PAA-Africa. "Here was a complete airline, from top executives to grease monkeys, operating side by side with the military organization," writes Oliver La Farge, ATC's wartime Historical Officer. "The airline had been there first, it had its own ways . . . its officers seem sometimes to have been impatient with military control. As happened in various parts of the world, the airline men were definitely not impressed by the Army way of doing things, and frequently enough with good reason. Pan Am-Africa procured many of its own supplies, ran its own communications. It was so well entrenched that at times the Air Forces men who were ultimately responsible for the success of air transport operations in Africa felt as if they were guests rather than employers."[14]

Militarization would be finalized in December of 1942, but the Air Transport Command was already setting up operations at Accra and elsewhere in Africa. The transition came at a key juncture in the battle for North Africa that precipitated the creation of Pan Am's South Atlantic and trans-Africa operation. By June the buildup began for British commander Montgomery's offensive in North Africa. By late summer, ferry deliveries had become a veritable flood of aircraft and arms. "Between June and the end of the year, 398 Lockheed and Martin medium bombers—including 120 B-34s, 153 A-28s, 45 B-26s, and 80 A-30s—were ferried to British forces in Africa by crews of Pan American Air Ferries or by American and British military crews," records the Office of Air Force History. "At the same time, the forces gathering under the leadership of General Brereton during the summer and fall . . . reached their battle stations in large part by use of the South Atlantic and trans-African ferry routes."[15]

That summer Rommel was at the gates of Cairo, and British forces were desperately short of anti-tank fuses to repel the advance. At midnight on July 3, British military headquarters made an urgent call to Accra—Montgomery needed fifteen tons of anti-tank artillery fuses and .50 caliber ammunition. Six PAA-Africa crews were awakened and prepared for immediate departure to the British port of Lagos, 3,100 miles away, to pick up the vital supplies then being unloaded. "Most of them [Pan Am-Africa pilots] were looking forward to a well-earned sleep, and fuses, which explode so easily, are the kind of cargo pilots prefer not to fly, but there was no hesitation on the part of any of them," La Farge chronicles. "The first plane took off at four in the morning."[16]

Khartoum was the last stop, for a crew change, before Cairo. The mission continued for thirty-three straight hours, delivering on a special day for Americans—fourth of July. (One of the PAA-Africa airmen was Ridge Hammel, who later survived crashing in the Himalayas.)[17] By 4:00 p.m. the first plane was contacting Cairo's Heliopolis Field, asking permission to land there or the battlefront. An incredulous RAF officer reportedly replied, "I say, old man, that really isn't funny. This is no time for spoofing."

By then, the second plane was arriving. The battlefront had no proper runways, so they landed at Heliopolis. The dangerous cargo was loaded onto trucks and immediately driven to the fighting. "In the course of the following hours, fifteen tons of fuses were brought in," La Farge reports. "They were delivered to the front, the gunners armed their shells and loaded their anti-tank guns, almost as the Germans moved to the attack. Rommel was thrown back, in no small part because of the fast action of the Command's soldier-civilian team."[18]

"All rules were off, airplanes were overloaded, with bad tires, with radios inoperative, airplanes flew with only one generator working," Pan Am's corporate history records. "For some of the young Captains, the pace got pretty fast. It was scary to go up . . . alone at the controls of the monstrous machine—the DC 3 was that, then—and loaded with explosive ready to flash. . . . This Fuse-Lift alone made the whole Africa line worth having."[19]

When the conquest of Cairo seemed imminent, PAA-Africa flew evacuation missions and forty-nine RAF ferry pilots from Cairo to Takoradi to facilitate delivery of British warplanes. Pan Am's communication system provided vital weather information during the planning of the North African invasion.[20]

"The militarization of PAA-Africa, Ltd. was but a month from completion when the gigantic North African invasion occurred in November, 1942," Voit Gilmore recorded in 1943. "Former Pan American personnel who had joined the Army played key roles in the opening up of the North African country. Equipment and aviation facilities previously obtained and established by Pan American were used extensively throughout the operation."[21]

Bill Taylor, who was part of Pan Am's Pacific pioneering, had been transferred to PAA-Africa's New York office as administrative assistant to John Yeomans. "All of us in PAA-Africa felt a sense of involvement and satisfaction in that our supply line to the Mid-East had helped in some small measure in the build-up of Montgomery's forces so that he could go on the offense," Taylor said. "By the summer of 1942 . . . there was no point in a commercial airline operating a military activity. So the Air Force announced that they would take over PAA-Africa. PAA employees in Africa were offered military rank appropriate to their jobs. John Yeomans elected to take a commission and stay in Africa; only a few months later he was in a Lockheed transport which crashed on take off; all were killed. In New York we phased out the PAA-Africa operation."[22]

The last Pan American Airways-Africa flight on December 15 was a round-trip from Accra to Teheran commanded by Captain Dwight L. Shrum.[23]

The Hump operation under the CBI and 10th Air Force was still struggling into the summer of '42. That June, Stilwell and Arnold, tired of projections of a hundred transports, asked that seventy-five be put in service. The Chinese government was unhappy with the trickle of supplies over the Hump, as was Stilwell. The Ferry Command only delivered 106 tons in June and seventy-three tons in July. "CNAC flying regularly when weather keeps us [AAF] grounded," a disgusted Stilwell wrote.[24]

In July, Stilwell proposed to Arnold that the U.S. Army take over the China National Aviation Corporation under military contract. Arnold, showing his kinship for commercial aviation, wired a reply recommending that CNAC take over *the entire* transport program and all military equipment, with military crews under CNAC direction until they could be replaced with civilians.

Stilwell delivered a blunt rebuttal on August 1. "For many reasons . . . the suggestion that CNAC handle all air transportation in this theatre is most unsound. . . . Placing civilians over military personnel in a zone of combat is not advisable," Stilwell wrote. "My control of air transport in this theatre is necessary both for political and military reason." Stilwell's recommendations included his having authority to contract CNAC for its entire "Lend-Lease capacity" and that the original projection for a hundred transports—seventy-five for Army Air Force, twenty-five to CNAC—be honored.

On August 5, General Marshall advised Stilwell that his proposal was accepted, and Chiang Kai-shek agreed. "The plan was put into effect, and became the basis of relations between the Air Transport Command and CNAC later," records ATC's history.[25]

The Air Transport Command was ready to take over. "It is not the province of historians of the Air Transport Command to lay blame upon the 10th Air Force or to attempt to justify it," notes ATC's historical report, but adds: "Opinion within the Command . . . was that the 10th Air Force had done badly."[26]

"The present Air Cargo System between India and China is in great need of overhauling and study," argued an ATC memorandum concerning the Dinjan to Kunming route, declaring the effort go beyond "the token stage into a serious project under a command instilled with the will to carry large tonnage into China in order to properly supply the American and Chinese combat forces." The lack of "will" was attributed to the "defeatist attitude" of the 10th Air Force and theatre commander. Stilwell reportedly declared that 5,000 tons a month "is fantastic" and the memo rhetorically agreed—"if only 18 aircraft are assigned to the job."[27]

The ATC historical report acknowledged that supply for the Dinjan-Kunming area—by air, land, or sea—was a critical problem. Even when planes weren't grounded, the 13,000-mile air route through Central Africa "passed through bases many of which were incompletely developed." The historical report added, "Cargo for India and beyond competed in priority with cargoes for the Middle East and the active front against Rommel. Boat shipments to Calcutta, the nearest seaport, had to make the loop south of Australia, forty days being the best time expectable." Getting cargo from Calcutta to Assam and elsewhere faced bad roads, limited river barges, undependable railroad service, and floods brought everything to a standstill. "In general it can be said that nowhere has the dependence of air activity upon ground supply been more emphatically demonstrated than in the India-China transport operation and the air operations within China which it serves, and nowhere at any time in the history of aviation has the maintenance of flight by air-borne supply been more fully tested," the report concluded.[28]

A September '42 survey report by Major Clifford Henderson to ATC Commander Harold George explained the return from Kunming to Dinjan "is considered by all experienced pilots familiar with the weather, altitude, and enemy hazards of this area to be the most strenuous flying transport mission now being accomplished by the American Air Forces. Each trip between these two points requires a flight over Japanese occupied territory of more than two hours. The rugged Burmese mountains require minimum altitudes of 19,000 feet. The turbulent storms and monsoons which must be encountered during each of these flights make each trip an episode in the life of every pilot and crew."[29]

Meanwhile, with leaves from U.S. armed forces expiring, former American Volunteer Group members were signing up with the CNAC. "[C]arrying essential supplies over the mountains and deadly-jungled CNAC route, Flying Tiger pilots will still find the odds terrific, will still know their courageous flying is giving immense support to the U.S. war effort," *New Horizons* reported.[30]

But that infusion of skilled personnel was delayed because "air priority" had not been given former Tigers who had to make air connections from Karachi before sailing home on leave. "Up until such time as the AVG pilots return to work for CNAC, there will be a lack of reserve of experienced flying personnel," explained the ATC memo on the Dinjan-Kunming Air Route. "A total of 55 flying personnel is expected to be on the CNAC payroll within the next three months."[31]

Finally, in October, ATC Chief of Staff C. R. Smith boldly weighed in with his own memo to General Arnold. He noted that even when "obstacles are taken into account, there is apt to remain doubt that full effectiveness has been gained from the personnel and equipment assigned to, and available for, this operation." Again, "lack of singleness of purpose" was assigned the theatre commander. "Based upon the facts available to us, it seems warranted to conclude that at no time did the India-China operation have the full benefit of the personnel, aircraft and material which were sent to that theatre for the purpose of transporting material to China." Mr. C. R. had a recommendation: "[T]his India-China ferry operation might more effectively be conducted by the Air Transport Command."

Smith proposed the Hump could be an extension of ATC's trans-Africa and Middle East operation, more likely its own Wing, adding, "the Command must have control of the operation; to work in close harmony with the Theatre Commander but not to be under his control.... The operation would be conducted by the Command, under the supervision of the Commanding General, Army Air Forces."[32]

That October, Stilwell accepted what he once deemed the "fantastic" delivery target of 5,000 tons a month as the goal for February of 1943, a target recommended in July by Bissell and Stilwell's air officer, Lt. Col. Edward H. Alexander. "In contemplating greater American effort in CBI, Stilwell was no longer required to think of the airlift to China as his direct command responsibility," explains a work by the Office of Military History. "On 1 December 1942, the airlift had become part of the world-wide Air Transport Command.... This step had been directed by the War Department in late October."[33] Command of the India-China Wing was given to Edward Alexander, who was promoted to Brigadier General.

But the ATC quickly learned why the Hump was considered the world's toughest transport operation. In 1943, Wing Commander Alexander testified to the hazards: "The weather here has been awful. The icing level starts at 12,000 feet. Today a C-87 went to 29,500 feet on instruments, was unable to climb higher, and could not get on top. It has rained seven and a half inches in the past five days. All aircraft are grounded." In addition to ice and monsoon season's 200 inches of rain, there was heat. In a separate report, Alexander explained that aircraft maintenance was usually done at night and rainy days because touching metal exposed to sun and 100–130 Fahrenheit temperatures caused second-degree burns. The heat was hell on engines and had an enervating, demoralizing effect on pilots and crews.

The ATC historical document quoted Alexander's report, adding, "If living and operating conditions were so difficult at the end of 1943, after the India-China Wing had been the subject of constant attention and improvement for a year and supply for the whole theatre had been greatly improved, one might well imagine what they were like in the summer of 1942."[34]

The summer of '43, "ATC's shortcomings," as historian William Leary, Jr., puts it, prompted an investigation. Roosevelt personally sent Major General George Stratemeyer to investigate, with ATC Commander Major General George and combat ace and airline executive Edward Rickenbacker participating. They concluded the India-China Wing was facing many of the challenges faced by the Ferrying Command. Rickenbacker noted another factor—the CNAC was out-performing the ATC due to its greater experience in flying the Hump.

In May of '43, Roosevelt ordered ATC to raise tonnage to 7,000 by July and 10,000 by September. The ATC failed to meet those numbers—in July, they only flew 4,500 tons, and six ATC transports were lost over the treacherous mountains. "The Air Transport Command record to date is pretty sad," Stilwell wrote in his diary. "The CNAC has made them look like a bunch of amateurs."

"ATC found its problems hard enough to bear, but the disparaging comparison to CNAC was the cruelest cut of all," writes William Leary, Jr. "But Stilwell was right. In June 1943, ATC carried 2,219 tons with 146 aircraft assigned, including nearly 100 C-46s and several four-engine C-87s. . . . CNAC operated 20 aircraft, all DC-3s, and moved 734.7 tons. In other words, ATC flying larger aircraft, transported 15 tons per plane to CNAC's 37 tons."[35]

The CNAC had known crisis—disastrous plane crashes, military takeovers, Japan's invasion, and constant risk from enemy fire, despite its civilian status. To survive, CNAC mastered the most dangerous airway in the world, flying in extreme weather at high altitudes without oxygen.

And the airline had emerged, experienced and battle-hardened.

# CHAPTER 23
# "THE FASTEST WITH THE MOSTEST"

"[T]he next time you see an Air Carrier Contract man wearing the 'ATC' insignia look at him with respect. Maybe he's forgotten more about flying than you'll ever know. And remember that fighting a war isn't all ribbons and fast pursuits and sorties with tons of bombs over the enemy. Remember that it takes supplies and men and vital materials to carry out these missions and they are needed in a hurry."
—Colonel Harold R. Harris, Commanding Officer, Domestic Transportation Division, Air Transport Command[1]

Militarization was still a raw, unpleasant reality for some (notably Franklin Gledhill), but General George declared it all squared with the president's request that Air Transport Command get maximum use of commercial airlines. The ATC wasn't taking over the airlines, George argued, "It is the other way, the airlines are taking over, taking over the biggest job they ever tackled and we of the War Department have the utmost confidence that they can carry out the task."

ATC had a new assignment for Pan Am—set up a transport service between the U.S. and the Middle East and India. Franklin Gledhill was selected to lead the new Africa-Orient Division, bringing experience "starting an air service from scratch over some of the most barren areas on earth,"

*New Horizons* noted. Its leadership included Manager H. W. Toomey, recently division engineer and assistant division manager for Pan Am's Miami-based operations, and Assistant Manager James H. Smith, John Cooper's assistant since 1937. Potential personnel were experienced in Army contract work from PAA-Ferries and trans-Africa, while Pan Am's "Masters of Ocean Flying Boats," the gold standard for commercial pilots, would lead flight crews. Flight and ground crews would wear uniforms prescribed by Secretary of War Stimson, the distinction from U.S. Army uniforms being special ATC buttons.[2]

Boeing Clippers, camouflaged since Pearl Harbor, were stripped of their "war paint," as Pan Am put it, beginning with the *Dixie Clipper*. The "de-camouflaging" required removing 260 pounds of camouflage paint per plane. Wartime chronicler Reginald Cleveland records that Pan Am's "silver wings had been returned to them," with the removal of camouflage providing an extra five miles per hour. There was a need for speed, particularly when the Africa-Orient Division began flying its "Cannonball" missions. "[The Cannonball] spread across two oceans," Cleveland adds, "touched four continents halfway across the world and back in seven days and was the world's first round-the-clock air transport service, with big planes scheduled out night or day regardless of wind or weather."[3]

The Africa-Orient Division began November 10, 1942, with the arrival in Miami of the first Army aircraft, a converted B-24 minus bomb bays and gunnery, with wooden partition flooring. That plane was followed by two more B-24s and two C-54s. On November 16, the five aircraft left Miami with passengers and cargo on the inaugural route survey to Accra. Among the pilots, Captain R. H. McGlohn flew that first B-24, with Captain Vic Wright flying the second B-24. Captain Basil Rowe, piloting a C-54, was first to land at Accra, the others arriving within the hour.

On the return, Captain McGlohn's converted bomber was carrying mica and passengers that included Army personnel and Toomey. Suddenly, forty-five minutes from Ascension Island, a fire threatened to burn off the B-24s right wing. A subsequent report observes Toomey "made himself useful in this critical situation," tossing out hundred pound mica packages, two at a time. McGlohn safely landed, although the plane never flew again. "Such was the inauspicious start of Africa-Orient," a report concluded.

But operating out of Pan Am's 36th Street Airport, an early Africa-Orient mission responded to a critical need for a radio station during the North African invasion, with Captain Rowe and his five-man crew delivering radio equipment in a forty-eight-hour turnaround from Miami to the battlefront. Subsequent cargo included Christmas mail to Accra for delivery to troops in North Africa. Sixty crews and fifteen planes were soon in service.[4]

Miami was one of wartime's busiest air transport centers. The focal point was the 36th Street Airport and, less than three miles away by car, an Air Transport Command base. The latter was a 3,000-acre operation initially dubbed "Little Egypt" for its sandy terrain and tents. But a virtual town had since sprung up, with trees and sidewalks, housing, police and fire protection, facilities for power, water, and sewage, a library, bank, post office, and facilities for recreation and religious services.

Africa-Orient aircraft were serviced at 36th Street Airport and towed to the ATC terminal where silver and camouflaged transports, newly arrived or outward bound, lined in military precision. The around-the-clock schedule made for a bustling atmosphere in the terminal dining area. During one visit, an observer spotted RAF and Pan Am flyers, Chinese officers, a kilted Scotsman, WACs, and a soldier with his parachute strapped on, gulping a last-minute cup of coffee.[5]

The Cannonball Operation officially started on February 7, 1944, and through April flew eighty-four missions. It appears the service was getting up to speed, literally, as a May report from Frank Hankins, Jr., of the Africa-Orient Operations Manager's office in Miami, noted few flights were arriving on schedule. However, on average it was a successful start thanks to a blistering pace in March, when twenty-seven planes made the Miami to Karachi round-trip in nine days. Hankins's report focused on the nickname, which fascinated press and company personnel "because it stirs the imagination into a concept of a large effort at speed." "Cannonball" appeared to have originated in Natal, he noted.[6]

One origin of the name has an operations rep named Jim Howley posting info for a new schedule on the board in the operations office, adding in parenthesis: "Cannonball." "Oh, this one's going through on the long haul like a 'Cannonball,'" Howley told curious crews. "That is how fast this new operation has got to keep moving, so you had better do your stuff quick when it comes through."[7]

The phrase, "get there fastest with the mostest," summed up the Cannonball spirit.[8] The Africa-Orient Division had a hundred transoceanic flight crews at the ready, with missions undertaken in five relays. A crew first delivered aircraft to be serviced and fueled, cargo loaded or unloaded. The next flew the plane 2,500-miles to the South Atlantic, where the third flew it to Africa, the fourth crossed Africa, and the final crew flew the Arabian Sea into India. "Each flight crew completed the circuit of twenty-one days and then went home for a period of rest," Reginald Cleveland reports. "Every thirty days they logged an average of a hundred hours of flying, equal to a flight around the equator. . . . The Africa-Orient Division was flying 1,100,000 miles a month, carrying loads at the rate of 170,000 ton-miles a day."[9]

By 1944, the *New York News* dubbed the Cannonball "Burma's Secret Weapon." The operation had set a record of seven-day round-trips from the U.S. to northern India, delivering war materials to General Stilwell's forces that were fighting to take back Burma. All told, relay crews by then logged an incredible 14,500,000 miles.[10] By 1945, an Africa-Orient transport flight from Casablanca to Miami chalked up the operation's 5,000th Atlantic crossing.[11]

★

Pan Am's Naval Air Transport Service (NATS) began with four Consolidated Coronados (PB2Y3R), 110 trained flight personnel—captains, flight engineers, navigators, radio operators, stewards—five Masters of Ocean Flying Boats, and forty-five ground personnel members at NATS ports. "The idea was to utilize the know-how, experience, and organization of PAA . . . in connection with training, organizing, and expanding the Naval Air Transport Service in the Pacific," Lt. Commander Gillespie noted. "At that time we would have fallen on our face if it had not been for PAA in flight control, engineering[,] maintenance. . . ."[12]

In 1940, Pan Am began a course in aerial navigation in Miami for Army Air Corps Cadets, graduating its first class on November 12 of that year. "Navigators are as essential to our bombers as are the pilots and gunners," General Arnold said of the program. "We would have lost months of valuable time establishing our own school and training our own instructors if Pan American had not been able and willing to cooperate by placing its facilities at the Army's disposal." In that tradition, Pan Am instructed naval personnel in meteorology, communications, maintenance, and airport operations. Pan Am's wealth of knowledge included meteorological data, radio and navigation systems, detailed charts of landing areas, and operating procedures. The airline flew special surveys, provided weather maps, flight logs, and route manuals, complete data on geography and populations of Pacific islands, navigational charts—even records of ocean swells at Wake Island and procedures for serving meals in the air.

But a 1944 Pan Am report notes, "Pan American was not satisfied, however, that such services as these constituted a sufficient contribution to the war effort by its Pacific Division, and the company's executive and technical personnel devoted a considerable amount of time and study to the formulation of plans for the delivery of essential personnel and material to areas of war operations."[13]

"[G]enerations who know 'the Pacific' as painted by travel posters and television . . . differs totally from what they faced," recalls Ernest Colant. "They found, instead, islands surrounded by barbed-wire, heavy camouflage, military installations, and less than desirable quarters for short layovers, after extended trips, attempting sleep within ear-shot of the fighting surrounding them. There was no way to keep these crews out of combat zones. . . . [Pan Am crews] were given no special treatment and none was expected. They flew the same routes and were quartered and messed together with the military personnel. They were co-mingled at one base one day and with the same persons the next day at another island. Uniforms worn were identical except for the insignia."[14]

In just over half a year of operation, Pan Am's NATS operation flew 457,790 route miles, 3,157,439 NATS passenger miles, and totaled 1,761,865 NATS cargo ton-miles. Pan Am flew armor plating for patching sides of ships, equipment for anti-aircraft batteries, replacement parts for heavy construction equipment, self-sealing gas tanks for fighter planes, radar equipment, and radio parts.[15] By the end of 1943, Pan Am's Treasure Island base was too small for both the Navy and the airline's NATS' Pacific operations. The island was also too small to be a commercial airport—the San Francisco Airport, still called Mills Field, was serving domestic routes from the peninsula south of the city and had a new seaplane harbor. After January 1, 1944, Pan Am transitioned to Mills Field.[16]

Pan Am often flew very important passengers. One mission, involving a mysterious "Mr. Jones," began at dawn of January 12, 1943, at Dinner Key. Captain Howard Cone was preparing the *Dixie Clipper* for departure when he saw Mr. Jones board—in a wheelchair. It was President Roosevelt, off to the secret Casablanca Conference in French Morocco. "Casablanca was filled with Vichyites and Axis agents; if the Germans discovered the site of the conference, protection could not be guaranteed," Doris Kearns Goodwin notes of the "agonizing" security concerns.

The *Dixie* took off, followed by Pan Am's backup, the *Atlantic Clipper*, with Captain Richard Vinal in command. The president betrayed no worries. "I sat with him, strapped, as the plane rose from the water, and he acted like a sixteen-year-old, for he had done no flying since he was President," trusted aide Harry Hopkins recalled. "The trip was smooth, the President happy and interested."

Atlantic Division Manager John Leslie, in charge of the airline's top-secret operation, was on the flight and at Bathurst saw a sight he never forgot, as the president came by boat alongside the U.S.S. *Memphis* and was hoisted aboard, boat and all. "Like the Navy man he was, the President, sitting in the stern of his open boat, turned toward the U.S. flag at the stern of the 'Memphis' and placed his white Panama hat over his breast as he came over the side," Leslie recalled. "This was not done for press photographers; there were none! In this very remote corner of the earth, at a fearsomely dangerous phase of a World War, bearing the lonely burden of defending his country against Hitler and Japan, there he was saluting the flag of his country in the time-honored fashion of the United States Navy."

An Air Transport Command C-54 took Roosevelt on to Casablanca, where he discussed unconditional Axis surrender terms with Churchill and General Charles De Gaulle of France. On Saturday, January 30, the Clipper was safely winging the president and his entourage homeward on the last leg of what the travel log calculated as a 16,965-mile journey. The Casablanca trip was the first in which a sitting president flew in an airplane, first to fly overseas—and first airborne presidential birthday party. The *Dixie Clipper* flew international signal flags marking Roosevelt's sixty-first and the Pan Am crew served a roast turkey dinner, with champagne and birthday cake.[17]

Earlier that month, on January 20, NATS Flight 62100 lifted off from Pearl Harbor with another important passenger. The aircraft was the *Philippine Clipper*, and veteran Pan Am pilot Captain Robert Elzey was flying Admiral Robert H. English and his staff to San Francisco. Admiral English, who commanded the U.S. submarine fleet that was turning the tide in the Western Pacific, was to confer with naval planners and was carrying top-secret material, including photographic surveys of potential landing sites on Japanese-held islands. Weather coming into San Francisco was bad, and Elzey wanted to fly to San Diego but relented because of the importance of English's meetings. But the Bay Area was being soaked in heavier than expected rains, with winds estimated at over one hundred miles per hour. Treasure Island's Flight Watch Office was monitoring the weather and advised Elzey, "San Diego is the only possibility," or he could "hold until after daylight." Elzey replied, "Roger, thank you." He remained noncommittal about his plans, even as the winds rushed the Clipper to the Bay Area.

The Clipper passed over the Bay Area and took a due west course toward the ocean. Elzey began his descent, not over the ocean, but over coastal mountains—blown far off course by savage winds, the 26-ton Clipper hit a mountain slope near Ukiah and exploded.

Chief of Naval Operations, Admiral Ernest J. King, ordered an all-out search and recovery mission. When they found the crash site in a ravine, "The scene was one of utter destruction," recalls Pan Am radio officer Almon Gray, who was assigned to NATS and took part in the search. All died instantly, most of the nineteen bodies burned beyond recognition. Gray searched for days to recover the Top Secret material. Finally, an Army demolition squad detonated explosives in the ravine, burying the wreckage. With the loss of the ship, the *China Clipper* was the only Martin M-130 remaining. Writing about the tragedy more than fifty years later, Gray and co-author John Elott discovered "rain water has washed away most of the detritus in which the *Philippine Clipper* was interred, exposing its sun-bleached metal fragments like the skeletal remains of a prehistoric beast."[18]

Pan Am was called upon to perform dangerous rescues at sea. One dramatic incident was the sinking of S.S. *Cape San Juan*, a War Shipping Administration ship. Three hundred miles away, a twin-engine Martin Mariner commanded by Captain W. W. Moss had just landed with important cargo at a Pacific base when word of the disaster arrived. Moss asked for volunteers—every crew member stepped forward. (To save weight, three were left behind.) It was raining, and the sea was roiling with ten-to-fifteen-foot swells when they sighted the downed ship and oil-coated survivors clinging to floating wreckage. Moss landed in rough waters, and the crew tossed out inflated life rafts attached by lines to the aircraft. Forty-eight survivors were brought alongside and pulled in through side hatches. Captain Donald F. Smith, U.S.N., director of NATS, commended Captain Moss for "praiseworthy judgment, courage and airmanship."[19]

In the chaos of war, Pan Am crews often encountered the unexpected. One moonlit night, Captain Robert Ford was flying a Clipper NATS mission when First Officer McRae spotted a flare to the east. They changed course and were within a half-mile of a burning ship when "it disintegrated in a tremendous explosion which sent a mushroom of incandescent flame to an altitude somewhat higher than ours," Ford recalled. "There was a sharp crack of detonation and our plane rocked and pitched violently. The sea for a radius of one half mile about the vessel was lashed white by flying debris and a steel girder . . . could be seen tumbling in the air . . . up the column of incandescent gas."

The sky cleared and they saw torpedo wakes and two lights signaling. The lights brought their attention to three lifeboats carrying seventeen survivors, including seven wounded. Ford dropped to a thousand feet and released a flare that illuminated a quarter mile area—an enemy submarine was seen riding the surface, but it quickly submerged. Ford and his crew were officially commended, as the flare had probably deterred the submarine crew from machine-gunning survivors. But after taking a celestial fix of the lifeboats, the Clipper had to resume its course. "My crew and I felt heavy-hearted indeed," Ford said, "that we were unable to tell the survivors when aid might reach them, but security reasons dictated otherwise."[20]

★

During the war, commercial upgrades and innovation were at a standstill. Wartime service was paramount, and airlines often suffered shortages. "It is well appreciated by the Army Air Forces that your Company, as well as other airline companies, does not have as much equipment as is desirable," Brigadier General Frederic Smith wrote John Cooper in October of '44, responding to a plane order that hadn't been met. Pan Am Assistant Vice President Anne Archibald replied to Smith on Cooper's behalf the next day: "We would appreciate any help that you may be able to give at the earliest possible moment in assisting us to obtain these aircraft which are so critically needed by us at the present time."[21]

At midnight on December 31, 1944, Pan Am's NATS contract was to expire. Pan Am's Atlantic Division announced the welcome news that with the termination of the military contract it would return to transatlantic commercial operations that January 1, 1945.[22]

Pan Am's 1944 annual report recorded another year devoted to war work, with expanded military air transport services. There were sobering numbers—214 employees had now died during wartime duties. Trippe also reported the company was looking ahead. That December additional stock shares had been offered to underwrite postwar transports orders with Douglas, Lockheed, and Consolidated Vultee. "These giant Clippers will make possible low fares which in turn will make worldwide, airborne mass transportation a reality for the average American," Trippe predicted. Pan Am also requested authority to operate domestic service, but only if the government "should reverse its long established policy by combining American domestic and international operations" (in other words, if domestic airlines were allowed to invade PAA's international turf).[23]

CNAC was pulling its weight: "Up to the end of 1944, CNAC had completed more than 35,000 trips over the treacherous mountains and during that year it transported 82,908,000 pounds of cargo," Reginald Cleveland wrote.[24] There were several positive developments in the CBI theater that year. "[F]irst, the Air Transport Command and China National Aviation Corporation were carrying supplies into China at a rate never approached before, and, second, on 15 October 1944 the Allied forces in north Burma opened an offensive with six divisions to clear the last Japanese from north Burma," an Army history records. "Such was Allied power in north Burma and so battered were the Japanese that the end was a matter of weeks."[25]

In July of '45, with Myitkyina reclaimed from the enemy, 71,042 tons of cargo flowed into China, eclipsing the optimum 12,000 tons T. V. Soong once dreamed of. After that peak, the war began winding down. The Hump operation would soon be over. "Once that remote wilderness carried a traffic such as La Guardia Airport has never remotely approached; in all likelihood never again will anyone save some explorer bring the sound of aircraft engines over those mountains," ATC historian Oliver La Farge wrote. "The last to leave, of course, were the men of the Graves Registration service, searching for the last of the dead."[26]

## CHAPTER 24
# INTO THE CONGO

*"When the desperate race was on to build an A-bomb before the Germans did and the two major problems were solved, i.e., how to separate U-235 from the natural U-238 and how to detonate an A-bomb, there was left a third problem: where to get the uranium and enough of it to make a bomb. It is found in pitchblende [a radioactive, uranium rich mineral] and about the [richest] source then known was in the Belgian Congo. Once again the government turned to Trippe."*

—Horace Brock, Pan Am pilot[1]

Leopoldville was not a typical airdrome. Its terminal was a riverboat anchored to the Congo River's shore, and seaplanes moored at buoys on the water. Outside the landing area were submerged rocks and sandbars. Upriver, jungle growth collected into "floating islands," particularly during the rainy season, that were carried downstream by the current and swept over a thunderous waterfall below town.[2] Pan Am's Miami to Leopoldville route had been dormant since 1942 when the Navy purchased the *Capetown Clipper*. But in 1943, Pan Am planned to revive Leopoldville for commercial service and repurchased the *China Clipper* from the Navy to fly it.

The flagship Clipper that made the historic Pacific crossing had been flying since it left the Martin plant in 1935 (it was the last to complete a transpacific crossing before Pearl Harbor), but was given a complete overhaul at Treasure Island in March of '42, including removal of its 130-foot wings. "Old timers had never seen anything like it," *New Horizons* reported. "[B]y nightfall the Clipper's stub-nosed hull, stripped of every appendage, lay in solitary state in its beaching cradle like a huge mechanical whale."[3]

By November of '43, Harold Bixby was proposing to NATS director Captain D.F. Smith that Pan Am's Eastern Division cover the costs of the revived route and administrate its ports of call, except for Fisherman's Lake and Leopoldville. Bixby wanted the operation "on a commercial basis" and requested a maximum of five personnel in Leopoldville before the first week of December.[4]

But a War Department letter on February 9, 1944, declaring Belgian Congo service was no longer required for "national defense," canceled Pan Am's plans. The Civil Aeronautics Board confirmed that ruling on February 22.[5]

The problem was the Top Secret Manhattan Project was ready to create an atomic bomb in the United States. To do so, it needed more uranium, and the best deposits in the world were in the Congo.

⭐

On August 2, 1939, a month before Hitler invaded Poland, the White House received a letter addressed to the president from physicist Albert Einstein. The letter reported that it would soon be possible "to set up a nuclear chain reaction in a large mass of uranium, by which vast amounts of power and large quantities of new radium-like elements would be generated.... This new phenomenon would also lead to the construction of bombs." Such bombs might be too heavy to be carried by air, Einstein noted, but if carried by boat to a port and exploded "might very well destroy the whole port together with some of the surrounding territory." Einstein explained that good uranium deposits were in Canada and Czechoslovakia, but the richest source was the Belgian Congo. What was disturbing was Nazi-controlled Czechoslovakia had stopped uranium sales—there was every indication that Germany might be trying to build the bomb.[6]

America's secret Manhattan Project was building an atomic bomb, a two billion dollar effort utilizing facilities across the U.S. and a workforce of more than 600,000. One historian compares the enterprise with the great engineering feats of human history, such as the building of the Pyramids and the Great Wall of China.[7]

The richest uranium source was Shinkolobwe mine in Congo's Katanga Province, owned by the *Union Minière du Haut Katanga* (UMHK). The Belgian firm controlled the world market and stockpiled sufficient demand for thirty years. By August 21, 1943, a report to Roosevelt from the Military Policy Committee noted the world's major uranium supply was "not under our control in any way." British commercial interests had a stake in UMHK and the Committee and Manhattan Project leader, Major General Leslie Groves, recommended to Roosevelt that America and Great Britain enter into a "joint control" agreement. The negotiations were "a somewhat ticklish situation," writes Army historian Vincent Jones, "for neither Secretary of State Cordell Hull nor anyone else in the Department of State knew anything about the existence of the Manhattan project."

To ensure continued secrecy about the building of an atomic bomb, Roosevelt set up a negotiating team that circumvented Secretary Hull and his State Department. The negotiations that took place in London would largely be between Sir John Anderson, Chancellor of the Exchequer, and Roosevelt's handpicked representative, U.S. Ambassador to Great Britain John G. Winant. Roosevelt further charged Secretary of War Henry Stimson with monitoring and overseeing the negotiations from Washington, effectively bypassing Hull. Stimson would advise Winant, with input from General Groves and Harvey Bundy, Stimson's special science assistant.

"For these delicate negotiations then, the War Department assumed a role normally accorded to the State Department," Jones noted. "Although highly irregular, the War Department continued to play this role in subsequent quests for overseas uranium and thorium resources."

The resulting joint pact between the U.S. and Britain was followed by an agreement with Belgium in the fall of 1944. The U.S. and Britain now had a contract to mine the ore at Shinkolobwe Mine.[8]

The Manhattan Project had been receiving supplies of Congo uranium. But there were fresh security concerns. Previously, shipments from Shinkolobwe

Mine were transported by rail to the Angolan port of Lobito, and by ship across the South Atlantic to Natal, Port-of-Spain, and the United States. But Angola, a colony of neutral Portugal, was swarming with Axis spies. An alternative plan was to transport the ore by rail and river barge to Leopoldville, and then by train to port—a harrowing 1,500 miles. Once at sea, ships were vulnerable to enemy submarines or accidents—an estimated 200 tons of uranium had already been lost in the Atlantic. The solution was to bypass all terrestrial obstacles and take the uranium to the U.S. by air, with Pan Am doing the flying.

But before the airline could transport the uranium, it needed the Leopoldville service reinstated. To Pan Am, the cancellation of the service by the War Department had been premature. And, of course, even the State Department was in the dark regarding the Manhattan Project. But Pan Am knew it could make a case for continued service to Leopoldville—a May of '44 internal Pan Am report noted a backlog of fifty-seven non-priority passengers wanting air travel to Liberia and various cities in Africa. Potential customers included missionaries, the Texas and Standard oil companies, the Firestone Plantation Company, and other firms.[9]

But a paper trail continually refers to "strategic materials." As with all internal documents regarding the resumption of Leopoldville service, the highest levels at Pan Am were copied on key correspondence, including vice presidents Bixby and Cooper, assistant VP Archibald in Washington, and former Wall Streeter and now vice president, Howard Dean. Also in the loop was Fife Symington, a longtime Pan Am operations and sales leader who moved into government relations with his prewar promotion as Pan Am's London representative.

On April 20, 1944, Cooper and Symington met at the State Department with Henry Villard of the Division of Near-Eastern and African Affairs. Cooper explained that Governor General Pierre Ryckmans and other Belgian Congo officials strongly supported Pan Am's resumption of service and if the War Department and CAB gave the go-ahead, Pan Am could be operational within two weeks. Both Villard and Stockely Morgan, of State's Division of International Communications, felt an impending visit by the Congo's Governor General was the perfect excuse to reopen the matter.[10]

An ally was the Foreign Economic Administration (FEA), an agency formed by President Roosevelt to facilitate wartime coordination of overseas operations of U.S. agencies. In early May, Symington hand delivered to FEA's Washington office a three-page outline for U.S. flag wartime service between the U.S. and Congo. "Depending on the nature of the 'War' load to be transported (whether the largest volume will be strategic materials, mail or passengers) the interior of the Clipper can be arranged for maximum available weight," Symington's outline noted. A key section was titled "STRATEGIC MATERIALS" and explained Clippers "will provide a sure facility for unhampered transportation of any of the following materials vitally needed in the allied war effort." The list included industrial diamonds, uranium, and columbite, a radioactive mineral—added in pen was "very confidential," with asterisks marking uranium and columbite.[11]

By July 15, Villard at the State Department called Anne Archibald to ask about the status of the Leopoldville Route and whether the matter could be talked over with the Navy.[12] By the end of the month, Bixby met with Leo Crowley, head of the FEA, a meeting arranged by Trippe. Bixby explained the War Department's mistake in not consulting the State Department, Navy, Post Office, or FEA on the Leopoldville matter, and that it might take months to go through CAB hearings to get Pan Am's Leopoldville service reinstated. Bixby proposed the simplest solution—have the War Department rescind its cancellation order. Crowley agreed to talk to the governmental departments and, once convinced of their support, would ask Under Secretary of War Robert Patterson to withdraw the letter.[13]

Pan Am lobbied the Office of Strategic Services (OSS), the wartime intelligence operation created by Roosevelt and headed by William Donovan. The day after the Crowley meeting, Bixby wrote Charles Cheston, assistant OSS director in Washington, noting that Pan Am's flying boat was ready to go and their request had the support of State, Navy, Post Office, FEA, and others. The next day, Cheston responded with full OSS backing: "We are preparing a communication to the appropriate government authorities which will express our interest in the early inauguration of your service between the Belgian Congo and this country."[14]

Support for Leopoldville service arrived from an unexpected quarter—American missionary groups. Dr. Emory Ross, of the Foreign Missions Conference of North America, cited "undoubted National interest" in restoring service to allow more than fifty Protestant missionary boards to send doctors, nurses, agriculturists, and educators to their old service posts in Africa, estimating 300 potential missionary passengers in 1945. Ross conveyed those points in an August 10 telegram to L. Welch Pogue at CAB and Mr. Murray, the State Department's head of the Bureau of Near Eastern and African Affairs. He also wired his telegram to missionary societies in Nashville, Richmond, Indianapolis, Chicago, Boston, and Philadelphia, urging them to forward the telegram, with their endorsements, to Pogue and Murray. "We believe Dr. Ross' quick action may have assisted in our Leopoldville problem," Symington noted in an internal memorandum.

A few days later Anne Archibald telephoned Pan Am headquarters that she had received a CAB order—as of August 12, the War Department retracted its earlier order and CAB effectively restored service between Monrovia, Liberia, and Leopoldville.[15]

★

In October of '44, "Lodi" Lodeesen, a colorful Clipper Captain who flew Boeing special missions and called himself "the Flying Dutchman," was called to chief pilot Horace Brock's office and given a top-secret special mission to fly the *China Clipper* to the Belgian Congo. He was selected, Brock explained, because he knew the route. Lodi would pick up cargo and Vice President Howard Dean would be the only passenger. "On the return flight, stop only for fuel," Brock ordered. "No overnights. I'll give you a double crew and Captain George Duff as co-captain . . . No questions, no answers. Dean knows what to do."[16]

Dean was in Leopoldville on October 16 and met with OSS agents, including Henry Stehli. "Dean told Stehli that Pan Am was extremely grateful to OSS for helping them get permission to land at. . . . Leopoldville," historian Susan Williams writes. "Dean had taken a key role in the shipping of uranium from the Congo. . . . both understood the importance of absolute secrecy."[17]

There's no evidence Dean knew exactly what Pan Am was flying out, its importance in building a super bomb. Only a handful of scientists could have known the implications of that payload of ore. Lodi was certainly unaware. Captain Lodeesen arrived with the *China Clipper* and his double crew, the unmarked crates were loaded, and Dean boarded, the only passenger, and they were off. Flying night and day, as ordered, they stopped only for fuel.

Back at his Manhattan apartment, relieved of the stress of a two-week long special mission, Dean was delighted to find his daughter, Nancy, home from Sarah Lawrence College. He casually mentioned the "odd looking dirt" they picked up in Africa. Nancy had studied the splitting of the atom in a science class taught at Sarah Lawrence by theoretical physicist and future Nobel laureate Maria Goeppert-Mayer, and she quickly put the pieces together and asserted, "That was uranium!" Dean promptly changed the subject.[18]

The *China Clipper* was then assigned mostly to the Caribbean. But the region Pan Am once used as a lab for flying the oceans was now a "backwaters" run, Lodi grumbled, likening the historic Clipper to "a wind-broken Kentucky Derby winner hacking tourists through Central Park. . . ." Not long after, Lodi was in Miami when he got a call from Dinner Key's airport manager—the *China Clipper* had crashed at Port-of-Spain while en route to Leopoldville. Most of the passengers and crew were dead. Lodi was asked to break the news to the widow of the second officer.

Afterward, Lodi headed to an all-night joint outside Coconut Grove. He loved flying the *China Clipper*, and he nursed a stiff drink and thought of the soothing song of its engines and the rattling rivets on the bulkheads, the smell of leather seats, gasoline, and sweat in the cockpit. "I saw her blunt bow and her honest lines, and the great, thick wing, spread wide like the wings of a soaring gull," he recalled.

Three decades later, Lodi learned the secret of the cargo on his last flight of the *China Clipper*. "I learned that the unmarked crates put in the Clipper's hold at Leopoldville contained the uranium ore for the first atomic bomb that was to destroy Hiroshima. . . . The spring water of the well of knowledge is clear and cold as the truth, but the taste is as bitter as tears."[19]

⭐

Franklin Roosevelt suddenly died of a cerebral hemorrhage on April 12, 1945. By May 8, Nazi Germany formally surrendered. That June, total victory was in the air. The Army had already deactivated Benson Field at Fish Lake, taking away their equipment and leaving what they didn't want with Pan Am.[20]

In China, General Claire Chennault learned that General Marshall and General Arnold wanted a reorganization of air forces in China, and their plans did not include him. On July 8, "eight years to the day that I first offered my services to China," Chennault made his second request for retirement from the Army. When the press made an issue of his retirement on the eve of victory, Under Secretary of War Patterson "announced that the changes were purely a China Theater matter, and the decision to supersede me had been made in the field," Chennault recalled. This and subsequent testimony "bore little resemblance to the facts," he added.

Chennault was heading home, bitter he would not be present at Japan's eventual surrender. He had a warm meeting with the Generalissimo and made a farewell tour of the Fourteenth Air Forces bases, ending up at Kunming, where his China adventure began. Along the way, he was met by adoring crowds. "I assured them that the final victory was already in sight and that the Japanese could not fight beyond Christmas," he noted. "I had no information then about the atomic bomb, although it was obvious that Russia would be jumping in for a share of the spoils almost any day. I urged the Chinese to expend the same dogged effort they used in fighting the war to build up their country during the peace and above all to fight to the end against any form of government that sought to enslave the individual at the expense of the state."

Chennault boarded his staff C-47 on the Kunming airfield, his pilot, Lieutenant Colonel "Tex" Carleton, at the controls. The runway was lined with hundreds of Yunnanese setting off firecrackers to scare away evil spirits. As Tex went airborne, Chennault could see black thunderclouds brewing over Burma to the south. "Below, the ripening green rice paddies of the Kunming Valley rolled by," he recalled, "and behind lay a record unsurpassed in the air annals of World War II—an air force that had grown from 250 men and 100 planes to 20,000 men and 1,000 planes, casting the shadow of its wings the length of the Asiatic continent."[21]

★

Bill Taylor saw the war to its end from the battlefield. Like many Pan Amers, he was a reserve officer and in mid-1943 applied for active duty. He served as a technical inspector for the VII Bomber Command, was appointed Captain, Air Corps, in December of '45. Brigadier General White would commend him for his service in the Gilbert, Marshall, Marianas, and Ryukyu Islands.

By November of '44, Taylor was at Ulithi, an atoll near Guam and launch site for MacArthur's attack on the island of Leyte and B-29 bomber strikes on Japan. They faced retaliatory strikes from Japan and Taylor was among a crew digging air raid trenches. One night he was awakened by explosions and rushed out of his tent. "The sky was crisscrossed by powerful searchlight beams, streams of tracer bullets from anti-aircraft guns, a burning Japanese aircraft falling, and a tremendous pillar of flame from a B-29 exploding on the air field." As a Japanese attack bomber seemed to dive straight for him, Taylor leapt into a deep trench he and his comrades had dug near their tents.[22]

The atomic bomb was dropped on Hiroshima on August 6, 1945, by order of the new commander-in-chief, President Harry Truman. Taylor and everyone on his island began testing their gas masks, certain of reprisals. "We all waited in trepidation, and then a couple of days later the second atomic bomb was dropped on Nagasaki," Taylor recalled. "That did it. The Japanese announced their surrender on 10 August. . . . We heard the news on the armed forces radio network about 10:00 in the evening. The whole island immediately burst forth in an orgy of celebrating by firing off guns of every type. The sky was criss-crossed with tracers. I grabbed my helmet, as did many others, and ran to my air raid trench."[23]

Even before Japan's surrender, territory was being liberated, and Pan Am's prisoners of war had begun returning home. The front page of the April 15 Pan Am Pacific-Alaska Division *Clipper* included a tribute to President Roosevelt and a photo of smiling Pan Amers Don McCann, Eugene Brush, and Ed Powers below the headline: "PAA WELCOMES INTERNEES: Families and Company Officials Crowd Docks, Meet Men Back from Philippines." Fifteen liberated internees traveling by ship to San Francisco arrived on Sunday, April 8, where the reception included a band playing, "Hail, Hail, The Gang's All Here." Among them was Rush Clark, the Manila airport manager captured at bayonet point on the way to a friend's wedding. He had been imprisoned at Los Baños internment camp in the Philippines, but today was a new day, as Clark's parents greeted him with adoring smiles.

Internees in Japan were freed after the surrender, and another wave of liberated PAA employees were bound for home. On September 13, a cablegram from Manila to Pan Am's Pacific-Alaska Division headquarters accounted for the last prisoner whose whereabouts were unknown: "Have been liberated. Am now in Manila. . . . Will be back soon. Waldo Raugust." The man captured at Wake flew to San Francisco on the *Honolulu Clipper* with eleven fellow Pan Am internees, landing at Mills Field on September 25. At the San Francisco Airport, Raugust, a North Dakota native, recounted driving wounded Chamorro personnel to Wake hospital after the Japanese air attack. "I missed the plane that evacuated Wake personnel after the attack by about ten minutes, but I was so busy that I hardly noticed it out there taxiing for the takeoff to Midway," he explained. It was noted those ten minutes cost him almost four years "of privation and near-starvation in Japanese hands."[24]

Another liberated Wake prisoner was Marine pilot John Kinney. His Pan Am leave of absence was still in effect, and he later tried to land a job with the airline. But pilots were unionized, and he would have to work his way up through the ranks. Instead, he worked as a test pilot and in 1959 retired from the Marine Corps with an honorary promotion to brigadier general. He wrote a book "to show families of future prisoners of war that a man's life need not end when he enters into an enemy prison compound. He can survive, recover, and lead a useful, productive life."[25]

On October 29, 1945, William Mullahey, the "human fish" and now a section superintendent with the Pacific-Alaska Division, returned to liberated Wake, where he once unloaded cargo and blasted coral, to report on conditions. Six hundred Japanese prisoners still remained and were "working for their conquerors" while awaiting transport back to Japan, he reported.

A military escort drove Mullahey, both strapped with sidearms, by jeep across the causeway bridge from Wake to Peale, where Pan Am had its operations. They saw the wreckage from both Japan's initial attacks and the American fight to reclaim the island. Along the beach, Japanese defensive positions were in ruins. Prewar Navy buildings "are now only a twisted tangle of rusted steel girders," Mullahey observed. The main powerhouse was partly completed when Japan attacked, but a direct hit from an American shell caused massive damage to its two-foot thick concrete walls. One water tower was standing, the other a mass of blasted steel. Mullahey's report concluded: "I would estimate Pan American's entire Wake Island capital investment to be a total loss."

When they tried to find Pan Am's hotel they saw only mounds of coral rubble. Mullahey then recognized the hotel's floor plate. "Nothing remains visible above ground and apparently a tank trap trench was dug through the length of the Hotel, possibly connecting up several bomb craters. A forlorn street light stanchion was partly hidden in the underbrush. It was difficult to believe that the Hotel building with concrete base could disappear so completely."

The isle that entranced Clipper voyager Dorothy Kaucher was no longer the innocent place "that belonged to the dim, silent centuries." But she had felt "strange, distorted images of impending doom" during her visit. War passed over Wake, and ruins remained.[26]

On Christmas day, Milton Caniff's *Terry and the Pirates* comics strip took a break from its normal storyline of intrigues in embattled China. Text appeared against a snowy night, a streaking plane heading off stage right. Caniff's text explained the character Dude Hennick was inspired by his old Ohio State University classmate, Capt. Frank Higgs. "During the bitter, barren war years he flew unarmed cargo aircraft over the Hump into China—until he was killed in a crash in the hills south of Shanghai . . . Today your mind will be on your particular good Joe who didn't come back for Christmas . . . But if you liked Dude Hennick you may wish to spare a thought for Frank Higgs . . . Dude died with him."

## CHAPTER 25
# NO DISTANT LANDS

*"Air transport achievements by Pan American under direction of the Army Air Forces are the most significant when their meaning is translated in terms of air power and national defense. The nation's airlines, of which Pan American is a leader, in the early days of war were the backbone of the Air Forces' system of aerial supply which so often meant the difference between victory and defeat and continued an indispensable element of support until the end. The Army Air Forces' interest in continued development of civil transport aviation is predicated upon this war experience in the sure knowledge that civilian air transport is an essential auxiliary to military air power in any emergency of the future."*

—LT. GENERAL HAROLD L. GEORGE, 1946 LETTER TO JUAN TRIPPE[1]

Pan Am began in 1927 with a single airmail route across less than one hundred miles of water separating Key West from Havana. In less than twenty years, the airline had crisscrossed the planet and was now known as Pan American World Airways. In the beginning, Herbert Hoover saw the potential for international trade, military planners saw strategic advantages, and by accident and design, Pan Am synthesized aviation's twin aspects of commercial and military potential.

The airline's pioneering achievements, including opening transoceanic airways and airdromes in foreign lands, served Allied air operations up to and through World War II. The Airport Development Program established the anchor in South America, while the South Atlantic ferrying and the trans-Africa operation moved troops and supplies to battlegrounds, and Boeing Clippers flew vital special missions. After militarization, the airline created the Africa-Orient Division, its Cannonball missions defining speed and efficiency. The China National Aviation Corporation pioneered the Hump and kept the aerial Burma Road going in partnership with the Air Transport Command. From the Pacific to the Atlantic, naval and air force operations were informed by Pan Am's experience and ability to get there "the fastest with the mostest."

A measure of appreciation came from bomber pilot Lieutenant Charles A. Young, Jr., who celebrated his fiftieth combat mission over Europe in September of '44 by posing for a photograph in front of his B-17G. In the tradition of combat aircraft fuselage painted with pin-up girls and movie goddesses, Young's was embellished with the words "Miss Pan-Am."[2]

In war, military necessity subordinated commercial innovation, often making for a difficult partnership. The month Young celebrated the success of "Miss Pan-Am," Harold Bixby drafted a letter to the Chief of Naval Operations, expressing frustration with the Navy's failure to carry its end of their NATS contract—"hundreds" of promised aircraft had not been delivered and Pan Am was often called upon at the airline's expense "and the weakening of our own organization." Bixby noted a recent United Airlines CAB proposal trumpeted their San Francisco to Australia C-54 service while denigrating Pan Am as "boat operators."

"Prior to Pearl Harbor we were tremendously proud of our accomplishments on the Pacific and we believe this pride was shared by the American Nation," Bixby's draft letter read. "We gladly gave everything we had to the Navy and frankly expected in return that the Navy, when able to do so, would help us to preserve our position on the Pacific."[3]

But author S. Paul Johnson was one of many wartime observers who understood that commercial aviation had been transformed by wartime service. "Although the war put a stop to all normal commercial development, the necessity of transporting our military materiel and personnel into all corners of the world has given a tremendous impetus to plans for eventual air routes on a global scale," Johnson wrote in 1944. "A colossal amount of over-water experience is thus being accumulated that will prove invaluable in post-war development."[4]

General Hap Arnold, the man whose first vision of the air was Blériot's fragile monoplane that had just conquered the English Channel, now imagined a future of faster than sound aircraft and guided missiles. Arnold still saw aviation's military and commercial possibilities as irrevocably linked. "No activity having to do with aviation in any form can be considered as being completely independent of national security," he wrote in 1946. "Civil aviation must be encouraged . . . and all arrangements, plans, agreements, and operations should be carried out with due regard for their military implications. . . . Air power must, in the future, be the business of every American citizen."[5]

Arnold wouldn't live to see that future. He suffered a number of heart attacks during the war but continued clocking twelve-hour workdays. As one account put it, Hap "eventually wore himself out." He died in 1950.[6]

With the war over, Pan Am could pick up where it had left off. Getting back to business included completing an order for Lockheed's Constellation that had been placed on June 11, 1940. The era of land planes had arrived, and the "Connie," as Lockheed's four-engine land plane was affectionately known, was designed to serve both the military and commercial airlines.

Transcontinental & Western Air was one of the airlines that would square off against Pan Am in the postwar fight for commercial air supremacy. TWA had never flown outside the U.S. until the war, but during it made some 6,000 crossings of the North and South Atlantic for the ATC. By 1945, TWA revealed its postwar ambitions in its rumored name change: Trans-World Airlines. Like Pan Am, TWA was anticipating the Connie, designed to fly forty-eight passengers or one hundred soldiers in bucket seats. "Within the next ten years we will have transport planes flying 400 to 500 miles an hour at an altitude of 35,000 feet," TWA president Jack Frye told *Fortune*. "Souped up models on demonstration flights will be able to fly around the world in thirty-six hours." The money and passion behind TWA came from wealthy owner Howard Hughes, a record-setting pilot, Hollywood movie mogul, and playboy. Frye and Hughes were young, new generation airman eager to take on Pan Am and Juan Trippe, even the U.S. Congress, to get what they wanted. As if to serve notice, Hughes and Frye co-piloted a 1945 Constellation test flight, spanning Los Angeles to Washington, D.C., in under seven hours.[7]

As if in response, Pan American World Airways broke in the Constellation in a big way, making the first scheduled around the world flight in Constellation model 749, dubbed *Clipper America*, on June 29, 1947.

The Clipper name was a tribute—the iconic flying boats were vanishing into history. The venerable Sikorsky *American Clipper*, the first to be called "Clipper," was interred in a Miami scrapyard during the war. In 1943, the year the *Philippine Clipper* hit a mountain in California, Captain R.O.D. Sullivan, misjudging an approach to Lisbon, cartwheeled the *Yankee Clipper* into the Tagus River, killing nineteen passengers and eight crew members— Sullivan survived but died three years later, a broken man. The *China Clipper* crash ended the Martin flying boats. The *California Clipper* was the last Boeing 314 to be retired in 1946, with the seven remaining B 314s purchased by a startup, World Airlines, in 1948. They sat idle for years at San Diego's Lindbergh Field. Six were sold for scrap in 1950. The last, the *Anzac Clipper*, was resold and scrapped in Baltimore the following year.[8]

There is a wartime tale about a veteran Pan Am pilot denied promotion who went to argue with André Priester. The esteemed engineer went to his office safe and pulled out a big black book and handed it to the veteran. It was the specs for the delayed Lockheed Constellation. Priester patiently went through pages and pages of graphs, diagrams, and details of the super plane's modern mechanics, its electrical and fuel systems. "The pilot thinks 'the man is crazy,'" Pan Am's corporate history recounts. "After a while [the pilot] takes his leave. It was Priester's way of telling the old-timer that it would take a new generation of men to fly the new generation of airplanes. The old-timer never understood him; and never understood that Priester himself . . . was being swept by time and tide."[9]

Despite the challenges, indomitable Juan Trippe was eager to lead his airline. Pan Am was modernizing, not only with the Connie, but arranging with American Telephone and Telegraph to hook up its reservation department with a nationwide "private line typewriter network."[10]

Trippe was first beguiled by flight when he watched Wilbur Wright circle the Statue of Liberty. He partnered with others similarly "born to the air," like C. V. Whitney and air warrior and visionary John Hambleton, lost too soon. Lindbergh's solo transatlantic flight and Hero of the Century stature lifted Pan Am and the entire aviation industry. Anne Lindbergh matched her husband as a trailblazing airwoman, and their Orient and Atlantic survey missions aided Pan Am's plans for crossing the Pacific and Atlantic. Pan Am harnessed elemental powers, with Hugo Leuteritz's mastery of radio waves pioneering aviation communications.

The airline had attracted personnel willing to adapt, including pilots that inherently knew the lone wolf barnstormers who flew "by the seat of their pants" wouldn't cut it if flying was to be a business. Pan Am pilots like Captain Musick and Captain Gray championed air safety, instrument flying, radio communications, and even the order and discipline of the Clipper system that assured the public they were in good hands—all that and more helped reduce risk to routine.

In a 1944 speech at the University of California at Berkeley titled "America in the Air Age," Trippe sounded his favorite theme, linking the nation's pioneering spirit to the first scheduled transpacific Clipper that set off not far from that very campus. Prior to the war, Trippe declared the airplane had shrunk the world; now he proclaimed, "Nor is this world view . . . that of a 'smaller world.' Such an expression cannot define America's destiny in the future, for as transportation and communication develop, the world before us grows, not smaller, but larger. . . . All over the world the roar of aircraft is awakening people and nations to new human destinies. A human being, whatever his past disadvantages may have been, is capable, in a few short years, of almost limitless progress. Who among us is wise enough to set a limit to man's capacity?"[11]

The war's end ushered in the Atomic and Space Ages, as well as the Cold War between America and its former ally, the Soviet Union. Pan Am was in the unaccustomed role as a competitor in international air travel—the "chosen instrument" argument would no longer fly. But Pan Am's indomitable leader still felt Pan American World Airways's future was as limitless as those possibilities he celebrated in his 1944 lecture.

The world had grown bigger, more complex, because aviation had conquered time and space. No longer were there distant lands. In the process, human consciousness was transformed. As Juan Trippe faced the postwar era, he must have felt that past was prologue. The power of wings had taken humanity across a once distant horizon, landing in the bright promise of The World of Tomorrow.

# NOTES

## PART I: AIR POWER
### Chapter 1: Visions of the Future

1. H. H. Arnold, *Global Mission* (New York: Harper & Brothers, Publishers, 1949), p. 115.
2. Robert Daley, *An American Saga: Juan Trippe and His Pan Am Empire* (New York: Random House, 1980), pp. 310, 507. One account claims Trippe was at his hotel packing to leave when summoned to meet Churchill. Daley says his interview with Trippe provided details, such as his and Arnold's presence on the hotel rooftop. Arnold's nickname of "Hap" was for his positive disposition.
3. Jenifer Van Vleck, *Empire of the Air: Aviation And The American Ascendancy* (Cambridge, Massachusetts and London, England: Harvard University Press, 2013), pp. 134–135; Editors Francis L. Loewenheim, Harold D. Langley, Manfred Jonas, *Roosevelt and Churchill: Their Secret Wartime Correspondence* (New York: Saturday Review Press/E. P. Dutton & Co., 1975), p. 146.
4. Daley, *An American Saga*, p. 311; Wolfgang Langewiesche, *Pan American Corporate History*, Section 16, pp. 5196–5198, San Francisco Airport Commission Aviation Library. Wolfgang Langwiesche's assignment to write the company history was approved by Pan Am's board of directors in May of 1957, and continued into the 1970s. It will be referred to as "Pan Am's corporate history," although Langwiesche's manuscript was never completed or published. Hereafter, references to San Francisco Airport Commission Aviation Library materials at SFO Museum will be noted, "SFOM."
5. Noel F. Busch, "Juan Trippe," *Life*, October 20, 1941: 111.
6. "Pan Am at War," *Time*, May 18, 1942: 73.
7. Juan Trippe statement, *Wings over the World—Annual Report for 1941*, Pan American World Airways System, May 2, 1942, p. 1, SFOM.
8. "Instrument of the nation," was the phrase Langewiesche used in the unpublished corporate history.
9. Arnold, *Global Mission*, pp. 1–2.

10. *The Fourth Annual Report of the Hudson-Fulton Celebration: Commission to the Legislature of the State of New York*, prepared by Edward Hagaman Hall (Albany, New York: J. B. Lyon and Company, 1910), Volume I, p. 486. A demonstration of dirigibles was considered, as was an International Aeronautical Exposition and an aviation float in the Historical Parade (p. 1149).
11. Arnold, *Global Mission*, p. 13.
12. *Fourth Annual Report of the Hudson-Fulton Celebration*, pp. 490–492. Wright flew in competition with rival Glenn Curtiss, but the latter did not record an official flight. On Wednesday, September 29, Curtiss reportedly launched before 7:00 a.m., but his twenty-six seconds aloft covered only 300 yards and was not officially recognized, having only been witnessed by a military officer and a friend of the pilot. Curtiss did not fly again until October 3, but he rose only sixty-to-one hundred feet, didn't brave open water, and circled back for a quarter mile and forty-five seconds in the air that wasn't judged official. *The Fourth Annual Report of the Hudson-Fulton Celebration*, Vol. I, Chapter XXX: Aeronautical Exhibitions, pp. 496–497.
13. Arnold, *Global Mission*, p. 13; Betty Stettinius Trippe, *Pan Am's First Lady: The Diary of Betty Stettinius Trippe* (McLean, Virginia: Paladwr Press, 1996), p. 6, SFOM; Daley, *An American Saga*, p. 6; Thomas P. Hughes, *American Genesis: A Century of Invention and Technological Enthusiasm 1870–1970* (New York: Penguin Books, 1990), p. 56.
14. The Department of the Army, *The Army Almanac* (Washington, D.C., Government Printing Office, 1950), p. 211.
15. Arnold, *Global Mission*, p. 15.
16. Ibid., pp. 27–28.
17. Thomas M. Coffey, *Hap: The Story of the U.S. Air Force and The Man Who Built It—General Henry H. "Hap" Arnold* (New York: The Viking Press, 1981), pp. 52–53.
18. Arnold, *Global Mission*, p. 20.
19. Ibid., p. 291; Assistant Secretary of State Francis White, "Aviation in Latin America," report to the Secretary of State, April 25, 1929, National Archives, Post Office Record Group 28, Box 2, file folder, "Awarding of Contracts," p. 1.
20. Dr. Wesley Phillips Newton, "The Role of the Army Air Aims in Latin America, 1922–1931," *Air University Review*, Sept.-Oct. 1967: 2, SFOM.
21. White, "Aviation in Latin America," p. 1, National Archives.
22. Edward S. Trippe, letter regarding genealogy to John H. Hill, February 28, 2017; "Three Killed By A Train," front page, *The New York Times*, Thursday, August 24, 1899.
23. Unidentified source on Trippe as a footballer from Langewiesche, *Pan Am Corporate History*, Section 1A, pp. 31–32, SFOM.
24. Ralph D. Paine, *The First Yale Unit: A Story of Naval Aviation 1916–1919* (Cambridge: Riverside Press, 1925), Volume I, p. 1, SFOM.

25. Ibid., Volume I, p. 84.
26. Langewiesche, *Pan Am Corporate History*, Section 1A, p. 71, SFOM.
27. *The Diary and Letters of Betty Stettinius Trippe: 1925 to 1968* (private edition, 1982), p, 290, collection of John H. Hill; Matthew Josephson, *Empire of the Air: Juan Trippe and the Struggle for World Airways* (New York: Harcourt, Brace and Company, 1943), p. 24.
28. "Colossus of the Caribbean," n.a., *Fortune*, April 1931: 47.
29. Langewiesche, *Pan Am Corporate History*, Section 1A, pp. 33–34, SFOM.
30. Ibid., Section 1A, p. 188; Charles Trippe's death from typhoid: *The Diary and Letters of Betty Stettinius Trippe*, John H. Hill collection.
31. Anthony J. Mayo, Nitin Nohria, and Mark Rennella, *Entrepreneurs, Managers, and Leaders: What the Airline Industry Can Teach Us About Leadership* (New York: Macmillan/Palgrave, 2009), p. 43, SFOM; Langewiesche, *Pan Am Corporate History*, Section 2A, p. 530, SFOM.
32. Ibid., Section 2A, pp. 503–504.
33. Ibid., Section 2A, pp. 548, 549a.
34. Ibid., Section 2A, pp. 538a–539a.
35. Mayo, Nohria, and Rennella, *Entrepreneurs, Managers, and Leaders*, p. 44, SFOM.
36. Avery McBee, "Pan American Airways' Musketeers," *The Sunday Sun Magazine*, Baltimore, Maryland, April 16, 1939.
37. Marylin Bender and Selig Altschul, *The Chosen Instrument* (New York: Simon and Schuster, 1982), p. 47.
38. Ibid., pp. 47, 57.
39. Ibid., pp. 46–47.
40. Mark Cotta Vaz, George Hambleton interview, New York City, April 2, 2008.
41. Bender and Altschul, *The Chosen Instrument*, p. 57.

## Chapter 2: Born to the Air

1. John C. Leslie, *Pan Am History*, Volume I, Chapter 1, p. 39, Research Manuscript, SFOM.
2. "Former Brigadier-General Mitchell Pays A Splendid Tribute To The Late Col. John Hambleton," letter to the *Baltimore Sun*, June 12, 1929, George Hambleton collection.
3. Bender and Altschul, *The Chosen Instrument*, SFOM; Marc Wortman, *The Millionaires' Unit: The Aristocratic Flyboys Who Fought The Great War And Invented American Air Power* (New York: PublicAffairs, 2006), p. 233.
4. Harold Buckley letter to Mrs. John Hambleton, from Leixlip Castle, Leixlip, Co. Kildare, August 3, 1931, Libbie Hambleton collection.
5. Merian Cooper letters to Wolfgang Langewiesche, May 31, 1961, p. 2, and June 12, 1961, p. 3, George Hambleton collection.

6. Emile Gauvreau and Lester Cohen, *Billy Mitchell: Founder of Our Air Force and Prophet without Honor* (New York: E. P. Dutton & Co., Inc., 1942), p. 167.
7. Gerald W. Johnson, "Warriors," *Baltimore Evening Sun*, June 13, 1929, Libbie Hambleton collection.
8. Vaz, *Living Dangerously*, p. 180.
9. John Hambleton's diary record of 1924–1925 provided by Libbie Hambleton.
10. Ibid., May 29, 1925.
11. Daley, *An American Saga*, p. 16.
12. Ibid., p. 15.
13. Langewiesche, *Pan Am Corporate History*, Section 10, p. 3533, SFOM.
14. Ibid., Section 1A, pp. 153, 159a.
15. Ibid., Section 1A, p. 219.
16. Hambleton diary entry, October 8, 1925, Libby Hambleton collection.
17. Ibid., entry, October 9, 1925.
18. Daley, *An American Saga*, p. 472; Hambleton diary entries, October 13–14, 1925, Libbie Hambleton collection.
19. Ibid., entries, October 15–16, 1925.
20. Ibid., entries, October 17–18, 1925.
21. Ibid., entry, October 19, 1925.
22. Ibid., entry, October 27, 1925.
23. Ibid., entry, October 29, 1925.
24. Ibid., entry, November 3, 1925.
25. Ibid., entry, November 9, 1925.
26. Ibid., entry, November 13, 1925.
27. Ibid., entry, November 23, 1925.
28. Langewiesche, *Pan Am Corporate History*, Section 2B, p. 924, SFOM.
29. Josephson, *Empire of the Air*, p. 28.
30. Harry Bruno, H.A. Bruno—R.R. Blythe and Associates, Public Relations, two separate letters to Juan Trippe, March 17, 1927, Series 4, sub-series 27: Others, Box 2, folder 5, University of Miami, Richter Library Special Collections, Pan American World Airways, Inc. Records Collection (hereafter "UM Richter Library Special Collections"); Harry Bruno, *Wings Over America: The Inside Story of American Aviation* (New York: Robert M. McBride & Company, 1942), pp. 168–169.
31. "Ten-Passenger Liner reaches City at 10:40, n.a., *Jacksonville Journal*, December 17, 1925, George Hambleton collection.
32. Langewiesche, *Pan Am Corporate History*, Section 1B, p. 382, SFOM; Josephson, *Empire of the Air*, p. 28.
33. Langewiesche, *Pan Am Corporate History*, Section 1B, p. 401, SFOM.
34. Josephson, *Empire of the Air*, pp. 28–29.
35. Charles M. Meister, "Fokker Plane reaches City On First Trip," *Tampa Telegraph*, December 19, 1925, George Hambleton collection.
36. Bruno, *Wings Over America*, pp. 169, 249.

37. Daley, *An American Saga*, pp. 18–19.
38. Juan Trippe, "Charles A. Lindbergh and World Travel," lecture at the Fourteenth Wings Club 'Sight' Lecture, presented at the Wings Club in New York City on May 20, 1977, p. 1.
39. Langewiesche, *Pan Am Corporate History*, Section 10, p. 3630; Section 1A, p. 137, SFOM.
40. Bender and Altschul, *The Chosen Instrument*, p. 73.
41. Leslie, *Pan Am History*, Vol. I, Chapter 1, p. 18, SFOM.
42. Paine, *First Yale Unit*, Vol. Two, p. 270, SFOM.
43. Langewiesche, *Pan Am Corporate History*, Section 1A, p. 218b, SFOM.
44. William A. M. Burden, *The Struggle for Airways in Latin America* (New York: Council on Foreign Relations, 1943), p. 11, SFOM.
45. Arnold, *Global Mission*, pp. 114–115.


## Chapter 3: Champions of Air Power

1. Burke Davis, *The Billy Mitchell Affair* (New York: Random House, 1967), p. 62.
2. Hauptmann Hermann, *The Luftwaffe: Its Rise and Fall* (New York: G. P. Putnam's Sons, 1943), pp. 11–12, SFOM.
3. Ibid., pp. 28, 81–82.
4. Langewiesche, *Pan Am Corporate History*, Section 10, pp. 3484–3485, SFOM.
5. Pan American Airways, Inc., Civil Aviation Board (CAB) Docket No. 525 *et al.*, *Outline of the History of the Latin American Services*, p. 4, SFOM.
6. Langewiesche, *Pan Am Corporate History*, Section 16, pp. 5013–5016, SFOM.
7. Ibid., Section 16, pp. 5016–5017.
8. Ibid., Section 16, p. 5026.
9. Ibid., Section 16, pp. 5020–5021, 5084.
10. For their work in the Amazon, Rice was honored with a gold medal from the Royal Geographical Society and von Bauer with a life membership. Describing von Bauer's malady in his unpublished manuscript, Langewiesche crossed out "malaria" and wrote "tropical fever" in the margin. Langewiesche, *Pan Am Corporate History*, Section 16, p. 5085.
11. Ibid., Section 16, pp. 5025–5026, 5030, 5033–5034.
12. Ibid., Section 16, pp. 5007a–5008, 5042–5043.
13. "Pan American Airways," *Fortune*, April 1936: 85.
14. Langewiesche, *Pan Am Corporate History*, Section 16, pp. 5053–5054, SFOM; White, "Aviation in Latin America," pp. 3–4, National Archives.
15. Burden, *The Struggle for Airways in Latin America*, p. 12, SFOM.
16. Francis White, "Aviation in Latin America," p. 3, National Archives.
17. Wayne Biddle, *Barons of the Sky: From Early Flight to Strategic Warfare: The Story of the American Aerospace Industry* (John Hopkins University Press, 2002) p. 106.

18. Editor John T. Greenwood with Von Hardesty, *Milestones of Aviation: Smithsonian National Air and Space Museum* (New York: Universe Publishing, 2008), pp. 28–30.
19. Arnold E. Briddon and Ellmore A. Champie, *Federal Aviation Agency Historical Fact Book: A Chronology, 1926–1963* (Federal Aviation Agency, Washington, D.C.: U.S. Government Printing Office, 1966), pp. vii–viii.
20. Gauvreau and Cohen, *Billy Mitchell*, pp. 61–64.

## Chapter 4: Prophet of a New Era

1. Trippe, Wings Club 'Sight' lecture, p. 3.
2. Arnold, *Global Mission*, pp. 117–118.
3. Ibid., p. 119.
4. Hambleton diary entries, September 18 and 28, 1925, Libby Hambleton collection.
5. Ibid., entry, October 2, 1925.
6. "The Mitchell Trial," *Aviation*, November 23, 1925: 746–747, SFOM. One of Mitchell's judges was Major General Douglas MacArthur, a future controversial military figure himself.
7. Gauvieau & Cohen, *Billy Mitchell*, pp. 150–151.
8. "Mitchell Trial," *Aviation*: 746, 748, SFOM; Newton, "Army Air Aims," *Air University Review*: 3, SFOM.
9. Edward V. Rickenbacker, *Rickenbacker* (Englewood Cliffs, New Jersey: Prentice-Hall, Inc., 1967), p. 256.
10. Ibid., pp. 189, 265.
11. The Air Corps Act authorized formation of an Army Air Corps and an Office of the Chief of Air Corps. Major General Mason M. Patrick was installed as first chief, and a new sub-Cabinet post of Assistant Secretary of War for Air was also created in the War Department. Yale First Unit founder F. Trubee Davison served in that position, although, by 1933, a presidential Executive Order abolished the sub-Cabinet post. Department of The Army, *The Army Almanac*, p. 213.
12. Quote on "legislative corner-stone" from *Federal Aviation Agency Historical Fact Book*, p. viii; Bender and Altschul, *The Chosen Instrument*, p. 141.
13. "Who Was John Hambleton?" No author, biographical paper, pp. 1–2, George Hambleton collection.
14. Cooper letter to Langewiesche, May 31, 1961, pp. 2–3, George Hambleton collection.
15. R. G. Grant, *Flight: 100 Years of Aviation* (Smithsonian Institution/Covent Garden Books, published in U.S.: New York: DK Publishing, 2009), p. 119.
16. A. Scott Berg, *Lindbergh* (New York: Berkley Books paperback edition, 1999), pp. 114–116.

17. Ibid., p. 114.
18. Trippe, Wings Club 'Sight' Lecture, pp. 1–2
19. Geoffrey Wolff, *Black Sun: The Brief Transit and Violent Eclipse of Harry Crosby* (New York: Random House, 1976), p. 260.
20. Berg, *Lindbergh*, pp. 142–143.
21. "The First Across Alone," May 21, 1927, from *Time* magazine *80 Days that Changed The World* (website reference).
22. Charles Lindbergh, *We* (New York: G. P. Putnam's Sons, 1927), pp. 283, 292–293.
23. George Buchanan Fife, *Lindbergh: The Lone Eagle* (New York: A. L. Burt Company, 1927), pp. 218–234.
24. Daley, *An American Saga*, pp. 62–63; Berg, *Lindbergh*, pp. 169–170.
25. Aeromarine's last flight, between Nassau and Miami, was May 1, 1924. Aeromarine was a training ground for such Pan Am stars as Captain Edwin C. Musick, Captain Wallace D. Culbertson, and D.G. Richardson; Leslie, *Pan Am History*, Volume I, Chapter 1, pp. 31–32, SFOM.
26. Arnold, *Global Mission*, pp. 117, 122.
27. "Pan American Airways," *Fortune*: 90.
28. Leslie, *Pan Am History*, Vol. I, Chapter 1, p. 24, SFOM; R.E.G. Davies, *Pan Am: An Airline And Its Aircraft* (New York: Orion Books, 1987), p. 4.
29. Hambleton diary entry, November 24, 1925, Libbie Hambleton collection.
30. Bender and Altschul, *The Chosen Instrument*, p. 85.
31. Leslie, *Pan Am History*, Vol. I, Chapter 1, p. 25, SFOM.
32. Ibid., Vol. I, Chapter 1, p. 26.
33. Bender and Altschul, *The Chosen Instrument*, p. 85.
34. Daley, *An American Saga*, p. 29.
35. Leslie, *Pan Am History*, Vol. I, Chapter 1, pp. 23, 26, SFOM.
36. "Colossus of the Caribbean," *Fortune*: 48.
37. "Pan American Airways," *Fortune*: 159.
38. Clair explains this information was given her during a phone call from an unnamed individual—believed highly placed in the intelligence community—referred to her by Mr. John Taylor, an archivist at the National Archives. Mark Cotta Vaz, interview with Kathleen Clair, New York City, March 29, 2008.
39. Langewiesche, *Pan Am Corporate History*, Section 1A, pp. 101–102, SFOM.
40. Ibid., Section 1B, pp. 258–259; "Pan American Airways," *Fortune*: 91; Davies, *Pan Am*, p. 4.
41. Leslie, *Pan Am History*, Vol. I, Chapter 1, p. 28, SFOM.
42. Bender and Altschul, *The Chosen Instrument*, p. 86; Fortune, "Pan American Airways," *Fortune*: 91.
43. Daley, *An American Saga*, p. 33.
44. "Pan American Airways," *Fortune*: 91.
45. Leslie, *Pan Am History*, Vol I, Chapter 1, p. 28, SFOM.

46. Accounts for the amount paid Caldwell vary, the $175 figure from: Bender and Altschul, *The Chosen Instrument*, p. 87, $250 from: Daley, *An American Saga*, p. 35.
47. Howell French, letter to "Anne and Richard," Sunday, November 5, 1961, George Hambleton collection.
48. Langewiesche, *Pan Am Corporate History*, Section 8, p. 2826, SFOM.

## Chapter 5: The Aviator and the Airline

1. Langewiesche, *Pan Am Corporate History*, Section 10, p. 3510, SFOM.
2. R. E. G. Davies, *Airlines of the United States since 1914* (London: Putnam, revised reprint edition, 1982), p. 213, SFOM.
3. Langewiesche, *Pan Am Corporate History*, Section 1B, pp. 412–413, SFOM.
4. Ibid., Section 9, pp. 3346b–3347, SFOM.
5. Ibid., Section 8, p. 2759.
6. Ibid., Section 8, pp. 2770–2771, 2829, 2831–2832.
7. Ibid., Section 9, p. 3055.
8. Ibid., Section 9, p. 3056.
9. Ibid., Section 9, p. 2972.
10. Ibid., Section 9, p. 2974.
11. Ibid., Section 9, pp. 2978, 2981.
12. Ibid., Section 9, p. 2986.
13. Ibid., Section 9, p. 2986.
14. Ibid., Section 9, p. 3034.
15. Ibid., Section 9, pp. 2985, 2988.
16. Trippe, Wings Club 'Sight' Lecture, p. 6.
17. Charles Lindbergh, letter to Wolfgang Langewiesche, November 19, 1967, p. 1, from Langewiesche's *Pan American World Airways Corporate History* Research Manuscript Supplement, SFOM.
18. Berg, *Lindbergh*, pp. 172–174.
19. Minutes of the First Meeting of the Interdepartmental Aviation Committee, November 23, 1927; three-part document, National Archives, Record Group 28, The Post Office, entry #152, Box 2, file folder, "Awarding of Contracts," pp. 1–3.
20. Bender and Altschul, *The Chosen Instrument*, pp. 93–94.
21. Langewiesche, *Pan Am Corporate History*, Section 1B, p. 422, SFOM.
22. Ibid., Section 1A, pp. 99–100.
23. "President's Report," Board of Directors meeting, Atlantic, Gulf and Caribbean Airways, Inc., December 17, 1927, Series 1, sub-series 8: Secretary (Morris and Macy), Box 2, folder 54, UM Richter Library Special Collections.
24. Langewiesche, *Pan Am Corporate History*, Section 1B, pp. 445–446, SFOM.
25. Bender and Altschul, *The Chosen Instrument*, pp. 124–125.

26. Langewiesche, *Pan Am Corporate History*, Section 1B, p. 432; Section 10, p. 3410, SFOM.
27. Lindbergh letter, *Pan Am Corporate History* Supplement, pp. 2, 7, SFOM.
28. "Col. J. A. Hambleton and Couple Killed in Airplane Crash," *Baltimore Sun*, June 8, 1929, George Hambleton collection.
29. Bender and Altschul, *The Chosen Instrument*, p. 97.
30. *Aviation*, February 20, 1928: 441, SFOM.
31. Gene Banning, *Airlines of Pan American since 1927* (Rockville, Maryland: Paladwr Press, 2001), p. 12, SFOM.
32. "The Air-Way to Havana," Pan American Airways first flight schedule, circa 1928, collection of Mark Cotta Vaz.
33. Langewiesche, *Pan Am Corporate History*, Section 10, p. 3456, SFOM.
34. Bender and Altschul, *The Chosen Instrument*, p. 96; Langewiesche, *Pan Am Corporate History*, Section Section 1B, pp. 433–435, SFOM.
35. Langewiesche, *Pan Am Corporate History*, Section 7, p. 2617, SFOM; White, "Aviation in Latin America," pp. 1–2, National Archives.
36. Pan Am, CAB Docket 525, *History of the Latin American Services*, pp. 4–5, SFOM.
37. Langewiesche, *Pan Am Corporate History*, Section 10, pp. 3496, 3502–3503, 3531–3523, SFOM.
38. Ibid., Section 1A, pp. 146–147, Section 10, p. 3503.
39. Ibid., Section 10, p. 3506.
40. Ibid., Section 1A, p. 146.
41. Ibid., Section 10, pp. 3507–3508.
42. Banning, *Airlines of Pan American*, p. 13.
43. "Pan American Airways" listing, *Moody's Industrials*, 1929, p. 3087.
44. "Name changed to Pan American Airways Corp" (from Aviation Corp. of the Americas), noted in *Moody's Industrials*, 1931, p. 3166; Langewiesche, *Pan Am Corporate History*, Section 1B, p. 361, SFOM.

### Chapter 6: An Accumulation
1. Langewiesche, *Pan Am Corporate History*, Section 1A, p. 126, SFOM.
2. Ibid., Section 7, pp. 2712–2713, 2717, SFOM.
3. Ibid., Section 7, p. 2724; Leslie, *Pan Am History*, Vol. I, Chapter 2, p. 8, SFOM.
4. Leslie, *Pan Am History*, Vol. I, Chapter 2, pp. 8–9, SFOM; Langewiesche, *Pan Am Corporate History*, Section 7, pp. 2722–2725, 2727, SFOM; Banning, *Airlines of Pan American*, pp. 87–88, SFOM.
5. Ibid., Section 7, pp. 2721–2722, SFOM.
6. M. C. Cooper, "The Airlines of Mexico," *Aero Digest*, Feb. 1931, reprinted in *Conquerors of the Sky*, edited by Joseph Lewis French (Springfield, Massachusetts: McLoughlin Bros., Inc., 1932), pp. 151, 153.
7. Langewiesche, *Pan Am Corporate History*, Section 7, p. 2748, SFOM.

8. Leslie, *Pan Am History*, Vol. I, Chapter Two, p. 15, SFOM.
9. Langewiesche, *Pan Am Corporate History*, Section 6, p. 2281b, SFOM.
10. Ibid., Section 6, pp. 2328, 2339b, 2351–2352.
11. Ibid., Section 6, pp. 2353–2354.
12. Ibid., Section 6, p. 2337.
13. Ibid., Section 6, p. 2296.
14. Ibid., Section 6, p. 2289.
15. Ibid., Section 6, p. 2298.
16. Ibid., Section 5, p. 1895.
17. "The Air-Way to Havana," brochure, Mark Cotta Vaz collection.
18. Vaz, *Living Dangerously*, p. 181.
19. Leslie, *Pan Am History*, Appendix section, Vol. III, July 1974 article, "An Informal Biographical Sketch of André A. Priester," p. 1, SFOM.
20. Ibid., pp. 2–3.
21. Langewiesche, *Pan Am Corporate History*, Section 8, pp. 2772–2773, SFOM.
22. Leslie, "Biographical Sketch of André A. Priester," p. 5, SFOM.
23. Langewiesche, *Pan Am Corporate History*, Section 9, p. 2037. SFOM.
24. William Stephen Grooch, *From Crate to Clipper With Captain Musick, Pioneer Pilot* (New York/Toronto: Longmans, Green and Co., 1939), pp. 1–2, SFOM.
25. Ibid., p. 35.
26. Ibid., pp. 36–41.
27. Ibid., pp. 43–44.
28. Bruno, *Wings Over America*, pp. 248–249.
29. Grooch, *From Crate to Clipper*, pp. 84–85, SFOM.
30. Bruno, *Wings Over America*, pp. 249–250.
31. Grooch, *From Crate to Clipper*, p. 106, SFOM.
32. Ibid., pp. 92–94.
33. Ibid., p. 95.
34. Langewiesche, *Pan Am Corporate History*, Section Ibid., Section 9, p. 2984, SFOM.
35. Ibid., Section 9, p. 2983.
36. Ibid., Section 9, pp. 3060–3061.
37. Grooch, *From Crate to Clipper*, p. 96, SFOM.
38. Cooper letter to Langewiesche, May 31, 1961, p. 3, George Hambleton collection; Pan Am CAB Docket No. 525, *History of the Latin American Services*, p. 9, SFOM.
39. "Aviation" address transcripts, J. T., Trippe, president, Pan American Airways System, delivered before The Junior League of New York City, Tuesday, December 11, 1934, p. 14, Trippe Family Papers, National Air and Space Museum, Smithsonian Institution.
40. William Van Dusen, *Log of the China Clipper*, n.d., probably circa 1936, pp. 14–16, SFOM.

41. Ralph A. O'Neill, with Joseph F. Hood, *A Dream of Eagles* (Boston: Houghton Mifflin Company, 1973), pp. 58–61, 125; Rand investment totals from *Fortune*, "Colossus," p. 128.
42. Ibid., pp. 55–56.
43. Ibid., p. 131–132; Grooch, *From Crate to Clipper*, pp. 121–122, SFOM.
44. Langewiesche, *Pan Am Corporate History*, Section 9, p. 3305, SFOM.
45. Reproduction of Lindbergh's February 2, 1929, letter to Juan Trippe, Jon E. Krupnick, *Pan American's Pacific Pioneers: The Rest of the Story* (Missoula, Montana: Jon E. Krupnick, publisher, 2000), p. 47, SFOM.
46. Josephson, *Empire of the Air*, p. 59; Langewiesche, *Pan Am Corporate History*, Section 16, p. 5103, SFOM.

## Chapter 7: The Miracle Year

1. "Colossus," *Fortune*: 132.
2. Transcript of Juan Trippe radio speech, under auspices of the "Aviation Activities Hour," radio station W.A.B. C., January 3, 1929, pp. 1–2, 4, Trippe Family Papers, National Air and Space Museum, Smithsonian Institution.
3. Banning, *Airlines of Pan American*, p. 19, SFOM.
4. White, "Aviation in Latin America," p. 5, National Archives.
5. Vaz, *Living Dangerously*, p. 181.
6. John Hambleton, vice president, Pan American Airways, "Air Transport for Commerce" speech, Official Report of the Sixteenth National Foreign Trade Convention, Baltimore, Maryland, April 17–19, 1929, pp. 198–202, George Hambleton collection.
7. Ibid., p. 202; Banning, *Airlines of Pan American*, p. 21, SFOM.
8. Ibid., pp. 23–25.
9. "Colossus," *Fortune*: 128.
10. O'Neill, *Dream of Eagles*, pp. 132–136.
11. Ibid., pp. 197, 200–203. In his autobiography, O'Neill places the christening date of the *Buenos Aires* as October 2, 1929. His date might be a little off as Juan and Betty Trippe were probably still on their way home from the Caribbean survey with the Lindberghs.
12. Langewiesche, *Pan Am Corporate History*, Section 9, p. 3024, SFOM.
13. McBee, "Pan American Airways' Musketeers," *Sunday Sun Magazine*.
14. "Pan American Airways," *Fortune*: 91; Grover Loening, letter to Merian C. Cooper, June 13, 1961, George Hambleton collection.
15. Hambleton & Company, Federal Aviation Corporation statement, April 4, 1929, George Hambleton collection; Vaz, *Living Dangerously*, pp. 180, 182.
16. Vaz, *Living Dangerously*, p. 184. Von Der Hayden died upon impact. Mrs. Hayden expired in an ambulance before it reached the hospital.
17. News clipping missing the full publication title, but appears to be *The Washington Post*, George Hambleton collection.

18. "Hambleton's Body is Due in City Today," newspaper clipping, publication unknown, George Hambleton collection.
19. Mitchell letter, *Morning Sun*, June 12, 1929, George Hambleton collection.
20. George Carey, letter, New Stanley Hotel, Nairobi, Kenya colony to Margaret "Peg" Hambleton, July 29, 1929 (copy), Libbie Hambleton collection. Carey and Margaret would marry, a union that lasted until Margaret's death in 1973.
21. Aviation Corporation of the Americas letter to Cooper, signed by Trippe as ACA vice president and Pan Am president, February 10, 1932, certified true copy, Hoover Institute Archives.
22. Vaz, *Living Dangerously*, pp. 186–187.
23. Juan Trippe "Dear Coop" letter, July 23, 1935, George Hambleton collection; Vaz, *Living Dangerously*, p. 259.
24. Vaz interview, Kathleen Clair, March 29, 2008.
25. Betty Trippe, *Pan Am's First Lady*, p. 29, SFOM.
26. Ibid., pp. 40–41.
27. Oliver Rickertson, Jr., and A. V. Kidder, "An Archeological Reconnaissance By Air In Central America," *The Geographical Review*, April, 1930, Vo. XX. No. 2: 177, 179, 202, 204.
28. O'Neill, *Dream of Eagles*, p. 211.
29. Ibid., pp. 212–213.
30. Josephson, *Empire of the Air*, pp. 73–74.
31. O'Neill, *Dream of Eagles*, pp. 268–270, 282–283.
32. Ibid., pp. 288–289.
33. Leslie, *Pan Am History*, Vol. II., Chapter 2, pp. 64–65, SFOM.
34. O'Neill, *Dream of Eagles*, pp. 293–294.
35. Langewiesche, *Pan Am Corporate History*, Section 7, pp. 2453–2454, SFOM.
36. Grooch, *From Crate to Clipper*, p. 124, SFOM.
37. Langewiesche, *Pan Am Corporate History*, Section 7, p. 2603, 2724–2725, SFOM.
38. Ibid., Section 7, p. 2454.
39. O'Neill, *Dream of Eagles*, pp. 307–309.
40. Leslie, *Pan Am History*, Vol. I, Chapter 2, p. 24, SFOM.
41. Ibid., Chapter 2, p. 25.
42. Ibid., Vol. I, Chapter 2, p. 26.
43. Ibid., Vol. I, Chapter 2, p. 24.
44. Langeswiesche, *Pan Am Corporate History*, Section 16, p. 5132, SFOM; "Confidential, Brief Outline Of Example Situations Which Might Be Adversely Affected By Public Hearing" (PAA document, no author or date), Series 4, sub-series 24: SCADTA, Box 2, folder 20, UM Richter Library Special Collections; Wesley Phillips Newton, *The Perilous Sky: U.S. Aviation Diplomacy and Latin America: 1919–1931* (Coral Gables, Florida: University of Miami Press, 1978), pp. 311–313, SFOM.
45. "Pan American," *Fortune*, p. 160; Pan Am CAB Docket No 525, *Outline of the History of the Latin American Services*, p. 7, SFOM.

46. Ibid., pp. 6–7.
47. William Van Dusen, *Log of the China Clipper*, pp. 17–18, SFOM.
48. Pan American Airways System release, "Trans-Atlantic Represents Goal Sought by American Aviation Since Lindbergh," July 1937, p. 4, SFOM.
49. Charles Lindbergh, *Autobiography of Values* (New York & London: Harcourt Brace Jovanovich, 1978), pp. 111–112.
50. Langewiesche, *Pan Am Corporate History*, Section 9, p. 2992, SFOM.
51. Pan Am CAB Docket 525, *History of the Latin American Services*, pp. 11–12, SFOM.
52. Ibid., p. 11.
53. Langewiesche, *Pan Am Corporate Papers*, Section 9, pp. 2995–2997, SFOM.
54. Juan T. Trippe speech, transcript "1932?" pp. 4–5, Trippe Family Papers, National Air and Space Museum, Smithsonian Institution. The "1932?" speech was probably delivered late in 1933—Trippe makes a reference to the Lindberghs' "recently completed" Atlantic Survey flight.
55. Ibid., p. 5.
56. Charles Lindbergh, Forward from Anne Morrow Lindbergh's *Listen! The Wind* (New York: Harcourt, Brace and Company, 1938), p. v.
57. Berg, *Lindbergh*, p. 52.
58. Mark Cotta Vaz interview, Kathleen Clair, New York City, March 29, 2008, p. 4.
59. Lindbergh letter to Langewiesche, Nov. 19, 1967, p. 5, *Pan Am Corporate History* Supplement, SFOM.

## Chapter 8: Life in the Air

1. Anne Morrow Lindbergh, *War Within and Without: Diaries and Letters 1939–1944* (New York and London: A Helen and Kurt Wolff Book, Harcourt Brace Jovanovich, 1980), p. xv.
2. Anne Morrow Lindbergh, *Hour of Gold, Hour of Lead: Diaries and Letters of Anne Morrow Lindbergh 1929–1932* (New York/London: Harcourt Brace Jovanovich, 1973), pp. 9–10; Berg, *Lindbergh*, p. 216.
3. Charles Lindbergh Forward from Anne Morrow Lindbergh's, *Listen! the Wind*, p. vii.
4. Anne Morrow Lindbergh, *North to the Orient* (New York: Harcourt, Brace and Company, 1935), pp. 210–211, 255.
5. Ibid., pp. 226, 229–232.
6. Berg, *Lindbergh*, p. 231.
7. Anne Morrow Lindbergh, *War Within and Without*, p. xv; Lindbergh letter to Langewiesche, November 19, 1967, *Pan Am Corporate History Supplement*, SFOM.
8. Lindbergh, *Autobiography of Values*, pp. 112–113.
9. Langewiesche, *Pan Am Corporate Papers*, Section 9, p. 3033, SFOM.

10. Anne Morrow Lindbergh, *Locked Rooms and Open Doors: Diaries and Letters: 1933–1935* (New York and London: A Helen and Kurt Wolff Book, Harcourt Brace Jovanovich, 1974), p. xviii.
11. Anne Lindbergh, *Listen!*, p. 231.
12. Anne Lindbergh, *Locked Rooms*, p. xvii.
13. Ibid., pp. xvii–xviii.
14. Anne Lindbergh, *Locked Rooms*, p. 51.
15. Berg, *Lindbergh*, p. 286.
16. Anne Lindbergh, *Locked Rooms*, pp. 74–75.
17. Anne Lindbergh, *Listen!*, pp. 102–103.
18. Langewiesche, *Pan Am Corporate History*, Section 15: "Crossing the Atlantic," p. 4814, SFOM.
19. Anne Lindbergh, *Locked Rooms*, pp. 79, 81.
20. This quote and what follows taken from Charles Lindbergh twelve page letter to Juan Trippe, from Reykjavic, August 18, 1933. The direct quotations present Lindbergh's text as he wrote it. All 1933 survey letters from SFOM, courtesy of the Pan Am Records Collection, University Of Miami Richter Library Special Collections.
21. Here Lindbergh misspelled Godthaab as "Goalthaab." He occasionally misspelled "Angmagssalik," which has been corrected throughout.
22. Langewiesche, *Pan Am Corporate History*, Section 15, pp. 4814–4815, SFOM.
23. Lindbergh "Dear Juan" letter, 1933, SFOM/UM.
24. Anne Lindbergh, *Locked Rooms*, pp. xviii, 50, 66.
25. Ibid., pp. xviii–xix.
26. Ibid., pp. xix, 95.
27. Ibid., pp. 104, 106.
28. Quote and following material from Charles Lindbergh six-page letter to Juan Trippe, Stockholm, September 15, 1933, SFOM/UM.
29. Quote and following material from Charles Lindbergh letter to Juan Trippe, Wales, October 16, 1933, SFOM. Lindbergh spells Bergen "Berger," which has been corrected throughout.
30. Anne Lindbergh, *Locked Rooms*, pp. 136–137.
31. Anne Lindbergh, *Listen!*, p. 103.
32. Lindbergh, *Autobiography of Values*, pp. 113–114; Anne Lindbergh, *Locked Rooms*, p. 170; Trippe radio address, "1932?" speech transcript, p. 3, Trippe Family Papers, National Air and Space Museum, Smithsonian Institution.
33. Anne Lindbergh, *Locked Rooms*, pp. 174–176.
34. Ibid., pp. 177–178.
35. Berg, *Lindbergh*, p. 290; Lindbergh, *Autobiography of Values*, pp. 114–115.
36. Anne Lindbergh, *Listen!*, p. 275; Berg, *Lindbergh*, p. 290.
37. Charles Lindbergh, Forward, Anne Lindbergh, *Listen!*, p. ix; Pan American Airways, Inc., CAB Docket No. 855, *et al.*, *History of the Transatlantic Air Services*, p. 4, SFOM.

38. Anne Lindbergh, *Hour of Gold*, p. 216.
39. Gregory Crouch, *China's Wings: War, Intrigue, Romance and Adventure in the Middle Kingdom During the Golden Age of Flight* (New York: Bantam Books, 2012), p. 272.
40. "Pan American Airways," *Fortune*: 79.

## PART II: WAR CLOUDS
### Chapter 9: Across the Pacific
1. Langewiesche, *Pan Am Corporate History*, Section 9, p. 3034, SFOM.
2. Lindbergh, *Autobiography of Values*, p. 108; Pan Am CAB Docket No. 851 et al., *History of the Transpacific Air Services to and Through Hawaii*, p. 2, SFOM.
3. William Stephen Grooch, *Winged Highway* (New York/Toronto: Longmans, Green and Co., 1938), pp. 166–167, SFOM.
4. Pan Am CAB Docket No. 547 et al., *History of Pan American's Air Services To and Through Alaska*, p. 2, SFOM.
5. "Pan American Airways," *Fortune*: 164.
6. Pan Am CAB Docket 851, *History of the Transpacific Air Services*, p. 8, SFOM.
7. Pan Am CAB Docket 547, *Air Services To and Through Alaska*, p., p. 8, SFOM.
8. Daley, *An American Saga*, p. 95; Trippe speech transcript, "1932?," pp. 3–4, Trippe Family Papers, National Air and Space Museum, Smithsonian Institution.
9. Grooch, *From Crate to Clipper*, p. 133, SFOM.
10. Langewiesche, *Pan Am Corporate History*, Section 5, pp. 2138–2139, SFOM.
11. Ibid., Section 5, pp. 2107–2109.
12. "Sikorsky S-42," *FAM 14*, November 2010, San Francisco Aeronautical Society.
13. Ibid., "Martin M-130."
14. Grooch, *From Crate to Clipper*, pp. 148–149, SFOM.
15. Lindbergh proving flight: Daley, *An American Saga*, p. 139; R.E.G. Davies, *Pan Am*, p. 37; Pan Am CAB Docket 851, *History of the Transpacific Air Services*, p. 11, SFOM.
16. Josephson, *Empire of the Air*, p. 105.
17. Grooch, *From Crate to Clipper*, pp. 135–136, SFOM.
18. Pan American Airways, Inc., CAB Docket No. 851, *History of the Transpacific Air Services*, p. 1, SFOM.
19. Langewiesche, *Pan Am Corporate History*, Section 1B, p. 290, SFOM.
20. Bender and Altschul, *The Chosen Instrument*, p. 273.
21. Josephson, *Empire of the Air*, p. 93.
22. Pan Am CAB Docket 851, *History of the Transpacific Air Services*, p. 5, SFOM.
23. Langewiesche, *Pan Am Corporate History*, Section 9, pp. 3014–3015, SFOM; "Adcock Antenna," from Wikipedia, Internet site.
24. Langewiesche, *Pan Am Corporate History*, Section 9, p, 3016, SFOM.
25. Henry W. Roberts, *Aviation Radio* (New York: William Morrow, 1945), p. 183.

26. Pan Am CAB Docket 851, *History of the Transpacific Air Services*, p. 5. SFOM.
27. Midway was so named because it is at the midway point around the world from Greenwich, England, a town on the Prime Meridian from Greenwich time and used as the basis for Standard time.
28. Don Cooper, "The Route of the China Clipper," from *Thanks for the Memories* program, p. 37, the China Clipper 75th Anniversary Celebration: "Honoring Pan America's Pacific Pioneers," San Francisco, California, November 17–20, 2010.
29. Langewiesche, *Pan Am Corporate History*, Section 12, p. 3992, 3999, 4001, 4003–4004, SFOM.
30. J. T. Trippe, President, Pan American Airways, letter (copy) to The Secretary of the Navy, October 3, 1934, from Appendix section, John Leslie, *Pan Am History*, pp. 1–3, SFOM.
31. Justin Libby, "Pan Am Gets a Pacific Partner," *Naval History*, September/October, 1999: 5–6, SFOM.
32. Borger, "PAA lays ground work for Pacific air service," *Clipper*, p. 1.
33. Pan Am CAB Docket, 851, *History of the Transpacific Air Services*, p. 21, SFOM.
34. Cooper, "Route of the China Clipper" from *Thanks for the Memories* program, p. 39.
35. Ibid., pp. 40–41.
36. Langewiesche, *Pan Am Corporate History*, Section 13, p. 4287, SFOM.
37. Pan Am CAB Docket 851, *History of the Transpacific Air Services*, pp. 6, 14, SFOM.
38. Langewiesche, *Pan Am Corporate History*, Section 14, p. 4633, SFOM.
39. Josephson, *Empire of the Air*, p. 106.
40. "Navy Replied to Protests over Airline: Purely Commercial, says Swanson, Denying 'Hidden Motives,'" United Press by radio article, April 4, 1935, clipping from unnamed Hawaii newspaper, Binder 90, SFOM.
41. Claude A. Swanson, Secretary of the Navy, letter to Juan Trippe at PAA's New York office, date stamped "November 12, 1935," p. 1, National Archives, Pacific Region, Box 363, file #A21/A2-12, Pan Am, San Bruno, California.
42. Libby, "Pan Am Gets a Pacific Partner," *Naval History*, p. 6, SFOM.
43. Taylor, *Memoirs*, Vol. I, pp. 4, 6–8, SFOM.
44. Ibid., Vol. I, p. 28.
45. Ibid., Vol. I, p. 31, SFOM.
46. Langewiesche, *Pan Am Corporate History*, Section 12, p. 4009, SFOM.

## Chapter 10: Island Stepping Stones

1. Letter, Swanson to Trippe, "November 12, 1935," p. 1, National Archives, Pacific Region, San Bruno.
2. Taylor, *Memoirs*, Vol. I, p. 31, SFOM.

3. "The North Haven Expedition," by John G. Borger, pp. 9, 11, SFOM; Langewiesche, *Pan Am Corporate History*, Section 12, p. 4013; Section 14, p. 4568, SFOM.
4. Taylor, *Memoirs*, Vol. I, p. 31, SFOM.
5. Ibid., Vol. I, p. 33; William Stephen Grooch, *Skyway to Asia* (New York/Toronto: Longmans, Green and Co., 1936), p. 67, SFOM.
6. Taylor, *Memoirs*, Vol. I, p. 32, SFOM.
7. Grooch, *Skyway to Asia*, pp. 54–55, SFOM.
8. Langewiesche, *Pan Am Corporate History*, Section 12, p. 4018, SFOM.
9. Grooch, *Skyway to Asia*, pp. 59, SFOM.
10. Borger, "PAA lays the ground work for Pacific air service," *Clipper*, pp. 2, SFOM; Langewiesche, *Pan Am Corporate History*, Section 12, p. 4017, SFOM.
11. Grooch, *Skyway to Asia*, p. 61, SFOM.
12. Langewiesche, *Pan Am Corporate History*, Section 12, p. 4016, SFOM.
13. Taylor, *Memoirs*, Vol. I, pp. 32–33, SFOM.
14. Grooch, *Skyway to Asia*, p. 99, SFOM.
15. Cooper, "Route of the China Clipper," from *Thanks for the Memories* program, p. 42.
16. Langewiesche, *Pan Am Corporate History*, Section 13, pp. 4290b–4291, SFOM.
17. Material from article for the April 18, 1935 edition of the *New York Times*, Edwin Musick byline, from Langewiesche, *Pan Am Corporate History*, Section 13, pp. 4293–4296, SFOM.
18. Ibid., Section 13, p. 4297.
19. Cooper, "Route of the China Clipper," from *Thanks for the Memories* program, p.
20. Langewiesche, *Pan Am Corporate History*, Section 13, pp. 4300–4301, SFOM.
21. Cooper, "Route of the China Clipper," *Thanks for the Memories* program, p. 43; Daley, *An American Saga*, p. 156.
22. Grooch, *Skyway to Asia*, p. 87, SFOM.
23. Taylor, *Memoirs*, Vol. I, p. 35, SFOM.
24. Grooch, *Skyway to Asia*, pp. 93, SFOM.
25. Taylor, *Memoirs*, Vol. I, pp. 35–36, SFOM.
26. Ibid., Vol. I. p. 36.
27. Pan Am CAB Docket 851, *History of the Transpacific Air Services*, p. 7, SFOM.
28. Borger, "PAA lays the ground work for Pacific air service," *Clipper*, p. 4, SFOM.
29. Taylor, *Memoirs*, Vol. I., pp. 36–37.
30. Grooch, *Skyway to Asia*, pp. 102–103, SFOM.
31. Ibid., pp. 108, 119.
32. Taylor, *Memoirs*, diary section, May 15, 1935, SFOM.
33. Ibid., Vol. I., p. 37.
34. Van Dusen, *Log of the China Clipper*, p. 110.

35. Dorothy Kaucher, *On Your Left The Milky Way* (Boston: The Christopher Publishing House, 1952), pp. 219–220.
36. Taylor, *Memoirs*, diary section, p. 38, SFOM.
37. Langewiesche, *Pan Am Corporate History*, Section 13, p. 4337b, SFOM.
38. Borger, "PAA lays the ground work for Pacific air service," *Clipper*, p. 4, SFOM.
39. "To Wake & Back," *Time*, September 2, 1935: 52.
40. Langewiesche, *Pan Am Corporate History*, Section 13, pp. 4333–4334, SFOM.
41. Josephson, *Empire of the Air*, p. 122.
42. "First 'China Clipper' Flying Boat Delivered to Pan Am With Flair and Elegance of a Hollywood Screenplay," October 9, 1935, pp. 32, 34, *Pan Am News* release from 50th Pacific Flight Anniversary material, 1985, SFOM.
43. Ibid., p. 35.
44. Trippe, Wings Club 1977 'Sight' Lecture, p. 4.
45. Pan Am CAB Docket 851, *History of the Transpacific Air Services*, p. 5, SFOM.
46. Swanson letter to Trippe, "November 12, 1935," National Archives, Pacific Region, San Bruno.
47. Grooch, *From Crate to Clipper*, pp. 189–190, SFOM.
48. Ibid., p. 161; (Langewiesche, *Pan Am Corporate History*, Section 13, p. 4308a–4309, SFOM.
49. Ronald W. Jackson, *China Clipper: The gripping true story of Pan American's flying boats and their role in the war in the Pacific* (New York: Everest House, 1980), pp. 132–134, SFOM.

## Chapter 11: Clipper Glory

1. Captain Edwin C. Musick, "Clipper Trimmed Scheduled Time," wireless to the *New York Times*, November 29, 1935, copyright exclusive, SFOM. In the author's opinion, Musick was too focused on his historic challenge to take time to send off, via wireless, well-crafted prose. The report is attributed to Musick but was probably prepared by the airline's public relations department.
2. Pan Am CAB Docket 851, *History of the Transpacific Air Services*, pp. 21–22, SFOM. Preparations included calibrating the direction finder that Leuteritz had built in Alameda, and having pilots familiarize themselves with the greater San Francisco Bay and the northern coastline up to Clear Lake, the designated alternate landing site if San Francisco was too foggy. Langewiesche, *Pan Am Corporate History*, Section 13, pp. 4305–4306.
3. Conrad, *Pan Am*, p. 87.
4. Pan Am CAB Document 851, *History of the Transpacific Air Services*, p. 22, SFOM.
5. "Transpacific," *Time*, December 2, 1935: 47; Daley, *An American Saga*, pp. 172, 174.
6. Kaucher, *On Your Left The Milky Way*, pp. 34–36.

7. Ibid., pp. 131–133, 135.
8. "Log of the China Clipper: Pan American Air Ways Pacific Supplement No. 2," Friday, November 22–Saturday, November 23, 1935, SFOM. This photo and text publication, which is without date and publishing information, is described: "A composite report which all crew members cooperated in writing." It was doubtless prepared by William Van Dusen's public relations department and appears to include material from the in-flight *New York Times* report published under Captain Musick's byline. Further references to the log are from this document.
9. Langewiesche, *Pan Am Corporate History*, Section 13, p. 4357, SFOM.
10. "Log of the China Clipper," Sunday, November 24, 1935, SFOM.
11. Ibid., Monday, November 25, 1935; Wednesday, November 27, 1935.
12. Taylor, *Memoirs*, Vol. I, p. 41, SFOM.
13. "Log of the China Clipper," November 29, 1935, SFOM.
14. Harold Bixby, *Top Side Rickshaw*, p. 287, unpublished manuscript, donated to the the San Francisco Airport Commission Aviation Library by the Bixby family, January 19, 2016.
15. Grooch, *From Crate to Clipper*, pp. 203–204, SFOM.
16. "Transpacific," *Time*: 47.
17. "Log of the China Clipper," Tuesday, December 3, 1935, SFOM.
18. Idem.
19. Taylor, *Memoirs* Vol. I, p. 42, SFOM.
20. "Log of the China Clipper," Friday, December 6, 1935, SFOM.
21. Pan Am CAB Docket 851, *History of the Transpacific Air Services*, p. 22, SFOM.
22. Ibid., p. 22, SFOM.
23. "Pan American Airways," *Fortune*: 79.
24. Schildhauer signed orders for the first hundred Pacific flights. Langewiesche, *Pan Am Corporate History*, Section 13, p. 4363b–4364, SFOM; Associated Press, "China Clipper Damaged in Attempted Take-off," January 5, 1936, as appeared in *Chicago Daily Tribune*.
25. Ibid., Section 13, pp. 4481a–4483.
26. Ibid., Section 13, pp. 4444–4445.
27. Ibid., Section 13, p. 4443.
28. Ibid., Section 14, p. 4671.
29. Ibid., Section 14, p. 4671.
30. Hamilton, who became chief pilot in Hong Kong, was once sent to Rio for six months and stayed three years. In Rio, he shared an apartment with colorful colleague Steve Bancroft, who loved snakes and kept a python in the apartment, until Hamilton (who hated snakes) finally got Bancroft to find it another home. Langewiesche, *Pan Am Corporate History*, Section 9, pp. 3148–3149, SFOM.
31. Ibid., Section 13, p. 4388b.
32. Taylor, *Memoirs*, Vol. I, p. 45, SFOM.

33. Libby, "Pan Am Gets a Pacific Partner," *Naval History*: 6, SFOM.
34. Taylor, *Memoirs*, p. 48, SFOM.
35. Elgen M. Long and Marie K. Long, *Amelia Earhart: The Mystery Solved* (New York: Simon & Schuster, 1999), pp. 75–76.
36. Ibid., p. 68.
37. Dorothy Kaucher, *Wings over Wake* (San Francisco: John Howell, Publisher, 1947), p. 98, SFOM.
38. Kaucher, *On Your Left The Milky Way*, p. 160; Grooch, *From Crate to Clipper*, p. 218, SFOM.
39. Langewiesche, *Pan Am Corporate History*, Section 14, p. 4530, SFOM.
40. Pan Am CAB Docket 851, *History of the Transpacific Air Services*, p. 14, SFOM.
41. Libby, "Pan Am Gets a Pacific Partner," *Naval History*, p. 6, SFOM; "strongbox" from: Frederick D. Parker, *Pearl Harbor Revisited: United States Navy Communications Intelligence: 1924–1941* (Department of the Navy, Naval Historical Center, and Center for Cryptologic History, National Security Agency, 1994), p. 33, from Internet site.

## Chapter 12: War in China

1. Langewiesche, Pan Am Corporate History, Section 3A, p. 1079, SFOM.
2. Josephson, Empire of the Air, p. 100.
3. Daley, An American Saga, pp. 119–120.
4. Pan Am CAB Docket 851, History of the Transpacific Air Services, p. 8, SFOM.
5. "Pan-American in Asia," *Scientific American*: 30; The China National Aviation Foundation, Wings Over Asia: A Brief History of China National Aviation Corporation (1971), pp. 9–10, Freedom of Information Act (FOIA); William Douglas Pawley, Memoirs, biographical page, FOIA.
6. Langewiesche, Pan Am Corporate History, Section 12, 4057–4058, SFOM; Pan Am CAB Docket 851, History of the Transpacific Air Services, p. 8, SFOM.
7. Langewiesche, *Pan Am Corporate History*, Section 12, p. 4042b, SFOM.
8. The purchase was made through a specially formed holding company, Pacific American Airways, although there was no illusion that "PAA" stood for anything other than Pan American Airways. Langewiesche, *Pan Am Corporate History*, Section 12, p. 4043, 4047, SFOM; Pan Am CAB Docket 851, *History of the Transpacific Air Services*, p. 8, SFOM; Crouch, Wings, pp. 35–36.
9. Bixby, *Top Side Rickshaw*, p. 59.
10. "Pan-American in Asia," *Scientific American*: 30.
11. Daley, *An American Saga*, p. 283.
12. Bixby, *Top Side Rickshaw*, p. 87, SFOM.
13. Langewiesche, *Pan Am Corporate History*, Section 12, pp. 4143–4144, SFOM.

14. Erik Just later left CNAC to fly for Chiang Kai-shek. Bixby, *Top Side Rickshaw*, pp. 61–62, SFOM.
15. Grooch, *Skyway to Asia*, p. 3, SFOM.
16. Pan Am CAB Docket 851, *History of the Transpacific Air Services*, p. 8, SFOM.
17. Langewiesche, *Pan Am Corporate History*, Section 12, p. 4053, SFOM.
18. Grooch, *Winged Highway*, p. 192, SFOM.
19. Josephson, *Empire of the Air*, p. 101.
20. Daley, *An American Saga*, p. 282.
21. "The Dragon in Flight," *Aviation*, April 1933: 115.
22. Bixby, *Top Side Rickshaw*, Chapter II, p. 6 (earlier manuscript), SFOM.
23. Theodore H. White and Annalee Jacoby, *Thunder Out Of China* (New York: William Sloane Associates, Inc., 1946), pp. 4–5.
24. Bixby, *Top Side Rickshaw*, p. 119, SFOM.
25. Langewiesche, *Pan Am Corporate History*, Section 12, pp. 4153b–4154, SFOM; Bixby, *Top Side Rickshaw*, p. 88, SFOM.
26. Bixby, *Top Side Rickshaw*, p. 97.
27. Ibid., Chapter VI, pp. 36–37.
28. Ibid., p. 120.
29. Langewiesche, *Pan Am Corporate History*, Section 12, pp. 4154–4156, SFOM; Bixby, *Top Side Rickshaw*, p. 133, SFOM.
30. Ibid., pp. 133–135; "Liu Xiang (warlord)," Wikipedia.
31. Josephson, *Empire of the Air*, p. 102.
32. Daley, *An American Saga*, pp. 124–125; Crouch, *China's Wings*, p. 56; William M. Leary, Jr., *The Dragon's Wings: The China National Aviation Corporation And The Development Of Commercial Aviation In China* (Athens, Georgia: The University of Georgia Press, 1976), p. 82, SFOM.
33. W. Langhorne Bond, edited by James E. Ellis, *Wings for an Embattled China* (Bethlehem: Lehigh University Press, 2001), pp. 97, 98, SFOM; Crouch, *China's Wings*, p. 63; Leary, *The Dragon's Wings*, pp. 82–83, SFOM.
34. Grooch, *Winged Highway*, p. 219, SFOM; "The Dragon in flight," *Aviation*, p. 114, SFOM.
35. "Minutes of the Thirty-First Meeting of the Board of Directors of China National Aviation Corporation," January 17 and January 21 (no year listed, probably 1935), Series 1, sub-series 8: Secretary (Morris and Macy), Box 2, folder 8, UM Richter Library Special Collections; Pan Am CAB Docket 851, *History of the Transpacific Service*, p. 9, SFOM.
36. Langewiesche, *Pan Am Corporate History*, Section 14, pp. 4629–4632, SFOM.
37. General editor I.C.B. Dear and consultant editor M.R.D. Foot, *The Oxford Companion to World War II* (Oxford/New York: Oxford University Press, 1995), pp. 210, 229.
38. Langewiesche, *Pan Am Corporate History*, Section 12, pp. 4125–4127, SFOM.
39. Ibid., Section 12, pp. 4195–4196.

40. Daley, *An American Saga*, pp. 283–284; Cloud Club description: Claudia Roth Pierpont, "The Silver Spire," *The New Yorker*, November 18, 2002: 79.
41. Ibid., p. 285.
42. Ibid., pp. 286–287.
43. White and Jacoby, *Thunder out of China*, p. 7.
44. Daley, *An American Saga*, p. 289.
45. Oral History Program Transcription, Captain Moon Chin interview, conducted by Mauree Jane Perry at Chin's home in Hillsborough, California, Feb. 9–11; March 5–April 30, 2004, p. 55, SFOM.
46. Daley, *An American Saga*, p. 288; Jackson, *China Clipper*, pp. 201–202.
47. Daley, *An American Saga*, p. 289.

### Chapter 13: The Colonizers

1. Juan T. Trippe speech, "Trying To Keep the Peace Through the Power of Wings," delivered Wednesday evening, October 26, 1938, at final evening session of the *New York Herald Tribune* "Forum on Current Problems," transcript, pp. 2, 4, from the Trippe Family Papers, National Air and Space Museum, Smithsonian Institution.
2. "Transpacific" brochure, section, "Beyond that sunset lies Cathay," (no date), Mark Cotta Vaz collection.
3. Kaucher, *Wings over Wake*, p. 11, SFOM.
4. Ibid., pp. 15–16.
5. Ibid., p. 37.
6. Kaucher, *On Your Left The Milky Way*, p. 216.
7. Ibid., p. 197.
8. Ibid., pp. 233–235, 240.
9. Kaucher, *Wings Over Wake*, pp. 99–101, SFOM.
10. Ibid., pp. 96–98.
11. "Southern Pacific Air Service Announced," Wellington, N.Z., Oct. 29 [Oct. 30, 1935, Reuters news service; Reynolds scrapbook Vol. II, SFOM.
12. Jon E. Krupnick, "Pan American's Pacific Pioneers," Spirit of Flight Lecture #4 (San Francisco: San Francisco Aeronautical Society, 2005), pp. 24, 26–27. Published transcript of Krupnick lecture presented on May 3, 2003, at the San Francisco Airport Commission Aviation Library, Louis A. Turpen Aviation Museum, SFOM.
13. Langewiesche, *Pan Am Corporate History*, Section 14, pp. 4570–4576, SFOM; Krupnick, "Pan American's Pacific Pioneers," pp. 25, 31–32.
14. Grooch, *From Crate to Clipper*, p. 229, SFOM.
15. Ibid., p. 226.
16. Ibid., pp. 234, 237–238.
17. Langewiesche, *Pan Am Corporate History*, Section 14, pp. 4537–4539, SFOM.

18. *Midway News* cables, January 12–13, and "San Francisco: Pan Americans, Hopeful, Discount Fire and Explosion Theory" (2:00 am) MRT, SFOM; Daley, *An American Saga*, pp. 198–200; Langewiesche, *Pan Am Corporate History*, Section 14, p. 4540, SFOM.
19. Taylor, *Memoirs*, Vol. I., p. 50, SFOM.
20. Langewiesche, *Pan Am Corporate History*, Section 14, pp. 4601–4602, SFOM.
21. Grooch, *From Crate to Clipper*, p. 242, SFOM.
22. Kathleen Clair account, as told to John H. Hill.
23. Langewiesche, *Pan Am Corporate History*, Section 13, p. 4467, SFOM.
24. The three-member board was chaired by Robert D. Hoyt, aeronautical inspector, Phil C. Salzman, Airline maintenance Inspector, and W. T. Miller, Airways Superintendent, International Section. "PRELIMINARY REPORT OF INVESTIGATION OF THE DISAPPEARANCE OF AN AIRCRAFT OF PAN AMERICAN AIRWAYS, INCORPORATED, IN THE VICINITY OF LATITUDE 12 (o)27' NORTH, LONGITUDE 130 (o) 40' EAST, ON JULY 29, 1938," presented to the Air Safety Board of the Civil Aeronautics Authority, p. 2. The seventeen page report is printed in its entirety in *Fix on the Rising Sun: The Clipper Hi-jacking of 1938—and the Ultimate M.I.A.'s*, self published by Charles N. Hill, SFOM.
25. Ibid., Air Safety Board, official report, p. 17.
26. Langewiesche, *Pan Am Corporate History*, Section 13, p. 4460, SFOM.
27. Libby, "Pan Am Gets a Pacific Partner," *Naval History*: 3, SFOM.
28. Langewiesche, *Pan Am Corporate History*, Section 14, pp. 4543–4545, SFOM.
29. Ibid., Section 14, pp. 4546–4548.
30. Ibid., Section 14, pp. 4548–4549.
31. Ibid., Section 14, pp. 4549–4550.
32. Ibid., Section 14, p. 4550.
33. Ibid., Section 14, pp. 4560–4561.
34. Ibid., Section 14, pp. 4551–4552.
35. Ibid., Section 14, pp. 4562–4565.
36. Juan T. Trippe speech, "Trying To Keep the Peace Through the Power of Wings," Trippe Family Papers, National Air and Space Museum, Smithsonian Institution.
37. The above and following references from PAA Annual Report—1938, for year ending Dec. 31, 1938, pp. 5–10, SFOM.
38. Pan Am CAB Docket 851, *History of the Transpacific Air Services*, p. 27, SFOM.
39. "Transoceanic Transport," *Life*, August 23, 1937: 34–35, 38–39, SFOM.
40. Pan Am CAB Docket 851, *History of the Transpacific Air Services*, p. 27, SFOM.
41. Josephson, *Empire of the Air*, p. 137.
42. Bender and Altschul, *The Chosen Instrument*, p. 297; Josephson, *Empire of the Air*, p. 137.
43. Bender and Altschul, *The Chosen Instrument*, p. 296.

## Chapter 14: The World of Tomorrow

1. Juan Trippe, "Aviation in the World of Tomorrow," speech before the Merchants Association of New York's "Banquet of the World of Tomorrow," New York, April 20, 1939, lecture transcript, Trippe Family Papers, National Air and Space Museum, Smithsonian Institution, p. 4, SFOM.
2. Daley, *An American Saga*, pp. 187–188.
3. Anne Morrow Lindbergh, *War Within and Without: Diaries and Letters: 1939–1944* (New York and London: Harcourt Brace Jovanovich, 1980), p. xv.
4. Berg, *Lindbergh*, pp. 353–354.
5. Anne Lindbergh, *War Within and Without*, p. xv.
6. Ibid., p. xvi.
7. Berg, *Lindbergh*, pp. 355–357.
8. Jean Cooke, Ann Kramer, and Theodore Rowland-Entwistle, *History's Timeline*, p. 208.
9. Charles Lindbergh, *The Wartime Journals of Charles A. Lindbergh* (New York: Harcourt Brace Jovanovich, Inc., 1970), pp., 72–73, 75.
10. Arnold, *Global Mission*, pp. 168–169.
11. Anne Lindbergh, *War Within and Without*, p. xvi.
12. Arnold, *Global Mission*, pp. 168–169.
13. Lindbergh, *The Wartime Journals*, pp. 182–183.
14. Arnold, *Global Mission*, pp. 188–189.
15. Lindbergh, *The Wartime Journals*, p. 204.
16. Josephson, *Empire of the Air*, p. 138.
17. Daley, *An American Saga*, pp. 238–239.
18. Josephson, *Empire of the Air*, p. 148.
19. John C. Cooper, *The Right to Fly: A Study in Air Power* (New York: Henry Holt and Company, 1947), pp. 38–39, 145–146, 148–149.
20. Langewiesche, *Pan Am Corporate History*, "Crossing the Atlantic," Section 15, p. 4832a, SFOM.
21. Cooper, *The Right to Fly*, pp. 146–147.
22. Pan Am CAB Docket 855, *History of the Transatlantic Air Services*, p. 13, SFOM.
23. Ibid., pp. 20–21.
24. Ibid., pp. 16–17.
25. Josephson, *Empire of the Air*, pp. 128–129.
26. Langewiesche, *Pan Am Corporate History*, "Crossing the Atlantic," Section 15, p. 4972, SFOM.
27. Cooper, *The Right to Fly*, p. 147.
28. Langewiesche, *Pan Am Corporate History*, "Crossing the Atlantic," Section 15, pp. 4910–4911, SFOM.
29. Pan Am CAB Docket 855, *History of the Transatlantic Air Services*, p. 23, SFOM.

30. #20–1939 America Unlimited, Juan T. Trippe speech transcript, pp. 5–6, Trippe Family Papers, National Air and Space Museum Smithsonian Institution, SFOM.
31. Pan Am CAB Docket 855, *History of the Transatlantic Air Services*, p. 23, SFOM.
32. "Treasure Island And the World's Greatest Spans of Steel," brochure from San Francisco Bay Exposition, published by The Crocker Company of San Francisco, 1939, Mark Cotta Vaz collection.
33. Reprint of 1940 Federal Writers Project of the Works Progress Administration Guide, *San Francisco in the 1930s: The WPA Guide to the City by the Bay* (Berkeley, Los Angeles, London: University of California Press, 2011), p. 47.
34. Jon E. Krupnick, *Pan American Clippers Unite the Pacific Rim: 1935 to 1946*, published for "Pacific 97," the World Philatelic Exhibition, San Francisco, California, May 29–June 8.
35. *WPA Guide to the City by the Bay*, p. 368.
36. Official Program Guide, Golden Gate International Exposition On San Francisco Bay, 1939, San Francisco Bay Exposition, p. 83, Mark Cotta Vaz collection.
37. Golden Gate International Exposition, Official Guide Book-1940, p. 44, Mark Cotta Vaz collection.
38. Golden Gate International Exposition, Official Guide Book, 1939, p. 60.
39. Golden Gate International Exposition, Official Guide Book-1940, p. 41.
40. Pan Am CAB Docket 855, *History of the Transatlantic Air Services*, p. 23, SFOM; Trippe, "Aviation in the World of Tomorrow," address before the "Banquet of the World of Tomorrow," April 20, 1939, pp. 3–4, from Trippe Family Papers, National Air and Space Museum, Smithsonian Institution, SFOM.
41. Pan Am CAB Docket 855, *History of the Transatlantic Air Services*, pp. 24–25, SFOM.
42. Ibid., p. 25.
43. Ibid., pp. 25–26, SFOM; Cooper, *The Right to Fly*, p. 147.
44. Peter Jennings and Todd Brewster, *The Century* (New York: Doubleday, 1998), p. 211.
45. Dear and Foot, *Oxford Companion to World War II*, pp. 787, 790.
46. Pan Am CAB Docket 855, *History of the Transatlantic Air Services*, p. 26, SFOM.
47. Cooper, *The Right to Fly*, p. 147.
48. "Carriers," *Time*, February 5, 1940: 51.
49. Pan Am CAB Docket 855, *History of the Transatlantic Air Services*, p. 27, SFOM; "The Month" section, *New Horizons*, February 1941: 9.
50. Ric Burns and James Sanders, *New York: An Illustrated History* (New York: Alfred A. Knopf, 1999), p. 457.

51. Richard, Reinhardt, *Treasure Island: 1939–1940, San Francisco's Exposition Years*, (Mill Valley, CA: Squarebooks, Inc., 1978), p. 168.

## PART III: WARTIME MISSIONS
### Chapter 15: The Secret Plan
1. Major General Clayton Bissell, Assistant Chief of Staff, G-2, Pentagon Building, Washington, D.C., reply to questions about the ADP to Chief of Engineering, War Department, Washington, D.C., March 15, 1945, pp. 3–4, Classified Secret, FOIA.
2. Grant, *Flight*, pp. 165, 168; Daley, *An American Saga*, pp. 187–188; Langewiesche, *Pan Am Corporate History*, "Juan Terry Trippe interviews," Section 3A, pp. 1080–1083, SFOM. Trippe places the letter's arrival from the summer of 1939 to 1940 or even 1941.
3. Army Air Forces/Air Transport Command, *The Official History of the South Atlantic Division*, classified "Secret," November 13, 1945, p. 64, FOIA.
4. Royce A. Wight and Frank R. Kelley, "Clipping the Axis Wings," *The Inter-American*, September 1943: 20, SFOM.
5. Army Air Forces/Air Transport Command, *The Official History of the South Atlantic Division*, pp. 65, 115, FOIA.
6. United States Department of State, Foreign Relations of the Unites States diplomatic papers, 1941. *The American Republics* (1941). pp. 403–412, University of Wisconsin Digital Collections from Internet site.
7. William A. M. Burden, *The Struggle for Airways in Latin America* (New York: Council on Foreign Relations, 1943), p. 75, SFOM.
8. Pan Am CAB Docket 525, *History of the Latin American Services*, p. 32, SFOM; "Anti-Axis Progress," *New Horizons*, September, 1941: 12.
9. Leslie, *Pan Am History*, Vol. I, Chapter 2, pp. 28, 34–35, SFOM.
10. Herbert Boy, *Story With Wings*, excerpt from Langewiesche, *Pan Am Corporate History*, Section 16, p. 5159, SFOM.
11. Daley, *An American Saga*, p. 294; Boy, *Story With Wings*, from *Pan Am Corporate History*, Section 16, p. 5160, SFOM.
12. Daley, *An American Saga*, p. 295.
13. Boy, *Story With Wings*, from *Pan Am Corporate History*, Section 16, pp. 5159–5160, SFOM.
14. Ibid., pp. 5145–5146.
15. Daley, *An American Saga*, pp. 297–298; Langewiesche, *Pan Am Corporate History*, Section 16, pp. 5150, 5152.
16. Ibid., Section 16, pp. 5151–5152, SFOM.
17. Ibid., Section 16, Boy, *Story With Wings*, excerpt from *Pan Am Corporate History*, Section 16, p. 5160.
18. Pan Am CAB Docket 525, *History of the Latin American Services*, p. 32, SFOM.

19. Army Air Forces, Air Transport Command, *The Official History of the South Atlantic Division*, pp. 73–74, FOIA.
20. "Two Days Less to Rio," *Time*, September 2, 1940: 55–56.
21. Daley, *An American Saga*, pp. 302–303; Military Appropriations Act funding noted in contract between the U.S. and Pan Am, November 2, 1940.
22. Langewiesche, *Pan Am Corporate History*, Section 16, p. 5180, SFOM.
23. Daley, *An American Saga*, p. 302.
24. Major General Clayton Bissell, letter in response to Chief of Engineers, War Department, March 15, 1945, pp. 3–4, FOIA.
25. Langewiesche, *Pan Am Corporate History*, Section 16, p. 5170, SFOM.
26. Major General Clayton Bissell to Chief of Engineering, War Department, March 15, 1945, p. 4, FOIA.
27. Army Air Forces/Air Transport Command, *The Official History of the South Atlantic Division*, p. 79, FOIA.
28. Langewiesche, *Pan Am Corporate History*, Section 16, p. 5162, SFOM.
29. Ibid., Section 16, pp. 5163–5166, 5172.
30. Ibid., Section 16, p. 5165.
31. The Army Air Forces/Air Transport Command, *The Official History of the South Atlantic Division*, p. 84, FOIA.
32. Ibid., p. 77.
33. "Contract between the United States of America and Pan American Airports Corporation," November 2, 1940, declassified, FOIA.
34. The Army Air Forces/Air Transport Command, *The Official History of the South Atlantic Division*, pp. 80, 82, FOIA.
35. "Anti-Axis Progress," *New Horizons*, September 1941: 12, SFOM.
36. "Pan Am in Brazil," *Time*, November 24, 1941: 92.
37. Sherman Miles, Brig.-General, U.S. Army, Acting Assistant Chief of Staff G-2, War Department, Military Intelligence Division, Washington, D.C., "Confidential" letter to Juan Trippe, August 28, 1940, and Trippe reply letter to Gen. Miles, September 4, 1940, Series 1, sub-series 5: Juan Trippe, Box 7, folder 11; Navy Department Office of Naval Intelligence, "Personal and Confidential" letter to Juan Trippe, September 20, 1940, and Under Secretary at the Department of State in Washington, letter to Juan Trippe, September 30, 1940, Series 1, sub-series 5: Juan Trippe, Box 7, folder 13, UM Richter Library Special Collections.
38. The Army Air Forces/Air Transport Command, *The Official History of the South Atlantic Division*, pp., 88, 90, FOIA.
39. Ibid., p. 115.
40. Ibid., pp. 134–135.
41. Ibid., pp. 110–111, FOIA; the mission members were Colonel Kenner F. Hartford, Colonel Willis Hale, Colonel Dennis McCunniff, and Colonel John B. Leonard.

42. Ibid., p. 88.
43. Ibid., pp. 86–87. Quoted from Harold W. Sims, U.S. Vice-Counsel, Natal, Brazil, to Jefferson Caffery, U.S. Ambassador to Brazil, "Confidential memorandum on Udiano Campagner, Panair Manager in Natal," May 5, 1941, FOIA.
44. Ibid., pp. 109, 117.
45. Ibid., p. 71, quotes from Jefferson Caffery, Accomplishments Report, U.S. Embassy, Rio de Janeiro, Feb. 11, 1943. FOIA.
46. Ibid., p. 135.
47. Alice Kearns Goodwin, *No Ordinary Time: Franklin and Eleanor Roosevelt: The Home Front in World War II* (New York: Touchstone, 1995), pp. 44–45, 47–48.
48. Ibid., pp. 194–195, 210, 212–213.

## Chapter 16: Air Carrier of the Arsenal of Democracy

1. The president's announcement excerpted from "South Atlantic & Africa," *New Horizons*, September 1941: 9–10.
2. "Flight 262," *New Horizons*, March 1941: 14, SFOM.
3. Ibid., pp. 14, 16–17.
4. Ibid., p. 15. The other two passengers were John Cowles, president of the *Minneapolis Star-Journal*, and Landon K. Thorne, a retired New York banker; Van Vleck, *Empire of the Air*, p. 134, SFOM.
5. Ibid., p. 17.
6. Goodwin, *No Ordinary Time*, pp. 213–214.
7. "Lend-Lease," *The Oxford Companion to World War II*, pp. 677, 680.
8. Busch, "Juan Trippe," *Life*, October 20, 1941: 111.
9. Pan Am CAB Docket 855, *History of the Transatlantic Air Services*, p. 26, SFOM.
10. "Through the Blockade," *New Horizons*, April 1941: p. 19, SFOM.
11. Pan Am CAB Docket 855, *History of the Transatlantic Air Services*, p. 26, SFOM.
12. Arnold, *Global Mission*, p. 210.
13. Ibid., pp. 212–214.
14. M.Y., "Flying the Takoradi Route: Pan Am goes to war," *Pan Am Clipper*, Newsletter of the Pan Am Historical Foundation, December 2006, Vol. 12, No. 3: 1, 4–5.
15. Dear and Foot, *Oxford Companion to World War II*, p. 1099.
16. Langewiesche, *Pan Am Corporate History*, Section 16, p. 5199, SFOM.
17. "Pan Am Stretches," *Time*, September 1, 1941: 20.
18. Army Air Forces/Air Transport Command, *The Official History of the South Atlantic Division*, pp. 93–94, FOIA.
19. Ibid., p. 93.
20. PAA Company Press release, 11/3/58 (no author), Series 9, sub-series 1: Africa Orient Division, Box 1, folder 2, UM Richter Library Special Collections;

Army Air Forces/Air Transport Command, *The Official History of the South Atlantic Division*, pp. 95–96, FOIA.
21. Ibid., pp. 97–98.
22. *Roosevelt and Churchill: Their Secret Wartime Correspondence*, Docs. 57 and 59, Roosevelt to Churchill, May 29; Churchill to Roosevelt, June 3, 1941, pp. 143–145.
23. Ibid., Doc. 62, Roosevelt to Churchill, June 17, 1941, pp. 146–147.
24. Juan Trippe, "Ocean Air Transport," Wilbur Wright Memorial Lecture before the Royal Aeronautical Society, London, June 17, 1941, transcription, pp. 3, 33, 36, SFOM.
25. H. M. Bixby, letter from Pan Am's Washington office to John A. Steele, Atlantic Airways, Ltd., Municipal Airport, Miami, July 29, 1941, UM Richter Library Special Collections; Editors Wesley Frank Craven and James Lea Gate, *The Army Air Forces in World War II: Volume One: Plans and Early Operations: January 1939 to August 1942* (Washington, D.C.: Office of Air Force History, 1983), p. 322.
26. Contract between the United States of America, Pan American, and "Ferries" and "African" corporations, August 12, 1941, World War II Contracts, SFOM.
27. Editors Craven and Cate, *The Army Air Forces in World War II*, p. 322. James V. Forrestal led negotiations for the government, while Trippe called upon Henry Friendly to assist him in sketching out a legal structure and contracts.
28. "South Atlantic & Africa," *New Horizons*, September 1941: 10.
29. Langewiesche, *Pan Am Corporate History*, Section 16, p. 5207, SFOM.
30. "South Atlantic & Africa," *New Horizons*, September 1941: 10.
31. "Pan Am Stretches," *Time*, September 1, 1941: 20.
32. Langewiesche, *Pan Am Corporate History*, Section 16, p. 5166, SFOM.
33. Ibid., Section 16, pp. 5213–5214.
34. Ibid., Section 16, p. 5210.
35. Tom Culbert & Andy Dawson, *PanAfrica: Across the Sahara in 1941 with Pan Am* (McLean, Virginia: Paladwr Press, second printing, 1999), p. 5, SFOM.

### Chapter 17: The Pan-Africa Corps
1. Voit Gilmore, *African Report: An Account of what the Pan Africans found and what they did while running the trans-Africa aerial life-line from September 1941 until December 1942*, manuscript has no page numbers; selection from section "Where They Lived and Worked," SFOM.
2. Langewiesche, *Pan Am Corporate History*, Section 16, p. 5209, SFOM.
3. Daley, *An American Saga*, p. 312 and footnotes, pp. 507–508. Daley ascribes the air mileage to a letter by Pan Am public relations head William Van Dusen that also reported the record high temperature at El Fasher.
4. Langewiesche, *Pan Am Corporate History*, Section 16, p. 5221, SFOM.

5. Frederick D. Sharp, Lieut. Col., G.S.C., "Subject: Special observation flight over coast of Liberia by Pan American Airways," to: The A.C. of S., G-2, War Department, Washington, D.C., July 22, 1941, p. 1, FOIA.
6. Ibid, p. 2.
7. Langewiesche, *Pan Am Corporate History*, Section 16, pp. 5212, 5214, SFOM.
8. Ibid., Section 16, p. 5212.
9. Ibid., Section 16, pp. 5215–5216.
10. Pan Am CAB Docket 855, *History of the Transatlantic Air Services*, p. 40, SFOM; Langewiesche, *Pan Am Corporate History*, Section 16, pp. 5222–5224, SFOM.
11. Colonel Frederick D. Sharp, G.S.C., Subject: Defenses for P.A. A. clipper base, Fisherman's Lake, and ferry base, Roberts Field, Liberia," To: The A.C. of S., G-2, War Department Washington, D.C. (Attention: British Empire Section), August 11, 1942, pp. 1–2, FOIA.
12. Military Intelligence Division, Military Attaché Report, Subject: Landing ground—Fisherman's Lake, Liberia, report 3930, May 7, 1942, report signed by Frederick D. Sharp, Colonel, G.S., FOIA.
13. Pan Am CAB Docket 855, *History of the Transatlantic Air Services*, p. 40, SFOM.
14. Gilmore, *African Report*, 1943, "Where They Lived and Worked," SFOM; Langewiesche, *Pan Am Corporate History*, Section 16, pp. 5221–5226, SFOM.
15. William B. Nash, "Flying the Boeing 314 'Clippers,'" *Airways*, May 2009: 42–45.
16. Langewiesche, *Pan Am Corporate History*, Section 16, pp. 5248–5249, SFOM.
17. Ibid., Section 16, p. 5239.
18. Gilmore, *African Report*, "Recruiting Employees," SFOM.
19. Langewiesche, *Pan Am Corporate History*, Section 16, p. 5238; Gilmore, *African Report*, "Ages of PAA-African Men," and "Outfitting Employees," SFOM.
20. Gilmore, *African Report*, "Number of Overseas Employees" and "A Day in Africa," SFOM.
21. Gilmore, *African Report*, "Where They Lived and Worked," SFOM; Langewiesche, *Pan Am Corporate History*, Section 16, pp. 5283–5284, SFOM.
22. Langewiesche, *Pan Am Corporate History*, Section 16, pp. 5281–5282, SFOM.
23. Ibid., Section 16, pp. 5229–5230.
24. Ibid., Section 16, pp. 5291–5292.
25. Ibid., Section 16, pp. 5244–5247.
26. Ibid., Section 16, p. 5293.
27. Ibid., Section 16, p. 5274.
28. Gilmore, *African Report*, "Overseas Canteens" and "Employees' Clubs," SFOM.
29. Langewiesche, *Pan Am Corporate History*, Section 16, pp. 5226, 5293, SFOM.
30. Busch, "Trippe," *Life*, October 20, 1941: 110–111.
31. Daley, *An American Saga*, p. 312.

32. "Pan Am in Brazil," *Time*, November 24, 1941: 88, 90.
33. "Pan Am in Brazil," *Time*, November 24, 1941: 90; Krupnick, *Pan American Clippers Unites the Pacific Rim*, p. 6.
34. Army Air Forces/Air Transport Command, *The Official History of the South Atlantic Division*, Ibid., pp. 87, 128–129, FOIA.
35. Ibid., pp. 100–101.
36. Ibid., pp. 111–113, 128–129.

## Chapter 18: Far Horizons

1. Clare Boothe Luce, "Destiny Crosses The Dateline: Report on a Flight Across the Pacific," *Life*, November 3, 1941: 99, SFOM.
2. "Catering Aloft," *New Horizons*, February 1941: 26, SFOM.
3. The "Jap" slur is emblematic of the cruelty of the wartime period. The reference is often unavoidable and is presented only for its historical veracity. "Life Line," *New Horizons*, April 1943: 22, SFOM.
4. "In China," *New Horizons*, December 1940: 10, SFOM.
5. Ibid., p. 11.
6. The Memoirs of Claire Lee Chennault, Major General, U.S. Army (Ret.), edited by Robert Hotz, *Way of a Fighter*, (New York: G. P. Putnam's Sons, 1949), p. 31; Vaz, *Living Dangerously*, pp. 297–298.
7. Ibid., pp. 72–73.
8. Ibid., p. 74.
9. "Life Line," *New Horizons*, April, 1943: 22, SFOM.
10. Ibid., pp. 22–23.
11. Chennault, *Way of a Fighter*, p. 85.
12. Ibid., p. 85.
13. Vaz, *Living Dangerously*, pp. 295, 297.
14. William D. Pawley, *Americans Valiant and Glorious: A Brief History of the Flying Tigers*, booklet, pp. 5–6, FOIA.
15. Pawley, *Memoirs*, pp. 1–2, 4, 9–10, 41, 47, FOIA; Chennault, *Way of a Fighter*, p. 132.
16. Olga S. Greenlaw, *The Lady and the Tigers* (New York: E. P. Dutton & Co., Inc., 1943), pp. 13–15, SFOM.
17. Ibid., p., 98.
18. Chennault, *Way of a Fighter*, p. 233.
19. Mauree Jane Perry, Captain Moon Chin, interview transcription, SFOM p. 68.
20. "10 Years of Adventure," *New Horizons*, December 1943: 23, SFOM.
21. Brig. Gen. John F. Kinney, USMC (Ret.), with James McCaffrey, *Wake Island Pilot: A World War II Memoir* (Washington: Brassey's, 1995), pp. 3, 11–12.
22. Ibid., pp. 13–15, 17.
23. Ibid., p. 49.
24. Ibid., p. 51.

25. Ibid., p. 54.
26. Pan Am Historical Foundation, "SM No. 1," Clipper picture and text.
27. "Rush from Japan," *New Horizons*, December 1941: 10, SFOM.
28. Clare Boothe Luce, "Destiny Crosses The Dateline," *Life*, November 3, 1941: 99–103, 108–109, SFOM.

## Chapter 19: Case 7: Condition A

1. Taylor, "Memories," Volume I, p. 62, SFOM.
2. Dear and Foot, *Oxford Companion to World War II*, pp. 870–871.
3. Ibid., pp. 871–872.
4. Pan Am CAB Docket 851, *History of the Transpacific Air Services*, p. 43, SFOM.
5. Kinney with McCaffrey, *Wake Island Pilot*, pp. 54–55; "Wake Escape," Transpacific section, *New Horizons*, January 1942: 20–21, SFOM.
6. Ibid., pp. 55–56.
7. Ibid., pp. 57–58.
8. Ibid., pp. 59–60; Pan Am CAB Docket 851, *History of the Transpacific Air Services*, p. 44, SFOM.
9. C. V. Glines, "Clippers Circle the Globe," *Aviation History*, March 2007: 36.
10. Pan Am CAB Docket 851, *History of the Transpacific Air Services*, p. 44, SFOM.
11. Glines, "Clippers Circle the Globe," *Aviation History*: 36.
12. Pan Am CAB Docket 851, *History of the Transpacific Air Services*, p. 44, SFOM.
13. "Hong Kong Drama," *New Horizons*, February, 1942: 9–10, SFOM.
14. Mauree Jane Perry, Captain Moon Chin interview, 2004, transcripts pp. 57–58, SFOM; Associated Press, "Captain Reports Jap Bombed Hongkong Clipper into Flames," from the *Baltimore Sun*, UM Richter Library Special Collections.
15. "Incredible Rescue," *New Horizons*, January 1942: 20, SFOM; "Hong Kong Drama," *New Horizons*: 10–11, SFOM.
16. Preceding material from "Japanese Internment Camp—Philippines 1942–5," May 1977 transcript by Rush S. Clark, Regional Managing Director, Far East, pp. 1–12, Pan Am World War II internees collection, SFOM.
17. Kinney and McCaffrey, *Wake Island Pilot*, pp. 75–79, 88–89, 118–119, SFOM.

## Chapter 20: Clippers at War

1. Trippe statement, "The Wings of Democracy," *Annual Report for the War Year 1942*, Pan American World Airways System, June 16, 1943, p. 1, SFOM.
2. Pan Am CAB Document 851, *History of the Transpacific Air Services*, p. 45, SFOM.
3. Ibid., pp. 45–46.
4. Carl Spaatz, Office of the Chief of the Air Staff, letter to Mr. H. M. Bixby, Pan American Airways, December 3, 1941, FOIA; John C. Cooper, letter to

The Secretary of War, December 8, 1941, FOIA; Daley, *An American Saga*, pp. 309, 338.

5. Secret Supplemental Contract—Service and Supplies, between the War Department and PAA/PA-Africa/PA Air Ferries, Pan American WW II Contracts, Contract Nine, December 13, 1941, SFOM.
6. Pan Am CAB Docket 855, *History of the Transatlantic Air Services*, p. 41, SFOM.
7. Army Air Force, ATC, *The Official History of the South Atlantic Division*, p. 123, FOIA.
8. Lieut. Colonel Arthur I. Ennis, Air Corps, Chief of A. A.F. Public Relations Board, letter to "President, Pan American Airlines" in New York, Series: 9, sub-series 5: General, Box 1, folder 12, UM Richter Library Special Collections.
9. H. L. George, War Department, memo for the Chief of the Army Air Forces, December 10, 1941, re December 8 CAB hearing, "Confidential," FOIA.
10. Gilmore, *African Report*, "Employees' War Psychology," SFOM; Langewiesche, *Pan Am Corporate History*, Section 16, p. 5294, SFOM.
11. Pan Am CAB Docket 855, *History of the Transatlantic Air Services*, p. 42, SFOM.
12. Ibid., pp. 41–42.
13. "Special No. 1," 3-page document, February 16, 1942, Series 9, Sub-series 5: General, Box 3, folder 1, UM Richter Library Special Collections.
14. J. D.M. Ford, letter (typed copy) to PAA at La Guardia Field, December 10, 1941, and John C. Leslie airmail letter to Col. Clarence Young at Treasure Island, December 12, 1941, both Series 9, Sub-series 5: General, Box 2, folder 44, UM Richter Library Special Collections.
15. Ed Dover, *The Long Way Home: A Journey Into History With Captain Robert Ford* (Albuquerque, NM: Valliant Press, 2008), pp. 56–57, SFOM; Glines, "Clippers Circle the Globe," *Aviation History*: 36.
16. Brock, *More About Pan Am*, and essay, "Around the World After Pearl Harbor—1941," John Steers diary, p. 72, SFOM.
17. Glines, "Clippers Circle the Globe," *Aviation History*: 37.
18. Trippe reported other special missions underway, including a Clipper leaving San Francisco for New York "with personnel and spares," and another Pacific Division Clipper bound for Singapore with urgent supplies for Burma. Juan Trippe, Pan American Airways System, New York, letter to General Arnold, Chief of the Air Forces, War Department, Washington, D.C., December 12, 1941, FOIA.
19. Glines, "Clippers Circle the Globe," *Aviation History*: 37, 39; Brock, *More About Pan Am*, Steers diary, p. 74, SFOM.
20. Brock, *More About Pan Am*, Steers diary, p. 74, SFOM.
21. Glines, "Clippers Circle the Globe," *Aviation History*: 40.
22. Ibid., p. 41.
23. "Epic," *New Horizons*: 13.

24. Glines, "Clippers Circle the Globe," *Aviation History*: 41.
25. "Epic," *New Horizons*: 11–13, SFOM; Glines, "Clippers Circle the Globe," *Aviation History*: 34, 41.
26. War Department Foreign Wing Air Force Ferrying Command, Washington, D.C., Special Operation Order No. 6, signed by Colonel T. L. Mosley, 12/20/41, UM Richter Library Special Collections; Daley, *An American Saga*, p. 314.
27. Various PAA confidential reports on "Special Mission #6," Series 9, sub-series 5: General, Box 1, folder 9, UM Richter Library Special Collections.
28. Chennault writes that the supplies arrived by March, but as Mission #6 was their first supply mission since Wake, it was probably several months earlier. Chennault, *Way of a Fighter*, pp. 118–119.
29. Pan Am CAB Docket 855, *History of the Transatlantic Air Services*, p. 43, SFOM.
30. "Tropical Triumph," *New Horizons*, November 1942: 7–9, SFOM.
31. U.S. Army Air Force, ATC, *The Official History of the South Atlantic Division*, p. 118, FOIA; "Civil Aeronautics Board Hearing On Pan American Airways Service To Replace LATI—Friday January 9 [1942], 3:00 P.M.," signed by A. M. Burden, Defense Supplies Corporation, "Confidential," FOIA.
32. Mr. Latchford represented State, and Lieut. Commander Morse the Navy. William A.M. Burden, Defense Supplies Corporation, Washington, letter to Major Eugene F. Gillespie, Munitions Building, Washington, D.C., January 7, 1942, "Confidential," FOIA; Major E. Gillespie, Air Corps, memorandum for Assistant Secretary of War, Subject: Elimination of LATI, and "For General Arnold," stamped January 11, 1942, "Confidential," FOIA.
33. Cauby C. Araujo, Rio, message to Pan Am VP Young in New York, Subject: LATI Gasoline Supplies, March 20, 1941, Series 1, sub-series 14: Competitive Airlines, Box 2, folder 21, UM Richter Library Special Collections.
34. Army Air Forces/Air Transport Command, *The Official History of the South Atlantic Division*, pp. 133–134, FOIA.
35. Ibid., pp. 135–141, 146.
36. Air Transport Command, *The Official History of the South Atlantic Division*, pp. 3–4, Appendix XI, excerpted from Pan Am Group Veteran Status Exhibits, Volume II No. 7–76, SFOM.
37. Harold B. Whiteman, Jr., report No. 12, March 5, 1942 and Report No. 13, March 15, 1942, PAA-Africa, Ltd.—Accra, to William Van Dusen, Series 9, sub-series 4: Pan American Africa, Ltd., Box 1, folder 5, UM Richter Library Special Collections.
38. Culbert and Dawson, *PanAfrica*, p. 7, SFOM.
39. Ernest J. Colant and Scharleen H. Colant, "Pan American Group Veteran Status Application," p. 56, SFOM.
40. A. T. Harris, Royal Air Force Delegation (British Air Commission), Washington, D.C., letter to Lieutenant General H. H. Arnold, U.S. Army Air Corps, War Department, Washington, February 2, 1942, FOIA.

41. Brigadier General Robert Olds, memo to Colonel Wolfinbarger, Chief Air War Plans Division, Air Staff, "Subject: Air Route to Far East," February 17, 1942, Secret, pp. 2–3, FOIA.
42. Chin had another surprise when he landed in Dinjan—eight more people crammed into the cargo area. Captain Moon Chin memories, Mauree Jane Perry interview transcription, "The Jimmy Doolittle Experience," pp. 78–84, SFOM; Bond, *Wings for an Embattled China*, p. 347, SFOM.
43. Vaz, *Living Dangerously*, pp. 289–290; Dear and Foot, *Oxford Companion to World War II*, p. 309.
44. Chennault, *Way of a Fighter*, pp. 168–169.

## Chapter 21: Hell Riders of the Himalayas

1. "Battle of Asia," *Time*, May 18, 1942.
2. White and Jacoby, *Thunder Out Of China*, p. 145.
3. "The Unbelievable Burma Road," *Fortune*, September 1941: 51.
4. Charles F. Romanus and Riley Sunderland, *The China-Burma-India Theater: Stilwell's Mission to China*, The United States Army in World War II (Washington, D.C.: Office of the Chief of Military History, Department of the Army, 1952), pp. 77–78.
5. Lt. J. B. Haines memorandum to Major R. M. Love, Subject: History and Present Status of the India-China Route, June 10, 1942 (memo headed by note: "General Arnold: A resume prepared of the China ferrying situation. H.G."), Appendix section dated June 9, 1942, India-China Air Route (Chronological Summary): 1/28/42 "Radiogram from General Magruder at Chungking to Adj. General Ammisco"; 2/3/42 "Letter from Col. Clayton Bissell to Major General Harmon," p. 1, FOIA.
6. H. H. Arnold, Lieutenant General, Deputy Chief of Staff for Air, Memorandum for the President: Subject: Cargo Planes for China, February 4, 1942 (copy), p. 1. FOIA.
7. Prepared by the Historical Officer, HQ AAF Air Transport Command, *Air Transportation to China Under The 10th Air Force: April-November 1942*, end date: 3/31/1945, p. 2, FOIA.
8. Ibid., pp. 3–4.
9. Robert Lee Scott, Jr., *Flying Tiger: Chennault of China* (Garden City, New York: Doubleday & Company, Inc., 1959), pp. 114–115, SFOM.
10. Captain D. B. Sherman, PAA-Africa, Ltd., Accra, report, "Observations of Joint Operations PAA-Africa, Ltd. and U.S. Army, Assam-Burma-China Ferry Command, Dinjan, India; April 6th to May 15th, 1942," to Chief Pilot, PAA-Africa, Ltd., Accra, May 26, 1942, pp. 1–3, 6; companion list of PAA-Africa personnel, Series 9, sub-series 1: Africa-Orient, Box 1, folder 2, UM Richter Library Special Collections.
11. ATC Historical Officer, *Air Transportation to China*, pp. 4–5, FOIA.

12. Langewiesche, *Pan Am Corporate History*, Section 16, p. 5295, SFOM; "Flight to the West," *Time*, May 18, 1942.
13. Brock, *More About Pan Am*, "4. Evacuation of Burma," p. 66; "Flight to the West," *Time*.
14. Brock, *More About Pan Am*, p. 67, SFOM.
15. Culbert & Dawson, *PanAfrica*, pp. 122–123, SFOM.
16. Sherman, "Dinjan Mission" report, May 26, 1942, p. 1, UM Richter Library Special Collections.
17. Culbert & Dawson, *PanAfrica*, p. 121.
18. Scott quoted in Merian C. Cooper letter to Wolfgang Langewiesche in San Francisco, July 19, 1961, from Merian C. Cooper Papers, Brigham Young University, Mss 2008, Box 34.
19. John Yeomans, PAA-Africa, Ltd., Accra, report to Vice-President Gledhill, PAA-Africa, Ltd., New York, re "Dinjan Mission," May 28, 1942, Series 9, Sub-series 1: Africa-Orient, Box 1, folder 2, UM Richter Library Special Collections.
20. T. J. Hanley, Jr., Air Corps, memorandum for the Assistant Chief of Staff, Subject: Contracts with Civilian Concerns for Overseas Facilities, January [date not legible] 1942, "Confidential," FOIA.
21. Greenlaw, *The Lady and the Tigers*, p. 284, SFOM.
22. Chennault, *Way of a Fighter*, pp. 171–172.
23. Boris Chaliapin cover art, *Time*, December 6, 1943; Chennault, *Way of a Fighter*, p. 176.
24. Colant, "Veteran Status Application" on behalf of Pan American Veteran Status Group, p. 47, SFOM; Chennault, *Way of a Fighter*, pp. 176, 183–184.
25. McBride excerpt, Horace Brock, *Flying the Oceans* (Lunenburg, Vermont: The Stinehour Press, 1979), p. 244, SFOM.
26. W. L. Bond, letter to Harold Bixby, February 2, 1943 (copy, typed), Series 9, sub-series 5: General, Box 1, folder 6, UM Richter Library Special Collections.
27. Captain C. Joseph Rosbert, "Forty-Six Days to Dinjan," excerpted in Brock, *More About Pan Am:* pp. 52–65, SFOM; "Return from the Dead," *New Horizons*, March 1944: 27, SFOM.

### Chapter 22: Militarization

1. H. H. Arnold, Lieutenant General, memorandum from the War Department, Office of the Chief of the Army Air Forces, Washington, D.C., to General R. C. Moore, noted "2/18/42" and stamped "Feb. 20, 1942," FOIA.
2. Howard B. Dean's Journal: April 22, 1942–May 7, 1943, John H. Hill collection.
3. Lindbergh, *The Wartime Journals*, Monday, January 12–Tuesday, January 13, 1942, pp. 579–584; Arnold, *Global Mission*, p. 189.

# NOTES

4. Ibid., diary entry, Monday, January 19, 1942, p. 587.
5. Ibid., diary entry, Monday, January 26, 1942, p. 588.
6. Ibid., journal entry, Tuesday, February 3, 1942, p. 590.
7. Dear and Foot, *Oxford Companion to World War II*, p. 690.
8. Lindbergh, *Wartime Journals*, journal entry, Tuesday, March 10, 1942, p. 601.
9. Oliver La Farge, *The Eagle in the Egg* (Boston: Houghton Mifflin Company, 1949), p. 13.
10. Lt. General Harold L. George, *History of the Air Transport Command*, manuscript, pp. 7–8, from Pan American Group Veteran Status Application Research Exhibits Volume I: No. 1–16, SFOM.
11. Ibid., pp. 2, 9.
12. Arnold, *Global Mission*, pp. 294–295.
13. Mark Cotta Vaz interview, Kathleen Clair New York City, November 13, 2011.
14. La Farge, *The Eagle in the Egg*, p. 91.
15. Editors Craven and Gate, *The Army Air Forces in World War II*, pp. 340–341.
16. Oliver La Farge, *The Eagle in the Egg*, p. 85.
17. Culbert and Dawson, *PanAfrica*, p. 126, SFOM.
18. Oliver La Farge, *The Eagle in the Egg*, p. 85.
19. Langewiesche, *Pan Am Corporate History*, Section 16, pp. 5304–5305, SFOM.
20. Pan Am CAB Docket 855, *History of the Transatlantic Services*, p. 47, SFOM; Culbert and Dawson, *PanAfrica*, p. 127, SFOM.
21. Gilmore, *African Report*, "Historical Perspective," SFOM.
22. Taylor was transferred back to San Francisco as Assistant Division Engineer. Taylor, *Memoirs*, Vol. II., pp. 69, SFOM.
23. J. H. Smith, Jr., Pan American Airways-Africa, Ltd., Divisional Offices, Accra, letter to Captain Dwight L. Shrum, from, December 12, 1942, from "Pan American Group Personal Statements Supporting Veteran Status Application," SFOM.
24. Romanus and Sunderland, *Stilwell's Mission to China*, pp. 165, 167.
25. ATC Historical Officer, *Air Transportation to China*, pp. 13–17, FOIA.
26. Ibid., p. 19.
27. Undated, probably late summer or fall of 1942, Memorandum Re Air Transportation System Dinjan-Kunming, China, True Copy prepared by Oliver La Farge, Major, Air Corps, Historical Officer, pp. 1, 6, FOIA.
28. ATC Historical Officer, *Air Transportation to China*, pp. 20–21, FOIA.
29. Ibid., p. 24.
30. "Tigers Change Spots," *New Horizons*, July 1942: 13, SFOM.
31. Dinjan-Kunming memo, p. 3, FOIA.
32. Colonel C. R. Smith, Chief of Staff (Smith held that rank when he enlisted after Pearl Harbor), The Air Transport Command, Memorandum For The Commanding General, Army Air Forces [,] Subject: India-China Ferry Operation, October 13, 1942 (copy), pp. 1, 3–6, FOIA.

33. Romanus and Sunderland, *Stilwell's Mission to China*, p. 267.
34. ATC Historical Officer, *Air Transportation to China*, pp. 25–27, FOIA.
35. Leary, Jr., *The Dragon's Wings*, pp. 160–161, SFOM.

## Chapter 23: "The Fastest With the Mostest"

1. Col. Harris, quoted by Africa-Orient Division Manager H. W. Toomey in personnel posting for "Uniforms & Insignia," July 28, 1943, as copied in "Pan American Group Personal Statements Supporting Veteran Status Application," SFOM.
2. "New Bridge To The East," *New Horizons* (no author or date), PAA Public Relations Dept., News Reference Files, pp. 2–5, Series 9, sub-series 1: Africa-Orient, Box 1, folder 3, UM Richter Library Special Collections.
3. Pan American World Airways, Atlantic Division, La Guardia Field, New York, press release—Thursday, October 19 [no year], Series 9, subseries 5: General, Box 3, folder 1, UM Richter Library Special Collections; Reginald M. Cleveland, *Air Transport at War* (New York/London, Harper & Row Publishers, 1946), p. 179, SFOM.
4. Untitled and unaccredited report on the Africa-Orient Division, pp. 1–4, Series 9, Sub-series 1: Africa Orient Division, Box 1, folder 53, UM Richter Library Special Collections.
5. Edward K. Titus manuscript, Chapter XIV: "Mr. Smith Goes to Chungking," pp. 1–4, Series 9, Sub-series 1, Box 1, folder 3, UM Richter Library Special Collections.
6. I. L. Lee, Jr., Assistant, PAA-Confidential Memorandum to Manager, Africa-Orient Miami, to Director, Public Relations Department, New York, May 18, 1944; Frank H. Hankins, Jr., Operations Manager, Africa-Orient, Miami, report to Airport Briefer, Africa-Orient, Natal, "Story Of The 'Cannonball,'" April 11, 1944, both Series 9, sub-series 1: Africa, Box 1, folder 3, UM Richter Library Special Collections.
7. Africa-Orient manager Toomey, PAA-Confidential report to Franklin Gledhill, re: "Cannonball," March 3, 1944, Series 9, Sub-series 4: Pan American Africa, Ltd., Box 1, folder 7, UM Richter Library Special Collections.
8. Ernest Colant and Scharleen Colant, "Veteran Status Application," Basil Rowe quote, p. 29, SFOM.
9. Cleveland, *Air Transport at War*, p. 180, SFOM.
10. "Cannonball" Burma's Secret Weapon," *New York News*, March 13, 1944, Series 9, Sub-series 1: Africa-Orient Division, UM Richter Library Special Collections.
11. The crew of the milestone flight: Captain R. A. Holman, co-pilot Kenneth Bresdal, navigator Robert Simmons, flight engineer John Grimshaw, and radio operator A. E. Deese.

12. Personnel Survey Group, Pan American Airways Atlantic Division, *Report on Personnel Requirements*, "Restricted" report, New York, N.Y., September 15, 1944 p. 3, part of Pan Am Group Veteran Status Application, Research Exhibits, Exhibit #30, SFOM; Gillespie quote from *History of Naval Air Transport Squadron, Pacific, 1942*, Pan American Veteran Status Application, Exhibit #9, p. 4, SFOM.
13. "National Defense," *New Horizons*, December 1940: 9, 11, SFOM; Pan Am CAB Docket 851, *History of Transpacific Air Services*, pp. 47–48, SFOM.
14. Colant, Pan Am Veteran Status Group, pp. 36–37, SFOM.
15. Personnel Survey Group, *Report on Personnel Requirements*, Pan Am Group exhibit #30, pp. 2–3, SFOM.
16. "Gambit," *New Horizons*, July, 1943: 18–19, SFOM.
17. "Passenger No. 1," *New Horizons*, January 1943: 7, SFOM; Conrad, *Pan Am*, pp. 144–145; Goodwin, *No Ordinary Time*, p. 401; "The Exploration of the Air," transcript of John C. Leslie speech at the Phillips Exeter Academy, New Hampshire Assembly, November 6, 1972, p. 8, provided authors by Peter Leslie; "The Log of The President's Trip to the Casablanca Conference 9–13, 1943, SFOM.
18. John Eliott, with Captain Almon A. Gray, U.S. Naval Reserve (Retired), "Where's Flight 62100?" *Proceedings*, published by the U.S. Naval Institute, January 1997: 69–71, SFOM.
19. "Naval Air Transport Service Plane Rescues 48 From Sea," Navy Dept. Press Release, April 23, 1944, Pan American Group Veteran Status Application, Exhibit 38, SFOM.
20. Pan American World Airways Press release, January 25, 1945, Series 9, Sub-series 5: General, Box 3, folder 2, UM Richter Library Special Collections.
21. Brigadier General Frederic H. Smith, Jr., Deputy Chief of Air Staff, letter to John C. Cooper, Pan Am, Washington office, October 24, 1944; Assistant Vice President A. M. Archibald, Pan Am Washington office, letter to General Smith, Headquarters of the Army Air Force, War Department, Washington, October 25, 1944, FOIA.
22. PAA Atlantic Division press release, Series 6, sub-series 4: Other, Box 7, folder 4, UM Richter Library Special Collections.
23. "Wings Over the World: Annual Report for 1944—PAN AMERICAN WORLD AIRWAYS: The System of the Flying Clippers," pp. 3, 6, 15, back page "Roll of Honor," SFOM.
24. Cleveland, *Air Transport at War*, p. 215, SFOM.
25. Charles F. Romanus and Riley Sunderland, *United States Army in World War II, China-Burma-India Theater: Time Runs Out In CBI* (Washington, D.C.: Office of the Chief of Military History, Department of the Army, 1959), pp. 12–13.
26. La Farge, *Eagle in the Egg*, pp. 127–128.

## Chapter 24: Into the Congo

1. Brock, *Flying the Oceans*, p. 285, SFOM.
2. Pan Am Cab Docket No. 1171, *et al.*, *Brief History of the Pan American Airways: Service to Africa*, p. 3, Series 9, Sub-series 4: Pan American Africa, Ltd., Box 1, folder 3, UM Richter Library Special Collections; Daley, *An American Saga*, p. 314.
3. "Dismantle Overhaul," *New Horizons*, March 1942: 25, SFOM.
4. H. M. Bixby, to the Attention of Captain D. F. Smith, Director, Naval Air Transport Services, Navy Department, Washington, D.C., November 17, 1943, Series 1, sub-series 1: Africa, Box 1, folder 8, "Operation Leopoldville" (1 of 2), UM Richter Library Special Collections.
5. Pan Am CAB Docket 1171, *Service to Africa*, 1964, p. 5, Series 9, sub-series 4: Pan American Africa, Ltd., UM Richter Library Special Collections.
6. Einstein letter reproduced: Susan Williams, *Spies in the Congo: America's Atomic Mission in World War II* (New York: PublicAffairs, 2016), pp. xxiii–xxiv.
7. "Atomic bomb" essay by R.V. Jones, from Dear and Foot, *Oxford Companion to World War II*, p. 73.
8. Vincent C. Jones, *Manhattan: The Army And The Atomic Bomb* (Washington, D.C.: Center of Military History, United States Army, 1985), pp. 8, 295–297, 300.
9. Charles N. Leach, District Traffic manager, Atlantic, in Natal, report to Division Traffic Manager, Latin America in Miami, re: Anticipated Martin Service to Leopoldville, May 23, 1944, Series 1, sub-series 1: Africa, Box 1, folder 8, "Operations Leopoldville" (2 of 2), UM Richter Library Special Collections.
10. "Memorandum for the Record," Symington report on April 20 State Department meeting regarding "Resumption of Leopoldville Service," April 26, 1944, Series 1, Sub-series 1: Africa, Box 1, folder 8 ("Operation Leopoldville" 1 of 2), UM Richter Library Special Collections.
11. It is not clear who added the asterisks and note, and when. "Suggested Direct U.S. Flag Wartime Service, U.S.A.—Belgian Congo," prepared by F. Symington, Washington, D.C., and stamped "PAA-Confidential," May 2, 1944, Series 1: Corporate and General, Sub-series 1: Africa, Box 1, folder 8, "Operation Leopoldville" (1 of 2), UM Richter Library Special Collections.
12. Anne Archibald in Washington, D.C., memorandum to Harold Bixby in New York, re Leopoldville Route, Series 1, sub-series 1: Africa, Box 1, folder 8, Leopoldville Operations" (2 of 2), UM Richter Library Special Collections.
13. Vice President Bixby, memorandum to President Trippe, July 26, 1944, Series 1, Sub-series 1: Africa, Box 1, folder 8, "Operation Leopoldville" (2 of 2), UM Richter Library Special Collections.
14. Harold Bixby, letter to Charles Cheston, Office of Strategic Services in Washington, July 27, 1944; Cheston response to Bixby (stamped "Confidential"), both references Series 1, Sub-series 1: Africa, Box 1, folder 8, "Operation Leopoldville" (2 of 2), UM Richter Library Special Collections.

15. F. Symington memorandum to Vice President Pryor, August 11, 1944; Emory Ross telegram to L. Welch Pogue; H. M. Bixby memorandum to Trippe, et al, August 15, 1944; all citations Series 1, sub-series 1: Africa, Box 1, folder 8, "Operations Leopoldville," (1 of 2), UM Richter Library Special Collections.
16. Marius "Lodi" Lodeesen, *Captain Lodi Speaking: Saying Goodbye to an Era* (McLean, Virginia: Paladwr Press, 2004), pp. 69, SFOM.
17. Williams, *Spies in the Congo*, pp. 206–207.
18. John H. Hill, interview with Nancy Dean Felch, Carmel, California, December 27, 2007. During the war, Maria Goeppert-Mayer worked for the Manhattan Project at Columbia University.
19. Lodeesen, *Captain Lodi Speaking*, pp. 69–71, SFOM.
20. C. W. McVitty, Assist. Manager, Atlantic Division, report to Harold Bixby. June 28, 1945, Series 1, sub-series 1: Africa, Box 2, folder 2, UM Richter Library Special Collections.
21. Chennault, *Way of a Fighter*, pp. 350, 352–354.
22. Taylor, *Memoirs*, pp. 72, 77–78, 80B–81A, SFOM.
23. Ibid., p. 80. Taylor was critical of the gunfire celebration, recalling several soldiers were killed or wounded.
24. "Internees Home At Last," *Clipper*, October 1, 1945: 1, 3, SFOM.
25. Kinney with McCaffrey, *Wake Island Pilot*, pp. 173, 181, SFOM.
26. Bill Mullahey report to manager, Pacific-Alaska Division, San Francisco: "PAA Installations—Wake Island," November 9, 1945, pp. 1–3, provided authors by Doug Miller.

## Chapter 25: No Distant Lands

1. Lt. General H. L. George, Air Transport Command, Office of the Commanding General in Washington, D.C., letter to Juan T. Trippe at Pan Am, New York, June 25, 1946, Series 9, sub-series 1: Africa Orient Division, Box 1, folder 53, UM Richter Library Special Collections.
2. Copy of photo and caption, Series 9, sub-series 5: General, Box 1, folder 1, UM Richter Library Special Collections.
3. Bixby, draft letter to Rear Admiral Wm. Radford, Assist. Admiral, Chief of Naval Operations (Air), in Washington, D.C., September 25, 1944. In pencil a note dated "10/17/44" and signed by Bixby adds, "Read to admir. Cassady," Series 9, sub-series 5: General, Box 3, folder 1, UM Richter Library Special Collections.
4. S. Paul Johnston, *Wings after War: The Prospects of Post-War Aviation* (New York: Duell, Sloan and Pearce, 1944), p. 61.
5. General of the Army H. H. Arnold, "Air Power for Peace," *The National Geographic Magazine*, February, 1946: 176, 193.
6. Dear and Foot, *Oxford Companion to World War II*, pp. 55–56.
7. "Chest Expansion of an Airline," *Fortune*, April 1945: 132, 138, 199.

8. Daley, *An American Saga*, p. 95; Pan Am CAB Docket 851, *History of the Transpacific Air Service*, p. 42, SFOM; Boeing 314 Clipper, details from Wikipedia.
9. Langewiesche, *Pan Am Corporate History*, Section 8, pp. 2765–2766, SFOM.
10. Letter from W. T. Jarboe, Jr., Division Communication Supt., to L. J. McVey, Div. Command Manager of American Telephone and Telegraph Company, December 3, 1946, Series 4, sub-series 5: Atlantic Division, Box 1, folder 34, UM Richter Library Special Collections.
11. #51–March 23, 1944, "Address Delivered at Charter Week Ceremonies, University of California, at Los Angeles and Berkeley: America in the Air Age," pp. 1–2, speech transcript, National Air and Space Museum, Smithsonian Institution.

# BIBLIOGRAPHY

**BOOKS CITED**

Arnold, H. H. *Global Mission*. New York: Harper & Row, Publishers, 1949.

Banning, Gene. *Airlines of Pan American since 1927*. Rockville, Maryland: Paladwr Press, 2001.

Bender, Marylin, and Selig Altschul. *The Chosen Instrument: Pan Am [and] Juan Trippe: The Rise and Fall of an American Entrepreneur*. New York: Simon and Schuster, 1982.

Berg, A. Scott. *Lindbergh*. New York: Berkley Books edition, 1999.

Biddle, Wayne. *Barons of the Sky: From Early Flight to Strategic Warfare: The Story of the American Aerospace Industry*. Baltimore, Maryland: John Hopkins University Press, 2002.

Bond, W. Langhorne, edited by James E. Ellis. *Wings for an Embattled China*. Bethlehem, Pennsylvania: Lehigh University Press, 2001.

Briddon, Arnold E., and Ellmore A. Champie. *Federal Aviation Agency Historical Fact Book: A Chronology, 1926-1963*. Federal Aviation Agency, Washington, D.C.: U.S. Government Printing Office, 1966.

Brock, Horace. *Flying the Oceans*. Lunenburg, Vermont: The Stinehour Press, 1979.

Brock, Horace. *More About Pan Am: A Pilot's Story Continued*. Lunenburg, Vermont: The Stinehour Press, 1980.

Bruno, Harry. *Wings Over America: The Inside Story of American Aviation*. New York: Robert M. McBride & Company, 1942.

Burns, Ric, and James Sanders. *New York: An Illustrated History*. New York: Alfred A. Knopf, 1999.

Chennault, Major General Claire Lee, with editor Robert Hotz. *Way of a Fighter*. New York: G. P. Putnam's Sons, 1949.

Cleveland, Reginald M. *Air Transport at War*. New York: Harper & Row Publishers, 1946.

Coffey, Thomas M. *Hap: The Story of the U.S. Air Force and The Man Who Built It—General Henry H. "Hap" Arnold*. New York: The Viking Press, 1981.

Conrad III, Barnaby. *Pan Am: An Aviation Legend*. Emeryville, California: Woodford Press, 1999.

Cooke, Jean, Ann Kramer, and Theodore Rowland-Entwistle. *History's Timeline*. New York: Crescent Books, 1981.

Cooper, John C. *The Right to Fly: A Study in Air Power*. New York: Henry Holt and Company, 1947.

Craven, Frank Wesley, and James Lea Gate, editors. *The Army Air Forces in World War II: Volume One: Plans and Early Operations: January 1939 to August 1942*. Washington, DC.: Office of Air Force History, 1983.

Crouch, Gregory. *China's Wings: War, Intrigue, Romance And Adventure In The Middle Kingdom During The Golden Age of Flight*. New York: Bantam Books, 2012.

Culbert, Tom & Andy Dawson. *PanAfrica: Across the Sahara in 1941 with Pan Am*. McLean, Virginia: Paladwr Press, 1999.

Daley, Robert. *An American Saga: Juan Trippe and His Pan Am Empire*. New York: Random House, 1980.

Davies, R.E.G. *Airlines of the United States Since 1914*. London: Putnam (revised reprint edition), 1982.

Davies, R.E.G. *Pan Am: An Airline And Its Aircraft*. New York: Orion Books, 1987.

Davis, Burke. *The Billy Mitchell Affair*. New York: Random House, 1967.

Dear, I.C.B., general editor, consultant editor M.R.D. Foot. *The Oxford Companion to World War II*. Oxford/New York: Oxford University Press, 1995.

Department of the Army. *The Army Almanac*. Washington, D.C.: Government Printing Office, 1950.

Dover, Ed. *The Long Way Home: A Journey Into History With Captain Robert Ford*. Albuquerque, New Mexico: Valliant Press, 2008.

Federal Writers Project, Works Progress Administration Guide (reprint edition). *San Francisco in the 1930s: The WPA Guide to the City by the Bay*. Berkeley, Los Angeles, London: University of California Press, 2011.

Fife, George Buchanan. *Lindbergh: The Lone Eagle*. New York: A. L. Burt Company, 1927.

French, Joseph Lewis, editor. *Conquerors of the Sky*. Springfield, Massachusetts: McLoughlin Bros., Inc., 1932.

Gauvreau, Emile, and Lester Cohen. *Billy Mitchell: Founder of Our Air Force and Prophet without Honor*. New York: E. P. Dutton & Co., Inc., 1942.

Goodwin, Alice Kearns. *No Ordinary Time: Franklin and Eleanor Roosevelt: The Home Front in World War II*. New York: Touchstone, 1995.

Grant, R.G. *Flight: 100 Years of Aviation*. Smithsonian Institution/Covent Garden Books, New York: DK Publishing, 2009.

Greenlaw, Olga S. *The Lady and the Tigers*. New York: E. P. Dutton & Co., Inc., 1943.

Greenwood, John T., editor, with Von Hardesty. *Milestones of Aviation: Smithsonian National Air and Space Museum*. New York: Universe Publishing, 2008.

Grooch, William Stephen. *From Crate to Clipper With Captain Musick, Pioneer Pilot*. New York/Toronto: Longmans, Green and Co., 1939.

Grooch, William Stephen. *Skyway to Asia*. New York/Toronto: Longmans, Green and Co., 1936.

Grooch, William Stephen. *Winged Highway*. New York/Toronto: Longmans, Green and Co., 1938.

Hermann, Hauptmann. *The Luftwaffe: Its Rise and Fall*. New York: G. P. Putnam's Sons, 1943.

Hughes, Thomas P. *American Genesis: A Century of Invention and Technological Enthusiasm 1870-1970*. New York: Penguin Books, 1990.

Jackson, Ronald W. *China Clipper: The Gripping True Story of Pan American's Flying Boats and Their Role in the War in the Pacific*. New York: Everest House, 1980.

Johnston, S. Paul. *Wings after War: The Prospects of Post-War Aviation*. New York: Duell, Sloan and Pearce, 1944.

Jones, Vincent C. *Manhattan: The Army And The Atomic Bomb*. Washington, D.C.: Center of Military History, United States Army, 1985.

Josephson, Matthew. *Empire of the Air: Juan Trippe and the Struggle for World Airways*. New York: Harcourt, Brace and Company, 1943.

Kaucher, Dorothy. *On Your Left The Milky Way*. Boston: The Christopher Publishing House, 1952.

Kaucher, Dorothy. *Wings over Wake*. San Francisco: John Howell, Publisher, 1947.

Kinney, Brig. Gen. John F., with James McCaffrey. *Wake Island Pilot: A World War II Memoir*. Washington: Brassey's, 1995.

La Farge, Oliver. *The Eagle in the Egg*. Boston: Houghton Mifflin Company, 1949.

Leary, Jr., William M. *The Dragon's Wings: The China National Aviation Corporation And The Development Of Commercial Aviation In China*. Athens, Georgia: The University of Georgia Press, 1976.

Lindbergh, Anne Morrow. *Hour of Gold, Hour of Lead: Diaries and Letters of Anne Morrow Lindbergh 1929-1932*. New York/London: Harcourt Brace Jovanovich, 1973.

Lindbergh, Anne Morrow. *Listen! The Wind*. New York: Harcourt, Brace and Company, 1938.

Lindbergh, Anne Morrow. *Locked Rooms and Open Doors: Diaries and Letters: 1933-1935*. New York and London: Harcourt Brace Jovanovich (a Helen and Kurt Wolff Book), 1974.

Lindbergh, Anne Morrow. *North to the Orient*. New York: Harcourt, Brace and Company, 1935.

Lindbergh, Anne Morrow. *War Within and Without: Diaries and Letters 1939-1944*. New York and London: Harcourt Brace Jovanovich (a Helen and Kurt Wolff Book), 1980.

Lindbergh, Charles. *Autobiography of Values*. New York & London: Harcourt Brace Jovanovich, 1978.

Lindbergh, Charles. *The Wartime Journals of Charles A. Lindbergh*. New York: Harcourt Brace Jovanovich, Inc., 1970.

Lindbergh, Charles. *We*. New York: Putnam's Sons, 1927.

Lodeesen, Marius "Lodi." *Captain Lodi Speaking: Saying Goodbye to an Era.* McLean, Virginia: Paladwr Press, 2004.

Loewenheim, Francis L., Harold D. Langley, Manfred Jonas, editors. *Roosevelt and Churchill: Their Secret Wartime Correspondence.* New York: Saturday Review Press/E. P. Dutton & Co., 1975.

Long, Elgen M., and Marie K. Long. *Amelia Earhart: The Mystery Solved.* New York: Simon & Schuster, 1999.

Mayo, Anthony J., Nitin Nohria, and Mark Rennella. *Entrepreneurs, Managers, and Leaders: What the Airline Industry Can Teach Us About Leadership.* New York: Macmillan/Palgrave, 2009.

Newton, Wesley Phillips. *The Perilous Sky: U.S. Aviation Diplomacy and Latin America: 1919-1931.* Coral Gables, Florida: University of Miami Press, 1978.

O'Neill, Ralph A., with Joseph Hood. *A Dream of Eagles.* Boston: Houghton Mifflin Company, 1973.

Paine, Ralph D. *The First Yale Unit: A Story of Naval Aviation 1916-1919.* Cambridge: Riverside Press, 1925.

Reinhardt, Richard. *Treasure Island: 1929-1940, San Francisco's Exposition Years.* Mill Valley, California: Squarebooks, Inc., 1978.

Rickenbacker, Edward V. *Rickenbacker.* Englewood Cliffs, New Jersey: Prentice-Hall, 1967.

Roberts, Henry W. *Aviation Radio.* New York: William Morrow, 1945.

Romanus, Charles F., and Riley Sunderland. *United States Army In World War II. The China-Burma-India Theater: Stilwell's Mission to China.* Washington, DC.: Office of the Chief of Military History, Department of the Army, 1952.

Romanus, Charles F., and Riley Sunderland. *United States Army In World War II. China-Burma-India Theater: Time Runs Out In CBI.* Washington, DC.: Office of the Chief of Military History, Department of the Army, 1959.

Scott, Jr., Robert Lee. *Flying Tiger: Chennault of China.* Garden City, NY: Doubleday & Company, 1959.

Trippe, Betty Stettinius. *Diary and Letters . . . 1925 to 1968.* Private edition, 1982, John H. Hill Collection.

Trippe, Betty Stettinius. *Pan Am's First Lady: The Diary of Betty Stettinius Trippe.* McLean: Virginia: Paladwr Press, 1996.

Van Vleck, Jenifer. *Empire of the Air: Aviation And The American Ascendancy.* Cambridge and London: Harvard University Press, 2013.

Vaz, Mark Cotta. *Living Dangerously: The Adventures of Merian C. Cooper, Creator of King Kong.* New York: Villard, 2005.

White, Theodore H., and Annalee Jacoby. *Thunder Out of China.* New York: William Sloane Associates, Inc., 1946.

Williams, Susan. *Spies in the Congo: America's Atomic Mission in World War II.* New York: PublicAffairs, 2016.

Wolff, Geoffrey. *Black Sun: The Brief Transit and Violent Eclipse of Harry Crosby.* New York: Random House, 1976.

Wortman, Marc. *The Millionaires' Unit: The Aristocratic Flyboys Who Fought The Great War And Invented American Air Power.* New York: PublicAffairs, 2006.

## SELECT DOCUMENTS AND UNPUBLISHED MATERIAL

Army Air Forces/Air Transport Command. *The Official History of the South Atlantic Division.* Declassified "Secret" report, November 13, 1945. FOIA.

Bixby, Harold. *Top Side Rickshaw*, manuscript. SFOM.

Chin, Moon. Interview by Mauree Jane Perry, Oral History Program Transcriptions, 2004. SFOM.

China National Aviation Foundation. *Wings Over Asia: A Brief History of China National Aviation Corporation*, 1971. FOIA.

Civil Aviation Board. Docket No. 525. *Outline of the History of the Latin American Services*; Docket No. 547. *History of Pan American's Air Services To and Through Alaska*; Docket No. 851. *History of the Transpacific Air Services to and Through Hawaii*; Docket No. 855, *History of the Transatlantic Air Services*. SFOM.

Clair, Kathleen. Interviews by Mark Cotta Vaz, November 13, 2001; March 29, 2008.

Cooper, Don. "The Route of the China Clipper," *Thanks for the Memories* program. China Clipper 75th Anniversary Celebration, San Francisco, November 17-20, 2010.

Dean, Howard B. Journal, April 22, 1942–May 7, 1943. John H. Hill Collection.

George, Lt. General Harold L. *History of the Air Transport Command*, manuscript. SFOM.

Gilmore, Voit. *African Report: An Account of what the Pan Africans found and what they did while running the trans-Africa aerial life-line from September 1941 until December 1942.* SFOM.

Hall, Edward Hagaman. *The Fourth Annual Report of the Hudson-Fulton Celebration: Commission to the Legislature of the State of New York.* Albany, New York: J. B. Lyon and Company, 1910.

Hambleton, John. Diary, 1924-1925. Libbie Hambleton Collection.

Interdepartmental Aviation Committee. Minutes of first meeting, November 23, 1927. National Archives.

Langewiesche, Wolfgang. *Pan American Corporate History*, manuscript. SFOM.

Leslie, John. *Pan Am History*, manuscript. SFOM.

Lindbergh, Charles. Atlantic survey report letters to Juan Trippe, 1933. UM Richter Library Special Collections/SFOM.

Mullahey, Bill. "PAA Installations—Wake Island," report, November 9, 1945.

"Operation Leopoldville" documents, 1944. UM Richter Library Special Collections.

Pan American Airways. Annual Reports. SFOM.

Pan American Airways (Atlantic, Gulf and Caribbean Airways, Inc.). Board of Directors meeting minutes, December 17, 1927. UM Richter Library Special Collections.

Pan American Airways. "Log of the China Clipper," Pacific Supplement No. 2, November 22-23, 1935. SFOM.

Pan American Airways. "Special Mission" and "Special Operation" reports. UM Richter Library Special Collections.

Pan American Airways. World War II contracts. SFOM.

Pan American Airways. World War II "Veteran Status Application" documents. SFOM.

Pawley, William D. *Americans Valiant and Glorious: A Brief History of the Flying Tigers.* FOIA.

Sherman, Captain D. B. "Observations of Joint Operations PAA-Africa, Ltd. and U.S. Army, Assam-Burma-China Ferry Command, Dinjan, India, April 6th to May 15th, 1942." UM Richter Library Special Collections.

Taylor, George W. *Memories*, manuscript. SFOM.

Trippe, Edward S. Family genealogy, correspondence with John H. Hill, February 28, 2017.

Trippe, Juan T. "Charles Lindbergh and World Travel." Fourteenth Wings Club 'Sight' Lecture, presented at The Wings Club, May 20, 1977, New York City.

Trippe, Juan T. "Ocean Air Transport," transcript of speeches, Wilbur Wright Memorial Lecture before the Royal Aeronautical Society, London, June 17, 1941. SFOM.

Trippe, Juan T. Transcripts of speeches, Trippe Family Papers, National Air and Space Museum, Smithsonian Institution.

White, Assistant Secretary of State Francis. "Aviation in Latin America," report to Secretary of State, April 25, 1929. National Archives.

## SELECT ARTICLES AND PERIODICALS

Arnold, General of the Army H. H. "Air Power for Peace," *The National Geographic Magazine* (February 1976).

Burden, William A. M. "The Struggle for Airways in Latin America." New York: Council on Foreign Relations (1943).

Busch, Noel F. "Juan Trippe." *Life* (October 20, 1941).

Elott, John, with Captain Almon A. Gray, USNR (Retired). "Where's Flight 62100?" *Proceedings* (U.S. Naval Institute). (January 1997).

*Fortune.* "Colossus of the Caribbean," (April 1931).

*Fortune.* "Pan American Airways," (April 1936).

Glines, C. V. "Clippers Circle the Globe." *Aviation History*, (March 2007). SFOM.

Libby, Justin. "Pan Am Gets a Pacific Partner." *Naval History*, (September/October 1999). SFOM.

Luce, Clare Boothe. "Destiny Crosses The Dateline: Report on a Flight Across the Pacific." *Life*, (November 3, 1941). SFOM.

*New Horizons.* Pan Am in-house magazine. SFOM.

Newton, Dr. Wesley Phillips. "The Role of the Army Air Aims in Latin America, 1922-1931." *Air University Review*, (Sept.-Oct. 1962). SFOM.
*Pan Am Clipper* newsletter. Pan Am Historical Foundation.
Rickertson, Jr., Oliver, and A. V. Kidder. "An Archeological Reconnaissance By Air In Central America." *The Geographical Review*, (April, 1930).
"The Mitchell Trial." *Aviation*, (November 23, 1925). SFOM.
*Transpacific*. Pan Am Pacific-Alaska Division newsletter.

# ACKNOWLEDGMENTS

★

The following institutions, research sources, and people were indispensable in the preparation of this book.

### SFO Museum
### San Francisco Airport Commission Aviation Library
### Louis A. Turpen Aviation Museum

The SFO Museum aviation history collection held at San Francisco International Airport was a major resource. This includes Wolfgang Langewiesche's unpublished Pan American World Airways Corporate History Research Manuscript, made available to the public in its entirety for the first time thanks to the Pan Am Historical Foundation; and the Tony Bill Aviation Library Collection. Julie Takata, head of Collection Management, and the museum and library staff were of invaluable help, particularly, Kenn Yazzie, Tomohiko Aono, Debbie Kahn, Gabe Phung, and Sandy Kwan. The support of Blake Summers, Director and Chief Curator, is also greatly appreciated. The creation and development of the aviation museum and library for the public benefit at SFO by the San Francisco Airport Commission is the result of the visionary leadership and ongoing support of three successive Airport Directors, Lou Turpen, John Martin, and Ivar Satero.

### University of Miami, Special Collections, Otto G. Richter Library
### The Pan American World Airways, Inc. Records Collection

The ultimate source on everything connected with Pan Am's history, our special appreciation to Cristina Favretto, Head of Special Collections. Her staff was impeccable, particularly Library Assistant Nicola Hellmann McFarland and Yvette Yurubi. A bow of appreciation as well to Beatrice Skokan and student intern Jean Paul Gilmour.

**Department of the Air Force, Air Force Historical Research Agency**
**Maxwell Air Force Base, Alabama**
**Freedom of Information Act material**
Our thanks to archivist Kevin Burge for his help in processing FOIA requests regarding Pan Am and its affiliate, the China National Aviation Corporation.

**Pan Am Historical Foundation**
The Foundation's resources were of great importance to the writing of this book, and several of it directors generously shared their knowledge, often first-hand, about prominent figures in the airline's history. These include Ed Trippe, the late Charlie Trippe, the indomitable Kathleen Clair, Pete Runnette, Peter Leslie, Doug Miller, Don Cooper, and Jeff Kriendler, who held the PAA flag high during the Miami research visit.

**The John Hambleton Family**
The family of Pan Am's cofounder provided diaries, personal letters, newspaper clippings, and other material related to John Hambleton's life. Special appreciation to George Hambleton (also a Pan Am Historical Foundation director) and Libbie Hambleton, who shared many of these rare and precious items. Thanks also to Diana Hambleton and John Hambleton (of "Islanders"), for supporting this project.

The historians and authors Gregg Herken and Robert S. Norris were most generous with their expertise on the war effort. A salute to our agent John Silbersack, and present and past assistants, Caitlin Meuser, Hannah Fergesen, and Rachel Mosner respectively, for never giving up on this "labor of love." Great thanks also to editors Joe Craig, Kirsten Kim, and Michael Campbell, and to tech-guru Michael Vaz.

# INDEX

Accra, Africa Gold Coast, 216, 220–21, 223, 261, 283–85, 292–93
Acheson, Dean, 210
Acosta, Bert, 19
Adcock direction finder, 114–15, 121, 333
Adcock, Frank, 114
*Aero Digest*, 61, 120, 327
Aeroflot, 141
Aeromarine Airways, 12, 42, 65, 325
*Aero Porto de Lisboa*, 207
Africa Gold Coast, 144, 209, 220, 223, 261
Air Commerce Act (1926), 38, 169
Air Corps Ferrying Command, 203, 210–11, 252, 256, 260, 262, 269, 272, 282
Aircraft Board (established by President Coolidge), 36, 38
Air France, 52, 88, 140, 192, 201, 203
Air Mail contracts, U.S. Post Office, 13, 18–19, 29, 52–53, 55–56, 70, 75, 83–82, 173
Air Mail Route No. 1 (New York-Boston), 18–19, 25–26
Air Ministry, Royal Air Force, 2, 210
Airport Development Program (ADP), 191, 198, 200, 217, 258, 314
Air Power philosophy, 5, 8, 37, 172, 272, 282, 315, 313
Air Transport Command (ATC), 268, 282–83, 286, 288–91, 293, 297, 300, 314
Air War Plans Division, U.S., 262
Alameda, California (Pan Am Pacific Division headquarters), 114, 118, 124–25, 129–33, 136, 140–43, 163
Alexander, Edward H., 289

Alfonso, Gus, 55
Allison, Ernest "Allie," 149, 152–53, 155
Amazon region, 103
American Airlines, 76, 252, 282
American Airways, 104
American Export Airlines (AEA), 198, 252
American International Airlines, 76
American Nitrates Corporation, 170
American Volunteer Group (AVG) (*see* Flying Tigers), 231–32, 273, 288
Anderson, John, 303
Andrée, Salomon August, 96
Angola, 304
Apra Harbor, Guam, 137, 139
Aquitania, 177
Archibald, Anne:
  role in resumption of wartime Leopoldville service, 304–06, as Washington fixture, 221, 299
Armistice, WW I, 7, 11, 14, 16–17, 28, 30
Army Air Corps, U.S., 21, 38, 177–78, 181, 185, 201, 210–11, 215, 221, 226, 229, 272, 295
Army Air Service, U.S., 26, 38, 229
Army Engineering Corps, U.S., 258
Army Signal Corps, U.S., 14
Arnold, Henry H. "Hap":
  as Air Mail pilot, 7
  Air Power philosophy, 4, 8
Air Transport Command, wartime organization of, 282
  Atlantic ferrying operations, support of, 209–11, 213

Air Transport Command, wartime
organization of (*continued*)
Blériot monoplane and thoughts of Air
Power, 5
Blitzkrieg of London, witness to, 1
Chief of the Army Air Corps, appointed
to, 177
China, wartime involvement with;
support of CNAC taking over
wartime transport program; opposes
General Chennault in air force
reorganization, 2, 286, 288
death of, 315
Hudson-Fulton Celebration, in
attendance, 5–6
Lindbergh, involves in intelligence and air
preparedness; appoints to Kilner-
Lindbergh Board; support of in
wartime, 177–78, 204, 281
militarization of overseas air operations,
252, 279
Billy Mitchell supporter and defense
witness, 33, 36–37, 272
Munich Pact, as "appeasement pact," 176–
77
Pan American Airways, forms airline and
envisions air routes; resigns from;
facilitates absorption by ACA;
witnesses christening of Yankee
Clipper; office assists in preliminary
plans for trans African ferrying
operation; praises navigation training
of Army Air Corps Cadets, 27, 43,
44–45, 295
Elliott Roosevelt, gives commission to in
the Air Corps, 209
SCADTA, crusade against, 8, 26
Trippe, interaction with, 1–2, 254, 281
Wright brothers, as student, 7
"Arsenal of Democracy," 204, 206, 214
Assam-Burma-China Ferry Command, 268–
69, 273
Assam, India, 234, 268, 271, 287
Astaire, Fred, 23
Atlantic Airways, Limited, 211
Atlantic Coast Line Railway, 18, 72

Atlantic, Gulf & Caribbean, 46, 53, 58
Atlantic Survey, Charles and Anne Lindbergh,
1933, 88–89, 117
Auckland, New Zealand, 165–67, 244, 253–
54, 256
Australia, 165, 167, 171, 226, 254, 287, 314
Aviation, 55, 120, 151
Aviation Corporation of America (ACA),
44
Aviation Corporation of the Americas
(ACA), 46, 48, 58, 77–79, 85
Aviation Day, New York World's Fair, 1939,
182, 184–85
Axis Airlines, the Americas, 192–93, 201, 225,
259
Azores Route, 33, 89, 156, 179, 185

*Bahia*, NYRBA S–38, 81
Balchen, Bernt, 39
Baltimore *Sunday Sun*, 77 Barnett, Ed, 236
Barranquilla, Colombia, 26, 30–31, 80–81, 87,
196
Barrows, Joe, 168
Bathurst, Africa, 2–3, 102, 104, 210–12, 214,
217, 219, 224, 296
Battery Park, New York, 8, 13
Belém, Brazil, 82, 197, 201, 210, 214, 225,
258–9
Belieff, Sam, 270
Belknap, Ralph, 89
Benson Field, Fisherman's Lake (Fish Lake),
Liberia, 216–9, 220–1, 261, 302, 308
Berg, A. Scott, 176
Bevier, Kenneth, 45
Bevier, Richard D., 43, 45, 76
Bingham, Hiram, 36
Bissell, Clayton, 191, 198–99, 265, 267, 289
Bixby, Harold M.:
Belgian Congo, wartime support for
service to Leopoldville, 302, 304–5
as China rep, PAA; purchases stake in
CNAC; out–maneuvers minister of
communications to win Airmail
Route No. 3; visits warlord country;
meets warlord Hsiang; expands service
to Chengtu, 147–49, 150–54, 264

# INDEX

Far East representative, PAA; negotiates landing rights in Manila; *China Clipper*, witnesses historic trans-Pacific landing in Manila Bay, 119, 138
Japan invades China; witnesses aerial assault on Shanghai; plans escape with Bond, 157–57
Lindbergh, support for *Spirit of St. Louis* flight; friendship with, 147, 282
as Pan Am vice president, 207, 314
South Atlantic, negotiates landing rights for Nouméa, French-held New Caldonia; involved in expansion of South Atlantic ferry service, 171, 207, 213
"Black Tuesday," October 29, 1929, 82
Blériot, Louis, 4, 41, 315
"Blind flying" (*see* "instrument flying"), 61–62
Bliss, Gerald D., 75
Blow, Margaret "Peg" (Mrs. Margaret Hambleton), 17–18, 22–23, 78–79
Bluethenthal Memorial Field, Wilmington, N.C., 78
Boeing "Super Clipper," 130, 166, 173, 181–82
Boeing 307 Stratoliner, 196
Boeing 314, *California Clipper* (renamed *Pacific Clipper*), 181, 183, 237, 253, 254–56, 316
Boeing 314, *Capetown Clipper*, 225, 256–57, 301
Boeing 314, *Dixie Clipper*, 207, 292, 296–297
Boeing 314, *Yankee Clipper*, 181, 184, 207, 316
Bogotá, Colombia, 26, 30–32, 85, 194–96
Bolama, Portuguese Guinea, 186, 206–07, 217, 219, 224
Bolivia, 193, 201
Bond, William Langhorne:
CNAC involvement, Curtiss–Wright and Pan Am; flight with Bixby to Chengtu; "damage control" for Pan Am; wartime control of CNAC, 149, 155, 158, 160, 229
Doolittle Flight, advice for, 264
Grooch tragedy, recollection of, 154–55
Hump, describes flight over, 274
Japan, during 1932 attack; *Kweilin* attack; Hong Kong attack and evacuation, December 8, 1941, 151, 245–246
Nanking, escapes from, 158
Trippe, contentious discussions with, 157–158
Borger, John G., 63, 117, 121, 123, 127, 129, 140, 143
Boy, Herbert, 194–95, 197
Braden, Spruille, 194–96
Branch, Harllee, 184, 214
Brazilian Decree-Law #3462, 225
Breckinridge, Henry, 71
Brereton, Lewis H., 272, 284
Briggs, Frank, 220
British Arctic Air Route Expedition, 96
British Overseas Airways Corporation (BOAC), 213, 218, 262
British Security Office, 221
Brock, Horace, 301, 306
Brooks, Jack, 166
Brownsville, Texas, 56, 60–62, 88
Brown, Walter, 77, 83
Bruce, David, 25, 52, 78, 174
Bruce, William C., 18
Brunk, Paul, 166
Bruno, Harry:
as aviation publicist, 22
Fokker survey, planning for, 22, 24
Eddie Musick, reflections on courage of; as "Cautious Ed"; airline safety vision of, 86
Trippe, working relationship with; recalls Key West to Havana plans of; recommends Musick to, 22, 24
Brush, Eugene, 310
Buckley, Harold, 16
*Buenos Aires*, Commodore aircraft, 76
Bundy, Harvey, 303
Burden, William, 259
Burdon, John (and Lady Burdon), 74
Bureau of Air Commerce, Department of Commerce, U.S., 69
Burma Road, 229, 238, 261, 266–67, 314

Busch, Noel, 3
Buskey, Henry, 73
Byrd, Richard E., 19, 24, 39

Caffery, Jefferson, 202–203
Calcutta-China Ferry Service, 267
Caldwell, Cy, 46–47
Campbell, Douglas, 193
Camp Colombia Field, Havana, 55, 66
Canaday, Harry, 117
Caniff, Milton, *Terry and the Pirates*, 230, 312
"Cannonball Operation" (*see* Pan Am Africa-Orient Division), 256, 292–94, 314
Canton, China, 110, 150–51, 154–56, 159, 244
Canton Island, 169–72, 182
*Cape San Juan*, U.S.S., 298
Carey, George Gibson, 79
Caribbean Sea, as ocean flying "Caribbean college," 113
Caribbean Survey (1929), 80–81
Carleton, "Tex," 308–09
Carrel, Alexis, 176
Casablanca Conference (1943), "Mr. Jones" cover; Pan Am preparations and flight; Roosevelt birthday, celebration of; 296–297
"Case 7, Condition A," 226, 242
Cavite, Manila Bay, 119, 238, 246–247
Central Aircraft Manufacturing Company (CAMCO), 232–233
Central America, 8, 13, 20, 26, 31–32, 37, 42, 45, 47, 52–54, 59, 67, 86, 219
"Central American Flight" (1924), 8
Central Pacific Route, 110, 115, 117, 165
Central Trust Company of China, 230
Certificate of Public Convenience and Necessity, 182
Chamberlain, Neville, 176
Chamberlin, Clarence, 39
"Chambers-Hoyt group," 43
Chambers, Reed M., 43
Chamorro people of Guam, 141, 244, 310
Chanin Building, New York, 47, 70, 89
Chapelain, A.M., 152
Chenea, Virgil, 73, 77

Chengtu, China, 151–54, 158, 172
Chennault, Claire:
 aerial combat theories of, 229–230
 American Volunteer Group, leader of; on "Flying Tigers" nickname, 231–232
 China, called to make confidential survey of China Air Force; trains American and Chinese pilots; reorganization of air forces; retirement from command, 230–31, 272, 308
 on CNAC, 257
 Doolittle Raid, criticism of mission command, 265
 the Hump, on operations and mastery of, 234–35
 Kunming, as base of operations, 230, 263, 308–09
 militarization, formation of China Air Task Force, Fourteenth Air Force; return to active duty as brigadier general, 273
 William Pawley, opinion of, 233
 supply problems, 273
 youth of, 229
Cheston, Charles, 305
Chicago World's Fair (1933-1934), 191
China Air Force (CAF), 156–58, 229–34, 308
China Air Task Force (CATF), Fourteenth Air Force, U.S., 273
China Airways Federal, Inc., 148
China-Burma-India (CBI) Theatre, 266
*China Clipper* (1936), 142
China National Aviation Corporation (CNAC), 110, 147–48, 154, 231, 286, 300, 314
China, Nine Power Treaty and Open Door Policy, 147
China Route No. 3, Shanghai to Canton, 110, 150–51, 154
Chin, Moon Fun:
 meets Doolittle, 263–264
 evacuation flights, 159
 the Hump, mastery of, 149, 235
 Japan's attack on Kai Tak Airport, witness of, 245
Chinn, Harold, 235

# INDEX 375

"Chosen instrument" policy, 318
Chrysler Building, New York, 3, 90, 117, 130, 157, 167, 215, 280
Chungking, China, 149, 151–53, 155–56, 158–60, 172, 229, 231, 235, 238, 263
Churchill, Winston Spencer, 2, 177, 197, 204–05, 211–13, 217, 297
Civil Aeronautics Act of 1938, 172–73, 179
Civil Aeronautics Board (CAB), 173, 175, 179, 181, 192, 207, 214, 224, 252, 259, 302
Clair, Kathleen, 45, 80, 168, 283
Clark, Rush S., 246–48, 310
Clay, Lucius, 217
Cleveland, Reginald, 292, 294, 300
"Clipper cocktail," 228
Clipper sailing ships, 113, 134
Clipper seaplanes, 3, 116
Clipper Special Missions, 251, 253, 257, 273, 306, 314
Cloud Club, Chrysler Building, 157, 178
Coates, P.C., 165
Coconut Grove, Miami, 82, 307
Coggeshall, Chester, 223
Colant, Ernest, 262, 295
Coli, François, 309
Colonial Airlines, 19
Colonial Air Transport (CAT), 19–20, 24–26, 42, 50, 55
Commerce Department, U.S., 51, 53, 69, 82, 114
Commercial Pacific Cable Company, 115
Commodore aircraft, 76, 82–83, 86–87, 159
"Community Company" (*see* Trippe, One Field), 57
*Compañia Mexicana de Aviación*, "CMA" (*see* "Mexicana"), 59–61
*Compania Nacional Cubana*, 200
*Compañía Nacional de Aviación Curtiss*, 148
Comstock mine, Whitney family holdings, 14
Condor (*see* Kondor Syndikat), 32–33, 53, 192, 201–3, 225
Cone, Howard, 296
Congo River, 257, 301, 304
Consolidated Aircraft Corporation, 70, 76
Consolidated Coronado (PB2Y3R), 294

Consolidated Instrument Company, 78
Contract Air Mail Act of 1925 (*see* "Kelly Act"), 18, 26
Cooke, John B., 242–43
Coolidge, Calvin, 25, 32, 36, 41, 51, 55, 70
Cooper, Don, 115, 117–18, 124–25
Cooper, John Cooper, Jr.:
  meets John Hambleton; 20
  international air law, expert of; negotiates landing rights in the Azores; on trans–Atlantic landing rights and negotiations, 156, 179, 186
  Leopoldville and strategic materials, 304
  as Pan Am vice president; signs secret ADP contract on behalf of airline, 200, 251, 280, 299
  as Trippe confidante, 80
Cooper, Merian C.:
  as combat pilot, World War I; shot down after bombing mission, 17
  as filmmaker, Chang, Flying Down to Rio, King Kong, 23, 38, 80
  Hambleton, friendship with; seminal Pan Am talks at Hambledune; on board of Federal Aviation Corporation; as pallbearer at Hambleton's funeral and reaction to friend's death; 16, 38–39, 78
  as Pan Am insider; early discussions with Trippe and Hambleton; airborne safety first policy discussion; describes Lindbergh/Hambleton Central America survey flights; Pan Am board of directors, member of; resignation from board; 61–63, 67, 79, 174
  Robert Scott, correspondence with; 271
Crosby, Harry, 41
Cross, Robert, 211
Crouch, Gregory, 148, 154–55
Crowley, Leo, 305
Crudge, Vernon, 218
Culbertson, Wally, 65
Culbert, Tom, 261
Cunningham, Winfield Scott, 236, 242, 249
Curtis, Cyrus, 171
Curtiss flying boats, 33
Curtiss-Wright Aircraft, 148–49

Dakar, West Africa, 198, 202, 209, 212
Daladier, Edouard, 176
Daley, Robert, 10, 24, 42, 149, 224, 178–79, 251
David, Noel, 39
Davis, Dwight F., 45
Davison, Frederick Trubee, 25, 52
Dawson, Andy, 261
Dean, Howard B.:
  Belgian Congo, uranium flight of, 306–07
  Pan Am, joins for wartime service; as part of inner circle; African Clipper flight; serious accident at 36th Street Airport, on scene of; 279–80, 304
  as Wall Street broker; 279
Dean, Nancy, 307
Defense Supplies Corporation, 193, 259
De Gaulle, Charles, 297
De-Germanization policy, 193–95, 197, 201, 259
Del Valle, Bill, 196
Deutsche Lufthansa (see Luft Hansa), 33, 53, 88, 140, 147, 176, 191–93, 202
Devereux, James P., 236
DH–4 Liberty Plane, 17
Dill, Marshall, 187
Dinjan-Kunming route, 268, 287–88
"Dinjan Mission," 269, 271
Dinner Key Airport, Miami, 82–83, 280, 296, 307
Direction Finder ("DF"), 66–67, 114–15, 123, 128–29, 132, 140, 145, 156
Donald, W.H., 158
Donohue, John, 132
Donovan, William J. "Wild Bill," 75–76, 82–83, 305
Doolittle, James H. "Jimmy," 263–65
"Doolittle Raid," 264–65
Dornier-Wal, flying boat, 32
Duff-Cooper, Alfred and Diana, 238
Duff, George, 306

Earhart, Amelia:
  Electra aircraft; goes missing while bound for Howland Island; 144–145, 164

St. Patrick's Day flight; coordination with PAA and Captain Musick; inspires Dorothy Kaucher, 143–144
36th Street Airport, at opening, 73
Eastern Air Traansport, 13, 18, 20
Einstein, Albert, 302
Eisenhower, David, 119
Elliott, George Blow, 18
Elott, John, 298
Elzey, Robert, 297–98
Emmons, D.C., 185
English Channel, 5, 315
English, Robert H., 297
*Essex*, British ship, 170

Fairchild, Sherman M., 13, 25, 43, 60
FAM 4 (Foreign Air Mail Route, Key West to Havana), 42–43
FAM 5 (Foreign Air Mail Route, Florida to Havana through Mexico to Panama Canal), 56, 86
Farley, James, 105, 130, 133–34
Farr, Louise, 9
Fatt, Robert, 67, 73
Fechet, James, 23, 37
Federal Aviation Agency, 34
Federal Aviation Corporation, 78–79
Federal Bureau of Investigation (FBI), 132, 221 Federal Writers Project, 182–183
Ferrying Command, 203, 210–11, 252, 256, 260, 262, 269, 272, 282, 289
Findlay, Tom, 166
Fisher, Colonel, commanding officer, France Field, Panama Canal, 75
Fisherman's Lake (or "Fish Lake"), Liberia, 216–18, 219–21, 261, 302
Fleet, Reuben H., 69–70
Fleming, Mr., 170–71
Florida Airways, 43
Florida East Coast Railway, 72
Flushing Bay, Long Island, 93, 95, 103
Flying Clippers, 2, 4, 113
Flying Tigers, (see "American Volunteer Group"), 231–34, 237, 242, 256–57, 266, 268, 273–74, 288

Fokker, Anthony:
 Federal Aviation Corporation, board member of, 78
 Fokker Tri-motor, reputation of; General Machado Fokker makes first scheduled flight to Cuba; Fokker christened General New by Mrs. Calvin Coolidge, 48, 55
 John Hambleton meets, 20
 John Leslie, as employee at Hasbrouck Heights plant, 63
 Lindbergh, flights in Fokker planes, 80
 as manufacturer of German war plane, 20
 manufacturing plant, Hasbrouck Heights, New Jersey, 20
 Philadelphia Rapid Air Transit Air Service, airline of, 66
 Pan Am, Fokker planes in fleet, 73, 86–87
 Priester, visits Hasbrouck Heights plant, 63
 at Roosevelt Field, witnesses Lindbergh flight to Paris, 39
 survey flight promotion, F–7; sets flight time record, Miami to Havana; rough landing, Key Largo, 22–4
 Trippe, negotiations with, 21–22
Fonck, René, 39
Ford Motor Company, Willow Run Plant, 282
Ford, Robert, 253–56, 298–99
Foreign Air Mail Act (1928), 55, 70
Foreign Air Mail routes, 47, 52–53, 56, 82
Foreign Economic Administration (FEA), 305
Foreign Missions Conference of North America, 306
*Fortune*, 11, 32, 44–45, 72, 75, 77, 105, 110, 266–67, 315
Fox Film Corporation, Movietone process, 39
France Field, Panama Canal Zone, 75
French, Howell, 47
Frye, Jack, 315–16

Gast, Bob, 150, 154–55
Gatty, Harold, 165, 170
Gelhaus, Fred, 46
*General Machado* (Fokker Trimotor), 49, 55
*General New* (Pan Am Fokker), 55
*Geographical Review*, 81
George, Harold, 252, 272, 280, 282–83, 287, 313
German Air Power, 28–29, 86, 176–77, 191
Gillespie, Eugene, 252, 259, 295
Gilmore, Voit, 216–17, 219–21, 223, 285
Gledhill, Franklin, 111, 215–17, 218–19, 271, 280, 291
Glenn L. Martin Company, 111, 213
Glover, Warner Irving, 25, 43–44, 51, 70, 77
Goddard, Robert, 175
Goeppert-Mayer, Maria, 307
Göering, Hermann, 176
Gold Coast Grill, Accra, 223
Golden Gate Bridge, 120, 134, 182–183
Golden Gate International Exposition (1939-1940), 182–84, 187
Gomes, General, air commander, Natal-Recife, Brazil, 203, 260
Goodwill Flight (1927-1928), 54–55
Goodwin, Doris Kearns, 204, 207–08, 296
"Goofy Goonie Club of Midway," 122
Governor's Island, "New York's first airport," 6
*Graf Zeppelin*, 191
Grant, David, 87–88
Gray, Almon, 298
Graybar Building, New York, 75, 84
Gray, Harold E.:
 Atlantic Division, chief pilot of, 181
 Boeing–314 Clipper test flights, 181
 *Capetown Clipper*, pilot of, "special operation order No. 6"; 256–57
 *Dixie Clipper* proving flight, pilot for homeward leg, 207
 instrument flying pioneer; as "new type of pilot," 61–62, 317
 Liberia, secret survey flight, 217–18
 Point of No Return flight, 142
Great Circle Route, 89, 92, 97
Greenland, 88–89, 95–97, 99–01, 104, 209
Greenlaw, Harvey, 233

Greenlaw, Olga S.:
    on "Old Man" Chennault, 234
    in wartime China; husband and AVG; transition to militarization, 233, 272
    CNAC, reflections on, 234
Green Spring Valley, Maryland (Hambleton family estate), 17
*The Grim Game* (1919), 23
Grooch, William S.:
    China, helps establish Pan Am affiliate in; as operations manager with Bixby; tragedy of wife and sons death; relationship with Bond; search for Gast; opinion of China air service; reassignment for colonization of Pacific bases, 109–10, 150, 154–55
    as Commodore pilot; at christening of Buenos Aires, 76–77
    Midway, lands at; unloading the North Haven, 122–23
    Eddie Musick, friendship with and reflections of, 67, 83
    Pan Am Pacific bases, expedition leader of, 118
    as NYRBA pilot, 76, 83
    Wake Island, lands at; proposes Peale as base; approves layout sketches; the shortest railroad in the world, 126–28
Grosvenor, Graham B., 251
Groves, Leslie, 303
Guam, 115, 118, 128, 131, 134, 137, 139–40, 156, 168, 242, 246, 250, 309
Guano Islands Act (1856), 170

Hall, Burton, 152
Hambleton, John A.:
    Aviation, vision of the future; separate air force, support of; Aircraft Board, testifies at request of Senator Bingham; as "trail-blazer," 17, 26, 36, 59, 77
    David Bruce, friendship with, 25
    Canal Zone flight, prepares fueling stops for, 73
    Merian Cooper, friendship with, 16, 80
    death of; statements of condolence, 78–79
    family roots; Hambleton & Company; Hambledune, 14, 18
    Federal Aviation Corporation, formation of, 78
    Florida, airway planning and exploring, 20–21
    Fokker aircraft, interest in; meets Anthony Fokker; F-7 survey flight, passenger of, 20, 22–24
    Foreign Air Mail service, lobbies for in Washington, 52
    Intercollegiate air meet, teammate with Trippe and Whitney, 11
    intercontinental Polar flight discussions, 38, 92
    Lindbergh, piloting duties with, Central American survey flights; co-pilot with on first Canal Zone airmail flight, 67, 73–75, 81
    Margaret "Peg" Blow, marriage to, 17–18
    Billy Mitchell, acolyte of; Mitchell court-martial trial, defense witness for, 33, 37
    Musick, co-pilot with on inspection tour flight, 66
    Pan American Airways; battle for FAM 4 route; with Trippe secretly negotiates landing rights in Havana; as vice president; "safety first" policy discussion with Trippe and Merian Cooper; Trippe-Hambleton-Whitney coalition and "Pan American Airways Musketeers," 13, 43–46, 62–63, 317
    Trippe, friendship with; invests in Colonial Air Transport; vision of CAT as domestic and international airline, 19, 25, 80
    Washington, political and military connections, 18, 52
    World War I; air combat experience; lieutenant and commander with 95th Aero Squadron; commander, 213th Squadron, 15–16
Hamilton, Bill, 242–43
Hamilton, John, 131, 142, 242, 244
Hamilton Standard propeller, 94
Hammel, Charles " Ridge," 274–78, 284

# INDEX

Hammer, Friedrich "Fritz," 30
Hangchow Bay, China, 154–55
Hankins, Frank, Jr., 293
Hankow, China, 148–149, 153, 155, 158–159, 229
Harriman, Averell W., 43
Harris, A.T., 262
Harris, Harold R., 291
Hart, Thomas C., 239
Harvard University, 10–11, 14, 215, 253
Hauptmann, Bruno Richard, 130
Havana, Cuba, 20, 22, 24–25, 32, 42, 44, 47–49, 51–52, 54–56, 57, 62, 66–68, 72–75, 77, 84, 86, 88, 313
Hawaii, 18, 35, 114–17, 124, 131, 136, 140, 181–82, 228, 238, 241–42
Haynes, Caleb V., 215, 268
Heliopolis Field, Cairo, 284
*Henderson*, observation ship (Mitchell aerial bombing demonstration), 34
Hermann, Hauptmann, 28–29
Hermes, British carrier, 93
Herrera, Enrique Olaya, 84, 194
Higgs, Frank "Dude":
   Milton Caniff, reflections on, 312
   CNAC, first flight with; evacuation flights to China's interior, 231, 246
   as model for Dude Hennick character, 230
   as trainer for Chinese air force cadets, 231
Himalayas, 149, 234–35, 268, 278, 284
Hiroshima, Japan, 307–9
Hitler, Adolf, 2, 85–86, 176–77, 192–4, 297, 302
Holbrook, Roy, 230
Homan (mechanic, 1933 Lindbergh survey), 97
Hong Kong, 113, 115, 119, 149, 156, 158–60, 164, 179, 229, 231, 233–34, 237–38, 245–46, 264, 268
Honolulu, 115, 117–18, 121–22, 135–36, 143–44, 165, 250–51, 253
Hoover, Herbert, 12, 25, 52, 56–57, 71, 76–77, 82–83, 313
Hoover, Lou Henry (Mrs. Herbert Hoover), 111

Hopkins, Harry, 204, 208, 296
Horton, Edward, 264–65
Houdini, Harry, 22–23
Howley, Jim, 294
Hoxsey, Arch, 64
Hoyt, Richard, 25, 43–5
Hsiang, Liu, 151–3
Hudson-Fulton Celebration, 5–8
Huebsch, Ken, 248
Hughes, Charles Evans, 55
Hughes, Howard, 315–16
Hull, Cordell, 105, 116–17, 170–71, 192–93, 237, 303
"Hump" (Himalayas), 234–35, 267–68, 273, 275, 286, 288–90, 300, 312, 314,
Humphrey, Woods, 101–02
Hutchings, W., 277, 157
Hutton, E.F., 157

Iceland, 88, 97–99, 100–01
Imperial Airways, 88, 101, 104, 165, 179–180, 209, 213, 215, 262,
Imperial Atlantic Airways, 180
India-China Wing, U.S., 288–89
Ingalls, David "Crock," 25, 215
Inter-American Airways (Von Bauer airline charter), 32
Interior Department, U.S., 170–71
"Instrument flying" (*see* "Blind flying"), 61–64, 66–67, 137, 139, 317
"Instrument of the nation," 4, 53
Intercontinent Aviation, Inc., 148
Interdepartmental Aviation Committee, U.S. (1927), 51–52
Inuit, 89, 95-100
Ireland, 180, 185, 186, 252

Jackson, Ronald, 132
*Jacksonville Journal*, 23
Jacoby, Annalee, 286
Japan, 18, 93, 110, 116, 119, 145, 147, 151, 154–56, 158, 160, 164, 169, 171, 183, 202, 229–30, 237, 239, 245, 250, 263–65, 267, 269, 297, 297, 309, 310–11
Jarboe, Wilson Turner, 97, 100, 117, 124, 134, 136, 139

*Jelling*, floating base camp, North Atlantic Lindbergh survey (1933), 94–00
Jenkins, Douglas, 193
Johnson, Gerald W., 17
Johnson, S. Paul, 314–15
Josephson, Matthew, 22, 71, 113–14, 119, 147, 178,
Jouett, Jack, 27, 43
Junkers F–13, 30
Junkers, Hugo, 28–29, 31
Just, Erik, 149–50

Kadoorie, Elly, 156
Kadoorie, Horace, 156
Kadoorie, Lawrence, 156
Kaemmerer, Werner, 30–31
Kahn, Gustave, 249
Kai-shek, Chiang, 145, 156–59, 169, 229, 232, 235, 266–67, 286
Kai-shek, Madame Chiang, 230–31
Kai Tak Airport, Kowloon, H.K., 245–46
Kaucher, Dorothy:
    Amelia Earhart, witnesses St. Patrick's Day flight of; as inspiration, 144
    *China Clipper*, witnesses historic Pacific flight, 134–35
    education of; as pioneering female aviation reporter, 135
    fascination with flight; among "air pilgrims" at Pan Am Pacific flights, 162–63
    as passenger on *Hawaii Clipper* Pacific flight, 163
    Wake Island; reflections on; as "island of my special dreams"; on history and colonization of, 128–29, 163–64, 311
Kellogg, Frank B., 25, 52, 84–85, 194
Kelly Act of 1925 (*see* Contract Air Mail Act of 1925), 18, 26
Kelly, M. Clyde, 18
Kennedy, Joseph, 176
Kent, Walter, 160
Kershner, Felix W., 258
Keys, Clement M., 148
Key West, 46, 49, 51

Key West-Havana route, 20, 24–25, 42, 44, 47–48, 52, 55–56, 62, 86, 313
Khartoum, Anglo-Egyptian Sudan, 209, 213–14, 216, 218, 221, 224, 251, 257, 284
Kilner-Lindbergh Board, 178
Kilner, Walter G., 18, 36, 178
King, Ernest J., 120, 298
King, George, 134
Kingman Reef, 165
Kinney, John, 235–37, 242–44, 148–49, 30–11
Kisaka, Yositane, 202
Kitty Hawk, N.C., 6
Klein, Julius, 30
Knox, Seymour, H., 43
Koch, Lauge, 96, 99
Kondor Syndikat (*see* "Condor"), 32–33, 53–54, 192, 201–03, 225
*Koninklijke Luchtvaart Maatschappij Voor Nederland an Kolonien* (KLM) (*see* "Royal Dutch Airline"), 46, 49
Kraigher, George, 61–62, 217
Krupnick, Jon E., 165
Kuhn, George, 118–119, 123, 171
Kung, H.H., 232
Kunming, China, 229–230, 234–35, 245, 257, 261, 263, 267–69, 272, 287–88, 308–09
Kurusu, Saburo, 237
*Kweilin* (CNAC DC–2), 159–160, 169, 229

La Farge, Oliver, 283–284, 300
La Guardia Field (or La Guardia Marine Air Terminal), 207, 237, 253, 256
La Guardia, Fiorello, 184–85
Lampert, Florian, 36
Landowne, Zachary, 35–36
Lands End, San Francisco, 134–35
Langewiesche, Wolfgang, 67
*La Niña* (Fairchild FC–2), 46
LaPorte, A.E., 184, 207
Lashio, Burma, 229, 267, 271
Latin American Division, Pan Am, 84, 198, 280
Lax, C.E., 277
Leach, Eugene, 253–54
Leary, William, Jr., 155, 289–90

# INDEX

Le Bourget airfield, 40
Leighton, B.C., 232
LeMay, Curtis E., 215
Lend-Lease (H.R. 1776), 204, 207–08, 213–14, 225–26, 260, 262, 268, 286
Leonard, Edmund, 17
Leopoldville, Belgian Congo, 3, 224–25, 237, 255–57, 301–03, 304–06,
Leslie, John C.:
    Africa, security concerns for "off record" survey flights, 217–18
    Atlantic Division, head of; greets *Pacific Clipper* at La Guardia Airport; on FDR Casablanca flight, 141, 180, 256, 296–97
    Fokker plant; as worker; meets Priester, 63
    Pan Am history; On Trippe, Hambleton, and Whitney; on FAM 4 route; on Priester's relationship with manufacturers; on Pan Am's secret relationship with SCADTA, 15, 42, 44, 46, 61, 85, 194
    as Pan Am Pacific Division engineer; oversees testing for Sikorsky Pacific survey flights; in charge of engineering and maintenance of Pacific bases; works out "bugs" in Martin Clippers, 114, 117, 141
Leuteritz, Hugo:
    Adcock Direction Finder, Pan Am capital appropriation for, 114–15
    Colonial Air Transport radio work for, 24
    Pan Am Chief Communications Engineer; meets Trippe; starts Radio Division in Key West, 49–50
    Radio Direction Finders, develops; pilot Musick on test program for radio communications, works with; compact radio set, development of; trans-oceanic radio communications, development of, and Pan Am control of, 66–67, 87–88, 118
    Lindbergh survey flights, organizes radio communications for, 93
    RCA career; as radio pioneer, 49–50
Leyte Island, 309
Libby, Justin, 143

Lidz, Cookie, 223
*Life*, 3, 173, 224, 237
Lindbergh, Anne Morrow:
    Atlantic Survey of 1933; as radio operator and co-pilot; Greenland, reflections of; on "life in the air"; works with *Jelling*, 92, 96–97, 99–00, 317
    as daughter of Dwight Morrow; learns of father's death, 51, 93
    diary entries of; as popular writer, 94, 96, 100, 102
    England, life in exile; at Long Barn; observes "cloud of danger" over Europe; visits Nazi Germany with husband, 175, 177
    kidnapping and murder of first child; on the "hell" of public life; the Buddha parable, 94, 104
    Charles Lindbergh, meets and marries; on Lindbergh in Paris, 51, 75, 102
    Orient survey flight of 1931; views flood conditions, 92–93
    Sirius test flights, 92
    survey flights, Caribbean and Central American survey and aerial archeological expedition (1929), 80–81
Lindbergh, Charles Augustus, Jr., 92–93
Lindbergh, Charles A. "Slim":
    air tour of continental United States, 1927, 51
    American aviation, promotion of, 41
    America First crusade; enmity with President Roosevelt; resignation from Air Corps; wartime service, 204, 279, 281–82
    Army Air Corps, colonel in, 178
    Atlantic commercial flight, vision of and predictions for, 139
    Atlantic survey of 1933; meets Dr. Koch and Danish expedition; "Dear Juan" letters; praises *Jelling* crew, 97–02
    Sirius named the *Tingmissartoq*; meets in London with Woods Humphrey of Imperial Airways; vision of high-speed and high altitude land planes, 96, 101

Lindbergh, Charles A. "Slim" (*continued*)
  Harold Bixby, supporter of *Spirit of St. Louis* flight; introduces to Trippe, 147
  Canal Zone, pilots first official airmail flight to, 73–75
  Caribbean and Central America survey flights, 50–51
  England, life in exile; work with Goddard and Carrel; eyewitness to war developments in Europe; inspects German air facilities; reports on German air power; return to America; provides intelligence to "Hap" Arnold; finances, management of by Dwight Morrow at J.P. Morgan, 51, 175–77
  "Good Will" survey flight; Havana stop for Sixth Annual Pan American Conference, 54–55
  kidnapping and death of first born, 93–94
  Kilner-Lindbergh Board, work for, 178
  "Lindbergh law," Foreign Air Mail Act (1928); Lindbergh and Pan Am as catalysts for advancing American aviation, 55–56
  Lockheed Aircraft, works with on development of prototype Lockheed 8 Sirius; with wife sets transcontinental flying record, 89, 92
  Morrow family; marries Anne Morrow, 92
  news media, aversion to and problems with, 94, 100, 177–78
  Orient survey flight (1931), 92–93
  Pan Am; as chair of technical committee; at dedication of 36th Street Airport; explores transoceanic flying ideas; helps develop next generation flying boat; completes proving flight in first S-42; inspects *China Clipper*, 70–71, 73, 87, 112, 116, 130
  radio, interest in for aviation, 24–25
  *Spirit of St. Louis* flight to Paris; takeoff from Roosevelt Field; landing at Le Bourget airfield; celebrated in New York; meets Trippe to discuss new airline; retires *Spirit of St. Louis*, 40–02, 89
  Vilhjalmur Stefansson, consults with on freezing weather flying, 89
  surveys with Anne Morrow Lindbergh; aerial archeological expedition of 1929; "personal ownership rule," 89, 94
  Trippe, meetings with; Caribbean survey flight with; opinion of, 42, 80–81, 130–31, 178, 281
Lindbergh, Land, 175
*Linee Aeree Transcontinentali Italiane* (LATI), 192, 201–02, 259–60
Lisbon, 33, 156, 185–86, 192, 207–08, 316
*Lloyd Aéreo Boliviano* (LAB), 193
Lockheed Aircraft factory, Burbank, California, 89, 197, 211
Lockheed Constellation ("Connie"), 315–16
Lockheed 8 Sirius (*see* "*Tingmissartoq*"), 89
Lodeesen, Marius "Lodi," 207, 280, 306–07
Loening, Grover C., 43, 77–78, 114, 167
Logan, Robert, 97–98
London, 1–2, 101, 173, 175–76, 205, 207, 212, 238, 303–04
Long Barn, England, 175
Long Island Airways (LIA), 11–13
*Los Angeles* (Navy dirigible), 24
Los Angeles International Air Meet (January 10-20, 1910), 84
Los Baños internment camp, Philippines, 310
Lotus Lake, China, 93
Lovett, Robert A., 268, 281
Luce, Clare Boothe, 228, 237–40
Luce, Henry, 157, 237
Lueder, Karl, 122, 217–18
Luft Hansa (*see* "Deutsche Lufthansa"), 33
Luftwaffe, 176–78, 202
Lunghwa Airport, Shanghai Municipal Field, 148–149
*Lusitania*, 6

Macao, Portuguese possession, 156
**MacArthur**, Douglas, 239, 247, 309
MacCracken, William P.:

as official at Commerce Department, 51, 69
as dignitary at opening of 36th Street Airport, 73
NYRBA, board chairman of; plots coup to depose O'Neil; negotiations with Trippe; on NYRBA merger with Pan Am, 82–83
Machado, Gerardo, 22, 24, 44–45
MacLean, Fred, 166
Maersk Line, 118
Magdalena River, Colombia, 26, 30
Malby's Globe, 3, 11, 90, 178–79, 224
Mallory, W.L. "Slim," 60
Manhattan Project, 302–04
Manila Bay, Manila, 119, 138, 238–39
Manila Hotel, 239–40, 247
Manning, Harry, 144
Marine Corps, U.S., 2, 65, 73–74, 201, 235–36, 311
Marine Fighter Attack Squadron, 236
Marshall, George C., 199, 286, 308
Marshall Islands, 144, 309
Martin, Glenn L., as aircraft manufacturer; bids for Pan Am "miracle" Clipper contract, 111
Martin M-130, 111–112, 117, 130, 250
Martin M-130 *China Clipper*, 130–2, 133–5, 138, 141–2, 163, 166, 172, 298, 301, 306–307, 316,
Martin M-130 *Hawaii Clipper*, 140, 143–144, 163, 168–169, 172, 181,
Martin M-130 *Philippine Clipper*, 140, 172, 236, 242, 244, 297–298, 316
Mason, George Grant, 43–44, 50
"Master of Ocean Flying Boats," 63–64, 292
Mayflower Hotel, Washington, D.C., 47, 83, 280
McAdoo, William, 133
McBride, Donald, 273–74
McCann, Don, 310
McDonnell, Edward O., 43
McGlohn, R.H., 292–93
McRae (First Officer with Robert Ford), 298
McVitty, Edward W., 256

Meacham Airport, Key West, Florida, 46, 55
Medellín, Colombia, 32
Mellon, Andrew W., 25, 52
Mellon, Richard, 52, 78, 174
Mellon, William L., 52
*Memphis*, battleship, 41, 296–97
Merriam, Frank, 133
Merritt, Raymond, 73, 75
Meuse-Argonne offensive (1918), 16–17
Mexicana (*see* "Compañia Mexicana de Aviación), 59–61, 200
Mexico City, 56, 60–62
Midway Island, 115–16, 118–19, 121–24, 128–29, 131, 134, 136–37, 140–41, 162–63, 171, 219, 239, 244, 310
*Midway News*, 167
Milch, Erhard, 176, 191–92
"Militarization" of wartime air forces, 271–73, 279, 283–84, 291, 314
Military Appropriation Act (1940), 197–99
Military Policy Committee, U.S., 303
Miller, Leland W., 260
Milling, Thomas, 7
"Millionaires Unit" (The First Yale Unit), 10, 215
Mills Field, San Francisco Airport, 296, 310
Mitchel Field, Long Island, 42
Mitchell, William L. "Billy":
Air Power demonstration; bombing demonstration to sink the Ostfriesland, 34
Air Power philosophy and crusade; criticism of "Air Trust" and DH-4 Liberty planes; supporters and acolytes, 8, 17–18, 28, 33, 79
court martial; aftermath of, 36–38, 43
death of, 272
Hambleton, recalls air combat report; tribute statement on death of; Mitchell, William L. "Billy" statement on death of Landowne and Rodgers, 15–16, 36, 79
World War I, as leader of American Air Forces; commands air attack for Meuse–Argonne offensive, 14–16

Mitsubishi Navy attack bombers, 243
Mittag, A.A., 122
Mitten, Thomas D., 12
Monrovia, West Africa, 3, 217–18, 306
Montgomery, Bernard "Monty," 283–85
Montgomery, John, 27, 43–44, 50, 76, 82
Morgan, J.P., 25, 36, 40–41, 48, 51,
Morgan, Stockely, 304
Morgan, Thomas, 178, 185
Morrow, Dwight W.:
   as Ambassador to Mexico, 51
   family; announces daughter's engagement to Lindbergh, 51, 75
   Lindbergh, handles finances for, 51
   U.S. aviation policy, involvement in; backs Trippe; as Aircraft Board chair, 25, 36
Morrow, Elisabeth, 93
Moses, George, 53
Moss, W.W., 298
Moulton, William, 258
Mullahey, Bill, 121–23, 127, 311
Munich Pact, 176–177
Musick, Cleo Livingston, 64, 66, 70, 131, 166, 168
Musick, Edwin C. "Eddie":
   aerial navigation, student of, 113
   Aeromarine Airways, chief pilot for; rescues flying boat pilot Culbertson and passengers, 65–66
   Harry Bruno, on "Cautious Ed," 66
   as daredevil pilot; air shows; solves mystery of air show crashes, 64–65
   Amelia Earhart, helps coordinate their respective St. Patrick's Day flights to Honolulu, 143–44
   Hambleton, 1928 inspection flight with, 66
   Dorothy Kaucher's Pacific flight, Clipper captain for, 163
   Cleo Livingston, marriage to; Cleo's concerns for husband's health, 64, 66, 166
   Los Angeles International Air Meet of January 10–20, 1910, attendance at, 64
   navigator on *General Machado*, inaugural service for Key West-Havana, 48, 55
   NYRBA, competition with; facilitates absorption of NYRBA crews into Pan Am, 70, 83
   Pacific route pioneer; leads survey flights; stays the course past "Point of No Return" on first round-trip Pacific survey flight; Lindbergh gives Musick the *China Clipper* demonstration flight; inaugural Pacific airmail flight to Manila, ferries *China Clipper* to San Francisco Bay, flies under Bay Bridge under construction, greets President Quezon at Malacanan Palace, 114, 117–18, 124–25, 129–31, 133–34, 136–40
   Pan Am; promoted chief pilot at; pilots inaugural flight to San Juan in 1929; as "Master of Ocean Flying Boats"; as Caribbean sea "short-cut" pioneer; Priester's choice for chief ocean flyer; inspects Sikorsky flying boat; South Pacific survey flights, 57, 63–64, 86–87, 110, 112, 165–68
   radio communications, support for; works with Leuteritz on communications system; reputation for maintenance and safety; Pan Am colleagues, respect for, 67, 131–32, 141–43, 317
   *Samoan Clipper* crash, 66, 167–68
   as *Time* cover subject; aversion to "big-time publicity," 131
Mussolini, Benito, 176
Myitkyina, Burma, 263–64, 267, 269, 271, 300

Nagaski, Japan, 309
Nagumo, Chuichi, 241, 242
Nanking, China, 93, 145, 147, 151, 153, 158
Nast, Condé, 157
Natal, Brazil, 186, 192, 201–03, 210–12, 214, 220, 225, 237, 255–56, 259–61, 294, 304
Nationalist government, China, 145, 147–48, 172, 229–30, 266
Naval Air Transport Service (NATS), 219, 244, 294–99, 302, 314

# INDEX

Naval Historical Center, 145
Navy Bureau of Aeronautics, U.S., 282
Navy Department, U.S., 36, 119, 202
Navy Department Office of Naval
  Intelligence, U.S., 202
N.B.C. radio network, 172
Neutrality Act, 185, 198, 214, 259
Newfoundland, 33, 95, 98, 179–80, 185, 197, 209
New Guinea, 144
New, Harry, 26, 32, 43, 55, 73
New Haven Railroad, 26
*New Horizons*, 187, 229, 231, 246, 255–56, 258–59, 270, 288, 292, 302
Newport, Bill, 141–42
Newton, Wesley Phillips, 85–86
New York City, 5–6, 8, 41, 75, 115, 117, 184, 225
*New York Herald Tribune*, 172
New York Life Insurance Building, 79
*New York News*, 294
New York Public Library, 12
New York, Rio & Buenos Aires Line ("NYRBA"), 69–70, 75–77, 81–84, 110, 150
*New York Times*, 9, 133
New York World's Fair, 1939-1940, 175, 182–84, 187
New York World's Fair, Aviation Day, 1939, 182, 184–85
New Zealand, 143, 158, 165–66, 170–71, 181, 183, 228, 253, 256
New Zealand survey flight, 143, 165
Nichols, Ruth, 39
95th Aero Squadron, John Hambleton in WWI, 16
Niblack, Albert P., 169–70
Noonan, Fred, 113, 117–118, 124, 134, 136–39, 143–45
North Africa, 2, 198, 213, 221, 226, 267, 283, 285, 293
North American Aviation Company, 233
  North Atlantic, 88–89, 94, 184–85, 209–10
Northcliffe, Alfred, 33
Northern Greenland Route, 89

*North Haven*, freight ship, 118, 120–24, 126–28, 140
Northrop, Jack, 89
Northwest Airlines, 104
Nosaki, Masakatsu, 203
Nouméa, New Caledonia, 171, 244, 253–54
Nungesser, Charles, 39

O'Connor, Basil, 60
Odell, Leroy L., 13, 20–22, 117–18
Office of Strategic Services (OSS), 305–06
Olds, Robert, 203, 260, 262, 282
"One Field" (*see* "Community Company"), 57
O'Neill, Ralph A.:
  animosity with Trippe and Pan Am, 76–77, 84
  Bevier and Montgomery, problems with, 76, 82–83
  as Boeing sales agent in Latin America; 69
  Consolidated Commodore, as state-of-the-art flying boat; reaction to Trippe at christening ceremony of *Buenos Aires*, 76–77
  President Coolidge, White House meeting with, 70
  "Wild Bill" Donovan, as connection to the president, 74–76, 82
  Foreign Air Mail Act; need for foreign airmail contract, 82
  *Fortune* reports on NYRBA success; assets of Commodore planes, routes, and Dinner Key base, 75, 83
  Assistant Postmaster General Glover, meets with, 70
  MacCracken, conflicts with, 82–83
  New York, Rio & Buenos Aires Line (NYRBA), inspiration and vision for; begins formation and as president of; works with Reuben H. Fleet and James Rand; Pan Am purchase of, 75, 83–84
  Pierson, as asset, 76, 82–83
  Stock Market crash of 1929, effect on airline, 81–82
  WW I combat ace, 69

Orient Survey, 1931, 89, 93, 110
Ormsbee, Frank, 75
Orteig Prize, 39
Orteig, Raymond, 39
*Ostfriesland*, demonstration ship (Mitchell aerial bombing), 34

Pago Pago Harbor, American Samoa, 165–69
*Panair do Brasil* (Pan Am affiliate), 199–200, 225
Panama Canal Zone, 8, 27, 32, 38, 51–53, 56, 68, 73–75, 84, 88, 191, 195, 198
Pan Am Africa-Orient Division (*see* "Cannonball Operation"), 291–94, 314
Pan Am Atlantic Division, 143, 173, 180–81, 218, 251, 253, 256, 296, 299
Pan Am Board of Directors, 46, 53, 78–80, 105, 113–14, 117, 167, 173–74, 186, 199
Pan Am Central Pacific Survey, 110, 115, 117, 165
Pan Am Divisions, 50, 60–61, 84, 87, 114–15, 125, 129, 143, 173, 180–82, 218, 221, 241, 250–51, 253, 256, 280, 291–92, 294–96, 299, 302, 310–11, 314
Pan American Air Ferries, 213–15, 251, 284, 292
Pan American Airports Corporation, 200
Pan American Airways-Africa, Ltd. (Pan-Africa Corps and PAA-Africa, Ltd), 213–16, 219, 221, 252, 261, 268–71, 274, 283–85
Pan American Airways East Greenland Expedition, 1932-1933, 89
"Pan American Airways System," 60, 115, 206
Pan-American Grace Airways ("Panagra"), 56, 193
Pan American International Airport, Miami (*see* "36th Street Airport"), 73
Pan Am Orient survey, 1931, 89, 93, 110
Pan American Pacific-Alaska Division, 310–11
Pan Am Pacific Division, 114, 125, 129, 180, 182, 241, 295

Pan Am radio stations, 88, 124, 137, 141, 156, 180
Paris, 5, 39–41, 48, 51, 102, 171
Passage, John, 270
Patrick, Mason, 21, 23, 36
Patterson, Robert, 305, 308
Paulhan, Louis, 64
Pawley, Edward, 232
Pawley, William Douglas, 148, 232–33
Payne, Robert, 258
Peale (isle of Wake Island), 115, 126–28, 236, 242–43, 248, 311
Pearl Harbor, 131, 136, 140, 157, 238, 241–42, 242
Peking, China, 151, 156, 159, 164, 266
Perisphere, New York World's Fair (*see* "Trylon"), 184, 187
*Pernambuco*, NYRBA S-38, 81
Pershing, George, 18
Philadelphia Rapid Transit Air Service, 66
Philippines, 5, 116, 119, 130, 133–34, 138, 168–69, 182, 238–41, 246–47, 250, 310
Pierson, Lewis E., 76, 83
Pitcairn, Harold, 21
Pogue, L. Welch, 306
Poindexter, John, 255
Poindexter, Joseph P., 133
"Point of No Return," 125, 142
Ponds, George, 22
Porter, Mr., Navy construction officer, 122, 127
Port of Trade Winds (also "Clipper Cove"), Treasure Island, 182
Portuguese Guinea, 180, 186, 206, 219
Port Washington, Long Island, 180, 184–85
Post Office, U.S., 8, 13, 19, 42, 46, 56, 60, 70, 73, 82, 208, 293, 305
Post, Wiley, 165
Powers, Ed, 310
Pratt & Whitney engines, 111–12
Pratt Institute, Brooklyn, New York, 49
Priester, André A.:
    background of; early life; with Royal Dutch Airlines, 49

Lockheed Constellation, as a "new generation" airplane, 316
flying boats, opinion of, 49
on "instrument flying," dispatches Gray to new Miami airport; supports instrument flying in Brownsville; creates rank of "Master of Ocean Flying Boats," 62–64
Musick, support for; reacts to death of, 64, 112, 167
Pan Am, as chief engineer; as first employee and "face of the company"; hires John Leslie; on technical committee with Trippe and Lindbergh; sends Grooch to China; works out logistics of Central Pacific airway, 46, 48–49, 63, 70, 77, 109–111, 114–17
radio communications, support for; hires Leuteritz; supports DF development, 49, 66–67
research and development, philosophy of, 63, 316
safety philosophy of; 62–63, 222
Pryor, Samuel F., Jr., 251
Putnam, Paul A. 236, 242, 244

Quezon, Manuel Luis, 134, 139

Radio Corporation of America (RCA), 49–50
Ralph, Fred S., 245–46
Rand, James, 70, 75, 81
Raugust, Waldo, 244, 249, 310
Read, Albert C., 33
Reid, Frank, 36
Remington Rand Company, 70
Republic of China, Nationalist government:
　Generalissimo Chiang Kai-shek, leader of, 145, 157, 159, 229–30, 232, 235, 266–67, 286
　Eurasia and China National Aviation Corporation airlines, stake in; CNAC operations in Nationalist territory; Communist insurgency, 145, 147–48, 153, 172, 266
　Holbrook, as government confidant, 230
　Nanking, as seat of power; Chungking as new capital, 145, 147–48, 151, 229
Reynolds, Harry, 64, 166
Reynolds, Jim, 81–82
Rice, Hamilton A., 31
Rickenbacker, Eddie, 33, 37, 43, 289
Rihl, George, 60, 196, 280
RKO Radio Pictures, 23, 79
Roberts Field, Liberia, 217, 219, 221
Roberts, Henry W., 115
Robertson Aircraft Corporation, 21, 24
Robertson, William Bryan, 21
Rockaway Beach (LIA maintenance yard), 12, 13
Rockefeller, William A., 18–19, 25, 43
Rodgers, John, 35–36
Rogers, Ginger, 23
*Rogerville*, 136
Roig, Harold J., 193
Rommel, Erwin, 2, 210, 222–23, 226, 284, 287
Roosevelt, Eleanor, 181, 204
Roosevelt, Elliott, 209, 212
Roosevelt Field, Long Island, 39
Roosevelt, Franklin Delano, 2–3, 60, 104, 116–17, 134, 139, 170, 181, 185–86, 197–98, 203, 204–06, 208–12, 214–15, 226, 251, 267–68, 281, 283, 289–90, 296–97, 303, 305, 308, 310
Rosbert, C. Joseph, 274–78
Ross, Emory, 306
Rossi, Angelo, 168
Rowe, Basil, 292–93
Royal Aeronautical Society (Twenty-Ninth Wilbur Wright Memorial Lecture), 1, 212
Royal Air Force (RAF), 2, 209–10, 219, 231–32, 254, 262, 268, 284–85, 293
Royal Canadian Air Force, 209
Royal Dutch Airlines (*see* "*Koninklijke Luchtvaart Maatschappij Voor Nederland an Kolonien,*" or KLM), 46, 49, 88, 102
Rummel, George, 150
Russell, Charles, 119, 122, 127

Ryckmans, Pierre, 304
Rymill, J.R., 89

"Safety First," Pan Am policy, 63, 66
Salomon, August Andrée, 96
San Francisco, 35, 112–14, 118, 132, 158, 166, 168–69, 181, 187, 202, 230, 244, 250, 296–97, 310, 314
San Francisco Airport (Mills Field), 296, 310
San Francisco Bay, 72, 119, 133
San Francisco-Oakland Bay Bridge, 120, 182
Santos, Eduardo, 194, 196
Schildhauer, Clarence "Dutch," 115–16, 141
Schnurbusch, Wilhelm, 30
Schoedsack, Ernest, 38
Schunemann, Carl, 51
*Scientific American*, 149
Scofield, F.H., 51
Scott, Emil, 230, 245
Scott, Robert, 268, 271
Seabright, New Jersey, 8–9
Selective Training and Service Act of 1940, 279
Selfridge, Lieutenant Thomas L., 7
Sellers, Cecil G., 149, 155, 166–67
Sewell, E.G., 73
Shanghai, China, 93, 110, 119, 148–52, 154–57, 159, 162, 164, 229, 263, 312
Sharon, Ohio, 35
Sharp, Charles L. "Chuck," 156–57, 159, 235, 245
Sharp, Frederick, 217, 219
Shea, "Hank," 196,
*Shenandoah* (Navy dirigible), 35–36
Sherman, Dallas, 269–71
Shrum, Dwight L., 285
Sikorsky, Igor:
  as aircraft manufacturer; tests first amphibian plane; works with Pan Am technical committee; develops "miracle" flying boat; shows Musick "the ship of his dreams;" Sikorsky Clipper as Pacific survey plane, 47, 53, 70, 111–12
Sikorsky S-38, 57, 74, 80
Sikorsky S-40, *American Clipper*, 111

Sikorsky S-42 *Hong Kong Clipper II*, 238, 245
Sikorsky S-42, *Pan American Clipper*, 118–19, 124, 129, 136
Sikorsky S-42B, *Pan American Clipper II/ Samoan Clipper*, 143, 166, 170, 172, 182
Sikorsky trimotor, 39
Simonds, George S., 51
Sims, Harold, 202–03
Shinkolobwe mine, Katanga Province, Belgian Congo, 303
Sino-Japanese War (1937), 155–56
Slessor, John, 232–33
Smith, C.R., 282–83, 288
Smith, Donald, 258
Smith, Donald F., (NATS director), 298
Smith, Frederic, 299
Smith, James H., 292
Smith, Jim, 217
Smith, Truman, 176
"Snafu Club," Accra, 223
Snow, George, 73
Snow, Gilda, 185
Snyder, E.J., 61
*Sociedad Colombo-Alemana de Transportes Aéreos* (SCADTA), 26–27, 29–32, 37, 51–54, 84–86, 192–196
*Sociedad Ecuatoriana de Transportes Aéreos* (SEDTA), 193
Soong, T.V., 156–57, 267, 300
South America, 2–3, 26, 29, 32, 47, 53, 56–57, 69–70, 72, 83, 85–86, 89, 94, 144, 150, 191–93, 197–198, 207, 219, 225, 250–51, 258
South Atlantic Ferrying Operation, 209, 211
Southeastern Air Lines, 43
*Southern Seas*, Curtis yacht, 171
South Pacific, 165, 172
"South Seas cocktail," 228
Spaatz, Carl "Tooey," 27, 33, 37, 43, 45, 178, 272
Spanish Civil War (1936), 176
"Special operation order No. 6," 256
Spencer, Lorillard, 13
Sperry-Gyroscope Company, 94, 178

*Spirit of St. Louis*, 40, 42, 50–51, 89, 120, 139, 147
Stackpole, Ralph, 183
State Department, U.S., 8, 32, 42, 51–53, 77, 85, 88, 160, 170, 192–94, 198, 202, 211, 257, 259, 303–06
Steele, John, 122, 213
Steers, John, 254–56
Stefansson, Vilhjalmur, 89–90, 97
Stettinius, Edward R., 48
Stettinius, Elizabeth "Betty" (Mrs. Juan Trippe), 48
Stevenson, Robert Louis, 182
Stickrod, John, 166
Stilwell, Joseph W., 266–67, 269, 286–87, 289–90, 194
Stimson, Henry Lewis, 33, 198, 200, 210–11, 251, 281, 292, 303
Stinson Detroiter, 152
Stock Market Crash, 1929, 82, 85
Stoeger, Don, 270
Stout, William, 12
Struthers & Dean, 279, 281
Sullivan, Robert Oliver Daniel ("R.O.D."), 117, 129, 134, 237, 316
Swanson, Claude, 116, 119, 121, 131
Sweet, Harold, 246
Symington, J. Fife, Jr., 38, 273, 304–06
Szechwan Province, China, 151–52

Taft, Robert, 204
Takoradi Route:
  Hap Arnold memo, "Ferry Plan-Takoradi-Cairo"; Arnold memo to Roosevelt on "Takoradi-Cairo-Ceylon Ferry Service," 2, 209– 10, 267–68
  British base on Africa's Gold Coast, 209–10
  British Overseas Airway Corporation, attempts to open old airway, 209, 213
  Gledhill survey of, 218–19
  as U. S. supply line from Brazil; as link to Western Desert campaigns; PAA-Africa evacuation missions, 2–3, 209, 210 2014–15, 223–24, 226, 257, 283–85, 314
*Tampa Telegraph*, 24

Taylor, C.H., 50
Taylor, George W. "Bill," 120–23, 126–29, 137, 139–40, 143, 167, 241, 285, 309
Terletzky, Leo, 168
Terry, Juanita, 9
Terry, Juan Pedro, 9
Terry, Lucy Adeline, 8
Thach, Robert, 13, 20, 43,
36th Street Airport (*see* "Pan American International Airport"), 73, 280–81, 293
Tietjen, Albert, 31
Tilton, Jack, 129
*Time*, 3, 129, 131, 139, 186, 197, 210, 214–15, 225, 237, 267, 269–70, 273
*Tingmissartoq* (*see* "Lockheed 8 Sirius"), 96, 103, 130
Tong, Chanchi, 235
Toomey, Humphrey W., 83, 292
Torre, Mario de la, 258
Toul airdrome, France, 15
Towers, John H., 185
"Transafrican Agreement," 214
Trans-Africa route, 214–15, 218
Transatlantic mail and passenger service, 1939-1941, 172–74, 179–81, 183–86, 208
Transcontinental and Western Airlines (TWA), 104, 175, 315
Transoceanic flying ideas, 38, 87–88, 97, 101, 105, 109, 111, 113, 115, 142, 173, 179
Trans World Airlines (TWA), 315
Treasure Island, San Francisco Bay, 182–83, 228, 238, 244, 251, 296–97, 302
Treaty of Versailles, 28
Trippe, Charles, 8, 11
Trippe, Charles White, 6
Trippe, Juan Terry:
  affiliate airline strategy; Mexicana; China National Aviation Corporation, 59–60, 147–48
  Africa, forays into; negotiates with Portugal for landing rights in Azores and Portuguese Guinea; CAB award for Leopoldville, Belgian Congo route, 180, 186–87, 206–07, 214–15, 224–25, 306

Trippe, Juan Terry (*continued*)
   Air Mail Route No. 1, competition for, 18–19
   Airport Development Program (ADP), meets with Roosevelt and Stimson; initial resistance to; concludes Pan Am has legal right to pursue program, 197–99
   Air Transport Command, declines offer to head, 283
   American Nitrates Corporation, sets up with C.V. Whitney, 170
   Hap Arnold, relationship with, 45
   Atlantic Airways, Limited, forms to assist U.S. Army ferrying operation; works with Lockheed President Cross, 211
   Atlantic Division, picks Leslie to head, 180
   Aviation Corporation of America (ACA); intrigues for FAM 4; Trippe-Hambleton-Whitney coalition, 41–45, 48
   childhood; tragedy at Seabright; witnesses Wright flight at Hudson-Fulton Celebration; early interest in aviation; father's inheritance, 6, 8–9, 11
   Caribbean operations, as lab for ocean flying; as "accumulation" of knowledge base, 59, 87, 109–10, 141
   Central and South America, forays into, development of airways, 47, 52–53, 67–69
   *China Clipper*, Pat O'Brien as composite character of Trippe and Priester, 142
   Chrysler Building, as Pan Am headquarters, 3, 89–90
   Churchill, meeting with, 2, 213
   Clair, personal secretary's memories of, 45, 80, 168, 283
   Clipper ships, vision of; accepts Martin and Sikorsky bids for "miracle" flying boat; develops "Super Clipper" with Boeing, 111, 136, 173
   CNAC as "welding a whole new nation"; directs Harold Bixby to purchase CNAC; as Pacific strategy; Bond, acrimonious Cloud Club lunch with, 109–10, 145, 147–49, 157–58
   commercial aviation; vision of, develops business model, 4, 11–12, 19
   Contract Air Mail Act of 1925 ("Kelly Act"), contributes to legislation, 18
   Merian Cooper, accepts board resignation of; John Cooper, confidant of, 80
   coup of by Pan Am board, 174, 179
   "de-Germanization" campaign against Axis airlines in the Americas, leader of; Braden accusation; orders SCADTA purge; alerts U.S. War Department to Nazi infiltration of Pan Am's operations in Brazil, 193–96, 201–02, 225
   *Dixie Clipper* proving flight, passenger on, 207
   Eastern Air Transport, forms; strategy for winning airmail contracts; bids for Air Mail Route No. 1; name change to Colonial Air Transport; CAT as business model for aviation industry; purchases Fokker transports, angers board, 13, 18–20
   Foreign Air Mail Act of 1928, involved in legislation; hails Act as "Lindbergh Law," 55–56
   Hambleton, friendship with; Hambledune meetings; on death of, 21, 38, 80
   Hong Kong, secures landing rights for, 156
   Hoover, meets with; discussions of "Community Company" and "One Field" philosophies, 56–57
   Secretary of State Hull, opinion of Trippe, 170–71
   Inter-Departmental Aviation Committee, works with, 52–53
   Anthony Fokker, business relationship with, 20–21, 78
   Key West to Havana, vision for, 24–25, 52, 56, 86
   Leopoldville, negotiates for resumption of wartime and "strategic materials" transport, 304–06

Lindbergh, meets at Robertson Aircraft Corporation; on pressures of fame and "curious view of life and risk"; witnesses *Spirit of St. Louis* take off from Roosevelt Field; friendship and association with; invites to join Pan Am, on Pan Am technical committee; Caribbean survey flight with; plans Lindbergh Orient and Atlantic survey flights; on pressures of Lindbergh's fame; failure to secure wartime role at Pan Am for, 14, 35, 39–40, 42, 70–71, 80–81, 89–90, 130–31, 281–82

Long Island Airways (LIA), beginning of and development; movie business of; as foray into international aviation, 11–13

media coverage of, *Time, Fortune, Life*; employs publicist Bruno; "publicity stunt" Fokker survey flight, 3, 11, 22, 44, 72, 186, 224

Merchado, negotiations with, 24, 44

Milch as Hitler's intermediary, 192

Naval Air Reserve commission, WW I, 11

Navy, relationship with in the Pacific; works with Secretary of the Navy Swanson in securing Pacific bases; cooperates with Naval Intelligence, 116–17, 119, 122, 131

as negotiator, 45

O'Neill and NYRBA, rivalry with; negotiates with and absorbs NYRBA assets, 69–70, 76–77, 83–84

PAA-Africa, forms and staffs; has operational ahead of schedule; as opportunity to penetrate Africa, 213–15, 224, 261

Pacific route; announces decision to fly the Pacific; change from North Pacific to Central Pacific route; "revolutionary" study of long range flight; inspects *China Clipper*, awaits news of historic round-trip Pacific survey flight; at launch of Pacific service, 105, 110, 117, 125–26, 130, 133–34

Pan Am board, criticism of; trusted board members; reaction to Pacific airway plan; votes to depose; votes to return Trippe to power, 113–14, 167, 174, 186

Pan American Airways, formation of; vision of flying the oceans; as "instrument of the nation"; Pan American Conference, attends sixth annual meeting in Havana as technical advisor to U.S. delegation; meets with Hambleton and Lindbergh; statements in PAA Annual Reports, 3–4, 43, 50, 55, 86, 111, 172–73, 194, 300

Post Office, U.S., relationship with; meets Assistant Postmaster Glover, 13, 19, 25, 46, 56, 60, 82, 105

radio communications; supports Adcock DF development, 24–25, 62, 94, 102

President Roosevelt, relationship with, 180–81, 283

South Pacific; Harold Gatty as "man in the South Seas"; Trippe pushes route from Honolulu to Pago Pago; statement on *Samoan Clipper* crash; strategy for Canton Island, 165, 167, 169–70

Speeches, "Aviation Activities Hour" radio broadcast speech, January 3, 1929; "Trying to Keep the Peace Through the Power of Wings," October 26, 1938; "America Unlimited," 1939; "Aviation in the World of Tomorrow," speech, New York "Banquet of the World of Tomorrow," New York World's Fair, April 20, 1939; "Ocean Air Transport," Wilbur Wright Memorial Lecture, June 17, 1940; "America in the Air Age," University of California at Berkeley, 1944; 1, 72, 162, 172, 181–82, 184, 212, 317

"Betty" Stettinius, marriage to, 48

Trippe-Hambleton-Whitney coalition, 13–15, 26, 43–44, 47, 52

Von Bauer and SCADTA, competition with; negotiations with and secret SCADTA deal; "Von Bauer situation" as Trippe talking point, 53–54, 60, 85–86, 197–197

Trippe, Juan Terry *(continued)*
    Wake Island, discovers "stepping stone" isle for Pacific route; directs Schildhauer to research Wake as potential base, 115
    Wall Street and Washington connections, 4
    Whitney, leads coup against Trippe, 174
    Yale; as football player; pursues aviation; as secretary of Yale Aeronautical Association; encourages wealthy classmates to invest in aviation; cultivates Yale connections, 10–11, 13, 19, 25
Truman, Harry S., 309
Trumbull, John H., 19
Trylon, New York World's Fair, (*see also* "Perisphere"), 184, 187
213th Squadron, Hambleton command of, WWI, 16

*Union Minière du Haul Katanga* (UMHK), 303
United Air Lines, 104
United Press, 119
University of Michigan-Pan American Airways West Greenland Expedition, 1932-1933, 89
Uranium mining, 301–05, 307
U.S. Defense Supplies Corporation, 193

Vanderbilt, Gertrude, 13
Vanderbilt, William H., 18, 43
Van Dusen, William, 68–69, 87, 128, 256, 261
Van Vleck, Jenifer, 207
Van Zandt, J.P. Parker, 125
Vargas, Getúlio, 203, 260–61
Vaughn, Charles "Chili," 149, 158
Vidal, Gustavo, 193
Villard, Henry, 304–05
Vinal, Richard, 296
Von Bauer, Peter Paul:
    Central America, interest in and explorations of; historic aerial survey of, 31
    childhood and education, 31
    Colombia, relationship with government; Bogotá, arrival in, 30–31
    Inter-American Airways, forms charter for, 32
    Lufthansa, relationship with, 33
    "mystery man" reputation, 27
    Nazi Germany, relationship with; threat of; Herbert Boy delivers Reich message, 194–95
    as promoter of commercial air travel, 32
    Hamilton Rice, joins expedition of, 31
    SCADTA, formation of; airmail contract with government; aerial land survey between Colombia and Venezuela; costs of modernization; effects of 1929 Wall Street crash on; infiltration by Nazi Party loyalists; nationalization of airline, 26, 31–31, 85, 192, 196–97
    Trippe, rivalry with; secret negotiations with, 53, 60, 85–86, 196–97
    U.S. relations with; fundraising and diplomatic overtures, 32, 53–54
Von der Heyden, J., 78
Von Krohn, Helmuth, 30
Vultee, Gerard, 89

Wah, Mr., China minister of communications, 151
Wake Island (and Wilkes and Peale isles), 115–16, 126–28, 162–64, 236, 242–43, 248, 295, 311
Waldorf-Astoria Hotel, New York, 172
Wall Street, 4, 9–10, 12, 21, 43, 81–82, 279, 281, 304
Walsh, Raycroft, and "Hawaiian Maneuvers," 8, 18, 37
War Department, 7–8, 34, 36–37, 52, 73, 192, 201, 217, 219, 224, 251–53, 259, 272, 281, 291, 302–06
Warner, Edward P., 51
Watkins, H.C., 89
Watkins, Henry George, 96
Wavell, Archibald, 210
Wei-shing, Lem, 158
Welles, Sumner, 170
Wells, Huestis "Hugh," 48, 55, 66

# INDEX

Wenhui, Liu, 153
Westervelt, George, 149, 151
West Indian Aerial Express Company, 46, 57
Westover, Oscar, 177
Whitbeck, J.E., 46
White, Francis, 8, 25, 32–33, 51–52, 54, 56, 73, 85, 194
Whiteman, Harold, 261
White, Theodore H., 266
Whitney, Cornelius Vanderbilt "Sonny":
    American Nitrates Corporation, sets up with Trippe;, 170
    Army Signal Corps, enlists as aviation cadet, 14
    Aviation Corporation of the Americas, chairman of, 46
    Eastern Air Transport, early investment in, 18–19
    FAM 4, effort to win contract; Trippe-Hambleton-Whitney faction, 43–44
    family history, wealth of, 13, 174
    Federal Aviation Corporation, on board of, 78
    NYRBA, negotiations with MacCracken, 83
    Yale scandals, 13–14
    Pan Am, formation of; as member of "Pan American Airways' Musketeers"; as "the financial man"; as board chairman; leads board coup, voted airline head, 13, 77, 174, 178
    Trippe, friendship with; betrayal of, 11, 174
Whitney, Harry Payne, 13–14
Whitney, John Hay "Jock," 43
Wilbur, Curtis, 35
Wilbur Wright Memorial Lecture, Royal Aeronautical Society, 1, 212
Wildcats (fighter planes), 236–37, 242–44, 248

Wilkes (Wake Island isle), 115, 126–28, 236
Williams, Susan, 306
Willkie, Wendell L., 205, 207–08
Winant, John G., 303
Wong, Li, 275–76
Wong, P.Y., 158
Wood, Junius, 122, 127
Woods, Hugh, 155, 159
Wooster, Stanton, 39
"World of Tomorrow," 175, 184–85, 318
World War I (the "Great War"), 7–8, 13–14, 36, 49, 37, 61, 69, 75, 149, 184, 194, 229, 232
World War II, 1, 4, 177, 208, 213, 309, 314
Wright, Chauncey D., 117, 134
Wright, Orville, 6–7
*Wright, U.S.S.*, 136
Wright, Victor D., 118, 124–26, 134, 136, 142, 166, 168, 292
Wright warplane, 7
Wright, Wilbur, Hudson-Fulton Celebration flight, 5, 7–8, 12
Wyman, Edward, 168–69

Yale-Accra Club ("Yaccra Club"), 223
Yale Aeronautical Association; 11
Yale University, 10–11, 13–14, 19, 25, 52, 194, 215, 223, 251, 279
Yangtze River trackers, 152
Yarnell, Harry E., 116–17
Yeomans, John, 217, 271, 285
Yerba Buena Island, San Francisco Bay, 182–83
Young, Charles A., Jr., 314
Young, Clarence, 114, 125
Young, Evan E., 88, 201, 280
Yuki, Shiroji, 237
Yunnan, China, 151, 156, 172, 230–31, 309

# AUTHORS

★

**MARK COTTA VAZ** is a *New York Times* bestselling author of over 35 books, including the critically acclaimed *Living Dangerously: The Adventures of Merian C. Cooper, Creator of* King Kong.

**JOHN H. HILL** is assistant director and curator in charge of aviation at SFO Museum.